THE
DRAMATIC WORKS
OF
DENIS JOHNSTON

Volume 2

COLIN SMYTHE LTD.
Gerrards Cross, 1979

*The Second Volume of The Dramatic Works of Denis Johnston
first published in 1979 by Colin Smythe Ltd., P.O. Box 6, Gerrards
Cross, Bucks., SL9 7AE.*

British Library Cataloguing in Publication Data

Johnston, Denis
   The dramatic works of Denis Johnston.
   Vol. 2
   I. Title
   822'.9'12   PR6019.0397A19

   ISBN 0–901072–53–2
   ISBN 0–901072–72–9 Limited signed ed.

Printed in Great Britain
Typeset by Watford Typesetters Limited
and printed and bound by Billing & Sons Limited,
Guildford, Worcester and London

THE
DRAMATIC WORKS
OF
DENIS JOHNSTON

Volume 2

Contents

Acknowledgements

The author wishes to thank the following for permission to reprint copyright material:

Faber & Faber, Ltd, for 'Fu-I loved the Green Hills' from 'Epitaphs' in *Personae* by Ezra Pound. Also William Alwyn for permission to publish and perform the music score of this poem.

PREFACE

TO THE *COLLECTED PLAYS* (1960)

One fine morning in the early 'thirties – in which expression I include both date and personal longevity – I was sitting at the feet of Bernard Shaw in Malvern, Worcs., receiving instruction on a variety of topics from this strictly non-alcoholic fountainhead. It was part of the routine of the local drama festival, and implied no contemporary importance in myself, except as a listener of some experience.

Two of his statements on this occasion struck me as being more than usually controversial, although uttered with that air of happy confidence that brooks no contradiction. Number one was to the effect that the second act of *The Silver Tassie* was the finest thing ever written for the stage. The other – with an admonitory finger pointed in the direction of Strindberg – was a warning that young dramatists ought never to marry actresses.

As I was already married to an actress, and this fact was within his knowledge, it occurred to me, either that old Father Neptune was being particularly roguish that day, or that there was something fishy about at least two prongs of his trident. Once a clock strikes thirteen, doubt is immediately cast not only on that particular pronouncement, but on all its previous ones as well. And although O'Casey's conception of the First World War, as embodied in Act II of the *Tassie*, might readily appeal to a pacifist as hostile to the whole subject as G.B.S., it could hardly be described as the best thing that Sean had ever written, much less as the greatest piece of theatrical literature of all time. Nor could it be argued that Strindberg's experiences in matrimony were any less valid than Chekhov's – or indeed that they were anybody's fault except his own.

So I thereupon adopted a practice that I have tried to follow ever since with regard to Shaw's advice. While listening to it with becoming respect, I have usually tried to do the opposite. In the case in point, I began by switching my colleagues on the board of the Gate Theatre to Yeats's adverse view of the *Tassie*. And I

married, not one, but two actresses, with tangible results that I
have never since regretted.

Another thing that Shaw used to urge was that all good play-
wrights ought – like himself – to explain themselves in prefaces.
What a pity, he said, that Shakespeare never wrote a preface to
Hamlet, thereby relieving Harley Granville Barker of this responsibility and incidentally ruining the livelihood of many generations
of front-rank lecturers. Herein Shaw displayed once again his
genius for giving cockeyed directives to those of us who happened
to be circulating perilously in his orbit. It is difficult to conceive
of a more disastrous palimpsest, dug out of some funk-hole in
Arden, than a preface to *Hamlet* written by Shakespeare himself.
And the fact that few of Shaw's own prefaces bear much relation
to the plays to which they are attached is evidence that he, personally, was wise enough to disregard the lure of this apple that he
was so freely offering to others.

Prefaces, however, present some temptations that it is difficult
for a Dubliner to resist. With the creditable exception of Sam
Beckett – who has professional help to do it for him – we all tend
to explain ourselves, regardless of the fact that this is usually a
feat beyond the capabilities of any writer with something on his
mind, and in any event is quite outside the scope of his duties.
Perhaps this urge to commit ourselves to paper on the subject
of our work is partly due to the state of domestic criticism. When
an Irish critic does not like a play or a book by one of his fellow
bar-flies – a not infrequent situation – he does not as a rule bother
to mention what is actually wrong with it. He prefers to invent a
set of facts about the work, the author, and the latter's intentions
that need not bear any resemblance to the actual truth. And then
he criticizes these. It is a handy form of self-expression, learnt
usually from a clerical education, and it enables the commentator
to make use, not only of any brickbats applicable to the immediate
subject, but also to employ all the material that he has forgotten
to make use of in his previous attack on somebody else. At the
same time, it encumbers an author with such a backlog of things-
to-be-set-right and matters-to-be-contradicted that prefaces inevitably follow. Or – more dangerous still – letters to the newspapers.

In my own case, I have long since given up the Augean task of
denying that I am a decayed relic of an ascendancy class, or that I
am attempting to raise a laugh at the expense of my singularly
unfunny country, or that I am a disciple of Ernst Toller, or about

to become a Catholic. Nevertheless I now find myself writing prefaces for various reasons that do not include any wish to obey the instructions of Good Old Wenceslaus of Ayot St Lawrence – a monarch who was always a pleasure to read, a headache to listen to, and utter confusion to agree with. Probably the most potent of these reasons is the fact that it is necessary to correct a widespread impression, put about by unscrupulous enemies, that I died of some unspecified disease in the summer of 1933, and have never written anything since.

Looking over such of my work as is here assembled for the first time in moderate bulk – an expressionist gesture of dissent, two antimelodramas about war, an exercise in character drawing, a costume piece for touring companies, and finally some sober reflections on my earliest and best-loved profession – I am a little puzzled as to whether there are any generalizations that can be applied to all of them, apart from the fact that they are by the same author, and that each in turn has been hailed as worse than the last – which is not a good selling point. Can they even be validly classified as Irish plays, in the sense of being acceptable in the island where most of them were first produced? It is true that the point of *The Old Lady* can be fully appreciated only in Dublin, where its meaning is only too evident to any ordinary intelligence. It is equally fair to say that at least three of the other plays are probably less intelligible to the Irish than to any other community that has yet performed them. From this generalization I should, perhaps, except the Belgians, who disapproved of what they considered to be the unpatriotic sentiments of *The Moon in the Yellow River*, and came to Erin's rescue – I am told – in a most gallant and voluble manner.

But whether or not there is any common denominator, I should perhaps say that the variety of style that the plays disclose is simply a reflection of my search for an adequate means of communication. In spite of some occasional chaff about obscurity, I have a great regard for communication, and do not hold with a current view that it is a sign of a lesser artist to disclose what he is talking about. Whether the stage is the proper place for me to be talking at all is another matter, for here we have a medium with a characteristic of which most practising dramatists must be conscious. Hardly anybody listens in the theatre to anything that he doesn't know already – a peculiarity of this powerful soundingboard that I have always found it very hard to cope with, as will appear from some of the individual prefaces that follow.

Maybe I should only write prefaces, and not plays; for as a poet or an essayist or a novelist I would not be considered difficult to follow in the slightest degree. On the other hand, I would not be in touch with theatre people, who as a rule are the best possible company, notwithstanding the fact that in no other creative field – if you will pardon the expression – are there so many pimps, crooks, exhibitionists and frauds, living off other people's earnings, putting their names to other people's work, and talking and writing nonsense under the guise of technical know-how, as there are cluttering up the stage doors.

My only objection to the theatre is this glamour that is progressivly making it less and less a place of entertainment, as it becomes increasingly difficult to gain admission without applying for tickets several months in advance. As an example of what I mean, I shall illustrate my point by telling a story about the greatest actor I have ever known – the greatest actor's actor, with the possible exception of Alec Guinness. It will not be believed, of course, by logical positivists; but it may ring a bell with an occasional neo-Franciscan with an Irish grandmother. F. J. McCormick – whose actual name was Peter Judge – used to play all the best parts at the Abbey Theatre, from Joxer to Lear, putting them on and taking them off as he would an overcoat, and then going home like any good pro to his tea and his radio set. He was always a little anxious about his stomach, but one of his more pressing fears was that his work on the stage might some day make him a celebrity like his old associate, Barry Fitzgerald, and thereby the pattern of his reasonably contented life might be ruined by the importunities of Hollywood and the attentions of autograph-hunters in the trams. The sincerity of this attitude is shown by the fact that, having by some error of judgment won international fame by his brilliant playing of a small part in a film called *Odd Man Out*, he was then pursued by Hollywod and by autograph-hunters, and promptly developed a brain tumour and died – one of the most deplorable, but by no means the only, victim of what is called Show Business, and of its horrifying glamour.

I, myself, though well acquainted with the Repertory Theatre, have had very little experience of show business. Only one of the following plays has had – for example – the full Broadway rewrite treatment, and the most disastrous parts of this did not survive the first printed edition, in which the pundits' idea of what is wanted as a second-act curtain may be studied by anybody who has a copy of that rare and valuable book. All plays, of course, require re-writing after their first presentation, for the obvious reason that they do not really exist until they have had to face up to the reactions of a sensible, objective audience; and I am, myself, an incurable addict to the pencil and the eraser. My only objection to the usual managerial rewrite is not that it is unnecessary, but that most of the Aristotles in the Big League of whom I can speak from any experience, are not by any means dumb, but as a rule are merely wrong. In the endless search for the best way of saying what he has to say, the dramatist has nobody to guide him except himself, and what he overhears in the vestibule. And even in the latter locale he has got to remember that one of the surest ways of not pleasing his public is to give it exactly what it says it wants.

I have one other small warning to give to practitioners who will in due course undertake the task of cutting these plays for this, that, or some other good reason. All plays can be cut to any required running time. Indeed, the obsession of radio and television with the clock often provokes a wonderment as to whether there is any compulsive need to perform a play at all. But with every script there comes a moment when further shortening requires the entire elimination of certain characters, and the contraction of the story-line itself. Otherwise the result is chaos.

Now this art of cutting is not always as simple as it seems, and although there is nothing sacrosanct about any of my lines, it is wise to remember that clever cutting does not simply consist in the removal of anything that looks irrelevant, or does not advance the plot. Plays do not live by story-line alone, and an apparently pointless passage, offering itself temptingly to the man with the blue pencil, may be performing an important function in the structure of an act that is not evident without the presence of an audience. Its removal may, for example, have a surprising effect on tempo, or it may eliminate a deliberate moment of relaxation that is a useful preliminary to something that is yet to come. Cut the gravediggers, and see what happens to the last act at Elsinore.

All these plays have been cut – some of them already to the bone so far as the present story-line is concerned. If you have to cut them very much more, you may do so of course. But if you approach this task saying to yourself 'Where's it getting us? Take it out,' you must not blame the author if what is left fails to make sense on the stage. What is needed in most cases is a radical, intelligent shortening of the plot, with probably the elimination

of a character or two. If you can manage to do this, good luck
to you.

A BRIDE
FOR THE UNICORN

A contemporary ARGOSY
in play form
intended for Music

The Theme

O Western Wind
When wilt thou blow
That the small rain down can rain?
Christ, that my love were in my arms,
And I in my bed again!

Anon. 16th Cent.

CONCERNING THE UNICORN

My interest in these enigmatic beasts goes back many years to a late night party that followed the performance of a play by Yeats on the merits of which some acrimony was then raging – a play which he had begun seven years earlier as a tragedy, but had now altered under the advice of Ezra Pound into a comedy. Tragedy – Pound had insisted – was the proper medium for Emotion, while Comedy provided the best approach to matters of serious Thought. The leading protagonist in the argument that followed was a somewhat intoxicated Intellectual who, in claiming to be an authority on the beast which figures largely in the play in question was alleging that: 'Nobody who has not had a Classical education can appreciate the Unicorn as it deserves'.

It fell to me to point out that this was a statement of doubtful validity, seeing that this particular beast does not feature in he Classics at all, but is a product of Mediaeval Romanticism, not-withstanding the fact that it is mentioned by name at least seven times in Holy Scripture. Anatomically speaking it is by no means an unbelievable animal. One might well have our doubts about the reality of the giraffe or the kangaroo were it not for their presence in our Zoological Gardens. On the other hand there is nothing peculiar about the appearance of the Unicorn in spite of its supposed value as a detector of poisons and its infallible power of recognising Virginity. Yet it has only been conceded within the last hundred years that the Unicorn is an entirely mythical crea-ture that does not, and never has existed. We know what it looks like thanks to Heraldry and pictorial Art, but there the matter ends regardless of the fact that it is not long since there was a profitable trade in portions of its horn for medicinal purposes.

In my own play, however, the Unicorn is not presented in any therapeutic way, but as a symbol of Man, himself – not the Economic Man, or the Average Man, or even as that imaginery miasma of the Law Courts – the Reasonable Man, all of whom are as mythical as the Unicorn, but as a creature that is born, that

13

struggles for its right to Be, that grows old and dies, and whose significance resides not in the Noun but in the Verb, and that spends his life seeking for what he conceives to be his Fulfilment, while at the same time professing his fears for the natural denoument of Death.

When I first attempted to depict this maze of contradictory urges in the form of a comedy, I had been greatly impressed by a curious book of woodcuts with no text entitled *God's Man*, in which the story is told of a mysterious Visitor, cloaked and top-hatted and wearing a mask, who makes a bargain with an impoverished Artist on the lines of the Faust legend, in which the latter's existence – or 'Soul' as Goethe would have it – is the apparent payment. After a successful career, the fatal moment arrives when the Stranger reappears to claim his price, and on removing his disguise, reveals the face of a grinning skull – a somewhat cynical parable on the subject of Life and Death which, in my thirties, I was inclined to scoff at.

Now, when approaching my Eighties, the question before the House is whether I am still inclined to scoff, on which point it is more appropriate for others to decide. At any rate all of this would appear to be a serious subject, and therefore – in deference to Pound – material for Comedy. In more juvenile days I originally built this play around the Jason story – a hero with his seamen-companions navigating his way through Life in search of some Golden Fleece – the reason for it all. In its present form it is not a disguised Bogey-Man who is being sought for, but a similarly cloaked Woman who, after a night of Love, disappears, leaving behind her false face – the open question being, which of the girls of College days – if any – is the Temptress who is being sought? And whether the bargain is worth the prize?

On such a point nobody is entitled to be didactic, so I leave the answer to my Audience, with one reservation, to which any Author is entitled. In the course of my life I have had the experience of knowing four professions, the first of which was the most enjoyable but also the least perilous. I have left home three times, ostensibly to seek my fortune and have never made one. And on my various returns I have been usually met by the greeting: Have you not gone yet? It has never been tragedy, but more in the nature of comedy. From which the conclusion must be drawn that it has all been 'Serious'. So I am not in the least disturbed at what I shall see when at last I raise some mask and take a look inside.

At the tender age of eight I was somewhat annoyed by the fact

14

that my parents did not bother to wake me from my slumbers in order to see Halley's Comet, which was then making one of its periodic visits to the Earth's orbit just in time to take part in the Funeral Rites of King Edward the Seventh. It had previously attended, amongst other events, the Battle of Hastings. This omission was waived aside by my Father who laughed it off with the remark, 'Oh that's all right. You can take a look at it the next time it's round'. It would give me great satisfaction to have the last laugh at that memorable old man by waving the apparition on its way about seven years from now, provided of course that my personal clock has not struck its thirteen strokes in the meantime.

If not, there will be no ill feeling about the matter, for I have been long convinced that the true face of Death is not a grinning skull – the mere detritus of a Boneyard. What seems to smile in Hamlet's hand has no more to do with Poor Yorick than his discarded shirt. Yeats knew a better meaning of Immortality when, with the perception of his later years, he wrote:

> Many times man lives and dies
> Between his two Eternities.

It was not the great W.B. who was borne back to Ireland on that gunboat, but merely his leavings. The man himself lives on in his own niche of Space/Time while the clock still ticks.

- - - - - - - - -

The stage directions in their present form are merely an indication of a type of presentation in the simplest form compatable with the Author's general intention. Having provided the text, it is beyond the function of a Playwright to trespass upon the functions of Director and Designer, who may have larger facilities at their disposal than are here indicated. These may include a revolving or shuttle stage, elaborate flies and indeed a full Orchestra under the inspiration of an imaginative Composer. As it stands here, with a minimum of scenery in the form of small, portable set-pieces, the play can be performed with only one interval which, for continuity's sake, is an advantage.

The play is not intended as a Constructivist or Expressionist Drama, and is not usually improved by this somewhat dated form of approach.

15

CAST

JASON (sometimes referred to as JAY) – A Leading Man.
ORPHEUS (a Drunk Bust) – A Pianist/Singer. A Harlequin.

THE COMPANIONS
DR TYPHIS – An ageing Character man.
THESEUS (otherwise ALIX) – A Military/Head-Boy type.
HERCULES (familiarly, LES) – A Businessman type.
BACCHUS (referred to as BARNEY) – An eccentric young character man.
GANYMEDE (otherwise MEEDY) – A sexy male.
CASTOR (called HAROLD) – A Political type.
POLLUX (known as ESME) – a character con-man.
OMPHALE (addressed as PHILLY) – a bossy sex-pot.
PANDORA (shortened to DORA) – a pessimistic juvenile.
PSYCHE – an unintelligent Ingenue.
CALLIOPE (called CALLIE) – an Intellectual.
HERA – a cynical wife.

EXTRAS
Stockbrokers, Students, a Policeman, an ageing Solicitor, Somebody's Daughter (aged about twelve), an elderly Mother, and half a dozen Dancers of both sexes who may also double-up in various supporting parts.

A Bride for the Unicorn

THE PERMANENT SET

The stage is permanently divided into two levels. The front two-thirds in depth including on one side, an alcove containing a Baby Grand Piano, on the closed lid of which stands the base of a Bust, the upper part of which can be occupied with the head and shoulders of a live Actor who, from time to time, can disengage himself and come out to take part in the Play. Alternatively, he may have a pedestal, breast high, placed well down stage at the side. In any event this object should bear an inscription on the base, reading ORPHEUM ACADEMIAE COMDITOR.

On the other side of the lower area stands a large Grandfather Clock with a woman-sized Door at present closed by a lock, and with an unlit clock face bearing Roman figures but (to begin with) no hands.

The upper level – one third of the depth of the stage is – to begin with – empty, and can be reached on a sloping ramp running laterally, with a short level section half way down. This level can be masked either vertically or laterally (according to the taste of the Designer) by a decorative curtain bearing, inter alia, *a pictorial Unicorn. It is important to have a gap between the rear side of the upper level and the back wall or cyclorama on which can be projected appropriate colour and shadows. To begin with, however, the general impression should be one of cold but colourful Daliesque spaciousness. (Dali should be the operative word.)*

It is immaterial whether there is a front curtain or not. Nor need there be a live Orchestra apart from the Piano, if satisfactory recordings can be made, and played where required.

PART ONE

When the first part begins the upper curtains are open and that part of the stage is empty. There is a small podium to one side of the lower stage on which stands a lectern together with a frame intended to support exhibits. Up centre there is a student's desk encumbered with a couple of large, impressive-looking volumes. Also on the lower level, on the opposite side to the Piano alcove, there is a light set-piece representing a pair of decorative gates.

While the Audience is still coming in, the Stage is unlit, but as the house lights fade an unseen Orchestra (or recordings if this is preferred) begin a cold and mysterious Introduction.

Then the stage lights rise, disclosing the Dancers already in position. They are dressed in the careless slop of modern Under-graduates of both sexes. We should also notice that the Bust-base on the piano (or wherever it is) is now inhabited by the head and shoulders of a live actor (ORPHEUS) in a white make-up to match the rest of the effigy.

As the dance develops, the music modulates into a modernistic rendering of the familiar tune of the GAUDEAMUS, and Voices sing offstage.

SINGERS (*off*).
      Gaudeamus igitur, Juvenes dum sumus.
      Gaudeamus igitur, Juvenes dum sumus.
      Post jucundam juventutem post molestam senectutem.
      Nos habebit humus. Nos habebit humus.

(The dance continues to some appropriate point where the Performers dance off, unmasking JASON *who now sits alone at the centre desk, searching in the pages of one of his books.)*

JASON.
      Here, between the pinnacles of night and morning,

Where yesterday, tomorrow and today are one,
Safe from the interchange of tide and planet,
I put my question to the firmament.

I am Jay – at work upon my books.
'Prepare for Life' – the Calendar remarks.
But what that is, does not appear.

(He turns a page – a grave and youthful Faustus.)

Statistics I have studied,
Plant Science and the Calculus of Conduct,
Personal Hygiene, Archaeology,
And even the contemporary Novel.
For four long years,
Pressed from the rear by academic toes,
Into the fundamentals I have poked my nose.
But what I am supposed to search for
No one knows.

(He looks away.)

Out in the widowed reaches of the street
The vaulted night is vast and terrible.
Seasonless, changeless, cold.

(A hand bell rings, and the COMPANIONS enter, carrying notebooks and pencils and singing to the unarranged tune of the Gaudeamus:)

THE COMPANIONS *(singing).*
> Eyes ab ille heres ego
> Fortibus es in aro
> O nobile themis trux
> Si vats enim
> Pesan dux.

(They are followed by DR TYPHIS in cap and gown who mounts the podium and arranges his books on the lectern, while bashing the desk with his cane.)

TYPHIS. Silence please, Ladies and Gentlemen. What is the assignment for today?

MEEDY. Virgins, sir. Very very Novo.

(*He clicks his lips and the Class giggles.*)

TYPHIS. Ttt. Ttt. I assume you are referring to the divine Areopogite. Allow me to find the place.

THE CLASS (*in unison*).

Vere novo. Gelidus canis
Cum montibus humor liquitur.

TYPHIS. Ah yes. Where we left off. Georgics 43. Construe if you please Mr What's-your-name.

LES. Vere novo. Mmm. Strange but true.

TYPHIS. Substantially incorrect. Next please.

DORA. Gelidus canis. Er – the cool dog?

MEEDY (*eagerly*). Cum montibus liquitur. It pees on the mountains?

CALLY. But he's left out the Humour! What about that?

TYPHIS (*disgusted*). Well?

BARNEY (*holding up his hand*). By way of a joke. (*Applause*).

JAY (*his eye on his book*). – God only knows.

TYPHIS (*turning to him*). Mr Phosphorus, while the rest of the Class has been lacerating this work of classical antiquity, I notice that you seem to have been engaged on independent study.

JAY. Yes sir.

TYPHIS. Is this the time for blatant inattention?

JAY. That is one of my problems, sir. What *is* the time? How can we tell anything with a clock like that? If it only had a little more of a face. Or would that be a mistake?

TYPHIS (*sarcastically*). Very interesting indeed. And do you imagine that the pursuit of such matters is going to assist you to graduate?

JAY. Probably not. At the same time –

TYPHIS. Ah yes. Time is fleeting. (*Indicating the clock*). Indeed it would now seem to be non-existent. But the more pertinent question is one of graduation.

JAY. Is that a matter of great importance?

TYPHIS. To graduate! A matter of importance? Are you suggesting that all these Students are wasting their time in studying here? Eh?

JAY. I don't know. Let's ask them. What have you been learning, Dora?

23

DORA. Me? (*Looking into her notebook*). Well – Mm – There's Boyle's Law.

BARNEY. Cookery. Well, that's important.

TYPHIS. It has nothing to do with Cookery.

DORA (*reading from her notes*). If any given volume of a gas is twice the pressure and the pressure is halved the resulting gas is twice the size it ought to be. Anyhow that's what I've got.

JAY. Don't you mean twice the size of the Bill?

DORA. Well yes. It's bigger anyway. The Bill always is.

CALLY. Oh do shut up, Dora. (DORA *wipes her eyes*). I've learnt that Exchange Values show themselves as the quantitative ratio in which Use Values of one kind are exchanged for Use Values of another kind, the ratio varying with changes in the Gross Product.

(*Sounds of admiration and dissent.* Jolly good. Pure drivel. She's certainly got something there. Trust Cally!)

JAY. Quiet everybody! Let's hear Hera.

BARNEY. Hear Hear.

HERA. Oh you mean me? Well, I'm doing Social Relationships and that's certainly important. I know why people want to get married. It's all due to Psychology.

MEEDY. Not with me, it's not. Let me show you ducky.

(*He frisks her skirt, and she slaps his face.*)

PHILLY. Serves you right.

DORA. He's disgusting.

BARNEY. Well I've got something really funny. The angles at the base of an isosceles triangle – you'll never believe this – are quite equal for the others, because if not let one be the greater than the other one must be all the worse for it which is UNFAIR. (*He laughs heartily*) Absolutely ridiculous!

(*An outburst of ad libbing, ended by* TYPHIS *banging with his cane.*)

TYPHIS. Silence everybody! This class is getting out of hand! (*Shouting*) Quiet please! (*The Students open their notebooks as* TYPHIS *unrolls a chart or diagram which he hangs up and indicates with his cane.*) This matter of graduation is simply one of viable objectives.

ALIX (*politely*). I beg your pardon?

TYPHIS (*louder*). Viable objectives! Dante tells us that the goal of the soul is Paradise. (*He points to it on his chart.*) A Cielo Quieto under which all other Spheres of the Universe revolve in heirarchical order. (*He points this out.*) The peril of the

Soul is Inferno (*He indicates this.*) – nine circles grouped around a central pit or Pozzo in which Lucifer is fixed with his head downwards towards Jerusalem. (*A Voice: Where's Jerusalem?*) Up there. These various circles are respectively called –

JAY. Excuse me, sir. Do you believe this?

TYPHIS. Believe it? Personally you mean?

JAY. Yes.

TYPHIS. Of course not. Not personally. But what's that got to do with it?

JAY. Then you're wasting our time, sir.

TYPHIS (*louder*). I am doing nothing of the sort, and you have not been listening to what I am saying. The essence of judgment is something that is or is not determined either as existing or as something in particular. Cogito ergo sum. I am. A Centaur is not. A square circle is impossible. Take any of these carelessly expressed propositions of ordinary life, and note that similar judgments are often differently expressed. (*A Voice*: Balls!) I shall ignore that interruption. Take for instance these two propositions: I, being a Man have a purpose in Life, and *If* I am a Man I have a purpose in Life. You see my point? (*Another voice*: No.) (*Raising his voice*) Conversely, different judgments are often similarly expressed. For example, when I say that every pupil must graduate –

JAY. Why?

TYPHIS. Why what?

JAY. Why must we graduate?

TYPHIS. To become Alumni. That's important. Don't interrupt me. It is because you must all be properly equipped for what you will meet with when you go through that gate.

JAY. What will we meet?

TYPHIS (*angrily*). How should I know? That is of minor importance and is for you to find out for yourselves. And look here – *I'm* supposed to be the one asking questions – not you.

JAY. We're supposed to be the ones getting useful information. Not you. And our immediate question is, What *is* outside that damned Gate?

TYPHIS (*fumbling in his bag*). You'll find out soon enough when you find yourself out there without one of these certificates, which everybody is going to get – except YOU. (*He produces a pile of coloured papers.*) Because, Mr Phosphorous, you've

25

flunked. And that's what you get for asking questions to which you don't know the answer!

(*He starts to distribute sheets of paper to the Class which they receive with shouts of delight.*)

VOICES. Our Degrees! Our Diplomas! Our Certificates! That's great. We've graduated. Cum Laude. Let's get packed. Out! Out! !

(*They tear off their gowns, and hurry off to get their luggage. The Bust emits a polite burp.*)

BARNEY (*on his way*). Out at last! What was that I heard? .

JAY. It wasn't me.

(BARNEY *goes over to inspect the Bust, the mouth of which is now open.*)

BARNEY. Did you make that noise? Look! It's mouth's open. Do you suppose it's – (*Another Burp.*) Wait a minute. Steady there!

(*He produces a hip flask and pours a little into the open mouth. The Bust smiles and emits a louder noise.*)

BARNEY. What a send-off! He likes it! (*He hands his flask to* JAY) Here. You keep him happy while I pack up.

(*He dashes off after the others, and is followed by* TYPHIS.)

ORPHEUS (*with difficulty*). Outside the Gate – is –

JAY (*giving him another sip which restores life*). What do you know about it? You're only –

ORPHEUS. Life is outside – Gate. Life!

JAY. What do you know about Life? You've got nothing down there.

ORPHEUS. What do you know about me?

JAY. No operative parts.

ORPHEUS (*refreshed, and quietly disengaging itself from its Base*). Do you think not.

(*He has now fully emerged, and comes round to the keyboard end of the Piano, revealing himself in the full-length black and white costume of a Harlequin.*)

JAY. Well I'll be – A Harlequin! My God!

ORPHEUS. No. I'm afraid you flatter me. A Harlequin maybe; but nothing like your God. No pretensions to divinity. But I may have an answer to your question.

JAY. Which question?

ORPHEUS. Wanted – to know something about – something about Outside the Gate.

JAY. Well?

26

ORPHEUS. Life.

JAY. What?

ORPHEUS. Life – outside the Gate.

JAY. Life? You said that before. What does it mean?

ORPHEUS. Whatever – you like – to make of it.

JAY. That's no answer.

ORPHEUS. Maybe not. But that's – funny thing. You're the answer yourself.

JAY. Me? Then what am I doing wasting my time in here?

ORPHEUS. Looking for instruction. Or maybe – just for Company. (*He laughs knowingly*).

JAY. Instruction from Dr Typhis! Don't be absurd. You're getting sober again. There's nothing here but Arguments.

ORPHEUS (*his mouth open*). Thasss so. But outside – Argonauts. Should be one – you should. Or even two.

JAY (*giving him another drink*). Here. Take this, and tell me sensibly what I ought to do.

ORPHEUS (*brightening up*). Simple. Go over there and take a look – inside – Clock.

JAY (*after getting rid of the flask by shoving it into the empty Bust-base*). That thing! It doesn't work.

(*He bangs on the door, having crossed to the Clock.*)

ORPHEUS (*holding up a key*). Needs a key.

JAY (*coming over and taking it*). Is this some sort of a trick?

ORPHEUS. Abso-lute-ly. A hell of a trick. Just open it and have a laugh. All depends on you.

(JAY *takes the key and gingerly places it in the lock. It sticks, but at last it turns over and the door creaks outwards. He steps back as if expecting something to fly out at him, but what emerges is a lovely-looking woman in a white cloak. Her face, however, is covered by a calm, seraphic mask. At the same time the face of the clock lights up, and* ORPHEUS *distinctly sobers.*)

ORPHEUS (*after playing a chord*). There she stands – her swift limbs whispering desire.

(*He starts to play and the* WOMAN *dances slowly and with great dignity, occasionally making a gesture towards the Clock.*)

JAY. What loveliness – whoever she is! Is it one of the girls? Which?

THE CAROLS (*off*).

My beloved spake, and said unto me

27

'Arise my love, my fair one, and come away.
'For lo, the winter is past,
'The rain is over and gone.'

JAY. So beautiful! What does she want?

ORPHEUS. You, Jason. Just you.

JAY. No. Nobody wants me.

THE CAROLS (*continuing*).

The flowers appear on the Earth –
The singing of birds,
And the voice of the turtle is heard in our land.
The fig tree putteth forth figs,
The vine a tender grape.

(BARNEY *and* MEEDY *have appeared on the other side,
muffled and hatted and carrying their bags.*)

BARNEY. Hi Jay, coming along?

MEEDY (*with a wolf whistle*). Who's the tart?

JAY. Just one of the girls – trying to make a fool of me.

MEEDY. Does it matter which? Looks like she's asking you to go
with her.

JAY. I must say, I'm tempted.

BARNEY. I love temptations. You can always give way to them.

JAY. If only I dared.

ORPHEUS. Hunger will make you dare. Hunger – the first and last
of living.

THE CAROLS.

Arise my love, my fair one, and come away.
Arise my love, my fair one, and come away.
For lo, the winter is past.
The rain is over and gone.

(*As the music concludes she ends the dance by dropping a
rose on the forestage, where it remains throughout the play.
She then makes a gesture towards the clock, and concludes
the dance, half way up the ramp, with a gesture of invitation
towards* JAY.)

ORPHEUS (*rising from the piano*). Ah yes, of course. I was almost
forgetting. There is one small condition.

JAY. I thought that would come. What is it?

ORPHEUS. Just a small service to oblige a lady. Over there – inside
the clock – you will find a pendulum.

JAY (*going to the clock*) .Yes. It's here. It's still.

ORPHEUS. Then set it swinging.

ALIX (*entering with the other men Companions*). Be careful, Jay. You never can tell what trick –

BARNEY. So what? There's always something about starting a clock.

ALIX (*with an imperious gesture*). Sssh! Quiet everyone. We've got a problem here.

BARNEY. He's going to do it . . . unless he's scared.

JAY (*staring at the* MASKED WOMAN). I'm not afraid.

(*He sets the pendulum in motion. The hands of the clock appear at six as a smile appears on the lighted face, and six strokes boom out. The woman has gracefully removed her shoes, which she leaves midway on the ramp, before beckoning to* JAY, *who joins her there.*)

BARNEY. Magnificent!

ALIX. Now he's done it!

ORPHEUS. He has sundered tomorrow from yesterday, and set free a golden butterfly – the present. He has endowed himself with the mystery of the hours and of the seasons, and sounded a trumpet to salute the Dawn.

(*The* MASKED WOMAN *leads* JAY *off on the upper level, as the Companions react in various ways – some with delight and others with disapproval.*)

VOICES. Where's she taking him? Does it matter? Anywhere with her! That's the last we'll see of him. Who do you suppose she is? Term's over. Do you see the time? Where's my Diploma? Did you take it?

(*This is concluded by the arrival of* TYPHIS *ushering in the girls, who have also arrived with their possessions.*)

TYPHIS. Now, now Ladies and Gentlemen. Commencement is over, and you're all bound for the Big Outside, with two thoughts that you will never forget. Your Class Slogan – and of course the Alumni Fund. We'll be getting in touch with you, never fear.

LES & MEEDY. That's right. Got to be off. Argonauts not Arguments. All we need is a Boat.

SHOUTS. A boat. A boat. Argonauts – not Arguments!

TYPHIS. Good bye. Good bye. I'll see you on your way.

(ORPHEUS *strikes up the College Song on the Piano.*)

COLLEGE SONG.

> Our College Courts are old and grey
> But ever new their joys
> While through its halls resound the bawls

29

Of happy girls and boys.
And we will strive unceasing
To honour her renown.
Be this our rule, the dear old School
Must never be let down.
Be this our rule, the dear old School
Must never be let down.
Ready, Aye Ready. This shall be our song;
Ready to be gentle. Ready to be strong.
Ready to defend the right, and redress the wrong.
Orpheum for ever!
Hip-Hip-hip-Hooray!

(*Meanwhile two distinguished gentlemen have risen from their seats near the front of the Stalls, and are stalking across below the Stage in evident disgust, in full view of the Audience.*)

1ST INTRUDER (HAROLD). Pollux, I must have a whisky and soda.

2ND INTRUDER (ESME-POLLUX). Oh Gawd, I could use one myself!

(*The Companions of both sexes, having formed up, commence to march through the Gate, soon to be followed by the two Intruders who, having failed to locate an Exit door, mount the stage at the side and find themselves involved in the procession. This causes some confusion in the course of which the Gate set-piece is knocked over and broken, and has to be dragged off as they go.*)

POLLUX. Oh Gawd! What have we done now? Where are we?

(*Presently the whole procession, having marched off on the lower level reappears on the upper level, including the Girls,* TYPHIS *and the Intruders (still looking for a way out).*)

POLLUX. Oh Gawd, where have we got to now? We were only creeping out for a little –

HAROLD. Seem to have got involved somehow. So sorry.

(*Meanwhile* TYPHIS *is directing the entire party into a statuesque group supposedly in the shape and outline of an ancient Galleon with* ALIX *as figurehead and* LES *as the mast and the other men sitting as oarsmen and passengers. With some grumbling and abuse the two Intruders are pushed into this too, while* TYPHIS *takes his place as helmsmen. There has been music throughout.*)

PHILLY (*shrilly*). Don't spoil the act!

LES. Sit down! We're short of men.

CASTOR (*indignantly*). I can't row!

BARNEY. Nobody's asking you to. Sit down there.

 (*More or less in unison.*)

MEEDY. Where the hell did you come from?

PSYCHE. You're tearing my dress!

POLLUX. I've only appeared in Pirandello.

BARNEY. Each man in his turn plays many parts.

HAROLD (*settling in*). I'm used to better parts than this, you know.
Even a Prime Minister once.

Professional people –

 (*As the music modulates into a Boating Song,* ORPHEUS
 plays the Piano, and the Orchestra joins in.)

ORPHEUS (*yelling from the piano*). Stop all that chatter, you
cretinous louts! Here's the Boat Song coming. THE BOAT
SONG!

STROPHE (*from the Crew*).

 Now with oars tempestuous sweep
 Stroke on stroke we face the deep.
 Loose ye skies your piping gales
 And wing our barque with fattening sails.

ANTISTROPHE.

 Until that day when labour's o'er
 We meet again at Colchis by the shore.

(*The music concludes as the curtains close on the upper
level, and when silence has fallen,* ORPHEUS *who has risen
from his Piano, comes to stare at the clock, which has now
advanced to 2.00, and is chiming accordingly.*)

ORPHEUS.

 Now is the hour when the night wind moans
 And gusty larches on the hills
 Shiver their supplications to the stars.
 Out in the widowed reaches of the street
 The vaulted firmament is vast and comfortless,
 Seasonless, changeless, cold.

(*He notices the shoes, abandoned half way up the ramp,
and goes to pick them up, and then listens at the curtains
as if at a door.*)

ORPHEUS (*with a wry smile*).

 The shoes stand sentry at the door
 While bachelors must shiver in the Hall.

(*He brings them down, as Music comes again from the
Orchestra.*)

31

ORPHEUS (*singing*).

> Was it for shuttered souls that Nature made
> This silken girl with sunlit hair,
> The benediction that is in her hands,
> Her soft, unhallowed smile?
> Rise Heart, and seize your heritage,
> Clad in the gifts that fools forbid.
> None but the great shall ever plant
> A rood in every shrine.
> While the Gods –
> For reasons better left unsaid –
> Provide a Night twixt every day.

(*As he broods smilingly on the shoes,* JAY *appears, bemused, at the other side of the stage.*)

ORPHEUS. Well, my Pupil, are you the better of that?

JAY. She's gone!

ORPHEUS. What? Without a word?

JAY. Who cares about words where she's concerned? Where has she gone! (*At the Clock, rattling the door*) It's locked again! Have you the key?

ORPHEUS. This is all I have. (*He places the shoes on the Piano.*) Cinderella – twice over. You'd better get the girls to try them on. Unless – of course – you saw her face?

JAY. I never saw it.

ORPHEUS. Not even when you – ?

JAY. For one hour – drugged by her slow, soft fingers, the stars were circling round my head. When I awoke, nothing was left – but this. (*He holds up the mask.*)

TYPHIS (*who has entered and has been listening*). Now this is very interesting. A Bride is lost upon her nuptial night. A very common occurence in folk lore and myth.

JAY. If only I knew!

ORPHEUS. Very careless of you not to have enquired. (*He opens his mouth for a moment*) You haven't a – drink by any chance?

JAY. I've got to find her.

TYPHIS. First there was Niamh of the Golden Hair, daughter of the King of Tir na nOg. She was stolen away from her lover.

ORPHEUS. Have to go and – look for a little – Dangerous signs of sobriety. You had a flask once. Where's it gone?

(*He wanders away, taking the shoes with him, and passing* BARNEY *on his way in, carrying a fishing rod. It is getting considerably lighter.* ORPHEUS *continues to search around his Piano, before sitting down wearily.*)

TYPHIS. And then there was Dietrich of Berne who spent many years searching for Virginal, the Ice Queen, imprisoned by Magicians.

BARNEY (*looking around*). Anything the matter?

TYPHIS. It seems that Mr Phosphorous has been having an affair with one of the girls.

BARNEY. And she's probably walked out on him. They usually do. Oh do cheer up, Jay. Meedy can give you some addresses. Who was it?

JAY. I don't know.

BARNEY (*undoing his fishing line*). Really! One usually does.

JAY. Don't be a fool. She was wearing this mask.

(*By now it is morning.*)

BARNEY. Oh I see. Well how about trying it on some of the girls? You might be surprised. How about Psyche? She's up there – mooning in a cornfield. I'd be glad to come along only I have to do some fishing.

JAY. You're supposed to be looking for a job.

BARNEY. So are you. Skirts for you. Fish for me.

(*By now the curtains have parted on the upper level, disclosing a pastoral scene, with* PSYCHE *sitting on a rustic fence staring at a tree on which somebody has inscribed* PSY LOVES JP *with two entwined hearts.* BARNEY *sits down on the forestage and fishes out into the Auditorium. Birds twitter. The clock now stands at nine.*)

JAY. What do you expect to catch out there?

BARNEY. Oh one never knows. Maybe a hip flask or two. Can't imagine what's happened to mine. Better be careful with Psyche. She slapped my face on the way down.

JAY (*mounting to the upper level*). Why did you do that, Psyche? Slap poor Barney's face?

PSYCHE. Because he's a fool. I hate boys who are fools.

JAY. What a lot of hates you must have. What's wrong with Barney?

PSYCHE. He's so abstruse.

JAY. Mm. Now there's another important piece of information not to be overlooked. (*He points at the inscription*) 'Psy loves somebody or other.' How did that get there?

PSYCHE (*somewhat embarrassed*). Oh that's just silly. I don't know who could have done that.

JAY. It is something that should not be allowed to slip from Public Attention. So carve it up on all the trees and walls along with the Coca-Cola advertisements. 'Somebody loves Psyche'.

BARNEY. Trespassers will be prosecuted. 'Orpheans rule O.K.' So he's sowed his wild oats after all?

JAY. Wild oats for tame asses! The moon was my mistress and I, the shepherd boy she ravished. Who was my rival, lovely Psyche? Who was it that stood between us?

PSYCHE. That's a secret. Secrets are important things.

JAY. How true. It was the secret of You that made me stand outside your house to watch the lights go on and off. I'd lie in wait to board your tram – just by accident – surprise, surprise – so that I might pay both pennies, reckless of all expense. You made me a very daring fellow with that quiet smile of yours, and that thrilling trick of saying nothing, simply because you were so very, very deep? Who was it that beat me, Psyche dear?

PSYCHE. I love my love with an Ess because he's Special. Some day, I said, I'm going to marry him. And I shall sit in the window each evening, and watch for him to come home.

JAY. Soon, I thought, we shall have children – wonderful kids all over two years old, playing quietly before a big nursery fire, where never a tear is shed, never a sick is slopped and nothing has to be dried before the fire on a wooden clothes-horse.

PSYCHE. Then of course I got more sophisticated and learnt to treat life as a matter of course. And I plucked my eyebrows and lay on a chaise longue in a black dressing gown with my initials on the pocket, and became more and more restless. And I smoked French cigarettes in a long holder and played 'Tales from Hoffman' on the gramophone and longed for the day when I would know everything.

JAY (*impatiently*). Psyche, if I were to ask you to do something for me – ?

BARNEY (*softly*). Man traps and Spring guns! Dirty dogs shot!

JAY. Will you please go away, Barney. How can I talk to Psyche with you sitting there?

BARNEY (*to the Audience*). Muzzles to windward, you gossips! Ears to the keyholes! Get out your coppers for the telephone.

JAY (*shouting*). Will you shut up, and get out of here!

BARNEY (*getting up and rolling up his line*). Oh very well, if you're so fussy. I shall just go and – um – I shall buy a bicycle. My

Mother used to say to me, If you have two loaves, sell one and buy a bicycle. Or was it loafers that she mentioned?

JAY (*rising*). Barney I swear I'll –

BARNEY (*hastily*). All right. All right. No swearing with ladies present. I've no wish to be an essential witness. (*He goes with a comic gesture of warning to* PSYCHE.)

JAY. Sorry about that, dear Psyche. It's just that I wanted you to try on something for me.

PSYCHE. What was he talking about?

JAY. Oh just a bit of nonsense. All I wanted you to do was to let me see you in this mask.

PSYCHE (*slightly suspicious*). Oh, is that all you meant?

JAY. That's all. Not very much.

PSYCHE. Practically nothing. (*Pause*) I'm afraid I couldn't do that you know.

JAY. Why not?

PSYCHE (*stiffening*). Well, I can't imagine what all those people out there would think of me if I went in for that sort of thing.

JAY (*puzzled*). What sort of thing? What do you mean?

PSYCHE (*after a pause*). If we ever got married, would you love me for ever?

JAY. Isn't that rather a change of subject?

PSYCHE (*in difficulties*). Well . . . Do you believe that love lasts?

(*There is a distant whistle from* BARNEY.)

BARNEY (*off*). Go on! What's the answer?

JAY (*aside*). Damn that fellow! (*Then after a pause*) Well, it all depends. After all, isn't the same true of any sort of Happiness? It usually has to have a beginning and an ending. You know – like good wine, it has to be drunk.

ORPHEUS (*opening his eyes at the piano*). Drunk! I knew there was something I was looking for.

(*He staggers to his feet, and starts to look around.*)

PSYCHE. All men don't talk like that about love. I know somebody who wouldn't agree with you.

(*She turns towards the* SCARECROW *and smiles at it sweetly.*)

JAY (*suddenly recognising his rival*). You mean – Mr Right up there!

PSYCHE. I met him one day in the cornfield. He stood there silently – holding out his arms to me. I knew at once that he was different. So lonely and misunderstood.

(*The scarecrow sways gently in the breeze as if in reply.*

Meanwhile ORPHEUS *has found* BARNEY'S *flask where it was left – inside the Bust-base, and delighted with this, he returns to the Piano to refresh himself.*)

JAY (*melodramatically*). A-ha! A rival stuffed with straw. Behold the food with which our dreams are fed! Only a –

PSYCHE. Don't you dare call him names, or I'll never speak to you again!

JAY. My darling Psyche – a beautiful thing that will never grow wiser! The same nervous pigeon fluttering from cocked triggers. I love you – but you are not my woman!

(*Music is heard as the* SCARECROW *dances for her, and from the surrounding fields come* BOBBYSOXERS *each carrying a* SCARECROW *to join in the behop. As the dance concludes* JAY *laughingly slaps the* SCARECROW *on the back and its head falls off.* PSYCHE *screams and kneels beside the wreck, and the Music comes to an abrupt halt.*)

JAY (*melodramatically*). Woman, I have slain your lover!

(*As the clock starts to strike eleven, the other scarecrows gently slide to the ground, and there is a despairing wail from the* BOBBYSOXERS.)

JAY. No more morning, kids!

(*The upper curtains close on the last stroke, and* ORPHEUS *starts to play.*)

ORPHEUS (*now greatly refreshed and singing*).

Sumer is icumen in. Lhude sing cuccu!
Splasheth slush and waileth wynde.
Fogs obscureth too.
Sing boo-hoo. Brollies best be new.
Not a bloody bus in view!

(*A lot of* STOCKBROKERS *have entered below dressed in business suits and carrying their own chairs which they place in a circle as they talk on the lower level. Some consult a noisy Ticker-tape machine which has appeared on one side, and gets kicked from time to time as it pours forth questionable information. Telephones ring and are answered, and the babble continues while the upper stage is cleared behind its curtain and a large blackboard containing columns for quotations is lowered into place. When this job has been completed a bell rings, the upper curtains part and the* BROKERS *take their seats with open notebooks.*)

BROKERS. Morning all. Any news from the Kerb? Oh I never believed that. They were good friends that's all. Paris on

36

the phone. Never expected to see you around after last Tuesday. What's all this about Funds? Soft Sale Worldwide. (*Etc. with an unending supply that may be had from the Morning Papers.*)

(*Meanwhile* TYPHIS, HAROLD *and* POLLUX *have entered and are mingling with the crowd. A* BROKER *tenders his overcoat and umbrella to* HAROLD *who indignantly passes it on to* POLLUX *who, after studying it for a moment, goes through the pockets before throwing it on the ground and opening up an embryo cloakroom.*)

TYPHIS. So this is the Money Market. We could do with some money at the Orpheum.

HAROLD. That fellow needn't think I'm going to play a Cloak Room Attendant. I distinctly said a Professional role or nothing else.

POLLUX. Actually it's not a bad idea. It may keep us from being asked to leave.

BROKERS. Kaffir possibilities. Further fall expected. The drop in Commodities. Gentlemen, take your seats please.

(ORPHEUS *has wandered off, while a somewhat bewildered* JAY *meets* BARNEY *returning with an Alarm Clock, which he winds and sets down beside him.* LES *soon appears accompanied by* ALIX, *carrying pamphlets and ledgers.*)

LES. And now the time is ripe to float the Company, and you shall be Secretary. Distribute these Prospectuses.

ALIX (*doing so*). I say, I hope this is all above board. I wouldn't like to get mixed up in anything shady, you know.

LES. In sound finance there is no need to be shady. The thing itself is shady. And while we're on the subject, kindly remember that although you may have been Head Boy at school, here in the larger world, *I* am Head Boy.

ALIX. So sorry, I know I shouldn't have suggested such a thing.

JAY (*to Barney*). What's the idea of the alarm clock?

BARNEY. Just a promise I made to my mother. It keeps me on the move. She always used to say, 'See that you never get stuck anywhere for more than half an hour! Particularly Bars and Stock Markets. You can't get into serious trouble in half an hour'.

(ALIX *has been on the telephone while* MEEDY *enters, peddling pills of some sort.*)

MEEDY. Try it sir. A sure and safe remedy for general weakness, exhaustion, nervous decay and loss of other abilities – only fifty pee a box, or extra strong to take effect within a few minutes fifty-five pee.

A BROKER. Throw that man out. No business to be here. (*But nobody does.*)

LES. Where's my overdraft now?

ALIX. At the Blue Bank so far as I can hear. It's pretty large, and they're getting a bit restless.

LES. Then move it round through the Red Bank and the Yellow Bank, paying off one Bank by overdrawing at the next. When my credit is firm, overdraw still further at all three, and if they want security, give them short term bills on Hercules Limited. Tell me when the Funds are doubled, and meanwhile get me some cash.

(ALIX *writes cheques and hands them to* MESSENGERS, *who dash away. Then he returns to the telephone.*)

BARNEY. Some day I'm going to buy a bicycle. Then one can really get around.

JAY. Your Mother's idea, too?

BARNEY. Oh yes. Better than making money in a place like this.

(*He picks up a currency note that somebody has dropped and studies it.*)

TYPHIS. This place roars like a beast. I wish I had some money.

BARNEY. I'll divide this with you. There.

(*He tears the currency note in half and gives a part of it to* TYPHIS. LES *has been observing this operation, and intervenes.*)

LES. That's a very good idea, young man. I can give you a job.

BARNEY. Is it an amusing job? Because I've only got half an hour.

LES. Never mind whether it's amusing. You'll be paid, and that's good enough for the likes of you. Mr Theseus, where's that cash I asked for?

(ALIX *takes a bundle of notes from the returning* MESSENGER *and brings them to* LES.)

ALIX. There's now twenty thousand in the Yellow Bank. But in the others –

LES. Never mind the others. Tomorrow, repeat the operation on a forty thousand basis, and buy the Bills back on the Market at discount rates. Meanwhile, you there (*pointing to* BARNEY *and* MEEDY) take these Notes over to that table and tear them all in half –

MEEDY (*astonished*). Tear them in half?

LES. Do as I tell you! And stamp each half with this endorsement.

38

(*He hands them a rubber stamp each.*) Then bring them back to me. Don't bother if you drop any.

BARNEY. Only too delighted. Come on, MEEDY.

(*They dash across to the Cloak Room table, where they are soon joined in their work by* POLLUX.)

ALIX. Look here, what is this Endorsement? And why are you throwing money about like this?

LES. Perfectly straightforward, my dear fellow. It simply reads: Redeemable for one pound sterling at any of the offices of Hercules Limited.

ALIX. What offices? There *are* no offices.

LES. There will be shortly. Now read that Prospectus to the Brokers. Go on! Interrupt them. You know how!

(ALEX *gets up on the platform and fires a revolver.*)

ALIX. Now Gentlemen, I am instructed to bring to your notice the Prospectus of Hercules Limited New Issue of Gold Bearing Preference Stock, issued at 97, registered and transferrable by Deed in multiples of One Pound. Present Capital disclosable to Stockholders only.

VOICES. Nonsense! Hercules Limited! Never heard of it. No good. The Slump.

ALIX (*turning the page*). This Issue is made in direct response to the conditions created by the Slump. In Hercules Limited you are lucky in having a concern unaffected by the deplorable conditions prevailing in the industrial world. Hercules Limited are fortunate in making nothing. They buy nothing and they sell nothing. They have no Labour troubles . . . no Overheads; . . . no costs of distribution . . . no advertising expenses. They are, in short, a perfect economic investment, affected only by the immutable laws of higher mathematics. The Issue is now open. Invest in the Big One.

SEVERAL BROKERS. Ah no! I don't want that sort of thing.

ANOTHER BROKER. Well, I'll try anything once.

(*He wanders over to the table where* BARNEY *and* MEEDY *have been working. The interest of the* BROKERS *begins to rise, as the* BLACKBOARD MAN *opens a column for Hercules Ltd. on the Blackboard, which* TYPHIS *is presently interfering with. More and more* BROKERS *begin to steal off towards the Hercules table, as the price on the Board shows signs of rising.*)

(*As this goes on,* JAY *approaches* LES.)

THE BLACKBOARD MAN (*to* TYPHIS). Hey you! What are you up to. You mustn't touch that board.

TYPHIS. I'm only correcting your figures, sir. You have made several mistakes already in your Arithmetic.

JAY. Look here, Les. It seems to me that you're starting something you're going to be sorry for. There are laws you know about the Currency.

LES. Of course, my dear fellow. But you don't understand Economics. I'm not breaking the Law. I'm building up credit, which is what we all need. Everybody will get paid for a very simple reason. They all want more money, and that's exactly what I'm giving them – more and more money.

JAY. That's the Government's business – not yours.

LES. Before this place closes the Government will be at it themselves. Hercules Ltd. will not only be a National Asset. It will be a National Necessity. It's either me, or more taxation. With me – more money for everyone. Mr Theseus – kindly announce the New Issue.

ALIX (*shouting*). That issue being now fully subscribed I am instructed to offer a New Issue of half a Million Hercules Ltd, Cumulative Preference 10% Stock at – let me see – at – what was the last figure? Oh! only 97! Better try the next at half price.

LES. Nonsense. People buy when prices are rising – not when they're falling. Say 125.

ALIX. 125!

MEEDY (*to the* BLACKBOARD MAN). That's all right, old man. What of the Depression? Epsom Salts are still working night and day!

HAROLD. I say, listen to this, Pollux!

BROKERS. At what? Second Preference at 125! What nonsense is this?

BARNEY (*spilling another bunch of divided notes over the floor*). Terribly sorry! Most careless I'm afraid.

BROKERS. Give me a block of this. Hey! – you've dropped – Might I? – I beg your pardon. . . . Just one moment . . . Allow me. Don't stand on my hand.

(*Several subscribers circle round the notes on the floor.* BARNEY *grins excitedly and a wild light dawns in his eyes.* MEEDY *chalks up further figures on the blackboard, while the* ATTENDANT *is distracted.*)

LES (*to* ALIX). Go on. Read that.

ALIX. Hercules Ltd. Cumulative being now fully subscribed there will be another small issue of a quarter of a million Hercules First Debenture at –

LES. A hundred and fifty.

ALIX. At a hundred and fifty.

SHOUTS. Hey! What's this? Cumulative over-subscribed! First Debenture at 150! I'll sell Ordinary at 115.

BLACKBOARD MAN (*frantic*). Wait a minute, gentlemen! I haven't got all this down. (*To* MEEDY) What are you doing? Go away.

MEEDY. All right, old Man. I'm only helping.

LES. Buy on the rising market, gentlemen. Hercules Limited is up and going up fast.

(*Paper money starts falling from the flies.*)

LES. There you are! Didn't I tell you! The Government's joining in. Money for everybody!

JAY. This can't go on, you know.

LES. Why not? Hercules Limited has saved the Market!

BROKERS. Hey! Give me £5,000 worth! Who's got First Preference for sale? Curse you, get off my hands!

(*As fast as they pick money up off the floor, it gets paid in and is flung in the air again.*)

LES. Didn't I tell you? All that we need is more money!

HAROLD. Pollux – return all those umbrellas.

MEEDY (*through the shouting*). Send in champagne! Crates of champagne to the account of Hercules Limited.

BARNEY (*to* LES). Do you mind if I keep just this small one for myself?

LES. Not at all my dear fellow. Keep a dozen.

BARNEY. Oh no – this is enough. I only want to buy a bicycle.

(*Crates of wine appear.*)

MEEDY. Drinks for everyone. And don't let us forget the drunk Bust!

JAY (*shouting*). This can't go on! It can't go on for ever!

(HAROLD *and* POLLUX *take top hats from the contents of their cloak room and put them on to shake hands with the cheering* BROKERS, *when the hands of the clock advance to twelve, and the chimes ring out, silencing all rejoicing in an awestruck hush.*)

TYPHIS. Noon! The voice of God!

(*All hats are doffed.* JAY *breaks through the crowd and falls on his knees before the flower, with a little sigh of despair.*

41

(From somewhere in the crowd a voice starts to sing. The Delphic Hymn to Apollo *in the key of the notes of the clock. This is taken up by more and more voices until all are singing except* JAY. *Meanwhile the lights fade slowly out to a blackout which coincides with the end of the song, except for the light in the clockface which remains throughout the Interval.)*

THE DELPHIC HYMN

Sing, sing O children of triumphant Zeus
To him who tunes his lyre upon the snowcapped heights.
Sing, fair-armed daughters of the trumpeting Gods.
Sing of your brother Phoebus of the golden hair
Who rules Parnassus and the Delphic Stream,
Flowing from the fair Castalian Hill.

(In the darkness the cast, including JAY *gets off as best it can, after which the House lights rise for the Interval, during which the mess on the stage is cleared up by the Stage Crew. The Rose remains on the Forestage.)*

PART TWO

During the Interval the stage lights are off, including the light in the clock face, and the upper curtains are closed. Meanwhile a small table and a couple of chairs are placed upstage on the lower level on the opposite side from the Piano.

At the end of the interval a short orchestral introduction leads to the voice of ORPHEUS *singing out of sight, and with him the voices of the wind, crooning on an open vowel.*

ORPHEUS.

> O Western Wind, when wilt thou blow
> That the small rain down can rain?
> Christ, that my love were in my arms
> And I in my bed again!

The lights rise on the upper level as the curtains part on a domestic Interior – a painted fireplace and overmantle with rubbery plants and photographs of dim nonentities, shoes on the hearth, and a cradle by an ironing board at which HERA *works.* JAY *sits beside the painted fire, reading newspaper and smoking his pipe. The mask hangs upon the wall behind him, and in a rocking chair, close to a Radio which is playing soft tea-time music, sits an elderly* RELATIVE *who knits and knits. The clock face smiles again, and the hands indicate five o'clock. Throughout the scene the business of the husband and wife continues with complete realism, without necessarily bearing any reference to what they are saying. (This will be found difficult in rehearsal, particularly as they speak the stage directions in addition to non-realistic dialogue.)*

JAY. A domestic Interior. Here, in the midway of our mortal life, where a warm fire burns in the hearth and our baby whimpers in the cradle, I contemplate this partner of my pilgrimage and I ask her who she is?

43

HERA. Ironing. I am the Universal Wife. I am Mrs Hera Somebody. Darby and Joan. We are King and Queen of our uncosy
Castle. The Home Life of Pericles and Aspasia.

JAY. Opening his evening paper. So now they are joined together
in Holy Deadlock.

HERA. Dampening the clothes. She has a Certificate to that effect
stored in a suitcase under the Spareroom bed. Upon her
finger gleams the plain gold band. Together they have grown
ripe and round in marketing and matrimony.

JAY. But what of this old bundle of fur and feathers that snuffles
and shivers in the most comfortable chair? He turns off the
Radio.

THE RELATIVE. Chuck chuck. Krrr-Krrr-Krrrrr. Talk – talk – talk.

HERA. The companion of our domesticity. An immoveable
Relative.

THE RELATIVE. Eggs today. Soup tomorrow. Don't forget to read
the meter. Talk-talk-talk. She turns up the Radio.
    (*She does so.*)

JAY. Looking for his shoes. How long, O Lord, How long?

HERA. Until tomorrow whenever that may be. Indicating his shoes
on the hearth. If he does not like it why did he marry her?

JAY. If she does not like it why did she insist? From his angle
there are the gametes. He liked the look of her. Psychologic-
ally: he required somebody to talk to in the evenings.
Economic: Her Father was a Mason. And of course the
Personal Allowances are better. Lacing shoes. On the other
hand she seemed anxious to marry him. I wonder why.

HERA. Mainly because of other women. Other women are narrow.
All they can talk about is what some man said to them, and
if you say the slightest thing yourself, they get quite cynical
looking. Fetching the fireguard. Has he succeeded, so far, in
identifying her with the woman of his dreams?

JAY (*taking down the mask*). Not so far. There has not yet been
any appropriate moment in married life to propose such a
test, without risk of an argument.

THE RELATIVE (*in ascending cadences*). Talk-talk-talk. Talk-talk-
talk. Where is the wild honey of their youth?

HERA. The Nereid dancing naked on the shore?

JAY. The shepherd boy who gave the shy young moon its round-
ness?

THE RELATIVE (*in a descending scale*). Gone-gone-gone.

HERA. And in their place are these two substitutes – a little wiser,

and a good deal better off. Hanging the clothes before the
fire.

THE RELATIVE. Krrr-krrrrk. Are they really better off?

JAY. Of course they are. Hasn't he learnt to suffer wrong for
profit's sake – to compromise with fools – bend to the breeze?
Now he has all that milk-fed wisdom of the middle-aged, and
the benefits that go with it. Commences to fill his pipe.

THE RELATIVE. Unstable as water, he shall not prevail. He should
have married that nice young Psyche girl. He's not the boy he
was in my time. *And* he has a very bad breath.

JAY (*coughing*). Well, what about her? Is she any the wiser?

(*The baby whimpers.* JAY *turns off the radio.*)

HERA. How could she not be wiser? Now she knows how to train
puppies and to persuade children to eat bread and butter when
they call for cake. Now she can explain why Santa Claus is so
much kinder to the horrid little girl next door. Now she knows
life as a Nursery Rhyme cherishing a hopeless longing for
Homeric Verse.

THE RELATIVE. Krrrk Krrrk! He has quite the wrong attitude
towards her!

JAY. It is defensive. It is necessary to preserve his mind as an
instrument functioning independently. Lighting up. And after
all, what about her attitude towards him?

HERA. Uninspired but practical. As he has proved himself
incapable of carrying her to emotional heights of rising
intensity, she has decided to train him to tasks of utility. She
hands him the hot iron. Indicating the fireplace.

JAY. Burnt! Ow! How is he trained to such tasks?

(*The* RELATIVE *turns on the radio.*)

HERA. By appealing to his better nature. She has, for instance,
given him the best years of her life.

JAY. Which have enriched him largely in responsibilities.

HERA. She is a good wife who knows her limitations. She relies
on his decisions in almost everything.

JAY. So long as he decides acceptably.

HERA. And yet he does not seem to be satisfied. If only someone
would tell her what it is that men really want she would
have tried to get it for him – to do it for him. But nobody
seems to know, and he knows least of all.

JAY (*after rising and turning off the Radio.*) Beloved enemy of
the spirit – seated in the holy of holies – knowing all his
futilities, and ventilating them every one at inappropriate

moments. As every action springs from many motives, so with unerring fingers she will seek out the meanest, and display it to his eyes as though it were the only one.

HERA. And yet, she means so well – she tries so hard. Living creatures longing to love – why must they wage this endless war – ears steeled against each other's cries, wrung out in love's despair?

JAY. Since bound together with a yellow band, they feed upon each other's hearts and minds, like captive eagles, till at last they have no longer any tears, and so they weep no more.

(The Baby whimpers.)

HERA. Yet, twined grotesquely, they have planted the tree of life.

JAY. Yes. Here, at least, they have done something that cannot be sneered at. But is it the produce of the lordly mind? Pah – that only hatches a brood of gargoyles! The clay alone conceives, and can create this miracle that clamours in the cradle.

THE RELATIVE *(turning on the radio)*. Talk-talk-talk. Spoil the child. Spoil the child. Nobody knows how to bring up children nowadays. And the cost of everything is ridiculous.

JAY *(turning it off)*. What does this intolerable third party know? The uncertainty of the weather – the causes of flatulence – the danger of draughts. You timber-tongued obstructionist! Is it not enough that you forbid the alteration of the position of any of the furniture, that you provide that only yesterday's newspapers shall be found on the table – never today's, that you collect useless cartons, bottles and tins with which to encumber the bathroom? Cursed be the nurse who nourished the craftsman, who fashioned the mattress on which your father kept your mother from sleep! He looks at the mask in his hands.

HERA. He seems restless. Why?

JAY. He is wondering whether he knows her well enough to ask her now to try it on.

HERA. On the other hand, maybe he knows her too well.

JAY *(putting the mask under his coat)*. No, perhaps it is not wise. The matter can wait till the right moment.

HERA. When is the right moment to ask a wife whether she is actually another woman?

JAY. Never mind. Let's think about other things. He looks at his watch.

THE RELATIVE. Why has he not been to see me? He was a nice

46

boy when I could make him wash behind his ears. Once upon a time. Once upon a time. Krrrk-Krrk!

HERA. In spite of this comforting postponement, he still seems restless. Why?

JAY. He is wondering what to do about his old friend Meedy, who is liable to arrive at any moment.

HERA. Clearing the table. Will his old friend Meedy not be welcome?

JAY. No. Meedy is a school friend of bachelor habits and of lax conversation, and prima facie, people in this category are not persona grata.

HERA. Will he, in fact, be shown the door?

JAY. Not at all. The wife will welcome him with an electric smile.

HERA. What then has the husband got to worry about?

JAY. The fact that if his old friend is invited in, he will be skilfully forced to eat what would otherwise be his host's breakfast. Hence, he prefers to prevent this disaster by meeting him in the street outside. Whence they will repair jointly to some neighbouring hostelry. He gets his hat and coat.

HERA. Informing her of this intention?

JAY. Certainly not. Upon the pretext of purchasing a packet of cigarettes. Putting on his coat. He hopes that this subterfuge will be successful?

HERA. It will not. Whenever he is particularly careful in his behaviour, she knows that he has been drinking. Whenever he is unctuous about her needs, she knows that he has been with another woman. She gives him his muffler.

JAY. Why, then, does she allow him to go?

HERA. Because she has a remark to make on his return, and if he does not go she will be unable to make this remark.

(THE RELATIVE *turns on the radio, loudly.*)

JAY. I can't stay here. I can't stay here.

(*He dashes out down the ramp, tripping at the bottom. There is a loud crash.*)

THE RELATIVE. Krrrrrk. What was that?

HERA. He appears to have fallen downstairs.

THE RELATIVE. Did he break his neck?

HERA. I don't think so.

THE RELATIVE. Ah! What a pity. What a pity. What a pity. What a pity . . .

(*Upper Curtains close. The Radio fades out into the ticking of the Minutes as the clock hands advance to 8.00.*)

47

THE MINUTES. Tick tock tick tock tick tock. (*They continue, to background for a while before fading away.*)

JAY (*on lower level*). I must hurry. I shall be late.

A DEEP VOICE (*half whispering*). It is later than you think.

JAY. What was that? Something is following me. (*Pause*) The minutes run, and in their train they bring a host of twisted things. I must hurry.

A DEEP VOICE (*mockingly*). Yes, hurry, Jay. Hurry.

JAY. Meedy, Meedy! Where are you?

MEEDY (*entering*). Hello, Jay. Aren't you looking a bit peculiar?

JAY. Somebody's been following me.

MEEDY. Think nothing of it. It was probably only me. I'm always following people.

JAY. How about a drink?

MEEDY. Just what I was going to suggest. There's a nice little bar somewhere over here.

JAY. Where?

MEEDY (*going to the ramp*). Up here. Come on. Open up. Open up.

(*They go up the ramp. The curtains open disclosing a small bar parlour. Behind the counter sits DORA, staring gloomily at her face in the mirror of a Beauty Box. At the only table, PHILLY and CALLIE are sitting over a couple of cocktails. They are now married women – the first somewhat smoother than the other, but still good friends.*)

MEEDY. Seems to be full up, but there's a table down here.

(*They turn around and go to the table and chairs on the lower level.*)

PHILLY. The trouble with me, Callie, is that I'm in a rut.

CALLIE (*sceptically*). Yes, I know. One of those Bermuda-Miami ruts.

PHILLY. Actually, Bermuda can be a terrible rut.

CALLIE. Listen, if you want a rut, you come and see my Shangri Lar. I'm the one that's in a rut.

PHILLY. Comment? Quelle blague.

CALLIE. And don't talk French to me. I find it hard enough to understand my children.

PHILLY. Let's have another little stimulant.

CALLIE. I shouldn't, really.

PHILLY. Nonsense. We're only middleaged once. I'll get you to that monstrous bus terminal. (*She signals to the Bar, and DORA comes across.*)

48

DORA. Excuse me, Am I interrupting you, or just myself?

PHILLY. Why, if it isn't our Dora! Surely you don't work here?

DORA. Certainly I work here. Why not?

PHILLY. Oh no reason at all. Except, of course, that it's rather a let-down for the College. I mean – you to be working here.

DORA. You drink here, don't you?

PHILLY. That's different.

DORA. Different? You mean that you can be drunk but I mustn't?

PHILLY. Now you mustn't be argumentative, Dora. If you had arranged your life properly without so many alibis, you wouldn't have to work at all.

DORA. I do my best, but everybody lets me down.

PHILLY (*sternly*). I said, without so many alibis.

CALLIE. After all, look at Philly. She never works.

DORA. She's got money.

CALLIE. You mean she's got Alimony.

PHILLY. Now Callie, that's not a very nice thing to mention.

CALLIE. It's a very nice thing to have.

DORA. Nobody's ever given me any Alimony.

PHILLY. That's just what I've been saying, Dora. You've obviously been badly advised. Not that money is everything.

DORA. No. Of course not. Not unless you've got it.

PHILLY. Now don't be confusing, dear. The real question is, has one managed to fulfil oneself? Now obviously you haven't. But Callie has.

CALLIE. Four children. Is that what you call fulfilling myself?

DORA. Well you've been fulfilling *them* anyway.

PHILLY. Maybe so. And think of her full and busy life out there in Shangri Lar. . . .

CALLIE. While you fritter away your time in Norman Hartnell's. It must be tough.

PHILLY (*getting a little shrill*). I was about to say, in and out of my Psychiatrist's. Neither of you can realise the strain of my life – the packing and unpacking, the trouble with servants, all those ghastly First Nights, the provincialism of that Beckett Set, – the avant-garde magazines one has to know the names of – the squash at the Private Views – the plumbing in Po. . . .

DORA. In what?

PHILLY. Now don't look like that, Dora. It's a charming little place near Biarritz that I'm referring to. My dears my life is just one long Brou-ha-ha.

CALLIE. Listen, drop that Berlitz stuff. I told you so before.

PHILLY. Oh God, I can see that I'm wasting my time with you two!

DORA. Me too.

PHILLY. Now be frank, Callie. What real troubles have you got? A pleasant little home – in its own way. A husband who is only there at regulated moments. And little ones growing up all around you.

CALLIE. Well I'll tell you. First of all there's teeth. They're all crooked and have to be straightened. Then there's hair. That's too straight and has to be curled. Whatever's curved has to be straighter and whatever's straight has to be curved and vicey versa. Why the hell can nothing come naturally at the proper angle?

PHILLY. Ah dear! I'm sure I would quite enjoy those little problems. Wouldn't you, Dora dear?

DORA (*wiping her eyes*). Oh I'm sure I would. But I'll have to go now. There's two fellows over there roaring for drinks. Drinks! Just imagine that! Who do they think they are?

PHILLY. Well just bring us two more Dry Martinis dear while you're at it. Very very dry, dear.

DORA (*going to* JAY *and* MEEDY *on the lower level*). Two very very dear Dry Martinis. Oh dear dear!

CALLIE. Then there's the P.T.A. You can fulfil yourself there all right with that bunch! And Philly – (*lowering her voice*) Have you ever heard of the Brownies?

PHILLY. Brownies? You mean those rather nice little cookies?

DORA (*to the men*). And the same for you I suppose?

MEEDY (*with a flashy smile*). Yes, love. I'm sure I know that face.

DORA. Well it's not the area you've been looking at.

CALLIE. No I don't. I mean a hellish organisation that we don't mention above a whisper. Crowds of little girls wrecking the Living Room.

JAY (*to Dora*). Just whatever you intend to bring us anyhow.

(DORA *goes back to the Bar*.)

PHILLY. Why of course. 'Lend a Hand' is their motto. Are you in that? A bit ripe for a Brownie, I'd have thought.

CALLIE (*venomously*). I'm NOT a Brownie. I'm what they call a Wise Brown Owl.

PHILLY. I say! That's rather cute. 'Wise' as well as brown?

CALLIE. There's nothing wise about it. If that's an Owl's life give me the Horse Marines.

PHILLY. Much better for you than Bridge.

CALLIE. Philly, it seems to me that there's only one thing wrong with both of us. I ought to be you, and you ought to be me.

PHILLY. Maybe there's something in that. How about changing around?

CALLIE. Do you think we could?

PHILLY. We can always try. Let's do it.

(*They change hats.*)

PHILLY. Well?

CALLIE. How does it suit me?

(DORA, *after having had some trouble with the bottles, brings them a couple of drinks.*)

PHILLY. Terrible. But you'll get used to it. Does this look all right on me?

(DORA *agrees and disagrees.*)

CALLIE. That depends on the effect you're after.

PHILLY. Maybe we haven't tried long enough. Let's concentrate.

CALLIE. O.K. Go away, Dora. We're concentrating.

(DORA *returns to the Bar.*)

JAY. I wonder what's going on up there? I think we know those two.

MEEDY. I guess we could if we wanted to.

JAY. They were in College with us. (*He rises unsteadily*) Coming up to speak to them?

MEEDY. Not me. Not with those Martinis to be paid for.

CALLIE. Philly, don't look now, but there's a man coming up. What do we do?

PHILLY. Oh, just remain nonchalant.

JAY (*who has come up the ramp*). Excuse me. Aren't we old friends?

CALLIE (*nonchalantly*). I don't know, I'm sure.

PHILLY. Why I believe it's that odious Jay Foss. You remember him.

CALLIE. Not the one there was all that scandal about?

PHILLY. What scandal?

CALLIE. He had some sort of an affair with a clock.

PHILLY. Why of course. Rather disgusting.

JAY. You're Philly, aren't you? Les's girl as I remember. And you're Callie.

CALLIE. Oh no. I'm Philly now.

JAY. That's strange. I could have sworn. . . .

PHILLY. Are you suggesting that we don't know who we are?

JAY. Oh No! I don't want to do that. But. . . .

CALLIE. You see, Callie, I don't think it's much good.

PHILLY. You're right, Philly. Anyhow, I don't think I want to be you. Shall we change back again?

CALLIE. Let's.

(*They change hats again. Everybody except* JAY *starts to sway slightly.*)

PHILLY. Didn't you like it either?

CALLIE. No. Not much.

PHILLY. That's the way of things. One thinks one would like to be somebody else, but one never really does. Even Dora there. I guess she prefers to be always in trouble.

JAY. Callie, may I . . . ?

PHILLY. Philly.

JAY (*looking at Callie*). Philly?

CALLIE. No Callie.

(*He sits down puts his hand to his brow for a moment. The swaying grows more noticeable.*)

JAY. But didn't you say you were . . . ?

PHILLY. Things were different then. Did you want to speak to me, particularly?

JAY. I was just going to ask whether – whether either of you happened to be somebody else. But if you're not quite certain about yourselves, I suppose it would be a waste of time.

CALLIE. What would?

JAY. To ask if you were somebody else. I mean – you see . . .

(*He produces the mask.*)

PHILLY. Not very lucid, I'm afraid. Have you been drinking?

JAY. Yes, but we're also waiting. I was just wondering if this mask belonged to either of you . . . if . . . ?

PHILLY. That depends on whether it fits, doesn't it?

JAY. If you aren't certain who you are yourselves . . .

PHILLY. I'm certain who I am. I'm Hunger.

JAY (*startled*). I beg your pardon? Please don't sway about like that.

CALLIE. I'm the opposite of Hunger. We're not swaying about. You are.

JAY. I think you both must be a little drunk.

PHILLY. Nonsense! It's you that's drunk. Not us.

JAY. Did she say she was Hunger?

CALLIE. Yeah, but don't mind her. That's ridiculous. I'm Hunger. She's Indigestion.

52

JAY. Meedy – would you please come over here and help.

MEEDY (*coming up*). It all depends on whether a man should say to a girl because as if he can't he has no right in the first place.

JAY. O God! You're all drunk now. I can't understand a word.

PHILLY. It was perfectly clear to me, which proves that it's you who must be drunk.

CALLIE (*gabbling*). And don't think I don't know what you'll soon be hinting at you want me to try that mask on and I shall tell my husband what you've suggested he'll be furious in fact everybody in Shangri La will be furious it's terrible to think that a girl can't come and have a quiet talk with one of her school friends in a place like this without having people coming up to her and making suggestions like that.

JAY (*in despair*). I'll never find her – never! Nobody will ever help me!

PHILLY (*gabbling*). I'd be glad to but we'll have to see my lawyer first he always insists on keeping me right and you can't expect something for nothing you know but then men always do don't they maybe if you would write me a letter first that can be read out in Court or if you're in such a state about it why don't you try Dora over there she's in very low water poor girl and would probably be glad to try it on for a Fiver or one of those things with Swift on them. What about Dora?

JAY. Dora? It couldn't be Dora, could it?

DORA (*coming over*). What do you mean by that? Why couldn't it be me?

JAY. I just thought . . . I was wondering –

DORA (*confidentially*). As a matter of fact, it *is* me.

JAY. You?

DORA. You needn't look so surprised. I suppose you think I'm not good enough.

JAY. All right – show me.

(*He hands her the mask. She hesitates.*)

JAY. What's the matter? What are you waiting for?

DORA. Why should I oblige you like this?

PHILLY. Just like a man. He expects her to do it for nothing!

JAY. Oh, is that it? Here, take this.

(*He tears off a ring, which he gives to* DORA.)

DORA. I don't as a rule do this sort of thing. Least of all for a ring. But just because you've doubted me, I shall.

(*She takes the mask, goes across to the bar followed by*

JAY, *and assumes a grotesque pose. A musical discord.* JAY *laughs hysterically.*)

DORA (*offended*). What are you laughing at?

JAY. At this parody – this revolting parody. Give it back to me.

(*He snatches the mask from her, and she goes behind the Bar in tears.*)

DORA. I was only doing my best. I might have known you'd let me down.

(CALLIE *and* PHILLY *rise, laughing like witches.*)

JAY. You're a nasty little fraud. That's all you are . . .

MEEDY. That's no way to talk to a girl who's doing her best.

DORA. They all do. Everybody lets me down. It must be my face.

(*She opens her beauty box and stares at it.*)

JAY. You're all mad or drunk or something.

(DORA'S *beauty-box empties its contents over the floor.*)

DORA. Don't bother to pick them up. They're the woes of the world. All the woes of the woeful world.

PHILLY (*dancing*). Which of us do you prefer? –

CALLIE. You don't have to say if it embarrasses you.

PHILLY. Pain convex or pain concave. Pain plus or pain minus.

CALLIE. We'll be glad to do what we can.

PHILLY. But always pain – pain – pain.

JAY. Leave me alone! Meedy help me. Oh, help me somebody.

(*He runs down below.*)

A NANNY (*entering below*). Is somebody yelling for his old Nanny? And has he got a pain? Open his mouth then, and we'll soon fix him up.

JAY. Go away, you horrible old woman! I don't know you.

THE NANNY. Oh yes, you do. I fed you and pinned you up, and dandled you before the fire. I locked the nursery door at night to keep out the family, and gave you tiny spoonfuls of gin whenever you wouldn't sleep, you silly boy. I told you little horror stories of an improving nature, and was your closest companion all the most impressionable years of your life. My monogram is stamped on your cranium. See!

JAY. Vampire! You fed me from the bottle with dogmas, creeds, catechisms and texts – fine food for babies. You tried to load my tiny limbs with chains before I had the strength to cry 'No! ', so that I should be shackled like yourself for ever.

(*He dashes away from her, back to the upper level, from which the other characters have already fled. But here he finds himself met by two groups of sinister figures, pointing and threatening from each side. Behind them the Bar, Table and chairs are struck.*)

THE NANNY (*below*). Ah, Sin! Sin! Nothing but Sin! The Sins of little children! The Sins of the Fathers!
(*She moves off, wailing.*)

THE SINS OF THE FATHERS (*Pointing and closing in*). We are the Sins of the Fathers. Cirrhosis – Gout – the pallid blood of Gentility. For their pleasures we prick him. Burn him up! Scald him! Tear his rotting flesh with pincers of red-hot steel – that their sins may be blotted out – that they may rest in Peace!

JAY (*dashing at them with flying fists*). No! No! I want none of you!
(*As he drives them off, cursing and spitting, he finds himself face to face with* HERA *who has entered behind them.*)

HERA. What about your own Sins? I watched them with cat's eyes. When you went out and when you came in. I wrote them all down in a tradesman's note-book with cash columns, subtracting and dividing the minutes and seconds so that I could prove to you that you loved me no longer. You have cheated me in marriage. There was always another that you loved.

JAY (*after a ghastly pause*). Yes, there was always another! If I could sweat her from my body I would do so. Were memory a thing of eyes and ears I would have been blind and deaf by my own hands long ago. I married you, but I still love her. (*He hears slow footsteps approaching*) .What are those footsteps?
(*As shadowy Doubts come gathering in the background,* HERA *speaks again.*)

HERA. You married me to make a mock of me. You promised me that nocturnal gymnastics could create a permanent Paradise.

JAY. I never did! At least I was sincere.

THE DOUBTS (*dancing*). We are Doubts. You doubt if you are sincere, but are you sincere in your doubts? Or even in doubting that you doubt that you doubt? Where is your own reality, and what the reality that doubts your own reality? Suppose the world is just a picture swimming before your eyes – each day a patch of white that grows and passes with the dark reality of night? What then may lie behind?

THE MINUTES. Tick tock. Tick tock. Tick tock.

JAY. Those footsteps once again!

(HERA *and the* DANCERS *have faded away, but now his* SHADOW *appears on the wall behind him. He tries to run, but it follows.*)

HIS SHADOW. Hark to an ass braying its unspeakable desires! Run – run. The World is wide.

JAY (*trying to dodge*). Stop following me! Leave me alone!

HIS SHADOW. I cannot leave you, Jay. You willed your shadow to grow tall until it lay across the Earth. So now I stride in grisly majesty behind you. Why run from me? I am as swift as you. Maybe a little swifter.

JAY. As swift as the fear of Death that will not leave me. Where can I run? Every acre is a graveyard!

HIS SHADOW. Wherever you may run I shall be there behind you. You willed your Shadow to grow tall; and now, as the sun sinks in a flaming sky, behold, your wish is granted: I grow, I grow with the setting sun!

JAY. Why should I be afraid of endings? Why should I love this thing called life – this thing that I have purchased from the clock? Is it to drug myself with lies, slaughtering reason and enthroning corpses in the name of faith, till deep in the grave I end the circuit of my longing in infinite farewell?

HIS SHADOW. No reason. Make your terms with Fate.

JAY. It is to meet her once again that I must live. It is to raise her mask and see her face. But now the years wrap round me like a winding sheet, and hope is dying in my eyes. I can see nothing but mortality. Rattle, wrinkle, drooping and decay. I run. I run. But what man can outstrip Death!

THE MINUTES.

> Tick tock. Tick tock.
> We run. We run.
> The minutes run.
> Tick tock. Tick tock.
> The little minutes run.

HIS SHADOW. Earth – Dust – Crumbling – And Decay.

JAY.

> Decay! If only I could love without sight or sound –
> Without the miracles of touch and sense,
> Then I would be mightier than Death
> And I could lie in peace.
> But when that studded door clangs to behind me
> How shall I love her then

When once my body is no more?
When eyes no longer see nor fingers feel?
What shall I do if, when she comes again
My prison is an unreprieving grave?

HIS SHADOW.

When eyes shall cup the roots of daisies
When with the mole
You creep back into the soil
Moss for a pillow
Life's troubled bubble broken.

THE MINUTES.

We run. We run. The Minutes run.
Tick tock. Tick tock.
The footsteps of the End.

JAY (*battering on the clock*) No, No! Not yet, you dirty thief! Keep those pilfering paws for other pockets. What do you want with me? Haven't you Swift and Shaw to goster with? And Cleopatra's charms to keep you quiet? Why can't you leave me with the Living in this ha'penny place where I have other business to attend to? (*The clock ticks louder.*)

THE SHADOW. Prepare the waxen lilies! Turn the sod!

JAY. No, no! Was it for the this the clay was sanctified – to be a home for all the crawling creatures in the grass?

HERA'S VOICE: Fumigate the house! This thing I loved must be removed – and quickly!

JAY. Stop thief! I am robbed! I am robbed!

(*He batters on the clock. There is a loud crash, and the lights go out except in the clock face. Police whistles sound.*)

VOICES (*in the dark*). What's happened? What's up? What's going on? Did you see what he did? Throw him out! Hold him down! Fighting drunk! Yes, he did it! Police! Have you got him? Ah be quiet and nobody will hurt you. Get him to the Bridewell. Is there much damage done? Who let him in in that condition? It's all right, gentlemen please. Please don't get disturbed.

A LOUD VOICE (*in the darkness*). Silence in Court!

(*As the curtains part, the lights rise upon a Court of Justice, and it is four o'clock. On the Bench (above) is Mr Justice Somebody, and* JAY *is in the dock below. His Counsel*

HAROLD CASTOR Q.C. (*with him* E. POLLUX B.L.). *The Jury consists of twelve stuffed dummies sprawling in their Box or alternatively twelve painted faces on a strip of wood. Various Solicitors, Criers and Clerks are sitting gloomily around a large table on the lower level.* CASTOR Q.C. *is on his feet, and a Constable is in the Witness Box.*)

CONSTABLE (*reading from a notebook*). Particulars of an Occurence. On Thursday the 21st inst. at 3.45 a.m. or p.m. in consequence of a report received by me, I proceeded to the licensed premises of Thomas Lennon, No. 23 Lower Abbey Street, where I observed the accused in the Select Saloon Bar striking at a piece of furniture, the property of the said T. Lennon, to wit an antique Grandfather clock, value £250, with a blunt instrument, with intent to do grievous bodily harm. I duly cautioned the accused who made the following statement, to wit: 'I am being robbed'. I then enquired from the accused whether he wished to prefer any charge against any of those present, to which the said accused gave an unintelligible answer, upon which I observed that he was under the influence of drink.

JAY. Was I doing that?

CONSTABLE. That and more.

JAY. Jesus!

HAROLD. I object.

THE LEARNED JUDGE (*opening his eyes*). Er – what exactly do you object to, Mr Castor?

HAROLD. I object generally, m'Lud, to the whole proceedings as scandalous and embarrassing. Most embarrassing.

PROSECUTING COUNSEL. That is a most improper remark.

HAROLD. If my learned friend does not like my remark he has my permission to take himself home to the bosom of his wife and five children, four of whom, to my certain knowledge are illegitimate.

PROSECUTOR. A fact which if true, nobody could be better aware than so old and intimate a guest of the family as my learned friend.

JUDGE (*interested*). Oh come now, Mr Longbottom. Is that quite fair?

LONGBOTTOM. M'Lud during a long and moderately successful career at the Bar I can pride myself on never having failed

JUDGE. That scarcely seems an adequate reason, Mr Longbottom, to call a spade a spade.

for throwing out a suggestion that our friend, Mr Castor, is a rake.

(*Laughter in Court, in which His Lordship joins.*)

HAROLD. An observation, if I may say so, in Your Lordship's happiest vein, surpassed only on that occasion during my student days, when Your Lordship first made the same joke.

A VERY OLD SOLICITOR (*rising*). M'Lud, I represent the Trustees –

JUDGE. Do you press your objection, Mr Castor?

HAROLD. I do, M'Lud.

JUDGE. Well I will note your objection. Do you wish me to rule on it?

CASTOR. That is a matter of comparative indifference to me, M'Lud. Any ruling that Your Lordship may make on this or on any other matter can prima facie be reversed on appeal.

LONGBOTTOM. Perhaps Your Lordship could get around the difficulty by a Rule Nisi on my friend's demurrer.

THE VERY OLD SOLICITOR. . . . . er, the Trustees of the Compound Settlement.

JUDGE. Just what I was about to suggest. You will appreciate, Mr Castor, that if you are prepared to argue that . . .

THE VERY OLD SOLICITOR. . . . which in Nisi Prius was held to include the er –

HAROLD. M'Lud, if I argue that A is A I have said nothing of any importance unless the statement happens to be untrue Phibbs versus Phibbs.

JUDGE. Ah! You follow Mr Castor's point, Mr Longbottom?

HAROLD. Piffle!

LONGBOTTOM. Then keep your piffle in your pants!

CRIER. Mr Blotter wishes to intervene, My Lord.

JUDGE. Who? Oh. What? Oh, Mr Blotter. Yes. Eh? What is it?

THE VERY OLD SOLICITOR. It may clear matters up if I remind Your Lordship that I represent the interest of the Trustees . . .

ALL. What Trustees? What's he talking about? Trustees of what?

THE VERY OLD SOLICITOR. Oh yes. I must make this clear. The Trustees of the Statute-barred Remainder . . .

JUDGE. Oh tut, tut. Kindly sit down, Mr Blotter.

HAROLD. Don't interrupt, you cretinous dolt! (*Then to* POLLUX *who is pulling at his gown from the rear*) And you shut up too!

JUDGE. I think we had better proceed with the evidence. We must not detain the Constable.

CONSTABLE. Thank you, my Lord. Damage to the said clock. The glass in the face was cracked. A large incised scar running from the left of the front base and crossing to the right of the upper section. Damage to the blunt instrument – None. I then took a number of names and addresses from various parties present or not present as the case may be none of whom made any statements and escorted the Accused to the Bridewell. The road was wet but in good condition.

JUDGE. Thank you, Constable.

CONSTABLE. A pleasure, sir. You may be sure I'll mention your name in certain quarters.

JUDGE (*bowing politely*). Thank you Constable. I'm sure you will. We all appreciate our Police. And now, Mr Castor, do you wish to cross-examine the Constable? Or perhaps you would prefer not to dispel the fog which I have no doubt exists in the minds of the Jury thanks to Mr Longbottom's masterly examination-in-chief?

POLLUX (*rising and speaking with great sarcasm*). May I ask how you identify the prisoner?

CONSTABLE. By his face, sir.

POLLUX. Ah! By his face! But can you remember his face clearly?

CONSTABLE. As clearly as I can recollect your own, sir, on a somewhat similar occasion.

(HAROLD *rises and strikes* POLLUX *over the head with his brief. The latter collapses into his seat as the* CONSTABLE *comes triumphantly out of the Witness Box.*)

HAROLD. Excuse my Junior, m'Lud. He suffers from varicose veins. I appear for the Accused, and I now propose to open the defence – if I can find it.

(*He picks up various papers with great distaste.*)

JUDGE. And by whom are you instructed, Mr Castor?

HAROLD. By an exceedingly shady firm of Attorneys, if I may say so, with an accommodation address in Little Mary Street, whose name though written in pencil at the bottom of this bundle of dismal documents alleged to be a brief, is quite illegible to me, and probably would convey little to Your Lordship even if it were decipherable. I should also mention that this sad faced gentleman here opposite me, though nominally the Managing Clerk, is in reality the whole firm himself, having been struck off the Rolls in 1930 nominally for champerty, but actually for making a series of expensive applications on behalf of certain supposed minors and lunatics who were afterwards discovered to exist only in the realm of the imagination. However, this is by the way.

JUDGE. Dear me! Well I hope – ahem – that you have been adequately instructed today, Mr Castor?

HAROLD. You may rest assured, m'Lud, that I have been inadequately instructed with five sticky Treasury Notes which I only received ten minutes ago by threatening to retire from the case altogether before I had the opportunity of misleading Your Lordship further. (*Turning to* POLLUX *who is pulling his gown*) Don't let me have to speak to you again.

THE VERY OLD SOLICITOR. With regard to the Trustees –

EVERYBODY. Wrong Court! Sit down! Shut up! Throw him out!

HAROLD. My good man, you are under some serious misapprehension. Go away at once.

JUDGE. Yes, you must really not interrupt, Mr Blotter, or I shall have to have you removed. Now Mr Castor, I presume you are about to make the usual application for an adjournment to enable you to examine the contents of your brief?

HAROLD. Your Lordship need have no fear that I shall manage to gather sufficient knowledge of the facts as the case proceeds as are likely to be necessary for the purpose of addressing Your Lordship. My learned Junior, who persistently interrupts me because he has not been paid any fee at all, has doubtless looked up several cases off and on the point – whatever it may be. As for my instructing Solicitor, we need not expect any signs of excitement from him until the question of costs is mentioned, when the whole Court, we may be sure, will be galvanised into activity for the first time. (POLLUX *pulls his gown*.) Excuse me m'Lud.

>   (*He throws various papers into* POLLUX'S *face and the latter disappears below while picking them up.*)

JUDGE. Well, Mr Castor, after that display of forensic activity, I am sure we are anxious to hear your defence to this very serious charge?

HAROLD. My defence, m'Lud, is based on Section 15 of the Local Government Act 1898 by reason of which (*The* JUDGE *rapidly turns over the pages of a fat Law Book.*) – I confidently submit that Your Lordship has no jurisdiction whatever to hear a matter of this kind, and consequently the whole case for the prosecution falls to the ground. I ask therefore for a Direction.

LONGBOTTOM. Piffle!

HAROLD. And don't use that word to me!

JUDGE (*triumphantly*). But Mr Castor, I am under the impression – correct me if I am wrong – that this section deals with the licensing of public baths and washhouses.

HAROLD. If Your Lordship has a volume of the Statutes before you and you have succeeded on this occasion in turning to the correct page, I agree that Your Lordship may be right. I only mentioned the Section in the hope that neither Your Lordship nor my Learned Friend – as was reasonably probable – had ever heard of the Act before. That m'Lud concludes my case.

(*His Lordship then delivers judgment.*)

JUDGE. I have listened without much enthusiasm to the arguments addressed to me in this matter by learned Counsel upon both sides, and I must say that they have not assisted me to any noticable extent in reaching any conclusion as to what the issues – if any – may be in this somewhat difficult and unusual case. I have little doubt that the members of the Jury feel much the same sense of bafflement – and indeed, lack of interest – that I feel myself. Indeed, looking at their faces – (*Pause while he does this*) – which I must say do not convey to me any great sense of intelligence I am satisfied that they have even less interest in the exceedingly grave charges set forth in the Indictment than I have myself. In view, therefore of the unsatisfactory conduct of this case by members of both professions who, unfortunately, I am not in a position to penalise, I feel that the usual course should be followed: namely that the matter should be withdrawn from this Jury, and that the Accused should go to jail for a few months after which he should be committed for trial all over again . . .

(*General shouting of* Costs! Costs!)

JUDGE. I was about to come to that.

CRIER. Quiet! Quiet please!

JUDGE. Including, of course, Costs in the Cause.

JAY (*shouting above the renewed babble*). What does that mean?

THE VERY OLD SOLICITOR. That it includes, of course, the Costs of the Trustees!

(*The Judge hurls a number of books at the Bar below, but the only thing that stills the tumult is the arrival of* ALIX *in full campaigning uniform.*)

ALIX. I proclaim this Court suspended by order of the competent military authority.

JUDGE. Suspended? By what right?

ALIX. Martial Law has been proclaimed this evening, and a state of National Emergency announced.

ALL. But why? What has happened?

ALIX. The Hercules Bank of International Settlements has suspended payments. Temporarily of course.

JAY (*as drums start off*). There! I told them this would happen!

ALIX. All able-bodied men are summoned to register. Clear the Court at once.

> (*Bugle calls off. The lower level is stripped of everything, while Counsel take off their wigs and gowns. JAY is hustled off.*)

JUDGE. The Prisoner is released for National Service. I myself shall not hesitate to offer my services to the State in any consultative capacity.

HAROLD. While my learned friend and I will be available to join any non-party Ministry.

POLLUX (*Giving their costumes to an Attendant*). Get the money back on those!

> (*The curtains close above, while drumming starts off. Everybody hurries away except ALIX. Presently a file of soldiers enters, followed shortly by JAY, now encumbered with Field Equipment, a steel helmet and a rifle and bayonet.*)

ALIX. Mark time! Pick 'em up smartly. Fasten up those buttons. A uniform is something to be respected. (*Then to the panting JAY*) You're late! Why is this?

JAY. Sorry, Alix. Had to get into all this nonsense.

ALIX. Squad halt!

> (*The troops halt and the drumming stops.*)

JAY. Hello Alix. Don't you know me?

ALIX (*after a moment's consideration*). Troops, report up the road to Company Headquarters. Tell the Company Commander I'm on my way. Off, at the double. (*Then to JAY*) Not you.

> (*The Soldiers run off, and presently the upper curtains part, revealing a barren landscape with some tangled masses of barbed wire and a few shattered trees behind which the sunset glows. The clock advances to 8.00.*)

ALIX. Private Foss, don't you know that you're supposed to say 'Sir' to me?

JAY (*confused*). Why – I'm sorry, sir; of course. You're Head Boy again – of course.

ALIX (*thoughtfully*). Yes. I was Head Boy once. And then for a few years I was just an Old Boy. What degradation in the prime of life to be just an Old Boy! But now my time has come again. In a crisis like this it is I whom they have to send for. I am a Leader once again.

JAY. Yessir. A Captain. A great Captain.

ALIX. Actually a Substantive Major. But never mind that.

JAY. Then what are we waiting for? Start the drums again, sir, for they make me mad, and that is how I want to feel. Start the drums and let schoolboys come into their own. The drums! So that we can get on with the War, so that I can use my bayonet on somebody.

ALIX. Just one moment. I was nearly forgetting. Headquarters have directed me to impress upon all ranks that this force is not engaged upon a War. These are to be referred to in all official documents as Precautionary Operations for the Preservation of Peace, officially abbreviated to P.O.P.P.

(*A distant cheer from the troops and a shot rings out from somewhere. The drums begin again.*)

JAY. A shot, sir! A shot! Is that the signal to advance – with Fixed Bayonets, sir?

ALIX. Possibly, Private Foss. One can never tell. But there is one thing that must be emphasised. These operations – whatever they may be – must on no account be referred to as a War. Kindly remember that whatever we may be called upon to undertake, we are not an Army, but a Peace-Keeping Force. Remember that.

JAY. Oh. I see. That's rather disappointing. You mean – no Medals?

ALIX. That remains to be seen. There might be some Peace-keeping Medals, but I'm afraid it's not a promise.

(*Another shot. Both of them jump.*)

JAY. Ow! Well – you won't mind if I fix my Peace-Keeping Bayonet?

ALIX I have no instructions on that point. I suppose it's up to you. Anyhow, I'm going now, so keep in touch.

(*As a shadowy figure appears behind the entanglements, lurking on all fours, ALIX hurries away.*)

JAY (*fixing his bayonet*). Up the Pole! – I mean Up the POPP!

(*For a little while the two figures stalk each other until they meet face to face – JAY with his rifle and bayonet uplifted.*)

THE FIGURE. Come on! What are you waiting for?

JAY. It's Barney! What are you doing here?

BARNEY. Fighting. I'm the enemy. That's funny isn't it!

JAY. It wouldn't have been funny if somebody had got hurt.

BARNEY. Oh I wouldn't have hurt *you*.

JAY. But you were shooting, weren't you?

BARNEY. Oh yes. But only to get you to shoot at me.
(*A whistle sound off.*)

JAY. What do you mean? I might have killed you.

BARNEY. That's right. That's the idea. Would you mind doing it now?

JAY. Certainly not.

BARNEY. But you were going to use your bayonet.

JAY. That's different. I didn't know that you were anybody in particular.

BARNEY. But Everybody's someone in particular.
(*Another whistle, off, followed by* ALIX'S *voice.*)

ALIX. (*distantly*). Hey!

BARNEY. There now! You're only going to get into trouble.

JAY. How?

ALIX (*Off*). What the hell's going on up there?

JAY. It's only Alix. (*Shouting back*) One moment, please.

BARNEY. You'd better do it. There'll only be trouble.

JAY. Don't be absurd. Sensible people don't want to die.

BARNEY. Oh but you're quite wrong there. Everybody wants to die. Only they don't usually know it.

ALIX (*closer*). Get busy up there!

BARNEY. There you are! I told you so.

JAY. Stop talking rubbish.

ALIX (*louder still*). What the hell do you think you're up to?

JAY (*shouting back*). Bugger off! Can't you see I'm busy? (*Then to* BARNEY) If you must die why can't you kill yourself?

BARNEY (*as they sit down together*) Oh, I wouldn't do that. That would be against the law. I used to have that idea once, and even tried it a few times before I knew better. But somebody always came along and stopped me and got his name in all the papers while I only went to jail.

JAY. I'm not surprised.

BARNEY. Then I saw that the law was perfectly right. You see, if one is disgusted with one's own humanity, how *can* one kill oneself, when the very act of suicide is so large an affirmation of one's own bravery? Besides, it has no psychological importance, has it? Unless one can be aware of it. And how

65

can you be aware of it once you're dead? You see my difficulty?

JAY. Yes. I mean No I don't.

ALIX (*appearing below*). Look here – what about these Operations?

JAY. Well, what about them?

ALIX. Aren't you going to stick him with your bayonet?

JAY. Why?

ALIX. Why? I never heard of such a thing! Your's not to reason why. Stick him with your bayonet at once!

JAY. Go away, please. Can't you see that we're all working to rules.

ALIX. I don't care what you're working to. This is a Peace-keeping force, so it's your duty to stick him with your Bayonet. Otherwise what are we here for?

BARNEY. He's right, you know. That's why War is such a good thing.

JAY. Who says it's a good thing. Look at these fields – sown with dragons' teeth, where only the fortunate are still and silent, and where the luckless lie, crying with crooked mouths for sleep. This is a sorry harvest home to mark the autumn of the year.

BARNEY (*as the sky reddens*). Autumn is a good thing. Sunset is the best time. For soon we shall all go to sleep. And in sleep we will each have our own world. Here we have only a world in common. And what a world!

JAY. To sleep? Perhaps never to wake.

BARNEY. You are against sleep?

JAY. Who isn't? When it may mean Eternity.

BARNEY. You want a Life without Death – a Joy without Pain – a Heaven without Hell?

JAY. Who doesn't?

BARNEY. But that's nonsense. You should cultivate a Sanity like mine, and then maybe you wouldn't contradict yourself so much.

ALIX. Look here for the last time are you both going to obey your orders or not? Turning serious operations into some sort of a farce. Sitting up there working to rule while everything that matters in the World is breaking down!

JAY (*dreamily*). Why should I kill to save the scheme of things for rogues to play with?

ALIX (*preparing to go*). Very well. I shall just have to go down and report you both to the Authorities, and this will mean another Conference and that's the end of everything. It's all very unfair to me. But I see somebody else coming up to talk to you, and soon you'll be sorry. She'll be able to tell you where you get off. Just you wait.

(*He grumbles off, still ad libbing out of sight.*)

JAY (*after a brief silence*). Look! Down in the plain the tiny troops are digging tiny graves, while – up there – the wreckage of a dying day! Why must all things have to end?

BARNEY. Including Love? Didn't a girl ask you once about that, and didn't you give her an answer?

JAY. That's so. 'Not for ever,' I said. 'That would not be love. That would be a feat of strength.'

BARNEY. You said more than that. Something about the importance of Endings and Beginnings. I wasn't paying much attention, but I dare say you were right. (*He sighs*) I guess I like endings.

JAY. I'd say the same, if only I could be sure of one thing – that I'll see that woman's face before I go.

BARNEY. Well here's a couple of them coming up the hill to talk to you. So I'll be off. After all, amn't I the enemy?

(*He gathers up his equipment and hurries off, as* CALLIE *arrives below with a solemn-faced girl of about twelve.* JAY *comes down to meet them on the lower level and the Curtains close behind him.*)

JAY. Well, if it isn't Callie! What are you up to in these parts?

CALLIE. More to the point – what are you doing – fraternising with enemy snipers? We've been watching you!

JAY. Oh that was only Barney. What I'm really considering is an attack on that damn clock.

CALLIE. Don't be a fool! Can't you see what will happen if you stop it. Do you think you can make the sun stand still? Because you want to live, you're trying to kill yourself. Does that make sense?

JAY (*hesitating*). I wonder if you're right.

CALLIE. Of course I'm right. I've had a tough time too, but I've been able to survive.

JAY. How brisk you've become, Calliope! Have you learnt that from your friend? Aren't you going to introduce me?

CALLIE. I will if you want me to. But you mayn't enjoy it.

JAY. You mean she's a bad child?

67

CALLIE. On the contrary. She'll probably make it clear that you're a bad father.

JAY. Me? You don't mean –? She's not the one was in the cradle? (CALLIE *nods*.) My –? God! How strange if in some way a child should have the answer.

> (*He approaches her. Up to this point she has been looking at the Audience.*)

JAY. My dear.

> (*She turns and surveys him calmly.*)

DAUGHTER. Who are you?

JAY (*ingratiatingly*). Don't you know me?

DAUGHTER (*not unkindly*). No.

JAY. Oh come! Who do I look like?

DAUGHTER. An old gentleman.

JAY. An old – Oh! (*Then to* CALLIE) Is she right?

CALLIE (*producing a pocket mirror*). Want to see?

JAY (*looking in it*). This thing plays practical jokes, you know. It slips a stranger into sight. But never mind. (*He hands it back.*) Youth is entitled to be a little tactless. You may kiss me, my dear.

DAUGHTER. How silly. Why should I kiss you?

JAY. Because you're mine. You're my daughter. Don't you understand?

DAUGHTER (*Stiffening*). Oh? (*Pause*) I didn't know that.

> (*He holds out his hands to her. She looks at them, and then places her own behind her back.*)

JAY. What's the matter, dear? (*She turns away.*) Why are you turning away? You're my –

DAUGHTER. I'm not anybody's. I'm myself.

JAY. Have I done anything to offend you. (*Pause. Then to* CALLIE) What's wrong?

CALLIE. Only your birthday. She doesn't approve of you, Jay. The young seldom approve of the old.

JAY (*to the girl*). Don't you want to have a father? (*Pause*) To love you?

DAUGHTER. How could you love me? I don't belong to people. I'm myself.

JAY. But I *do* love you. I know that I love you.

DAUGHTER. You only love a Daughter. I'm not just somebody's daughter. I'm Me.

JAY (*to* CALLIE). What does she mean by that? Isn't she my child?

CALLIE. Rather say, she is the daughter of Life's longing for itself. Who was it remarked: 'You may house their bodies, but not their souls. For their souls dwell in the house of Tomorrow, which you can never visit – not even in your dreams'?

JAY. Rather a pompous remark in the circumstances.

CALLIE. Only because you wouldn't like it to be true.

JAY (*with a wry smile*). And mayn't I even kill a fatted calf? Just a small fatted calf – or two?

CALLIE (*shaking her head*). I'm afraid there's no known procedure for Prodigal Fathers. But cheer up, Jay. It's a lucky man whose children are disappointed in him. It probably means that he's leaving behind something that's a bit bigger than himself. And that's a matter for congratulation.

JAY. So this is the kind of thing you teach them?

CALLIE. No. That's what I teach the Parents. I have more suitable remarks for the real Customers.

JAY. And do they believe you?

CALLIE (*smiling*). On the whole – No.

JAY. Obviously a futile occupation. But let's get out of here. After all, isn't that why you were sent up – to tempt me back to that loony bin?

POLLUX. Ladies and Gentlemen, pray silence for the Right Honourable Harold Castor – the Lord Incumbent!

HAROLD (*entering below*). Ah yes, gentlemen. Quite a crowd here this evening! Have you introduced everybody, Mr Private Secretary?

POLLUX (*looking round for the nearest person who happens to be* JAY). Allow me to present you to the Incumbent – Mr Er –

HAROLD (*affably*). Ah yes. I remember you well. Let me see now –

JAY. I think we were at College together, sir.

HAROLD. Oh really? At College. Um – well in that case you'd better have some sort of a decoration. Give me an Order, somebody.

(*There is some searching of pockets.*)

JAY. I wouldn't presume to order you in any way, sir.

HAROLD. No, No. Not that sort of an Order. And it's *I* who am giving it to *you*. This will probably do.

(*He takes a decoration of some sort off* POLLUX'S *tray, and tries to read it.*

HAROLD. The Order of what? Ah – General Excellence. Will that be all right?

JAY. Anything you say, sir.

69

HAROLD. I have followed your career with considerable interest, Mr Er – Pin it, Pollux.

JAY (*as* POLLUX *does so*). Oh thank you, sir. I'm sure I don't know how I deserve this.

HAROLD. Probably not. But who does?
(*He moves off to centre rear of the Table and sits down. The members of the Cabinet, who have been standing since his entrance, sit down too.*)

POLLUX (*confidentially*). Pipe, sir.

HAROLD (*taking it out and starting to fill it*). Oh yes. Thank you Pollux.

HAROLD (*when ready*). And now to business. My Bullox, Mr Speecher. I mean – um my Speech – um Mister –

POLLUX. This side up, sir. Gentlemen, pray silence for the Right Honourable the Incumbrance – Incumbent.

HAROLD (*reading it*). Er – Confucius tells us that the first step towards an adequate reform of the State is a rectification of names – a very profound observation, I may say, wherever it comes from. There is really nothing wrong with the world, gentlemen, except the names of things. Change the names at properly chosen intervals, and everybody will be satisfied. (*General agreement.*)

TYPHIS. There was a time when I was told that all the troubles of the times were due to the Sunday Papers.

HAROLD (*raising his voice and relights the pipe*). As Founder and Leader of the National Nominalist Party I can confidently claim that since taking office I have changed the names of almost everything I could lay my hands on without once altering the delicate balance of anything. I have consequently retained a comfortable majority and made millions happy. An estimable achievement if I may say so.
(*Applause.*)

BARNEY. And stayed in office!

HAROLD (*lighting his pipe again and becoming conversational*). Believe me, my dear fellow, I have no thirst whatever to be at the top. Is it my fault that I have been driven there by an extraordinary congestion at the bottom? If we have stayed in office, it is by following the fundamental democratic principle of giving everybody whatever they ask for. How else can we expect them to vote for us? (*Voices*: Hear, Hear!) SO – (*He rises and declaims*) let it never be said that we have not explored every avenue and left open every door – broadening down from precedent to precedent so that freedom may not perish from the earth. (*Emotionally*) Gentlemen, the ship is at last entering harbour. Full steam ahead!

(*Uproar and applause*).

(*He sits down and puffs triumphantly.*)

POLLUX. Now the financial provisions of the settlement, Lord Hercules. Minister for Money.

LES. Well, to be brief I have a different call on my attention. Industry must be kept on its feet, with the wheels turning and turning and turning and – well you know all of that. And all that this needs is money, simply that. So what we have to do is to get rid of all crippling debt payments and strikes and inflation, and start afresh with what everybody's got, plus productivity deals, and of course free collective bargaining, a general Moratorium, and equal cash for equal jobs including the Unemployed. As I have said before on many occasions – it's all just a matter of money. (*Then aside to* PHILLY *who has entered and is signalling.*) Yes my dear. Just coming.

A VOICE. Where are we going to get it?

LES. From the Banks, of course. What do you suppose they're for? (*Loud applause mixed with minor sounds of dissent which are stilled by* HAROLD, *as* LES *slips off under the command of* PHILLY.)

HAROLD. Much more important – and intelligible – than these technical matters is the question of General Disarmament, with the guarantee of Peace for everybody through mutual understanding. I give you General Theseus.

ALIX (*rising*). On temporary pay during the present crisis. (*Then reading*) It is agreed between the High Contracting Parties that, as from a date later to be settled, all offensive armaments shall be totally abolished and Peace universally declared. (*Enthusiastic response.*) As from the appointed date yet to be agreed, all Land Forces shall maintain only Small Arms and ceremonial bayonets – (*Voices*: Jolly Good. About time too!) – together with strictly defensive Artillery and Tanks, Napalm and Gas. Ships of War of all Powers shall only be permitted to carry defensive Projectiles and Torpedoes, while Air Forces shall universally be limited to Long Range Bombers intended for Police purposes only. While all existing Cease Fire Agreements shall be reintroduced at intervals of Six Months.

71

(*General Applause while* BARNEY *begins to laugh hysterically, and* JAY *advances on the Table in a menacing manner.*)

JAY. I am now going to twist somebody's arm in a purely defensive manner. It was going to be you (*Indicating* LES) but I think we had better begin with you (*Indicating* ALIX).

HAROLD. Now, now! There's no need to get personal. The General bears honourable scars.

BARNEY (*shouting*). Whereabouts? Let's see them!

HAROLD. In respectable places I'm sure.

ALIX. Not a General, sir. Still a substantive Major.

HAROLD. Never mind. That will be seen to. Make a note, Pollux. All Majors to be Generals – substantive of course.

BARNEY (*pointing at Harold*). He's the one to hit, Jay. All he cares about is Law and Policemen. Nothing about the Facts of Life.

HAROLD (*producing his pipe with great assurance*). Listen, Mr Whatsyourname, I know this much about the Facts of Life – that they are not only lethal, but – on the whole – in very bad taste. I don't know who invented them, but it wasn't me. And you needn't suppose that I enjoy Policemen any more than you do. But I also know this, that if you don't have Policeman you'll soon have something worse. And the same goes for me and my Government. (*Voices from around the table*: Hear Hear) If we are the fools and racketeers you seem to take us for, our worst foolishness lies in allowing ourselves to be elected to a rotten job. So there! (*He lights his pipe again amidst applause.*) Any comment?

(*There is an awkward silence.*)

JAY (*thoughtfully*). You know – he's got something there.

BARNEY. If he has, why does he have to keep on lighting that damn pipe?

HAROLD. It inspires confidence. Notice how calm I am. You'd vote for me rather than for him – now wouldn't you? Even though he's a – By the way, do I know you?

JAY. That depends on whether you still imagine that we were at school together.

HAROLD. Thank God I was never at school with anyone. That's one of the reasons why people insist on voting for me. If I had one of those damn ties, I'd be glad to tear it off and fling it in your face.

JAY (*smiling*). Then I would certainly vote for you.

HAROLD (*after some consideration*). Good man! How did you manage to get into this production?

JAY. Oh just merit, I suppose. I was one of the Ugly Sisters in last year's Pantomime. How about you?

HAROLD. I haven't the faintest idea. It just happened that way.

JAY. Well that's good! You seem to have finished up with a top part.

HAROLD (*pleased*). You think so? Who is this fellow, Pollux? He seems to have got some sort of a decoration.

POLLUX. Yes sir. You gave it to him.

HAROLD. What for?

POLLUX. Nobody knows.

HAROLD. What's in the book?

POLLUX (*fingering through a card index*). B – C – D – E Name: J. Jason Foss alias Phosphorous. Nothing here to indicate Religion.

HAROLD. That doesn't matter. What else?

POLLUX. Nothing about Parents, Politics or Income. Social background given as 'amorphous'. But he seems to have had some experience in Long Distance Cruising.

HAROLD. Why? Running what? That may be significant.

POLLUX. Doesn't say, sir. Simply 'Objectives and Destinations unknown' That's about all.

HAROLD (*taking the card*). Um. The Bureau seems to have been a little lax in this particular Dossier. No mention of what he wants?

POLLUX. Nothing so far as I can see sir. Except – er – he –

HAROLD (*irritably*). Come on, man, come on! Surely some gossip! Some questionable Liaisons? Is he married?

POLLUX (*searching through the fiile*). Well hardly. Well – there's this rather peculiar story about him having had some sort of a ceremony – um – with a Clock.

HAROLD. A clock! What nonsense is this?

POLLUX. . . . and the rumour goes that his most frequently expressed wish is to see the . . . the unknown face of some unidentified female before he dies.

HAROLD (*amidst general laughter from a number of eavesdroppers*). Well I never! That's a new one on me! A Clockomaniac!

POLLUX (*upset*). I'm sorry sir, but that's all it says.

HAROLD. Probably just wants to see the works! (*He joins in the laughter*) Well, I'm sure that can be arranged to his satisfaction! See to it at once, Pollux. We might need him one of these days in the Cabinet.

POLLUX. Certainly sir. But I've no idea where to begin.

(*Various fingers point in the direction of* ORPHEUS, *slumbering at his piano.*)

HAROLD. Who? Over there? Well, maybe you'd better begin with that peculiarly dressed character at the piano.

VOICES. That's right. Him over there. Name of Orph – would you believe it!

HAROLD. Sounds Lebanese, but one never can tell.

MEEDY (*intervening*). Can't you see he's stone-cold sober! You'll have to give him a drink.

HAROLD. Absurd! But do what he says.

(HAROLD *signals imperiously to a Waiter, who promptly brings a glass of wine to* POLLUX *who places it to* ORPHEUS'S *lips.* ORPHEUS *relaxes, smiles and takes the glass before entering into an inaudible conversation with* MEEDY *and* POLLUX *which obviously is concerned with the clock. He then produces the key which both men try to grab, which scuffle ends in* ORPHEUS *throwing it across the stage into a group where* JAY *has been talking to four of the Girls, who for some time have been offering him various reasons and inducements to come away.* POLLUX *dashes after the key, which he grabs and brings to* JAY, *leaving* BARNEY *organising a small community sing-song around the piano.*)

BARNEY (*as* POLLUX *dashes off*). Do nothing till you hear from me.

(LES *and* PHILLY *arrive together – the latter in a new hat. She joins the other girls.*)

MEEDY. Will you look at Les! Even Hercules is the slave of Omphale!

JAY. We all stand in a gigantic circle – each eating each other's tails!

(*Meanwhile* POLLUX *has retrieved the key which he brings to* JAY *who pushes the girls aside and strides to the clock where after a brief struggle with the lock, he gets the door open and reveals the swinging pendulum.*)

THE FIVE GIRLS. No. No! Don't touch it! It's just another trick! Leave it alone! Please listen to us, Jay!

(ORPHEUS *stops the sing-song – rising to his feet.*)

ORPHEUS (*shouting*). Was it a trick the last time? Didn't you get what you bargained for?

74

JAY. It was a gracious bargain, and she honoured it! I am ready for another.

(*The five Girls shriek and run from the stage.*)

ORPHEUS (*shouting*). Good man! Let them go! You'll soon know what to do!

HAROLD (*shouting*). Do what? Can't you say what you want!

ORPHEUS. The opposite of last time! Stop the Pendulum! That damned Pendulum!

(*The hands of the clock, which at the start of the scene were somewhere around 11.45 are now almost at midnight, having advanced slowly throughout the action.*)

(*As JAY stops the pendulum they arrive at midnight and a bell starts to toll twelve strokes, while the cast spreads out on the lower level, looking wildly round in all directions. After the twelfth stroke there is a brief hesitation after which another stroke is added and the light in the clock-face goes out. At the same time a spotlight from underneath the upper level throws the shadow of a woman upon the Cyclorama or back wall – small at first but growing larger as she comes forward, and mounts some invisible steps that bring her to the upper level from the rear. JAY sees her first and points, at which the whole cast turns around and faces up stage. As she appears she is picked up in a halo of light from a spotlight at the rear of the Auditorium. She is masked as before, and wears a voluminous cloak with a hood that covers her head and each side.*)

JAY (*Pointing*). The mask! She has it once again! How –?

(*She makes a gesture towards JAY, as ORPHEUS plays a short arpeggio on the piano.*)

JAY. You –?

ORPHEUS (*quietly*). Now she has done *her* part. Ask for what you want.

JAY (*turning and picking up the flower from the forestage*). That mask! Let her remove it that I may see that face.

(*She bows slightly in compliance, and in complete silence she descends the ramp, BARNEY stepping forward to take her hand and guide her down the last perilous steps. The crowd draws aside into a wide semicircle facing her as she passes, and with a polite gesture of thanks to BARNEY as she leaves him she comes alone down centre to the front of the stage, where she turns her back to the Audience, removes her mask, and holds it above her head with its face to the*

Public. There is a gasp of astonishment from the Cast, while
JAY'S *face, on the other hand, is filled with exultation.*)

JAY.

Why have I run, screaming from Shadows?
What need to be dismayed – to fight for breath?
For if my Fate is You, what have I got to fear?
Take then this Song –
This little lust of words.
Take then this load of years –
This tapestry of terror and of tears.
Loosen the bonds that link me to the Earth
And let me rise, unshackled by mortality!

MEEDY (*in agony*). Jason!

JAY (*as* ORPHEUS *starts to play together with Orchestra*).

On with the dance, while Dionysos strikes the lyre!
On with the dance! Why should we say Good-bye?
Here is the Queen of all the Argosies –
Who, on the thirteenth stroke,
I shall embrace with exultation!

(*As the music builds he gives her the flower and she replaces
her mask, leading him as they dance back to the ramp, on
which they ascend to the upper level. Here she casts her
cloak around him, and when this is dropped he has vanished
from sight. She places the flower on the cloak, and swiftly
descends to where she came from – out of sight. After a
brief, surprised silence,* BARNEY *speaks. The music has
stopped.*)

BARNEY. What? No mourning? No crepe upon the door? No
grave obituaries?

(*With an imperious gesture from* HAROLD *he is silenced, as*
ALIX *leads the male Companions back to the upper level,
and an unaccompanied Chant comes from the crowd.
Darkness is growing on the Cyclorama, and presently the
Moon and some stars appear,* ORPHEUS *returns to his base.*)

CHORUS.

Woe, woe! Adonis is dead!
Rend the cloak, and still the lyre.
Thou hast conquered, Proserpine!
Woe to Aphrodite!

TYPHIS (*now very old*).

Pick up the corse, Companions. Spread the cloak,

And bear him as the Paladins bore Charlemagne
To lie at last amongst the mighty names!

CHORUS (*continuing*).

Woe, woe! Adonis is dead!

(*The Six Companions form up behind* TYPHIS *and having reverently rolled the cloak into a tubular shape they raise it upon their shoulders, and prepare to carry it off.* TYPHIS *places the flower on the top. Some distant bugle calls, and artillery fire, accompany quiet orchestral music, and as they move off,* HERA *speaks from amongst the girls who have reappeared below.* BARNEY *should be noticed winking at the Audience as they go.*)

HERA.

Over the far horizon lies a cave,
And in the mouth, a rock of massive stone
Guarding the sepulchre in which he sleeps.
There, all that has been is for evermore.
Save us, O Phoebus, from the fear of Endings!

(*In the distance we hear the rest of the cast singing the Delphic Hymn to Apollo. (Sing, sing O children of triumphant Zeus). The lights fade out, leaving only the Stars and the Moon. That is the end of this play.*)

P.S. *It is of importance, in the event of curtain calls, that the Masked Lady does not appear as such, but in whatever costume she has otherwise appeared in, during the play. This keeps her identity a secret only known to the cast, which of course, will have seen her face.*

THE MOON
IN THE YELLOW RIVER

A Play in Three Acts

LET THERE BE LIGHT

AN Irish play, taking its title from an American poet's translation from the Chinese, a play in which the references range from Slovakian convents to Paraguayan railway bridges, in which the commentator is a German, and the theme is international industrialism, can hardly be considered to have the same limited target as *The Old Lady*. Indeed, I have sometimes wondered whether the fact that its setting suggests the Liffey or the Shannon, and that it contains incidents drawn from the conflict of Irregular and Free Stater, is sufficient to constitute *The Moon in the Yellow River* as an Abbey play at all.

Although there is a good deal of talk about theology in the course of the dialogue, it is not as easy as it should be in an Irish play to determine the religious persuasion of most of the principal characters. It may also be noticed that the only reference to England is a passing sneer at the lion as 'a very middle-class beast'. So without either the odour of sanctity or of England, it may be asked what this play has got to do with the Emerald Isle. Yet in Dublin it has always been suspected of harbouring a superior ascendancy smile at the expense of the noble native, and it has never been popular there on that account.

It was gently sabotaged by most of its original Abbey cast who until 1938 played it with that subtle air of distaste with which experienced actors can dissociate themselves from the sentiments expressed in their parts. On its first night it had one of those very mixed receptions that usually presage a riot on the second. However, this never quite materialized, although I waited in some apprehension in the green room for another of those summonses to the stage that have nothing to do with a curtain call. All that it got was a rough deal from the newspapers, which complained that its humour was feeble, that it had no visible plot, and that it 'introduced some coarse levity on the subject of childbirth'.

In fairness to Dublin, it must be admitted that the play does propound a problem which was difficult, in those days, to face

81

without a certain feeling of depression. Although no physical assault was ever actually launched against the Shannon Hydro-electrical Power Plant, a very determined effort had been made by an armed minority to make majority government unworkable. This had been effectively stopped by the use of methods equally rough, but very practical in their results. In short, the recrudescence of murder as a political argument had been brought to a sudden stop by means of the counter-murder of prisoners in the hands of the new native Government. There was no legal or moral justification for such measures on the part of the infant Free State. But the melancholy fact remained that it had worked, and that an Irish Government had proved to be much tougher with the Irish than the English had ever dared to be. Nor did the glamour of patriotic martyrdom attach itself to the victims. This was all very sobering and disgusting. Yet it is hard to see what other answer could have been made to a continuance of underground warfare, provided of course that we were to have any government at all.

When Captain Jack White, the founder of the Irish Citizen Army, accosted me outside the theatre and accused me of justifying these methods in my play, I invited him to tell me what the proper answer was, and I would put it in.

'There is no answer,' said Jack White, 'and you know it. That's why you are a traitor and a renegade.'

So I wrote the operative part of this remark into the play, where it is still to be found in the last act.

As I have already mentioned, *The Moon* was the first, and is still the only one, of my works to have undergone the standard processing by which a script is rendered fit for Broadway production. Whether this is a good or a bad thing is a question that has long puzzled me. I have little doubt that, as a rule, it is a very good thing when practised by producers who are themselves either writers or directors. But the trouble is that this so seldom is the case. One of the two moments in the theatre when the Nuisances are most in evidence is whenever a dramatist is being told how to rewrite his script. The other, of course, is during casting, which is heaven for these chaps, but is hell for most of the regulars, who understand the heartburnings that are involved.

In my own case I was lucky in having only to deal with a committee of reputable theatre people. Even so, the sense that was talked with regard to making the play intelligible outside

Ireland was sometimes outweighed by the vulgarity of some of the technical suggestions as to how this excellent purpose was to be effected.

I was summoned to New York – as many a writer has been before and since, with much the same experience. It was explained to me that here was a more sophisticated audience than any that I was probably used to – an audience that had been trained by my present producers to expect a high state of care and accuracy in anything that they were to see upon the stage. Would I therefore please begin by drawing a plan of the fort in which the play was set, and add to this a sketch-map of the countryside for some miles around.

This was a pleasure. I drafted out a plan of the Pigeon House, together with all the topographical aspects of the surrounding slob-lands of Sandymount. But there were other things that they wanted to know. How many people were hurt in the explosion? How far away did the life-saving exercises take place? How old was Blanaid's mother when she died?

This was in the days before the Method, and – ponderous as it may seem – it was not a bad test by which to find out whether an author had really visualized what he was writing about. Indeed, a few more direct quotes from these conversations – which I wrote down in the Taft Hotel after each session – may be the simplest way of commenting upon some of the main points of the play, on how it first struck Broadway, and on how I failed to answer some of Broadway's more searching probes. The verbiage today is, of course, different from that of the days of the soup queues in Times Square, at which date 'Motivation' was one of the great Things. Nor is the catch-phrase 'I'm from Missouri' still in current use. But the same longing to leap to melodramatic assumptions, and to misinterpret human behaviour in terms of what is imagined to be Good Theatre (but is usually only Good Cliché) is still prevalent today – a fact that suggests that we are none of us probably quite as sophisticated as we like to imagine.

MR L. Well, I think this last Act is interesting philosophically, but it seems to me that nothing further happens. Just explain to me what this scene between the father and the daughter has to do with the play about the power house.

ME. The play isn't about a power house. It's a play about people.

MR L. Don't be afraid to say that it has nothing to do with it. I was reading a play of Dryden's last night that had three plots, and none of the characters in each ever meet each other.

ME (*doggedly*). It's not that I'm afraid to say it. All my characters meet each other.

MR M. What's missing is the motivation. This playing for time by Tausch has got to be motivated. The shooting of Blake must be motivated. You see, I'm from Missouri. Do you know what that means?

ME (*lying*). Yes. But I'm not sure that I know what 'motivated' means.

MR M. Well for example, how about Blake making some taunting remark after his song to Lanigan to make Lanigan mad at him so that he shoots him?

ME. But he doesn't shoot him because he's mad at him.

MR M (*surprised*). He doesn't? Then why does he shoot him?

ME. He shoots him because it is the only thing to do.

MR M. Splendid! That's a great idea. But why don't you say so?

ME. I thought I did say so. I'll say it again if you think I should.

MR M. Do. Always remember, we're all from Missouri.

MISS W. I don't understand what exactly Blake wants. I mean – why exactly should he *wish* to blow up the works?

MR M. I have no difficulties with that. You see, they're all after some sort of Arcady. That's why the aunt objects to factories and says that . . .

ME. No, no! The aunt doesn't want any Arcady. All that she objects to is being dominated by people like Tausch.

MR M. That's all right by me. Only why don't you say so?

ME (*frantically turning over some pages*). But I *do* say so. I mean – what about this speech here?

MR M. Doesn't come across. Simply doesn't come across, old man.

ME. Will it be all right if I give her an encore?

MR L. This still doesn't answer Helen's question about Blake. Doesn't he want Arcady?

ME. Not exactly. But he *is* against industrialism.

MR L. Why?

ME. Why? I suppose because he's that kind of person.

MR L. You mean because he's not very bright? He can't see all the good it would do to the country?

ME (*getting cross*). I doesn't necessarily follow that industrialism does good. That's like assuming that everybody wants to live in New York, which is far from being the case.

MR L. (*after a pause*). Oh.

MR M. Well apart from all that, I'd like to know what *side* Dobelle is on?

ME. Neither side.

MR L. He must be on some side. Does he or does he not want the works to be blown up? Answer me that.

ME. He would say that there's no point in wanting either, because whatever happens will happen anyhow. If they don't belong in Ireland they will go. What he really objects to is Tausch's attitude of mind.

MR M. Of course. Don't you see, he objects to being patronized. He doesn't like to hear Tausch calling the country backward.

ME. No, no! He doesn't feel the slightest patronized. By some damn German who reads his old magazine articles! Why should he give a damn what Tausch thinks about Ireland? It's something far more important than that. Tausch is what he calls a Servant of Righteousness, and those are the most dangerous people of all. He feels that all that they ever bring is misery.

MR M. Grand, grand! But . . .

ME. I know! I know! Why can't I say so?

A few years ago, I happened to pass through a reception room in the handsome premises of my old friends, and stopped to admire a plaque celebrating the jubilee of their organization, and listing some of their memorable past productions. My own play was there, but with the title misquoted. This is what I find so endearing about the American theatre. It is so right about motivation, and so wrong in its facts. It thrives on a series of crises that would never be permitted in a less businesslike community. And after all, why couldn't I have *said* what the title of my play was?

In addition to these operations in the United States, *The Moon* has been translated into Polish, French, Scandinavian and German, and been performed in these several tongues. It slipped into London by the back-door of the Malvern Festival, and if its varying reception over the years can be regarded as any index of audience receptivity it may be of interest to note that in England nowadays there are noticeably many more complaints and mutterings of 'What is all this about?' than there used to be twenty-five years ago. Maybe this is a sign of the times; or perhaps it is just another peculiarity of *The Moon,* that it becomes less familiar with longer acquaintance.

In the course of its productions on many stages and in various mediums, its cast has included such distinguished names as Claude Rains, Donald Wolfit, James Mason, Cyril Cusack, Barry Fitzgerald, F. J. McCormick, Errol Flynn, Jack Hawkins, Esmé Percy and Jean Anderson – though never, be it regretted, all in the same production. It blew a hole in the roof of one theatre, and on another occasion an efficient stage manager discovered just before Lanigan's entrance that his gun, by some error, had been loaded with live ammunition.

Occasionally the curtain falls on the second act without as much as a clap of a hand from the audience. And, oddly enough, this phenomenon is regarded by those who know the play well, not as a disgrace, but as an indication of a really fine performance.

The Moon in the Yellow River

This play was first produced at the Abbey Theatre, Dublin, on April 27th, 1931, with the following cast:

Agnes	MAUREEN DELANY
Blanaid	SHELAH RICHARDS
Tausch	FRED JOHNSON
Aunt Columba	EILEEN CROWE
George	ARTHUR SHIELDS
Captain Potts	MICHAEL J. DOLAN
Dobelle	F. J. MCCORMICK
Willie	U. WRIGHT
Darrell Blake	DENIS O'DEA
Commandant Lanigan	P. J. CAROLAN

The action of the play takes place in an old fort, now used as a dwelling-house, near the mouth of a river in Ireland.

ACT ONE	The Living-room
ACT TWO	The Armoury
ACT THREE	The Living-room

Time: About the year 1927.
        The play opens on an evening in late September.
        Act Two overlaps Act One by about five minutes.
        Several hours elapse between Acts Two and Three.

ACT ONE

The house was once the officers' quarters of the fort covering the river mouth. But it is now a long time since racks of small arms decorated the stone walls, and for a number of years it has done duty as a fairly comfortable, if out-of-the-way, modern residence. The room is furnished sparsely with good heavy furniture upon which the sea air has left its mark, and it is shockingly untidy. A large book-case is filled with books on technical engineering mixed with a hotchpotch of modern and classical literature. A cupboard filled with old blue-prints hangs open, and a small heap of fishing-tackle lies in the corner. To one side of the rear wall the massive door opens on to the court. It still carries some of the relics of its warlike past in the shape of rusty chains and bolts. To the centre the original aperture has been enlarged into a big window with iron shutters, opening outwards and hung with heavy curtains. These now stand open and we can see out and across the court to a whitewashed wall in which is a cannon port. Shortly after the scene opens it grows dark outside. Whenever the hall door is open, the distant hum of turbines can be heard. To one side of the room a short flight of stairs runs up to a gallery, off which the bedrooms open, of which the door of the first is visible. And down towards us, on one side, is an unpainted wooden table, running off stage out of sight, upon which is a toy railway station, signal box, signals and siding and a set of tracks which emerge from an aperture and disappear again.

As the Curtain rises a ship's siren can be heard from the river. It is an evening in late September, and an enormous red-faced woman wearing an apron is laying a few plates on the centre table. Although she has strong, domineering eyes and a commanding voice, there is nothing masculine about her. Quite the reverse, for her ample breasts and figure bear witness to a triumphant, all-enveloping matriarchy. Through the open door of the first bedroom we can see an angular, elderly lady who is

*seated at a typewriter on which she slowly clicks. In the window
seat a young girl of about thirteen dressed in a short cotton frock
is reading a book. She is an incredibly thin, solemn, untidy little
girl with short, tangled fair hair and bright, intelligent eyes.*

SERVANT. Well, about Mrs Mulpeter. Did I tell you about Mrs
Mulpeter, the poor lamb? (*She goes to the sideboard and then
returns.*) Ttt-ttt-ttt. Three days she's been now and three long
nights. Think of that now, isn't it a shocking, oh, a shocking
thing! (*She works vigorously for a time.*) Such a time as we've
had. God knows it's a terrible thing to be a woman. (*There is
a knock at the door.*) That was a knock at the door. (*But she
pays no attention to it.*) If some of them fellows could be
made to suffer half what a woman has to put up with! Oh,
my blood boils whenever I think of poor Mrs Mulpeter lying
there in pain. Ttt-ttt-ttt.

> (*She goes out. The click of the typewriter, which had
> stopped during her remarks, recommences and continues
> until her return with the tray.*)

Well, I censed the room a bit then, and I gave her a spoonful
of holy water. 'Take this, Mrs Mulpeter,' says I, 'take this
between your poor lips and it'll be as good as a novena to the
blessed St Margaret, the friend of all women in your condition.' (*The knock is repeated louder.*) There's that knock
again. Maybe there's someone at the door. (*She goes as if to
open it, but stops on the way.*) Isn't it a terrible thing for me
to be quietly laying the supper-table here as if there was no
trouble in the world to torture and torment a decent woman!
I think I'll go across now and see her, supper or no supper.

> (*She goes out again and the typewriter recommences. The
> girl peers out the window. Presently the* SERVANT *comes
> back with her hat and coat on.*)

SERVANT. Yes, I'm off now, supper or no supper, and you can
tell them that with my compliments.

> (*The knock is repeated still louder. The girl draws the
> curtains about her. The* SERVANT *goes to the hall door and
> flings it open.*)

Now, now, what's all this? What's going on here?

VISITOR. Excuse.

SERVANT. Are you the ignorant bosthoon that's banging and
hammering away at my knocker?

(*Upon the threshold is a pleasant-faced gentleman whose clothes suggest his continental origin. He has close-cut, greyish-fair hair and steady blue eyes. He is in the early forties, and a general air of physical well-being is set off by the punctilious charm of his manner. He has a scar upon one of his cheeks and speaks excellent English with a clipped, meticulous pronunciation, occasionally accenting the wrong syllable and having a little difficulty with his 'th' and his 'w'.*)

VISITOR. Pardon, I hope that I have not inconvenienced the Herr Doktor?

SERVANT. You ought to know better at your age than to be clattering and thumping on respectable people's hall doors.

VISITOR. But, excuse. I am a visitor. I wish to come in.

SERVANT. Not to speak of the clattering racket of them mechanicalisms out there driving the blessed sleep from her poor tired eyes.

VISITOR. Perhaps you will kindly take my card.

SERVANT. Oh it's little I can do to ease you in your trouble, poor Mrs Mulpeter, little and all.

VISITOR. Pardon?

SERVANT. Ttt-ttt-ttt! Shocking, shocking!

(*She goes out, leaving the door open. He stares after her in some bewilderment. He peers into the room and slowly enters.*)

VISITOR. Herr Doktor.

(*A sudden click of the typewriter makes him start. Finally he goes across and proceeds to examine the toy railway in a tentative manner. The* GIRL *emerges from behind the curtain and approaches him silently.*)

GIRL. Nobody's allowed to touch that.

VISITOR (*with a start*). Himmel!

GIRL. What does that mean?

VISITOR. It means, my dear young lady, that you gave me a surprise.

GIRL. I suppose you don't know who I am?

VISITOR. I am afraid not. But they say that Beauty is a good letter of introduction, eh?

GIRL. I thought you wouldn't know me, but I know you. You're the man from the Power House. Sometimes I look in through the windows and see you working.

VISITOR. So? You do?

GIRL. Hh-hh!

VISITOR. I will certainly look out for you tomorrow.

GIRL. You're a German, aren't you?

VISITOR. That is so, indeed.

GIRL. I was born in Germany.

VISITOR. *Ach!* Then we are compatriots. You are perhaps the daughter of the Herr Doktor?

GIRL (*nods*). At least it was somewhere out there. I'm not very good at geography. Perhaps you know a place called Bratislav?

VISITOR. I know the place well. I have passed by in the boats many times on the trip to Budapest. So that is where you were born!

GIRL. Well, there's a convent near there. Father was doing something to a bridge at the time, but of course I was too young to remember. I say, aren't you going to sit down?

VISITOR. *Bitte sehr.* But, as you say, Ladies first!

GIRL. Oh, I'm not a lady.

VISITOR. *Nicht wahr!* but a very charming one.

GIRL. I'm afraid not. But it's my father's fault. He calls me a little slut, but I think it's calling people things that makes them it, don't you? Oh, what's that little thing on the back of your hat?

VISITOR. This? Oh, it is nothing. We wear them so at home.

GIRL. It's awfully funny. (*She takes his hat.*) Just like a little brush . . . Oh, it comes in and out!

VISITOR. *Nein – Nein!* It . . . *Ach,* yes. I see now that it comes in and out.

GIRL. Isn't it meant to? I haven't broken it?

VISITOR. Not at all, my dear young lady. It is quite all right.

GIRL. I'm afraid I *have* broken it. You're not telling me the truth.

VISITOR. Please do not bother. *Das macht nichts.*

GIRL. Can you mend it?

VISITOR. I can procure another. It is nothing.

GIRL. I'm rather unlucky with things, but it's not really my fault, you know. At least, hardly ever. They always say it is, though.

VISITOR. One's parents never do understand, do they?

GIRL. I haven't any parents.

VISITOR. No parents? But . . .

GIRL. Not unless you count Father.

VISITOR. One usually counts one's father.

GIRL. Not ones like mine. We don't get on very well, I'm afraid.
I can't remember my mother.

VISITOR. So.

GIRL. But there's a picture of her out in the armoury. She has
fair hair and the loveliest hands. I think she's pretty, but we
don't know much about her. Except Father, and of course he
says nothing. Have you got any parents?

VISITOR. No, I am afraid not.

GIRL. Then, I suppose we're both orphans in a sense. But I
daresay you've been better brought up than me?

VISITOR (*laughing*). Well, that is a very difficult question. What
would you say was being . . . well brought up?

GIRL. Oh, going to a proper school instead of being taught by
Auntie and George. That's Auntie typing up there. She knows
medieval history and Latin, and George knows a lot of awfully
good sea shanties. But you can't go far on that, can you?
Nowadays, I mean.

VISITOR. Well, it all depends upon what you want.

GIRL. I think that every girl needs an education nowadays in order
to prepare her for the battle of life. She wants to be taught
deportment and geography and religious knowledge and – oh
– mathematics. I adore mathematics, don't you?

VISITOR. *Ach,* but you are the daughter of a great engineer. Most
young ladies of my acquaintance try to avoid these things
and to stay away from school.

GIRL. Perhaps that's because they have got more suitable parents.
My father says that education poisons the mind, but I say he
was educated himself, so his mind must be poisoned, and if
it's poisoned, how can he know what's good for me?

VISITOR. And what has he got to say to that?

GIRL. Nothing. He just looks at me – the way he always does. I
don't know why. Don't you think it must be wonderful to
have proper lessons and sleep in an enormous dormitory with
twenty other girls and go for walks in a long line like geese?
Tell me, have you ever looked through a convent keyhole?

VISITOR. *Ach!* No – I have not had that experience!

GIRL. Well, you can see them in there. Walking about in the
garden, always in threes – never in pairs. That's how I know
all about it. I wish you would take a look some day. Then
you might be able to tell me whether you think they're very
much more advanced than I am.

VISITOR. But have you no other young friends?

GIRL. No. There isn't anybody much out here except the men going out the wall to the lighthouse. I think that Darry Blake is my only real friend. Do you know him?

VISITOR. No.

GIRL. He used to come across the bay a lot when he had the water-wag, and sometimes he'd take me up to the pictures. But he hardly ever comes now. I think he must have dropped us. We're not awfully good, you know – socially, I mean.

VISITOR. I am sure that it cannot be that. But perhaps, when we are better acquainted, I may be permitted to take you up to the pictures instead.

GIRL. Oh, would you? How lovely! When? Tomorrow?

VISITOR. I would be charmed. But first we must ask the permission of your distinguished father.

GIRL. Oh, he won't care.

VISITOR. *Ach,* but you see, I do not know the Herr Doktor very well. This is the first time I have had the honour of his invitation to supper.

GIRL. Oh, supper! Is that why you called?

VISITOR. Then, you do not expect me?

GIRL. Oh, I'm sure it's all right. People do sometimes come to supper. Perhaps I'd better go and tell Father.

VISITOR. You are very kind. But if I am not expected . . .

GIRL. Oh, I wouldn't mind that. (*Turning at the bottom of the stairs.*) I think you were wonderful about the pictures. I do hope you're not annoyed about that little thing I broke?

VISITOR (*distressed*). Not at all, I assure you. Perhaps it would be well for me to call another time.

GIRL. I didn't think you would be annoyed, really. But don't tell Father, please. He'd only say it was what he expected of me or something. I'll get him now.

(*She goes upstairs. He takes a step after her, but decides to wait, and sits down uncomfortably in a big chair with his back to the stairs.*)

AUNT (*from her room*). Blanaid!

GIRL. Yes, Auntie?

AUNT. Who's that?

BLANAID. The man from the Power House.

AUNT. What does he want?

BLANAID. He wants to stay to supper, and for me to come to the pictures tomorrow.

AUNT. Was he asked?

BLANAID. He says so.

AUNT. I don't believe it for a minute.

BLANAID. Hush, Auntie! He's listening.

AUNT. Well, listeners never hear any good of themselves.

BLANAID. I'm supposed to tell Father.

AUNT. Well, if he stays, I go.

BLANAID. Ss-ssh! (*With a glance at the speechless foreigner*) It's all right. I don't think he heard.

(*She goes off down the gallery. Presently the* AUNT *emerges from her bedroom and comes quietly downstairs. She is a lean and vigorous woman of about fifty, with bright fanatical eyes. She wears a tweed skirt and a Fair Isle sweater that comes to the throat. Her hair, once very beautiful and still uncut, is now streaked with grey and is untidily done. She comes to the table in the centre and removes a silver flower vase which, with a look of deep suspicion at the* VISITOR, *she brings back to her room. She is almost at the table before he notices her and springs to his feet bowing politely. After she has gone he decides to steal away, but before he has got as far as the open hall door, there is a sound of voices outside and two men enter. They are* GEORGE *and his friend and crony,* CAPTAIN POTTS. *They are both well-seasoned and weather-beaten salts — the former a tall, lean man with brown wrinkled skin, dressed in a loose-fitting double-breasted grey tweed suit. He still has the face and carriage of an incurable romanticist, which he has never ceased to be since he ran away to sea from a comfortable home and a good family fifty years ago. Since then he has been all over the world, fought in half a dozen campaigns and come through them all unscathed both in mind and in body. The only regular feature in his life has been its unvarying lack of money, for on the occasions on which he has managed to acquire any, he has always lost it promptly, thanks to his uneconomic enthusiasms and his impulsive habit of backing bills for insolvent friends. For the last seven of his ripening years he has more or less settled down in a Government appointment that takes him about the coast, drilling crews and inspecting the life-saving*

apparatus. His old friend, CAPTAIN POTTS, is storekeeper.
The latter, a fat old Cockney with a heavy grey moustache,
is dressed in his best blue serge with collar and tie and a
sailor's cap and has a black crape band on his sleeve. He
carries a large bunch of flowers. Neither of them at first
takes any notice of the foreigner.)

GEORGE and POTTS (*singing off*).
> O whiskey is the life of man,
> O whiskey Johnny!
> I'll drink whiskey when I can,
> Whiskey for my Johnny.
>
> O whiskey makes you feel so gran',
> O whiskey Johnny!
> Whiskey from an old tin can,
> Whiskey for my Johnny!

GEORGE (*as he enters*). Bring 'em in, Potts, bring 'em in. Don't
be shy, old man, there's nobody here. We'll get something
for them over here. (*He goes to a cupboard and selects a glass
jar.*) Perhaps we'd better put some water in it.

POTTS. Ri'. (To VISITOR.) Better for a drop o' water, y' know.

GEORGE (*filling the jar from the carafe on the table*). There now,
shove 'em into that, old man. Much too late, don't you think?

POTTS. Sure. Gent 'ere, George.

GEORGE. What's that? Who? Why, so there is, b'gad. Friend of
yours, Potts?

POTTS. Nope.

GEORGE (*as they carefully arrange the flowers*). Suppose we'd
better have a word with the fellow. No good in being stand-
offish, eh?

POTTS. Just as you say, George.

GEORGE. Meet my friend Captain Potts. In charge of my store.

VISITOR. I am delighted to meet you, Herr Kapitän.

POTTS. 'At's aw ri'.

GEORGE. You're the fellow from the Power House. I know you.
Like to shake hands?

VISITOR. With pleasure.

GEORGE. *Gooden tag!* Shake hands with Potts, too. Shake hands
with him, Potts, old man. These fellows love shaking hands.

(POTTS *does.*)

POTTS. *Gooden tag.* (*Laughter.*)

VISITOR. I know you and your friend by sight. You manage the rocket apparatus. You save lives from the ships in distress, eh?

GEORGE. That's right. Do you like these flowers? (*Whispering.*) Say you do. For the old man.

VISITOR. You are fond of flowers?

GEORGE. They're not for himself, you know. (*Whispering.*) His wife's dead.

VISITOR. *Ach,* I am so sorry! A recent demise?

GEORGE. About sixteen years. Sixteen – is that right, Potts?

POTTS. Sixteen eggsackly.

GEORGE. Very sad for the poor old fellow.

VISITOR. (*rather at a loss*). Oh . . . yes. Er, I like your flowers, Herr Kapitän.

POTTS. Think they'll do?

VISITOR. *Sehr schön.*

GEORGE. Say you like his suit, too. Only puts it on once a year. Wife's anniversary. It was her favourite suit. Poor old Potts. (*He sniffs.*) I wonder is there anything in here. (*He inspects the cupboard again and produces a whiskey bottle.*) How about it, Potts, old man? Drink, Herr Splosch?

VISITOR. Tausch is my name.

POTTS. Ri'. I'll 'ave a small 'un.

GEORGE. You'll have to share a glass with Potts, I'm afraid. Mind sharing a glass with Herr Splosch, Potts?

POTTS. Naw. 'Salls same.

TAUSCH. I thank you, but I do not take spirits.

GEORGE. What? No spirits?

TAUSCH. No, thank you.

GEORGE. Really?

TAUSCH. Unfortunately they do not agree with me.

GEORGE. Most extraordinary! Well, you know yourself best. There you are, old man.

POTTS. 'At'll do.

GEORGE. Pour it down, Potts.

POTTS. Well – 'ere's looking at yer.

GEORGE. We got as far as the Scotch House, you know. But I said to Captain Potts here, 'Potts, it's all very well, old man, but I think we've started too late. Take a taxi and we'll have no damn money to get home. Take a tram and the damn cemetery'll be closed by the time we get there. It's no good bringing flowers to a cemetery when it's closed, is it?'

TAUSCH. You bring these flowers to the tomb?

GEORGE. Yes, you know the poor old fellow's wife's dead. Anniversary. We always go.

POTTS. Yes, mush too late.

GEORGE. So when we left the Scotch House, I said, 'Come on back to the store, Captain Potts, and we'll put these flowers in water and try again tomorrow.'

POTTS. 'Ave to go again.

TAUSCH. The Scotch House is closed tomorrow, I suppose?

GEORGE. Oh no, Sunday. Different hours, that's all. Well, when we saw the door open on our way back, we thought we'd come in to look for some water. And, by God, we got it, eh, Potts old man?

POTTS (*refreshed*). You betcher life!

GEORGE. Good thing we came in, Potts, or we wouldn't have met Herr Splosch. Are you sure now you won't have a splash, Splosch?

TAUSCH. No, thank you.

GEORGE. Well, you must step across to the store some time and we'll give you a rosner. You know – just next door in the old armoury.

TAUSCH. I think that I know the place.

GEORGE. Everybody welcome. Just like in this house. Eh, Potts?

POTTS. Liberty 'All.

GEORGE (*singing*). 'Sally Brown, she's a bright Mullatter.'

BOTH. 'Way – ay – y, roll and go.'

GEORGE. 'She drinks rum and chews tobacker.'

BOTH. 'Spend my money on Sally Brown.'

GEORGE. Steady, Potts old man, steady. Can't make a row in other people's houses, you know.

POTTS (*abashed*). 'At's ri', George. Shouldn't do that.

GEORGE (*mysteriously*). Listen! You're a foreigner. Are you at all interested in guns?

TAUSCH. Guns?

GEORGE. Don't mention it much. But come along some time and I'll show you something will surprise you. Just next door in . . .

(*The* HOST *and his* DAUGHTER *appear at the top of the stairs. He is a distinguished-looking elderly gentleman with a refined sensitive face and the delicate nervous hands of an artist. There is a certain ruthlessness – one would almost say, cruelty – about his fastidious lips and chin that seems to be perpetually at war with his eyes, which are imaginative and sympathetic. He dresses carelessly in tweeds, but with good taste, and his manner betokens an inborn restlessness. He comes down the stairs quickly, his hand outstretched.)*

HOST. Why, my dear sir, I had no idea that you were here. You must accept my sincerest apologies. Put on the light, Blanaid.

TAUSCH. Good evening, Mr Dobelle. I am afraid I have called unawares.

DOBELLE. Not at all, not at all. I was buried in the library, and nobody dreamt of telling me you were here. Deuced unmannerly house this.

TAUSCH. *Im gegenteil.* I have been entertained most charmingly by your daughter.

(BLANAID from the stairs flings him a smile, points to her head and places a finger to her lips.)

GEORGE. We thought you'd like us to give him a drink. So we did.

DOBELLE. Well, thank God for that! I hope there was enough.
(He lifts the empty decanter and looks at TAUSCH in some surprise.)

GEORGE. Oh yes, lots, old man, lots.

DOBELLE. You have met George, then?

TAUSCH. We have introduced ourselves. Oh, I assure you, I have – how you say – I have been done proud.

DOBELLE. Let me take your coat.

TAUSCH. Believe me, sir, since first I came to reside at the Power House, I have been looking forward to the pleasure of this visit.

DOBELLE. Very handsome of you to say so, I'm sure. We haven't much to offer, I'm afraid.

BLANAID. You can't stay to supper, George. There's only just enough as it is, and Agnes has gone off somewhere.

GEORGE. That's all right, my dear. We're not staying. Only dropped in to entertain Herr Splosch. Come along, Potts, old man.

POTTS. Well . . . Bye . . .

GEORGE. So long, everyone.

TAUSCH. *Auf Wiedersehen.*

GEORGE. *Auf Wiedersehen?* Did you hear that Potts? That was German. And don't forget what I told you. Any time you're

passing. Like to show you what I mentioned. Wiedersehen!
Ha-ha! Ha-ha! Damned silly language. Ha-ha-ha!

(*They go and are heard singing off for a moment,* POTTS
*after a moment's hesitation in the door coming back for his
flowers and removing them vase and all.*)

DOBELLE. Do sit down, sir.

TAUSCH. With pleasure.

DOBELLE. I'm very glad George gave you a drink. He's a dear
fellow, but rather a rolling stone. Very good company out
here where company is scarce.

TAUSCH. It is farther from the town than I had imagined. This
place is very old?

DOBELLE. No, just a relic of the Napoleon scare. Derelict for
about fifty years before I took it for my hermitage. Darrell
Blake could tell you all about its history.

TAUSCH. I do not think that I have met him. But your daughter
mentioned his name.

DOBELLE. He's one of our few regular visitors. But lately he's got
a little involved in other things and we don't see him so often.
It is a pity. I find, Herr Tausch, that there are very few people
in this world that are at all tolerable to talk to.

TAUSCH. I respectfully agree. That is why I feel so honoured in
being invited to share your hospitality, Mr Dobelle. You – a
distinguished railway engineer – I have so often in my student
days read your articles in the technical journals. Little did I
think that one day I would have you as my neighbour.

DOBELLE. Tut, tut. No man should be reminded of the articles
that he has written.

TAUSCH. When first I decided to come to this part of the world
my friends they all say: 'But why do you wish to go there?'
I answer, 'Ha-ha, I know what I am doing.' And now I write
home and I say, 'I told you so. I am the neighbour of the man
whose works I have studied for so many years – Mr Dobelle.'

DOBELLE. Still, that scarcely answers their question, does it? Why
should you wish to come here?

TAUSCH. *Ach,* how can one say. It is the call of the west wind.
One grows tired of those places where everything has been
done already. Then one day comes the call of romance. I
answer. You understand.

DOBELLE. I certainly do not. It sounds like nonsense to me.

TAUSCH. *Ach,* but I cannot believe that. You wish me to believe that you smile at sentiment, but that is only a charming conceit. I know that you can appreciate the charm of the West, Mr Dobelle, and I had spent but a very few weeks upon my course before I realized how right I had been.

DOBELLE. Oh, you took a course?

TAUSCH. But naturally. When one goes to live in a strange land, one should try to acquaint oneself with the customs of the people.

DOBELLE. We have some customs here that I fancy it would be difficult to understand in München. But be specific now and tell me frankly what is there here that can possibly interest an intelligent hydro-electrical engineer?

TAUSCH. Might I not put that question to you, Mr Dobelle? You seem to find something to interest you.

DOBELLE. My wander-years are over. I have come home to renounce them.

TAUSCH. Precisely. You have travelled the world and have come to the conclusion that your own place is the best after all.

DOBELLE. No, I doubt if I could explain to you, Herr Tausch. It's a purely personal point of view. But I find that the world you speak of maddens me.

TAUSCH. I think I understand. You prefer the life of the spirit. You long for – how does it go? –

> '. . . magic casements opening on the foam
> Of perilous seas in faery lands forlorn.'

DOBELLE. Ridiculous. Nobody but a Cockney could have conjured up such a picture. Don't be deceived, Herr Tausch. Here by the waters of Lethe we may believe in fairies, but we trade in pigs. No. I think it was those very pigs that called me back. It takes one a long time to find one's spiritual home, but revelation comes at last, my friend. Isn't it Goethe who tells us that when we are old we must do more than when we are young? Don't believe a word of it, my dear sir. Once I served Righteousness with that intense desire for service that one has in one's youth. I studied hard, read everything that came my way, and built railway bridges anywhere from Hungary to the Gran Chaco. But since my revelation I amuse myself with toy trains instead of real ones and read little else but the *Encyclopaedia*. And, believe me, I find it much more satisfactory.

TAUSCH (*smiling*). I suspect, Mr Dobelle, that you visited China as well as the Gran Chaco.

DOBELLE. I suppose every cock crows loudest on its own dunghill. Here it is still possible to live on one's own mind. Even if usually it proves a mighty poor diet. And speaking of diet, I did ask you to supper, didn't I?

TAUSCH. If it inconveniences you in any way . . .

DOBELLE. No, no; he who works may eat. Agnes! I wonder where Agnes is?

(*The* AUNT *appears at the top of the stairs. She has put on her hat and coat.*)

AUNT. Agnes has gone. (*She goes away again.*)

DOBELLE. Gone! Damnation!

BLANAID. It's all right. The table's nearly laid. Mrs Mulpeter is going to have a baby.

DOBELLE. Not again? I never heard of such a thing!

BLANAID. The supper is on the range. (*To* TAUSCH) Do you mind finishing the table while I go and get it?

TAUSCH. *Ja gewiss.* With pleasure.

DOBELLE (*making no effort to help*). This is too bad! too bad! Leaving the table half laid! And the supper on the range! Without as much as with your leave or by your leave!

TAUSCH. It is a privilege, I assure you. I enjoy the helping very much indeed.

DOBELLE. Servants are insufferable. Why can't we do without them? (*The* AUNT *appears again at the top of the stairs carrying a bicycle which she brings down with her.*) What the devil has happened to supper? I ask Herr Tausch here to supper. I give notice to you all. He comes. There is nothing to eat and he has to lay the table himself. Don't answer me back.

AUNT. Who cares about supper! Maybe there'll be more than supper to bother about by the time this night is out.

DOBELLE. A nice way to treat a guest. Oh, Herr Tausch, may I introduce my sister, Columba.

TAUSCH (*bowing*). *Gnädige Frau.* I think that we have met already tonight.

AUNT. I daresay you expect me to shake hands with you; but even if I would, I can't with this bicycle.

TAUSCH. Perhaps you will allow me to assist you with it.

AUNT. Leave it alone, please. I know how to look after my own bicycle.

TAUSCH. I am so sorry.

DOBELLE. She doesn't like people to touch her things, Tausch. That's why she keeps it in her bedroom.

TAUSCH. I see.

AUNT. And take my advice, my good man, don't leave any of your property round here if you ever want to see it again. A word to the wise.

DOBELLE. Columba, you're not going out before supper?

AUNT. I am. I have work to do. Sometimes there are too many strangers in this house.

DOBELLE. Oh well, have it your own way. Better let her go, Tausch, if she wants to.

TAUSCH. My dear sir, I had no intention of interfering with her departure.

AUNT. I'd just like to see you try. (*She pauses at the door and feels in her pocket.*) You'd better take one of these. They'll all be gone when I get back. (*She hands him a typewritten pamphlet.*)

TAUSCH. *Danke sehr.*

AUNT. Ah yes, the turbines are humming merrily now. The dynamos are turning and the water piles up behind the sluices. You think you have done well. But you haven't accounted for everything. No, you haven't accounted for everything, my good man.

(*The* AUNT *goes.* BLANAID *enters with a tray.*)

TAUSCH. *Grüss Gott.*

BLANAID. Supper!

DOBELLE. At last. Sit down, Tausch, and let us atone for our laxity with a bottle of hock. Where's the corkscrew? (*He takes a bottle from the cupboard.*)

TAUSCH (*reading*). 'Our existence is not the aftermath of a past revolt. It is the presage of a future one. We shall rise again.'

DOBELLE. What's that? Where's the corkscrew?

TAUSCH. 'We shall rise again.' What is this?

DOBELLE. Oh, that? Just propaganda. She types them herself and pastes them up on the tram posts in town.

TAUSCH. *Ach, Fliegende Blätter.* Politics.

DOBELLE. Here's the corkscrew. Yes, she's been in jail once or twice. You mustn't mind it.

TAUSCH. In jail? So interesting.

103

DOBELLE (*drawing the cork*). Oh yes. In and out. But she's not typical of the country.

TAUSCH. I do not think that I have met many people who have been often in jail.

DOBELLE. It's one of the best qualifications for a public appointment. Hock?

TAUSCH. With pleasure.

DOBELLE (*filling his glass*). I always say it's a pity she never got married; but her only serious affair ended in rather a row. Something about a mowing machine. And, by the way, while I remember, better not mention the matter to her. She's rather sensitive on the subject.

TAUSCH (*drawing another typewritten document from his pocket*). My dear sir, I would not think of doing so. But I wonder does what you tell me throw any light upon a strange communication which I received a few days ago?

DOBELLE. Let me see. (*He takes it.*) Oh-ho! A threat to the works! You got this a day or two ago?

TAUSCH. Yes. One of my men found it pinned to the door of the switch house.

DOBELLE. Were you at all put out by this?

TAUSCH. I did not understand it, my dear sir. Some people object because I supply power and light to the military barracks. I did not think it of much consequence, because when I notify the police they say that it will be quite all right. I am more than relieved to learn that it may only be your charming sister.

DOBELLE. I wonder. The situation is a little different from what you are accustomed to. In most countries the political idealist is merely a bore, but here he has a disconcerting tradition of action. He usually has his own Government and his own army as well, you see.

TAUSCH. You mean to say that he does not recognize the machinery of democracy?

DOBELLE. He would say that you don't understand democracy. The Will of the People is a tender delicate bloom to be nurtured by the elect few who know best. The icy blasts of a general election are not for it. There's some sense in it – when you know that you know best.

TAUSCH. That is a little metaphysical for me.

DOBELLE. Metaphysical? My dear fellow, it's simply Christian Science applied to politics. If you don't like the Government you deny its existence – a state of affairs which is sometimes a little embarrassing for the likes of you and me.

BLANAID. Willie's out tonight. I saw him go off with his whistle and his water-bottle.

DOBELLE. Oh? I suppose it's useless to say anything to Darrell.

TAUSCH. And your other acquaintance – the gentleman whose friend has suffered the so sad bereavement – would he be one of these too?

DOBELLE. Who? George? Well, not really. He's a barbarian, but an amiable one. When did Willie go off?

BLANAID. About half past six.

DOBELLE. Oh well, there's nothing can be done now. A little more hock, Tausch?

TAUSCH. With pleasure. And what will you have, young lady?

BLANAID (*taking the carafe*). Only this, thanks.

TAUSCH. 'And Roman women were of old for drink content with water.' Eh?

DOBELLE. Prosit. (*They rise.*)

TAUSCH. Prosit.

(*They drink.*)

Go muh shocht noora nees farr hoo bleeun oh nyoo.

DOBELLE (*after a surprised pause*). Part of your course, no doubt?

BLANAID. That's Irish. He was only trying to say, 'May you feel better next year.'

TAUSCH. And this is the little Miss who pretends to have no education!

(DOBELLE *looks at her silently for a moment and then sits down.*)

DOBELLE. I suppose that's what Columba teaches you. Well, after this display of erudition, perhaps we may get on with supper.

(AGNES *enters by the hall door.*)

AGNES. Tt-ttt-tt-tt.

DOBELLE. So here you are!

AGNES. Yes, here I am. I thought I'd come back for a short bit. But she's very bad.

DOBELLE. I'm afraid there's not much more for you to do.

AGNES. That's just as well. They may want me back any minute. They've sent for the doctor. So I propped her up on the pillows and I wrapped a vinegared handkerchief round her poor head. 'Poor Mrs Mulpeter,' says I, 'isn't that nyummy nyumm? God help you, it won't be long now.' And neither it will. I'd be ashamed and me a man to be quietly eating supper and drinking strong drink and poor Mrs Mulpeter so near to her great trouble. (*She goes into the kitchen.*)

DOBELLE. Well, I suppose we must be thankful for small mercies.

TAUSCH. I understand. A lady is in childbirth. It is a very trying time. Yes. One can excuse a lot at such moments. I remember when my dear wife was –

AGNES (*putting her head in the door*). Now, now! I'll have none of that sort of talk while I'm about, if you please. Think shame to you – a couple of men to be gostering and making chatter about the trouble and misfortune tormenting a poor woman.

TAUSCH. Pardon.

(*They eat in silence for a few minutes.* AGNES *enters again.*)

AGNES (*putting a plate on the table*). I made them move her downstairs, so I did. In the top room of the gate-house she was. But I said No. That child must not be carried downstairs until it's carried upstairs first or I'll know the reason why, and if the poor mite starts at the top of the house, how can it go upstairs first? So down to the sitting-room poor Mrs Mulpeter had to come. The agony the poor creature suffered! Tt-tt-tt – (*She goes.*)

DOBELLE. Oh, by the way, Tausch, I should have mentioned it before, but do be careful what you say in front of Agnes. She's very puritanical. You understand?

TAUSCH. I will try to remember that too.

DOBELLE. We find it best to attune our conversation to the tastes of our servants. Let's go back to George. He's quite a non-committal subject. Have a sausage? George, you know, is the best of fellows. Calls himself a Christian Communist and wants everybody to be free and happy and at peace. But every time that the people try to be free and happy and peaceful it seems to George that somebody comes along and stops them with big guns.

TAUSCH. So?

DOBELLE. Well, a few years ago George, the most practical of men, decided to make a big gun for himself so that the next time the people won't be so badly off. He's been at it on and off ever since.

TAUSCH. To *make* a big gun?

DOBELLE. Exactly. And with quite surprising results. Of course nobody knows what will happen when it's fired. But we all hope for the best. Naturally, this is all in the strictest confidence. You must get him to show it to you the next time you're passing the armoury.

TAUSCH. I certainly will. But what industry! What enthusiasm!

DOBELLE. And why not, if one believes as George does? If you, Herr Tausch, a complete stranger, can come here to harness our tides for us, why be surprised when George tries to do something for the country too?

TAUSCH. But, my dear sir – to make a big gun! It is a year's work!

DOBELLE. About four years, as a matter of fact. And about a year extra for each projectile. Yes, they started on the fourth shell in the spring.

TAUSCH. Colossal!

DOBELLE. Oh yes, in about twenty years' time we'll be getting quite formidable.

TAUSCH. Ah now, sir, I am afraid you are jesting. Of course it is not the application that I admire. I am not so materialistic. But the spirit – the praxis – it is an example. Please excuse while I make a note in my book for my next letter to my son Karl.

DOBELLE. Well, well, I'm sure George would be delighted to know that he had been a help to Karl. You have a large family?

TAUSCH. Not very large. Four children only. They are still young and at school. That is why I have to leave them behind when I come here.

DOBELLE. You must miss them all.

TAUSCH. I confess that sometimes I do. In the evenings especially I miss the music.

DOBELLE. You are fond of music?

TAUSCH. But naturally. We all love music in Bavaria. You are musical, too, perhaps?

DOBELLE. Oh, very.

TAUSCH. What instruments do you play?

DOBELLE. None, I'm afraid.

BLANAID. We had a piano once, but it got stuck.

TAUSCH. Stuck?

BLANAID. Yes. It's out in the armoury now.

TAUSCH. The sea air, I suppose?

DOBELLE. You play yourself, of course?

TAUSCH. Oh yes. We all play. I play the 'cello and my dear wife she plays very beautifuly upon the piano. My daughter – the eldest one, Lotte – she is the violinist of the family.

DOBELLE. Quite a little orchestra, in fact.

TAUSCH. Oh, that is not all. Karl, my first son, he plays the viola, and Herman, the second boy, plays the flute. And even my little Greta – she is only five years – we are teaching her to accompany us upon the triangle.

DOBELLE. Charming.

TAUSCH. We were to buy an electric organ when I decided to come away. Just a small organ, but a beautiful instrument. However, we found that the vibration would be dangerous for a wooden house. So this winter they are laying down a concrete foundation and that will make it all right, I think.

DOBELLE. A concrete foundation? For the organ, you mean?

TAUSCH. Yes.

BLANAID. Oh, how lovely!

TAUSCH. Each evening in my room at the works I play to myself when I can afford the time, just to keep in practice. I am afraid you will think me a little sentimental. But the melodies that we are fond of, what else can bring back to us in the same way the mountains, the lakes, the wife and children that one loves? You understand.

DOBELLE (*after a pause*). I don't think you should ever have come here. I shudder to think what is before you.

TAUSCH. I only hope that I may be able to help you. I love your country and would serve it even in some small way.

DOBELLE. Yes, that is what I feared, and I know that I should resent it, but I haven't the heart. You are in higher hands. Still, I can't help being sorry for you.

TAUSCH. Sorry for me? May I ask why?

DOBELLE. Because, Herr Tausch, I like you, and at the same time I see with infinite pathos the not far distant date when, if you stay here, you will find yourself out. And that to my mind is always a pity.

TAUSCH. I do not understand.

DOBELLE. It is not the destiny of a man like you to be buried in this accursed hole. Take my tip before it is too late. Leave your Power House and go.

TAUSCH. Leave my Power House? What joke is this?

DOBELLE. Have you ever heard of the bogey man, Herr Tausch?

Well, here we have bogey men, fierce and terrible bogey men, who breathe fire from their nostrils and vanish in the smoke.

TAUSCH. You have what?

DOBELLE. And we have vampires in shimmering black that feed on blood and bear bombs instead of brats. And enormous fat crows that will never rest until they have pecked out your eyes and left you blind and dumb with terror.

TAUSCH. Come, come, Mr Dobelle.

DOBELLE. And in the mists that creep down from the mountains you will meet monsters that glare back at you with your own face.

TAUSCH. Ah now, Mr Dobelle, you cannot frighten me with parables. You forget that I am a German, and what you say only convinces me how much you really need my work.

DOBELLE. I know that nobody will ever listen to me; but, remember, I have warned you.

TAUSCH. I think, if I may say so, that you are a little afraid of life and that is why you live here. But we are not like that in Germany. There we still have the virile youth of a new nation: hope, courage, and the ability to rise again. Put Germany in the saddle and you will find that she can ride. Just a little organization here and you will see the change. Do not please think that I am preaching the doctrines of material prosperity. That matters nothing. (*The sound of a motor-car comes from outside and headlamps throw a beam of light on the blinds of the window.*) It is here, in the brain, that we find all that is of any value. It is the change of mind that only power can bring that will be the justification for all my work here. As Schiller tells us, freedom cannot exist save when united with might. And what might can equal electrical power at one farthing a unit? (*On the blinds appears the shadow of a man in an overcoat holding something in his hand that closely resembles a revolver.*) I see in my mind's eye this land of the future – transformed and redeemed by power – from the sordid trivialities of peasant life to something newer and better. Soon you will be a happy nation of free men – free not by the magic of empty formulae or by the colour of the coats you wear, but by the inspiration of power – power – power. And in that day I shall say in the words of Horace . . .

(*He notices the silence of the other two and follows their eyes to the window. Presently a* GUNMAN *enters silently through the door. He wears a waterproof coat and a soft cap and the lower part of his face is masked by a handkerchief. He carries a revolver. The two men sit in silence, the* HOST *limply, the* VISITOR *rigid. Then the older man eats a piece of bread.*)

GUNMAN. All the men in this house will have to be searched for arms.

(*Silence.* BLANAID *at last rises and runs out. For a terrible moment it looks as though she may be shot.*)

GUNMAN. Have you any arms or ammunition?

(*Silence. The* GERMAN *makes a move, but the other with a quick movement restrains him.*)

GUNMAN. Come on, now.

DOBELLE. Now, we're not going to have any shooting here, are we?

GUNMAN. Oh, I'm not so sure of that.

DOBELLE. Well, perhaps you'd better come back another time. When supper's over, maybe, or when I haven't any visitors.

GUNMAN. I'm sorry. I have my orders – from battalion head-quarters.

DOBELLE (*standing*). Well . . .

GUNMAN. The house is surrounded.

DOBELLE. Probably. (*He rings the bell on the table.*)

GUNMAN. Leave that bell alone.

DOBELLE. Certainly. I just thought that as you have to search the men, you might like to see the women, too.

GUNMAN. I don't want to see the women.

DOBELLE. Then you can send them away.

(*There is a pause during which the* GUNMAN *shifts uneasily, and the* COOK *enters.*)

DOBELLE. Oh, Agnes, here's somebody who says he wants to search us all for arms.

GUNMAN (*gruffly*). Everybody ought to put up their hands.

AGNES. If I put up my hands, it'll be to take you across my knee and give you a good skelping where you least expect it.

DOBELLE. An excellent suggestion.

AGNES. Take that old rag off your face at once, Willie Reilly. And who, may I ask, let you in here with them boots on?

GUNMAN (*sheepishly removing his mask and displaying an honest, pink face*). Aw, I didn't know you knew me.

110

AGNES. Do you hear me asking who let you in with them dirty boots?

GUNMAN. I have me orders, Ma.

AGNES. Well, you have your orders now, and out you go before I lam you with the flat of my fist.

WILLIE. Ay, easy now, Ma.

DOBELLE. Just a moment, Agnes. It seems that Willie's here on military business, and I think it's scarcely fair to pack him off without hearing what it's all about.

WILLIE. That's right, Mr Dobelle.

AGNES. Military business! Indeed! And what sort of military business gives him the right to come trapesing into my clean living-room with the mud of three counties on his boots, I'd like to know? Go 'long owa that, ye ignorant yuck, before I military business your backside.

WILLIE. Ay, keep off me, Ma.

DOBELLE. Agnes, please. If you don't mind. There's no use being violent. Personally, I'd like to hear what it's all about.

WILLIE. That's right. Now, violence never did any good, Ma. You know that.

AGNES. Oh, very well, very well. Have it your own way. It's no concern of mine if you turn the place into a pigsty. But don't ask me to clean up after you. You can do that for yourselves. (*She goes off with a slam into the kitchen.*)

WILLIE. God looka what can a man do with a mother the like of that, tormenting and disgracing him and he on active service! Looka now, I ask you what harm in God's name is my boots doing?

(*The* GERMAN *rises and mops his brow.*)

DOBELLE. Not much, I'm sure, Willie. Don't mind your mother. I'll put in a word for you and any mess you make you can sweep up before you go. (*The* GERMAN *whispers to him.*) Oh yes, and Willie, now that we're talking on a friendlier basis, don't you think that you might put that revolver away?

WILLIE. Ah sure, there's nothing in it. But I'll put it in my pocket if you like, sir.

DOBELLE. That's good. This is Mr Tausch of the Power House. Herr Tausch, Willie Reilly, Agnes's first-born.

TAUSCH. I see – Good day.

WILLIE. How-are-ye?

DOBELLE. Won't you sit down, Willie?

WILLIE. Ah no, I can't, thank you very much, sir. I have to be off in a tick. The boys is all outside.

DOBELLE. And what have the boys got on hand, Willie?

WILLIE. Well, the idea is to blow up the works.

TAUSCH. *Gott in Himmel!*

WILLIE. You know – the Power House.

TAUSCH. You are going to blow up the Power House!

WILLIE. Yes. D'ye know.

TAUSCH. *Almachtiger Gott!* What is all this?

DOBELLE. Just a moment, Tausch. Perhaps you'd better let me talk to him.

TAUSCH. Perhaps I had better!

DOBELLE. Listen, Willie. Why are you proposing to blow up the Power House?

WILLIE. I'm sure I don't know, sir. Battalion orders, d'ye know.

TAUSCH. But it is monstrous! Outrageous! There must be some mistake.

DOBELLE. You realize, Willie, that this is all rather upsetting for Mr Tausch. They are his works, you know.

WILLIE. Indeed, I'm sure he'd have a right to be a bit put out, and I'm sorry indeed to be fixed the way I am. But I have my orders as a soldier, d'ye know, and I've got to obey orders, sir. But there's no ill will at all.

DOBELLE. I know, Willie, I know. I suppose it can't be helped.

WILLIE. You know that, Mr Tausch, don't you? There's no ill will at all.

TAUSCH. Ill will? What is that? I think I go mad!

WILLIE. We'll do the least damage we can, you may be sure.

DOBELLE. I'm sure of that, Willie. But this doesn't explain what you want here. These aren't the works, you know.

WILLIE. Well, sir, the fact is the stuff we have is a bit damp. I think somebody must have left it out last night, because we can't touch it off at all. So some of the boys thought if we were for to burn the place a bit first it might go up that way. D'ye know!

DOBELLE. That seems quite a practical notion.

WILLIE. So they sent me up to commandeer a few tins of petrol. There's a couple in the shed by the sea wall, we thought was Mr Tausch's.

DOBELLE. I see.

WILLIE. We'll pay for them, of course. That's what I want to do.

112

DOBELLE. Just what I would have expected of you, Willie.

WILLIE. Let me see now. 1s. 3d. a gallon – two gallons a tin – two times 1s. 3d. is . . .

DOBELLE. 1s 3d. from the pump, Willie. 1s. 3½d. in the tin.

WILLIE. Aw, that's right. One and threepence ha'penny, it is. Two one and threepence ha'pennys is two and seven, and two tins will be twice seven are fourteen, one and two – five and twopence. Isn't that right? (*He counts the money.*)

TAUSCH (*pulling himself together*). I think I ought to say that one of the tins is not quite full.

DOBELLE. Very handsome of you, Tausch, I'm sure.

WILLIE. Oh, is that so? (*He considers.*) Ah, well, we'll take it all the same. Or supposing we make it the even five bob? (TAUSCH *inclines his head and receives the money.*) And I'm sure you know how sorry we are to have to trouble you, sir. But orders is orders. D'ye know. (*Confidentially.*) And you can have the fire brigade out in no time.

TAUSCH. I see. (*He looks round the room and notes the telephone.*) You say you are a soldier. May I speak to your commanding officer?

WILLIE. Oh, I don't think so, sir. This is all very secret, d'ye know.

DOBELLE. Don't be silly, Willie. We all know who it is. Ask Mr Blake to come in and have a drink.

WILLIE. Well, sir . . . I don't know if . . .

DOBELLE. Come in, Darrell, for God's sake.

(DARRELL BLAKE *enters. He is a young man of about twenty-eight with great grace and charm of manner. He is well dressed in an ordinary lounge suit and wears an overcoat, but no hat. He has an air of reckless indifference which – at a distance – is rather fascinating. There is no external evidence of any weapon about his person. The quick nervous movements of his hands betray a highly-strung and sensitive disposition. He carries a small parcel under his arm.*)

BLAKE. Did somebody mention refreshments? Well, that's always a pleasure. (*He bows.*) Ah! (*He blesses the decanter.*) Benedictus benedicat.

DOBELLE. Herr Tausch – Mr Blake. Let me pour you out something.

BLAKE. *Sehr angenehm,* Herr Tausch.

TAUSCH (*crossly*). Good day.

BLAKE. Enough, enough, coz. What will the visitor think of me?

113

DOBELLE. Sit down, Darrell. (*He goes to the model railway and works with it.*)

BLAKE. Thank you, but I only sit on formal occasions. This is a strictly informal one. Herr Tausch will appreciate.

TAUSCH. I quite appreciate.

BLAKE. I knew you would. Here's health. (*He drinks.*) I'm sorry now we sent Willie in to you. I can see that there's only been a sordid family scene. By the way, I hope you don't think that Willie is our show desperado? Did you, Herr Tausch?

TAUSCH. I hardly know what to think.

BLAKE. Then don't bother at all. Thought is shocking bad for the brain. You should be a man of action like me, Herr Tausch. Terribly desperate, I assure you. You should see the blood I've spilt in my time!

TAUSCH. Mr Blake, I am in no mood for flippancy. I insist upon knowing at once whether it is seriously intended to interfere with my Power House?

BLAKE. Why, most seriously. Hannibal is at the gates! You didn't think we were pulling your leg, I hope?

TAUSCH. Then it is true what this man says?

BLAKE. That the wicked shall be burned with fire? Oh yes! Unfortunately it rained last night, and rain is damn bad for explosives, when left in Willie's charge. So you see us temporarily embarrassed.

TAUSCH. Then I go to the Power House, and I will see that nothing of the kind occurs.

BLAKE. Back, back! Regretfully not. Please regard that as out of the question.

TAUSCH. You propose to hold me by force?

BLAKE. That's right.

TAUSCH. But – but why?

BLAKE (*airily*). Oh, Revolution.

TAUSCH. What do you mean?

BLAKE. Just that.

TAUSCH. Revolution! What do you mean? That is just a word!

BLAKE. A beautiful word. So few people appreciate beautiful words nowadays!

WILLIE. Up the rebels! That's all, d'ye know.

BLAKE. Willie, I think we've had enough of you. Outside and guard something. We've got a better idea than we had. Where's George, coz?

(WILLIE *goes out.*)

DOBELLE. I'm not sure. Across in the armoury, I suppose.

BLAKE. This will be a great night for George. Excuse me, while I bring good news to Aix.

(*He goes.* TAUSCH *is galvanized into activity. He springs to the door and makes sure that nobody is about. Then a finger to his lips he beckons to* DOBELLE.)

TAUSCH. S-sh! There are men out there. Keep them engaged three minutes, and I will call assistance. See. *Wo ist das Telefonbuch?*

(*He hurries to the telephone and* DOBELLE *indicates the directory on a side table.* TAUSCH *feverishly turns over the pages and then waves* DOBELLE *away. The latter goes to the door, pauses, looks out, then in, shakes his head and finally disappears.* TAUSCH *throws the book away impatiently and takes up the receiver. After a while he glances out of the window and rattles the instrument.*)

TAUSCH. *Allo, Allo! Mein Gott!*

(*He rattles again. The* AUNT *enters carrying her bicycle. He slams down the receiver and turns away in affected innocence.*)

AUNT. Oh no, nobody would pay any attention to me. But maybe they'll listen now. The hour of the poor and the defenceless and the down-trodden comes sooner or later. The dynamos are turning. (*Shouting as she goes upstairs.*) But the proud in their pride shall be laid low. They didn't account for everything. Not for everything!

(*She goes into her room. The* GERMAN *makes sure that she is gone and returns hastily to the telephone. From upstairs the click of the typewriter starts once again. At last he gets a response.*)

TAUSCH (*in a loud whisper*) *Allo! Allo!* Yes, give me the police – *caserne.* No, I cannot speak louder . . . What? I do not know the number. Surely you can – No – *Gott in Himmel!* Never mind the Inquiries . . . I want the military – troops – *hilfe* – I say, are you listening? *Allo!* (*There is a distant burst of laughter from outside. Disconcerted, he glances out of the window before continuing.*) *Allo!* . . . Are you there? . . . *Allo? Allo!*

(WILLIE *enters quietly.* TAUSCH *holds the receiver behind him, breathing heavily, with thoughts of violence in his mind.*)

WILLIE. Did you press button 'A'? (*Pause.*) Maybe I could get it for you. I know the girl below. What is it you want? The fire brigade, I suppose? (*He takes the receiver from the speechless* GERMAN.) Well, take my tip and – and – Hello, miss, is that you? Oh, I'm well, how are ya? . . . Oh, I will indeed. Looka, will you give me double two double two one . . . thanks very much . . . (*To* TAUSCH) And I tell you what, you'd better give a call to the guards. There's often a lot of rough sorts and tinkers, you know, that comes hanging around the place where there's a fire. They'd be out in half an hour. Would you like to speak to them yourself? Hello, miss . . . (*He bangs the receiver.*) Ay, for God's sake, can you not get me the fire brigade!

(*The* GERMAN *drops into a chair with a string of expletives. A ship hoots in the river. The turbines hum merrily in the distance through the open door.*)

SWIFT CURTAIN

ACT TWO

This room was once the premises of the Army Ordnance Corps, but it is now used (officially) as a store of the Coast Life Saving Service and (unofficially) as a dumping place for old trunks and furniture belonging to the Dobelle family. There is a wide stone hearth over which the Royal Arms are still to be seen. To the rear is a big double door and a high barred window. Numerous Government circulars relating to distress signals at sea, fog-horns, and the like are pinned and pasted upon the walls, together with a picture of a full-rigged sailing ship cut from a tobacco advertisement. There is a desk against the wall near the window on which are a couple of ledgers. On the one side, opposite the fireplace, is a workman's bench covered with tools, amongst which stand four polished four-inch projectiles. From a door upon this side protrudes something that might be the muzzle of a gun. The room is full of coils of tarred rope, collapsible wooden tripods, a few big life-saving rockets and numerous lanterns of all sizes and shapes. Amongst the stored furniture is a cottage piano, and one or two pictures, all of which are covered with sacking, and on the wall, plainly visible to all, is a large kitchen clock. It stands at five to nine, and keeps going throughout the scene.

When the Curtain rises, CAPTAIN POTTS *is seated on a high stool with his back to the audience, making entries in one of the ledgers, and* GEORGE *is seated near the bench binding the stopper of a glass bottle, into which has been inserted a model of a full-rigged ship.* BLANAID *is seated on the ground beside him. The scene commences about six minutes before the conclusion of* ACT ONE.

GEORGE. Well, kid, we got into Cape Town, and the captain he drew a chalk line across the deck abaft the fiddley door and he said to me: 'Quartermaster,' he said, 'the doctor and I are going ashore on important business. See that none of those women cross that line.' 'Ay, ay, sir,' said I. So off he and the doctor went in a hansom cab.

BLANAID. And how many women had you on board?

GEORGE. Hundred and thirty-two. All cooks and housemaids. Government emigrants for Sydney. Never such a cargo known before, my dear.

BLANAID. Well, what happened then?

GEORGE. Well, I sat at the end of the gangway chatting with the little brown-eyed one, and by and by along comes the one called Scotch Annie, at the head of twenty-five whopping great females. 'Annie,' said I, 'you can't go ashore. Captain's orders.' 'George,' said Annie, 'we like you. You're a good sort. And me and these girls don't want to have to sock you one on the jaw.' 'O.K., Annie,' said I, 'I like you too.' And with that up the gangway and ashore they went and the whole hundred and thirty-two after them. All but the little brown-eyed one who stayed chatting with me.

BLANAID. And did they ever come back?

GEORGE. Come back! About an hour later up drives a hansom cab at the gallop with the captain and the doctor hanging out and shouting bloody murder. 'Quartermaster,' yells the captain, 'what the hell does this mean? Whole town's had to close down. Those damn women are everywhere.' And then up drives another hansom cab with two policemen and one cook in it. (*He gets up and acts the part with many gestures.*) 'Emigrant from the *Triumph*, sir.' Shove her on board. Salute. Off. Another hansom cab. Two more policemen. Two housemaids. 'Emigrants from the *Triumph,* sir.' Shove 'em on board. Salute. Off. All night. Hansom cabs. Policemen. Cooks and housemaids. Shove 'em on board. Salute. Off. Sailed next morning twenty-nine short. Next year the Boer War.

POTTS. Will you fire a rocket at the Greystones drill?

GEORGE. Greystones? When's that?

POTTS. Wednesday is when you said. Them rockets cost seven pounds apiece.

GEORGE. Um. Lots of kids at Greystones usually. Better let them have a rocket, old man. They like 'em.

BLANAID. May I come and watch you practising, George?

GEORGE. Delighted, kid. Like to go across in the breeches buoy? It's quite safe.

BLANAID. Oh, I'd love to. May I?

GEORGE. Wednesday, then, at Greystones. Artificial respiration too.

(WILLIE *enters and* BLANAID *rises.*)

WILLIE. May I come in?

GEORGE. Of course. Take a seat.

WILLIE. Ah, I won't sit down, thanks very much. I'm on active service, d'ye know.

BLANAID. I knew it was only you, Willie. What's happening?

WILLIE. Nothing much, miss. Mr Blake is over there now – talking.

BLANAID. Oh, Darry? Who to?

WILLIE. Ah, to no one special, miss. They were all talking when I left them.

BLANAID. What were they talking about?

WILLIE. They didn't say, miss.

BLANAID. Then I'm going over to see. Oh, hello!

(*She meets* BLAKE *in the doorway.*)

BLAKE. And how is my friend Blanaid?

BLANAID. Very well, thank you. You haven't been to see us for ages.

BLAKE. I know. But I want to atone for my past with a present. (*He hands her a small parcel.*)

BLANAID. Oh, Darry. (*She examines it.*) I'm so glad there's paper round it. Do you mind if I don't open it for a little?

BLAKE. Of course not. That's much the best part of a present.

BLANAID. I can't imagine what it is. It feels very interesting.

BLAKE. It's really most commonplace. Hello, George. Good evening, Captain.

GEORGE. Well, Blake, old man. Some time since we've seen you.

BLAKE. Yes, I've been rather busy lately. And, by the way, it's you I really want.

GEORGE. Anything to oblige, Darry.

BLAKE. Concerning this loud speaker of yours we've heard so much about.

AUNT (*off*) . . . proud in their pride shall be laid low. They didn't account for everything. Not for everything.

GEORGE. The gun you mean? Why, man, she's a beauty. Want to see her?

BLAKE. What do you suppose that was?

BLANAID. It sounds like Auntie. (BLAKE *smiles.*) What's the joke, Darry?

BLAKE. She must be abusing poor Tausch. Can you see?

(BLANAID *goes to the door and looks out to the side.*)

BLAKE. Have you met Tausch, George?

GEORGE. Oh yes. Potts and I were just giving him a drink about half an hour ago. Peculiar chap, I thought. Still we've got to make allowances for these foreigners. Come on, Potts. Let's get the cover off the gun for Darrell. (*They go off.*)

BLAKE. Listen, Willie, never mind the petrol. This job is worthy of a bit of style, so we're going to land a shot in the place with the gun. Besides, we want to please the old men.

WILLIE. The gun? Oh, that'll be very interesting for the boys.

BLAKE. Well, what's happening?

BLANAID. He's telephoning.

BLAKE. No! (DOBELLE *enters.*)

DOBELLE. Really this is too bad. I will not have my guests baited like this. The man's ringing up town.

BLAKE. Marvellous. (*They all crowd round the door and look out.*)

DOBELLE. It mayn't be so marvellous for you when somebody comes out.

BLAKE. By God! He's telephoning all right.

BLANAID. Golly, isn't he excited.

BLAKE. Willie, go across and ask if you can help.

WILLIE. I will indeed, Mr Blake. (*He goes.*)

BLAKE. Watch now everybody. Three to one in pounds that he hits Willie on the jaw. (BLANAID *and* BLAKE *laugh heartily.*)

DOBELLE. It's all very well to laugh. But what's going to happen when Lanigan gets out?

BLAKE. I don't give a damn for Lanigan. What sort of a fool do you suppose that German takes me for? Ringing up town when he thinks he's got me out of the way. And now I suppose he'll come across and try to distract us for half an hour with bright, helpful conversation until the lorries can get out with the Staters. I do dislike having my intelligence insulted.

DOBELLE. Darrell, this is intolerable behaviour. You know quite well what it will mean in the end.

BLAKE. Listen, I've got an idea. Is the tide out, my dear?

BLANAID. Yes. Why?

BLAKE. Then I think I'll give Mr Tausch all the cat and mouse he wants and bit to spare. We'll get the gun out on the sea wall, loaded and trained on the works, and then, by God, Tausch shall have all the distracting conversation he asks for.

We'll keep him on the hop for ten, fifteen, twenty minutes until we hear the rumble of the lorries. God, what a scheme! I'll be laughing for months. The rumble of the lorries, and the Bosch thinking he's caught us. And then bang goes the gun, up go the works to hell, and off we trot across the sand to the shore on the far side. What do you think of that?

DOBELLE. Exactly. And leave us to take the consequences.

BLAKE. They can't take the lorries off the road. We'll have them on toast.

DOBELLE. You know perfectly well what it will mean. The ruin of our privacy for weeks. The inquiries – the cross-examination – the statements – the alibis! Some of these days, my boy, I damn well will make a statement and where will you be then?

BLAKE. Don't worry. You'll have much the best part of the evening's entertainment. You'll be able to see the German's face. I'd give my soul for that. I do hope Willie hasn't discouraged him.

BLANAID (*opening her parcel and disclosing a small book*). Oh, how lovely! Did you have to buy it, Darry?

BLAKE. There. That's all the thanks a criminal ever gets! I always said you were badly brought up.

BLANAID. The Girl Guide's Diary. (*Laughing.*) Oh, it's perfect.

DOBELLE (*grumbling round amongst the Dobelle impedimenta*). Insufferable! Monstrous! Nobody ever has any consideration for me.

(*A ship hoots in the river.*)

BLANAID. With a pencil and everything. It's full of useful information.

BLAKE. Come on, George. About this gun. May I show it to the boys?

GEORGE (*reappearing*). Only too delighted, old man. Know anything about guns?

BLAKE. No, but I'm always ready to learn. This is the dangerous end, I suppose?

GEORGE. In theory, old man. At present we can't say more. Come along, Potts. We'll have to show him.

(POTTS *appears.*)

BLANAID. I suppose I could be a Lone Guide if I learnt all these knots?

DOBELLE. Of course, you must upset the fellow when he's my guest. Some of these things seem familiar.

GEORGE. This gun is what we call a muzzle-loading, four-inch-slow-firing-Potts-shot. Now explain, Potts. You've got it all learnt off.

POTTS (*in a steady sing-song*). Well, sir, beginning at this end, first the steel barrel is strengthened with wrought iron 'oops shrunk over one another so that the inner toob or barrel is placed in a state of compression and the outer portions is in a state of tension.

BLAKE. You don't say.

POTTS. Furthermore, by forming the outer parts of wrought iron bar eviled round a mandrel and then welding the coil into a solid 'oop, the fibre of the iron is arranged what we calls circumferentially, and is thus in the best position to resist the stress.

DOBELLE. Who the devil brings all these things of mine over here? No wonder I never can find anything!

BLAKE. One moment – just before you go any further. You mentioned a mandrel. Now, what exactly is that?

POTTS. A mandrel?

(*An uncomfortable pause.*)

GEORGE. Better come inside, old man. Able to explain better there. Eh, Potts?

POTTS. Inside? Oh, yaw. Much better inside.

(*They go out.* DOBELLE *has taken the sacking partially off one of the pictures, disclosing the portrait of a young woman dressed in the clothes of about thirty years ago.* POTTS *returns to collect a corkscrew and a couple of glasses from the bench.*)

POTTS. Forgotten something, George. (*He goes.*)

(*There are sounds of movement off followed by the clink of glasses.* BLANAID *stands looking at her father.* WILLIE *enters.*)

WILLIE. Where's Mr Blake?

BLAKE (*off*). Busy, Willie. (*Pop of a cork.*)

WILLIE. Oh, are you there? He doesn't seem to want anything. He sent me across and says he'll be after me.

(*He goes into the adjoining room. There is the sound of flowing liquid.*)

DOBELLE. Now there's something I've been looking for for months. How did it get here?

122

BLANAID. I don't know, Father. A lot of the things from the house get left over here.

DOBELLE. Well nobody has any business to do it no matter how full the place is.

(DOBELLE *stares out of the window. Siphon off.* BLANAID *approaches him tentatively.*)

BLANAID. Father . . . Did you see what Darry gave me?

DOBELLE. No.

BLANAID. It's a diary . . . I love it.

DOBELLE. You'll lose it, I expect.

BLANAID. No, I won't. Guides don't lose things . . . Father, do you think that giving presents to a person is a sign of friendship?

DOBELLE. I really don't know.

BLANAID. I think so. I haven't very many friends, I'm afraid . . . (*Silence.*) . . . Daddy, would this diary be of any use to you?

(DOBELLE *turns his head and looks at her for a moment.*)

BLANAID. You don't want it?

DOBELLE (*shakes his head and turns away*). No, thank you.

BLANAID. I see. (*Choking it back.*) Well . . . I think . . . I want something . . . in my room.

(*She turns and runs out.*)

POTTS (*off*). The castings are annealed by placing them in a furnace or hoven until red 'ot, then allowing them to cool gradyerly. The exterior of the body must be ground by a hemery wheel or turned on a lathe. (*Pop of a cork.*) 'Ere's looking at yer. (*Pause. Then briskly.*) The groove for the driving band is also turned an' the fuse 'ole fitted with a gun-metal bush.

BLAKE (*off*). And the same to you.

(TAUSCH *enters. He has an air of suppressed excitement and crosses swiftly to* DOBELLE.)

TAUSCH. *Ach,* so you are here! (*He whispers loudly.*) Listen, *Fünf-und-zwanzig Minuten.* When I have got rid of the young man I call the barracks. They come in lorries. Twenty-five minutes and all will be well.

DOBELLE. I expected as much. This is all most distasteful. (*He goes to the door.*)

TAUSCH (*misunderstanding him*). *Nein, nein.* Courage, *mein Freund.* Courage! See, until nine hours thirty! *Frisch gewagt ist halb gewonnen, eh, Kamerad!*

(*Enter* BLAKE, GEORGE, POTTS *and* WILLIE. *They go to the shell cases.*)

BLAKE. How many did you say you've got?

TAUSCH (*conversationally*). *Ach,* so here we are!

GEORGE. Hello, Splosch, old man. Four.

POTTS. The last one needs a bit o' greasing. We only got it done last week.

BLAKE. Four. A beautiful number. Like the gospels.

DOBELLE (*calling.*) Columba, come over here, please.

GEORGE. We'll have more in a year or so. Takes time to get down to them, you know.

BLAKE. Four are quite enough to save our souls. Do you mind if we take everything outside?

GEORGE. Not at all, old man. What's it all about?

BLAKE. Crime, George! Enough said, for your own sake. Tonight I am Dick Deadeye, the boy burglar! I'll call the boys to help to get it out the door. Willie, you bring one of those things.

DOBELLE. Columba, will you kindly come when I call you.

(*He disappears out the door, carrying the picture with him.*)

TAUSCH. Er, perhaps I also can assist in some way.

BLAKE. Of course, Herr Tausch. We were just saying you would. Bright, helpful conversation.

WILLIE. Will I take this one?

BLAKE. Any one. And for God's sake be careful. Remember they go off.

WILLIE. Oh, I'll walk like a cat.

(*Half-way to the door, the shell spins in his grasp, he catches it again, loses it once more, and finally lets it fall.* TAUSCH *drops flat on his face.* BLAKE *covers his head with an arm.* GEORGE *and* POTTS *fall into a locked embrace. The shell bounces dully and then lies still. Pause.*)

WILLIE. Oh! I dropped it.

BLAKE. He dropped it! He tells us he dropped it.

(GEORGE *and* POTTS *come slowly forward and bend over the object on the ground.*)

GEORGE. That was strange, Potts.

POTTS. Don't understand that, George. (*They prod it gingerly. Nothing happens.*)

WILLIE. Did it not go off?

BLAKE. O God, give me patience!

GEORGE. Ought to do better than that, old man. (*He picks it up and shakes it to an ear.*) I don't know. Some carelessness some-where.

POTTS. Watcher mean, carelessness?

GEORGE. Did you bring the water to the boil?

POTTS. Of course I brought the water to the boil.

GEORGE. Doesn't look like it, old man.

WILLIE. I hope I didn't break it on you.

POTTS (*indignantly gets out a dog-eared notebook*). There's the nitrate, ain't it – mercurous nitrate, sol-soluble in 'undred an' thirty times its weight o' boiling water.

GEORGE. Well let's bring it over and have a look.

POTTS. 'Ave as many looks as you like, but I don't like them insinuations, George. D'ye think I don't know 'ow ter boil water?

GEORGE. Now, now, Potts, there's no use crying over spilt milk. Maybe the stuff's not shaken down in the bag.

POTTS. Well, it's not my job to shake it, is it?

BLAKE (*dusting himself*). So much for Matthew. I suppose we may expect equally good performances from the other three?

GEORGE. No, no, not at all. You see, this one was the first we made. Probably a bit on the old side by now. Or maybe Potts here . . .

POTTS (*threateningly*). Atcher!

BLAKE. In any event, we'll excuse you, Willie. Go and help the boys to get that thing out. I'll handle the next myself.

WILLIE (*most willingly*). Right ye are, Mr Blake. Where's it to go?

BLAKE (*in a low voice*). Across the yard behind that parapet. And then you're to train the muzzle very carefully through one of those loopholes on to the roof of the turbine house. Now, do you understand me? Because say so, for God's sake, if you don't.

WILLIE. Oh, I do indeed. That'll be very interesting. (*To the earnest workers at the bench, as he passes*) I hope it'll be all right. (*He goes.*)

TAUSCH. *Alles zu seiner Zeit*, Mr Blake. You think it is necessary for us to risk our poor lives again?

BLAKE. It's all for the cause, you know. Did you see my glass anywhere?

(TAUSCH *fetches it and fills another for himself, which, how-ever, he does not drink.*)

125

TAUSCH. I would like so much to talk with you for a little. To ask you some questions about yourself.

BLAKE (*smiling*). Well, why not. There's no hurry, is there?

TAUSCH. Oh no. No hurry at all.

GEORGE. Try the screw in the base plug.

POTTS. D'ye not know that's the centrifugal bolt.

BLAKE. I suppose they're all right with that damn thing?

TAUSCH. We are in the hands of One above.

VOICES (*off*).

Come on in boys.

That's right, get the door open.

Ay, will you look where you're going?

BLAKE. Well, what do you want to know about me?

TAUSCH. Mr Blake, I am very glad I have met you. I think you are the most interesting person I have known since I have come to your most interesting country.

BLAKE. Oh, come now. Flattery.

TAUSCH. Yes, indeed. But, believe me, it is not quite the compliment. For, you see, I am much more interested in my enemies than in my friends. And I feel that you are my enemy.

BLAKE. I only hope, Herr Tausch, a foeman worthy of your steel.

TAUSCH. I think so. I think so.

BLAKE (*raising his glass*). Then may the worst man win. (TAUSCH *bows and drinks a sip also.*)

GEORGE. Take the needle pellet out of another one. This is no good.

POTTS. Picric, ain't it?

TAUSCH. You see, I have every sympathy with your National Movement.

BLAKE. Ah, national movements are only a means to an end. We're not such parochial politicians as you seem to take us for.

TAUSCH. But why, then? Why all this?

BLAKE. Why not? Look here, Herr Tausch, you are our guest, and I declare that in a way I like you. Let me give you a word of advice. Don't let yourself be deceived by life. She's fooling you.

TAUSCH. In what way, pray?

BLAKE. My God, man, go out and take a look at your works and then ask yourself that question again. Listen to the noise of your turbines and then come back and give me any adequate reason for it all. The rest of the world may be crazy, but there's one corner of it yet, thank God, where you and your ludicrous machinery haven't turned us all into a race of pimps and beggars.

TAUSCH. Machinery, my dear sir, does not make pimps and beggars.

BLAKE. It makes proletarians. Is that any better?

(*For some time* WILLIE *has been pushing vigorously at the muzzle of the gun.*)

A VOICE (*off*). Say when you're ready to shove.

WILLIE. Ah God! haven't I been shoving for the last ten minutes.

(*The gun is heaved out of sight.* WILLIE *falls after it.*)

TAUSCH. But, Mr Blake, must we not have some regard for progress?

BLAKE. My good man, how do you know what progress is? Tell me, if you dare.

TAUSCH. Well, perhaps I may put it this way without offence. Surely you must admit that there are such things as backward countries?

BLAKE. There are countries where, incredible as it may seem to you, some of us prefer to live.

WILLIE (*off*). If you go through there you'll be stuck in the jamb of the door.

BLAKE. If man has anything to boast of that the ant, the bee and the mole haven't got, surely it's his greater capacity for enjoying life. To me it is progress just to live – to live more consciously and more receptively. Herr Tausch, do you never see yourself as rather a ridiculous figure trying to catch life in a blast furnace?

TAUSCH. It seems to me that the blast furnace is just the thing that leaves us all the freer to enjoy life.

BLAKE. Excuse me – does it leave *you* any the freer? Does it leave your dirty workmen any the freer? That's just where you allow yourself to be deceived. It's just another shackle on your limbs, and a self-inflicted one at that. I might be like you, Herr Tausch, if I chose, and this country might be like yours if you had your way. But I don't choose, and you won't have your way. Because we intend to keep one small corner of the globe safe for the unfortunate human race.

TAUSCH. Very interesting. And so you are a machine wrecker? We are engaged in a *Kulturkampf*. Well, I have heard of such before. You are a man of courage, Mr Blake.

127

BLAKE. To challenge you? Tausch said 'Let there be light,' And the evening and the morning were the first day.

TAUSCH. There have been others.

BLAKE. Elsewhere maybe. But here we believe that the dawn will break in the west. You bring us light from the wrong direction.

(GEORGE *is holding the shell, and* POTTS *is rapping it smartly on the nose with a wooden mallet.*)

GEORGE. Give it a good hard one, Potts old man.

BLAKE. Really, I do think this has gone far enough. Can't you do that somewhere else?

GEORGE. Quite safe, old chap.

BLAKE. If it goes off it'll spoil that suit of yours, Potts.

POTTS. My suit? You know, George, I'd forgotten all about the poor old missus.

GEORGE. There now, you've reminded the old fellow!

BLAKE. Anything to stop him fiddling with that damn bomb. And look here, what have you been doing to this other one? It's all in bits.

GEORGE. Had to take out the needle pellet. And she just came apart in my hands.

BLAKE. Damn it, then there's only two left!

POTTS. Think I'll have to go and have a drink, George.

GEORGE. I don't blame you, Captain. I'm going to get one myself. Come along. (*He leaves by a door on the fireplace side.*)

BLAKE. Oh, do cheer up, Potts. Did you ever tell Herr Tausch the story?

POTTS (*hesitating in the door.*) I don't think as 'ow I did.

TAUSCH. I am sure it would be very painful for the Herr Kapitän on such a day as this.

BLAKE. Not at all. We often discuss it. You should listen to this, Tausch. It's rather illuminating. Go on, Potts. Here's a fresh cosmopolitan mind for you.

POTTS. Well, you see, sir, we was all out in the old *Mermaid,* and we found out we only 'ad the one lifebelt as soon as she turned out to be sprung. Well, I was for drawing lots for it. But George, 'e says, 'No, Potts, women and children first, Potts,' 'e says. So I says, 'You're right, George.' So we fixes the lifebelt around the old missus and pitches her overboard.

TAUSCH. Ah, your ship was sinking!

POTTS. Well, yes, sir, in a way. So we thought at the time. But that's just the queer thing, sir, for when the fog lifted and we could see what was what, there we was aground in about 'alf a fathom 'ard by Fairview.

TAUSCH. Ach, so. That was fortunate for you. You escaped?

POTTS. Sure. We just waded ashore. All but the old missus, poor soul. We didn't get 'er till the next day.

TAUSCH. She was safe in the lifebelt?

POTTS. Sure she was safe in it. Floating a cable or two off Salthill. The wrong ways up. Poor Maggie. I often wonders whether we was wrong, sir. George 'e says not, and 'e ought ter know. But sometimes on 'er anniversary I thinks of poor Maggie, and, you know, I 'as my doubts. I do indeed. (*He shakes his head and follows* GEORGE *off.*)

BLAKE. Well? You don't feel inclined to laugh?

TAUSCH. Mr Blake, I never feel inclined to laugh at a man because his wife is dead. I am amazed that a man of some sensibility such as yourself could be so cruel.

BLAKE (*thinks for a moment and at last raises his glass.*) To death, Herr Tausch, that makes the whole world kin. (*He drinks.*) There's nothing cruel about her. (*He sits.*) Quite the reverse. (*There is another pause while he sinks into a brown study.*)

TAUSCH. Come, my friend. Perhaps I have been unjust. I am sorry.

BLAKE. It's all right. I'm partially intoxicated, that's all. (*Angry voices rise outside.*)

VOICES:

A bucketful will do.

Try it the other way round.

Ah, will you leave it alone?

Etc.

BLAKE. (*pulling himself together*). What are those damn fellows up to now?

TAUSCH. Wait, I will see. (*They both look at the clock.*)

BLAKE (*rising*). We can't fool about here any longer. *Fronta capillata,* as the elder Cato says. If Matthew and Mark fail us, then Luke must do the trick.

(BLAKE *takes the third shell and goes out.* TAUSCH *hastily fills his glass from the bottle and hurries after him.*)

TAUSCH (*following*). Mr Blake, you have forgotten your glass.

WILLIE (*off*). Ay, will ye looka. I say the bloody thing goes the other way round. (*Altercations till* BLAKE'S *voice quietens them. After a moment* DOBELLE *and* AUNT COLUMBA *come in.*)

DOBELLE. I don't care how full the house is. Nobody has any business to leave any of my things over here.

AUNT. Don't raise your voice at me, please. You can't intimidate me with loud speeches.

DOBELLE. I wish to God I could intimidate somebody in the house.

AUNT. Well, now that we're on the subject of intimidation, what have you been saying to Blanaid?

DOBELLE. Nothing. Why?

AUNT. She's retired to her room in tears. Whatever it is this time, I've had to tell you before that you're doing that child a great injustice.

DOBELLE. Well, hasn't she done me an injustice?

AUNT. You mean – Mary? How can you blame her for that? She didn't ask to be born.

DOBELLE. It seems to me that she was most insistent about being born.

AUNT. Roddy, you're unbalanced on that subject.

DOBELLE. Next you're going to tell me that I'm off my head, I suppose.

AUNT. Sometimes I wonder. But that doesn't make any difference to your duty to instruct her.

DOBELLE. Don't I leave that to you?

AUNT. Yes. But you don't allow me to teach her about you-know-where. (*She points downwards.*)

DOBELLE. I don't see why that should be an essential part of her instruction.

AUNT. Don't be ridiculous, Roddy. Doesn't the Bible say: 'Suffer the little children to come unto me'? Well, if one adopts your absurd attitude, supposing they won't come, where can you tell them to go to?

DOBELLE. My dear Columba, if your instruction depends on that – as indeed all instruction ultimately does – then it only confirms what I say – that ignorance is bliss.

AUNT. She's entitled to be told.

DOBELLE. Well, I won't have it. And if I find she knows, you can leave this house.

AUNT. It is every parent's duty and privilege to tell his child about that.

DOBELLE. I deny all duties and privileges where Blanaid is concerned. I will feed and clothe her, but there my interests end.

AUNT. What possible complaint can you have against her? She's a most mild-mannered child.

DOBELLE. Her existence . . . that was bought and paid for at Pressburg. Isn't that enough?

AUNT. That's a most outrageous thing to say. I'd like to know what Mary would think.

DOBELLE. Columba, you're a most unscrupulous woman. What right have you to bring Mary into it when you know I can't bear the subject?

AUNT. Well I can't say I've ever noticed any great tact on your part where my feelings are concerned. Aren't you always hinting to me about mowing machines?

DOBELLE. Be quiet. They're coming back.

AUNT. I won't be quiet.

DOBELLE. S-sh!

(*They continue to converse in low undertones amongst the luggage.* TAUSCH *enters. He smiles nervously as they glare at him, and he crosses swiftly to the door through which* GEORGE *and* POTTS *have gone out. He looks out and then closes it, coming back centre as* BLAKE *enters rather loquaciously tipsy.*)

BLAKE. Come and show us which way up this – oh! Where's George?

TAUSCH. He is not here. (BLAKE *looks out the wrong door.*)

BLAKE. Oh, hell!

TAUSCH. Well, Mr Blake. You were to tell me what you thought of me.

BLAKE. Was I? Well, I'll tell you how I regard you. As a demon pantechnicon driver. Old worlds into new quarters, by road, rail and sea.

TAUSCH (*with a look at the clock*). But surely that is a most praiseworthy occupation?

BLAKE. Maybe. Do what you like with your own world. But I insist that you leave me mine. I am Persephone, weary of memory, putting poppies in my hair.

TAUSCH. This world is neither yours nor mine. It belongs to all these people. Have you the right to say that I may not help them?

BLAKE. Nobody wants your help, Tausch. Why can't you just go away?

TAUSCH. How do you know they don't want it? Have you ever asked them?

BLAKE (*incredulous*). Asked them? (*Then with a laugh.*) Well, ask them. I don't mind.

TAUSCH. The verdict of democracy.

BLAKE. God bless the dear old people. The majority is always right. O.K. Let's try.

TAUSCH. Mr and Miss Dobelle, may we put this question to you?

DOBELLE. Still fishing the troubled waters of a dry well, eh?

BLAKE. We ought to get them all. (*Shouting at the door*) Willie! Blanaid! Come over here.

TAUSCH. It is a matter of great importance. (*Whispers*) Twelve minutes more.

(*Enter* GEORGE *and* POTTS.)

BLAKE. Come on in, George. You'll enjoy this.

GEORGE. Hullo, Splosch, old man, still here?

BLAKE. I think Potts should take the chair. He's the most impartial.

POTTS. What's all this? (*He sits and smokes his pipe, phlegmatically.* WILLIE *enters.*)

AUNT. I suppose we must have that door open all night regardless of the temperature.

(BLAKE *and* WILLIE *close it.*)

BLAKE. Have you been able to fix that, Willie?

WILLIE. Oh, I think so. It looks all right to me now.

BLAKE (*opening the window and again speaking in a low voice*). Well, stand there by the window and listen for you-know-what. And the minute you hear them coming tell me at once.

WILLIE. But are we not going to . . .

BLAKE. Do what I tell you, and stop making remarks, Willie. I know what I'm doing.

(WILLIE *stands at the window. For some time* TAUSCH *has been speaking earnestly to* GEORGE.)

GEORGE. But did I ever call you 'Splosch', old man?

TAUSCH. It is a small matter. Just if you can remember.

GEORGE (*ruminatively*). Tosh – Tush – (*He puts the bottle beside Blake's chair.*) Good for the voice, old man.

BLAKE. Thank you, George. How about keeping some minutes, Aunt Columba? An affair like this will be nuts and wine to you.

AUNT. Many a minute I've kept that people have regretted when sober.

(*She draws forward a small chair and sits down.* BLANAID *comes quietly in and sits on the ground. She takes out her diary and starts to write in it.*)

BLAKE. Dearly beloved, the situation is a straightforward one. Our German brother stands indicted before the bar of this court on the gravest of charges. He has outraged the sacred person of our beloved mother – Cathleen ni Houlihan. I say let him be condemned and his works be a deodand. In other words, I propose to blow them up. We leave it to you.

TAUSCH. To express your views without force or unfair influence.

BLAKE. *Nihil obstat.* What are you working at, my dear?

BLANAID. I'm filling in my personal memoranda. (*She produces a tape and takes a few measurements of her span, breadth of thumb, etc.*)

TAUSCH. Perhaps you will allow me to begin with a few words.

AUNT. Just one moment, please. I understood that this was to be some sort of a public discussion. Now it appears to be more like a court martial.

BLAKE. Oh, need we go into that?

AUNT. It is of importance as to who should speak first.

TAUSCH. It is all the same. It makes no difference.

AUNT. Excuse me, it makes a very big difference.

TAUSCH. It is just what you choose to call it. That is of no importance.

AUNT. Herr Tausch, if you call its tail a leg, how many legs do you say a cow has got?

TAUSCH. Really, Miss Dobelle!

AUNT. Answer me, please.

TAUSCH. If you call its tail a leg? Well, five, I suppose.

AUNT. Wrong, four. Because calling its tail a leg doesn't make it one. Blanaid, you're the junior. Begin.

BLANAID. Me? Well, I think it would be a shame to blow them up.

AUNT. Reasons, please, if any.

BLANAID. Because I like Herr Tausch and I think you're all being beastly to him.

BLAKE. For acquittal. Well, that's one point of view. (*Drinks deeply.*)

TAUSCH. Thank you, *Mein Herzchen.* It is not a reason that I had expected, but I appreciate it.

133

AUNT. Now, Willie?

WILLIE. Ah, sure there's no good asking me. I'm on active service.

AUNT. But if you weren't on active service?

WILLIE. I'm always on active service. I took an oath, you know, and I can't go back on that.

TAUSCH. What kind of an oath?

WILLIE. To obey my superior officers, and not to recognize the Government until the country's free. Isn't this a Government works?

TAUSCH. Pardon me, but what is the difference between the 'Government' and the 'country'?

(All laugh.)

DOBELLE. All the difference in the world if you're out of office. I thought I'd made that clear.

TAUSCH. But, pardon me, Willie. If it were not for your oath, do you think that to blow up the works would do a lot of harm to the country?

WILLIE. Ah, it would and it wouldn't. Wouldn't it help a lot of lads out of work if they had for to build them up again? I'm dead against unemployment, d'ye know.

BLAKE. That's enough. Conviction. Who's next?

TAUSCH. But may not the accused speak a word upon his own behalf?

AUNT. Don't interrupt, please. I'm next. And I wish it to be quite clear that I have as yet no personal objection to Herr Tausch.

TAUSCH. I am so glad.

AUNT. He may be a most estimable man for all I know, although he does try to get young girls to go with him to the pictures, and as for his morals, well, they don't concern me. I can be as broad-minded as anybody.

TAUSCH. I beg your pardon . . .

AUNT. Nor have I any objection to any ordinary factory as such. But this building is a power house, which is quite a different thing. Some people, I know, are inclined to scoff at the significance of power houses and to dismiss them lightly as just a small matter. But it is those very people who before they realize it have become dependent on the very thing they tried to laugh off. They think that they can give them up at any time. But they never can. Never.

TAUSCH. The lady is surely speaking of alcohol!

BLAKE. But this is eloquence, Aunt Columba. There's not a dry eye.

AUNT. Now once you become dependent upon anything, you are the slave of the man who controls it. Expected to bow the knee to some place-hunting industrialist with a small technical education and with neither culture nor religion to guide them. And if anybody thinks I am going to do that he is very greatly mistaken. I will not be dominated or controlled by anybody, and I am very grateful to Darry Blake for what he suggests, although I don't pretend to approve of him in other ways.

BLAKE. Thank you, Aunt Columba. You see, Tausch, I am appreciated too.

TAUSCH. Really, Miss Dobelle, I am none of these things you call me, I do not expect you to bow the knee.

AUNT. Order, please.

TAUSCH. You misunderstand me, I assure you.

AUNT. You are persistently interrupting, Herr Tausch. Please understand I will not be trampled on by you.

BLAKE. Yes, stop trampling on Aunt Columba, Tausch, and sit down. Now George?

(TAUSCH *shrugs his shoulders and sits down with a glance at the clock.*)

GEORGE. Well, you know I haven't the gift of the gab the way you people have, but when I was in Birmingham I sometimes used to watch all those women and young girls coming in and out of the factories. And, you know, I was touched – more touched than I can say. All those women and young girls having to work night and day, with their poor, pale, pasty faces that they have to make up with rouge and all that, brought tears to my eyes, old man. They ought to be kept out of doors and have proper homes of their own, you know. No life for young girls.

BLAKE. Two up and one to play. (*He stands.*) Well, George, your young girls will have to thank you for their green fields from this out.

GEORGE. Me? How do you make that out?

BLAKE. You and your gun. That's the idea. Why bother with damp cheddar when the Third Evangelist is waiting by the sea wall to do the trick for us.

GEORGE. I say, old man, you don't mean you're thinking of actually firing that gun?

BLAKE. Precisely.

GEORGE. Oh, I didn't know that. Did you, Potts?

POTTS. No. I didn't know that.

BLAKE. My dear man, we've been talking of nothing else all evening.

GEORGE. Oh well, I didn't hear you say that.

BLAKE. You don't seem pleased?

GEORGE. Well, it's all very well, you know. But it's a bit of a surprise. After all, those shells. Took a year each to make. And now to see them go up in a flash! And the gun. Four years' work, old man. Supposing something happens to it?

BLAKE. George, you're not trying to back out, are you?

GEORGE. Well, what do you think, Potts?

POTTS. Oh, I didn't know they was going to fire our gun.

GEORGE. We won't get it back, you know. Once they hear about it, it's gone for good.

POTTS. Yes, that's a bit thick, I think.

GEORGE. Anything in reason, old man. But, all these years' work!

BLAKE. George, I'm sorry. We thought you'd be pleased if we used it. But it's too late to change now. That's understood.

GEORGE. Oh, well, I'm against it, then.

POTTS. So'm I.

AUNT. You're in the chair. You've only got a casting vote.

POTTS. Casting what?

AUNT (*shouting*). Vote!

BLAKE. Then it all depends on you, coz. What's the verdict?

TAUSCH. Yes, Mr Dobelle, it depends on you.

DOBELLE. I'm against you.

TAUSCH. *Davor behüte uns Gott!*

BLAKE. Thumbs down!

DOBELLE. My reasons are – (*Enter* AGNES *with a tray. Everybody relaxes except* DOBELLE *and* TAUSCH.)

AGNES. Of course, if you must sit up all night across here in the cold while the fire is roaring in the sitting-room it's no concern of mine. Here's your tea anyway, and you needn't expect me again this evening, for I'm not coming back till poor Mrs Mulpeter is over her trouble.

BLANAID (*taking the tray*). Thank you, Agnes.

AGNES. I've a bottleful of Lourdes water and a string of charmed knots to undo. I've unlocked every door in the house and taken the braids out of my hair. If the tide's coming in, it will be a boy, but once it's over the turn – Who left that brown paper and string there? Was it you, Miss Blanaid?

BLANAID. I'm awfully sorry, Agnes. But I'd like the string to practise a few knots with.

DOBELLE. I would like to give you my reasons . . .

AGNES. You know quite well I must have any brown paper and string. You've no consideration at all. Willie, put that in the drawer of my dresser.

WILLIE. I'm wanted here, Ma.

AGNES. Be off, ye yuck, before I level you.

WILLIE. But Ma, looka . . .

AGNES. Be off, I tell you! (*He runs.*) Goodbye now. The doctor's on his way up, so I must run.

BLAKE. Agnes, just before you go, may I ask you one question?

AGNES. Well, what is it? You'll have to be quick.

BLAKE. We're thinking of blowing up the Power House. What would you say to that?

AGNES. Now there's another thing. The whirring thrum of them mechanicalisms is very disturbing to poor Mrs Mulpeter. You'll have to stop it and the sooner the better. All I say is, whatever you do, do it quietly or you'll hear from me. Good night so. I'll not be back now till it's over for good and all. (*She goes.*)

DOBELLE (*taking his cup*). Some day, God willing, I shall strike that woman.

AUNT. There was nothing to prevent you this evening, was there?

DOBELLE. Nothing to prevent me! Sometimes you ask damn silly questions, Columba.

AUNT. There's no need to be any more offensive than usual. If you can't get on with her, why don't you get rid of her?

DOBELLE. You can't get rid of Agnes. She'd only come back under a different name. Once you surrender to servants you have no right to live.

AUNT. She's a very efficient woman.

DOBELLE. She's a damned dragon.

BLAKE. A dragon? Well, St George, they say, was a dishonest beef contractor. I'll find you one of his descendants, coz.

DOBELLE. I have not given you my reasons yet. This man Tausch comes here with the most high-hatted motives and . . .

AUNT (*giving tea to* TAUSCH *and* BLANAID, GEORGE *and* BLAKE *having refused*). Cold as usual.

GEORGE. I propose a vote of thanks to the chairman for the very able way he has conducted this meeting.

BLANAID. Hear, hear. (*Clapping.*)

DOBELLE. I was once like Herr Tausch here. I too built barrages and constructed power houses, until one day I found myself to be a false friend. So we parted company.

BLAKE. Oh, cheer up, Tausch. You gave me a much better run than I expected.

DOBELLE. I beg your pardon, will you kindly listen to me?

TAUSCH. I am listening, Mr Dobelle.

DOBELLE. But nobody else is. However, I will tell you, Herr Tausch, why we can never be friends. Because you are a servant of righteousness, whilst I have sworn allegiance to the other side.

BLAKE (*to* GEORGE). I didn't even think he'd save his deposit.

DOBELLE. You wish to serve something you call progress. But progress – whatever it is – is never achieved by people like you who pursue it. Progress is the fruit of evil men, with sinister motives. You and your kind can only make misery.

TAUSCH. I am sorry. I do not follow.

DOBELLE. I don't blame you. Very few people will see what I mean.

BLAKE (*studying the Royal Arms over the fireplace*). We have here the eternal struggle of the Gall with the Gael – of the lion with the unicorn. But, while the lion is really a very middle-class animal, the unicorn is a beast of great virility that is subdued to gentleness at the sight of a virgin.

DOBELLE. Have you ever studied Aquinas?

(TAUSCH *rises and listens, a smile spreading over his face.*)

BLAKE. A lonely, chaste and noble beast in many ways very like myself.

DOBELLE. Quite so. Aquinas tells us that in order that the blisses of Paradise may be more delightful to them the blessed in Heaven will be expected to view the tortures of the damned and to rejoice.

(*From outside comes the sound of engines and of distant shouting. Then there is a stampede of men past the window and* BLAKE *springs into activity.*)

BLAKE. Christ, the lorries! Where's Willie? Why wasn't he listening?

(*He rushes to the window and shouts.*)

BLAKE. Hi, wait! Fire the gun first, you fools! It's all set! Willie . . . Get back you goddam imbecile. No, in the fuse hole. The other end. Quick . . . you've still got time. All right. Got it? Now give her hell . . . One . . . two . . .

(*He gets down and covers his ears. Several others do likewise. Eventually there is a dull clank as of falling metal. All straighten up and listen, but there is no further sound.*)

BLAKE. I give up! Oh, I give up! Really this is too much.

VOICES (*off*). Hi, you! Put up your hands. Stand back there!

GEORGE. Did anything happen?

BLAKE. Did anything happen! Oh my God!

GEORGE. He can't have put it in right. Ought to do better than that, you know. Come on, Potts, and we'll see.

(*He opens the door. On the threshold stands a soldier in a green uniform. GEORGE and POTTS turn on their heels and walk rapidly off into the adjoining room.*)

Oh, excuse me.

(*The SOLDIER comes in. He is a man of about thirty-seven, with a pale saturnine face and sunken cheeks. His pale blue eyes contrast strangely with the incipient beard and shock of wiry black hair. His expression is one of haunted melancholy. He carries a holster and revolver slung from his Sam Browne belt under his greatcoat which hangs open. The GERMAN greets him with quiet satisfaction. AUNT COLUMBA slips the tea-cosy over the remaining shell.*)

TAUSCH. *Ach, so!*

SOLDIER. Good evening.

BLAKE. Go away Lanigan! You're here too soon.

SOLDIER. Mr Tausch?

TAUSCH. All is well. Commandant, I am so happy that you have arrived in time to prevent any foolishness.

LANIGAN. The works are safe, Herr Tausch. All necessary steps have been taken.

TAUSCH. I am sure. (*The AUNT proceeds to go out.*)

AUNT (*in LANIGAN'S face as she passes*). Scum!

LANIGAN. I'm sorry, but you can't leave here.

AUNT. Detain me! Detain me if you dare! (*She marches out carrying the tray with the hidden shell.*)

139

BLAKE. Lanigan never could cope with the ladies, could he?

TAUSCH. Commandant, I am more than grateful for your so prompt arrival. But I would like to say, now that it is all over, that we have all been the best of friends, and that I will make no charge.

LANIGAN. No charge?

TAUSCH. Let bygones be bygones. Eh, Mr Blake?

BLAKE. Well, well – going to win our hearts by kindness eh?

TAUSCH. I think you and the commandant are old friends, eh?

BLAKE. Friends! Why it was I brought him into the movement in the old days, when we were all one against the British. And now behold my handiwork! A wee State – a Free State, held up by this bile green clothes-prop.

LANIGAN. He has more respect for me than he pretends.

BLAKE. The greatest respect. Don't you carry a gun? (*To* BLANAID.) My dear, once upon a time there was an ass laden with sacred relics. 'Behold,' said the ass to himself, 'how all the people kneel down as I pass by. O noble ass! O excellent ass!'

LANIGAN (*darkly*). All right, Blake.

BLAKE. Come, come. Give Frankenstein his due. (WILLIE *enters.*) Well, if it isn't Liam Reilly, my left-hand man! Where the hell did you go when you were supposed to be on guard?

WILLIE (*indignantly*). Didn't you hear my mother send me on a message? The Staters out there say they have me under arrest.

BLAKE. Naturally.

WILLIE. Under arrest! What's natural about that?

TAUSCH. It is all right, Willie. You go home quietly. I arrange that nothing more will be said.

WILLIE. Go home? But what about the works?

TAUSCH. We will say no more about it.

WILLIE. But do they not go up?

TAUSCH. No, Willie.

WILLIE. You called in the Staters?

TAUSCH (*a little crossly*). That is so.

WILLIE. But that's might against right.

TAUSCH. Well, if you wish to put it that way.

BLAKE. Thus spake Zarathustra.

WILLIE. Oh, that's a terrible thing. Might against right. That's not playing the game, you know.

TAUSCH. That is not a game to me, Willie. It is my business. I have a right to defend myself.

WILLIE. And what about my oath?

(TAUSCH *shrugs his shoulders.*)

Oh, yev tricked us! Without force, says he. Force or unfair influence! Didn't you hear him? And then he calls up the Staters when my back is turned. Oh, there's a thing. But the people of this country can't be cowed by threats.

BLAKE. Oh yes, they can, Willie. Every time. But I'll tell you the right answer to these people. Lanigan can stop us from touching the place tonight. He can lock you and me up if he likes, and in spite of the Bosch. But he can't lock us up for ever. And so long as there's the will in our hearts and the likes of him can only pollute as much of this earth as the area of their own boot soles, so long will the future be before us.

WILLIE. That's right. Up the rebels!

TAUSCH. But what is this? I protest, sir! What right have you to discuss so calmly whether you will blow up my works? They are mine. I have a right to take steps.

BLAKE. Very well. The next time I call, Herr Tausch, we will dispense with the discussion. I shall have nothing more to say to you.

TAUSCH. But I, sir, will have a great deal to say to you.

LANIGAN. Mr Tausch, I suppose that security for these works is essential?

TAUSCH. Essential! Of course it is essential. I do not understand such a question.

(LANIGAN *nods to himself and starts to put* BLANAID *quietly out of the room.*)

BLAKE. Do I see a piano? Well, well. Would anybody be entertained if I were to render the Chinese National Anthem? Those in favour indicate in the usual way.

(BLAKE *commences to play the Introduction.*)

TAUSCH. The Chinese – ! *Lieber Gott!* I will not be treated like this. I refuse to listen. (*Then quietly*) *Ach so.* I understand. You make a joke of me. I am the fool of the family! I should have known better than to respond. It is how I have been treated ever since I have come to this place. But I will not be deceived again. Here you will talk a lot, but it comes to nothing. You and your guns that will never fire. I will not be put out again.

141

BLAKE (*singing*).

> Fu-I loved the green hills
> And the white clouds.
> Alas he died of drink.

TAUSCH. You will discuss this and that, but I am the only one who will ever *do* anything in this place. Mr Blake, it does not matter to me whether you are in jail or not, because you can sing songs and make speeches as well in jail as out of it. And always to the same effect!

BLAKE (*as he plays*). Oh, Willie. Next parade will be the day I come out. And do see that the stuff isn't damp the next time.

> (*Singing next verse.*)
> And Li-Po
> Also died drunk
> He tried to embrace a Moon
> In the Yellow River.

TAUSCH. This is no country! It is a damned debating society! Everybody will talk – talk – talk –

BLAKE (*rising after a flourish of chords*). Died drunk! A pleasing thought. But needing a Nero to do it justice. *Qualis Artifex pereo.*

TAUSCH. But nothing ever happens.

> (LANIGAN *without any demonstration shoots* BLAKE *dead. The latter falls with a little sigh of surprise. Then* LANIGAN *slowly puts up his revolver as* BLANAID *appears again in the door and the heads of* GEORGE *and* POTTS *are stuck out of the side door. All are turned to stone.* TAUSCH *springs forward and makes a brief examination.* LANIGAN *turns and walks slowly out, all eyes following him. Then* TAUSCH, *with a sharp intake of breath, rises, bows slightly, and follows him swiftly out. The four other men look on, and crossing to the door, they stare out after them with some excitement.* BLANAID *alone stares at the body on the floor with wide eyes.*)

BLANAID (*coming forward*). Oh!

> (*She sinks down as the men continue to gaze out the door.*)

SLOW CURTAIN

ACT THREE

The Scene is the same as Act One. Several hours have elapsed since the conclusion of the previous Act. The hall door is open and the shutters at the window are drawn. The supper things are still on the table and amongst them is the tea-tray from the armoury upon which stands the last shell concealed under the tea-cosy. The picture taken from the armoury is leaning against the wall. POTTS *is standing in the open doorway peering out. Presently the model train emerges, and runs round the tracks.* AUNT COLUMBA *appears at the head of the stairs and comes down. She is wearing a hat but no coat.*

AUNT. Somebody has taken my coat from my bedroom. Nobody has any right to touch my things. Nothing is safe in this house. (*She looks around for it and then goes upstairs again, pausing for a moment on the landing.*) You needn't think I don't know where you are.

    (DOBELLE *appears from behind the railway and presently he speaks.*)

DOBELLE. Well, can you see what's happening?

POTTS (*gloomily*). It's gone.

DOBELLE. What? The lorries?

POTTS. Naw. Only one of 'em. Gun's gone.

DOBELLE. But Lanigan?

POTTS. Oh 'im? 'E's still down there postin' guards. 'Orrible fightin' and arguin' there's been.

DOBELLE. What do you mean?

POTTS. That furrin chap. Gone balmy, I guess. Seems to expec' the commandant to arrest hisself or somethin'. (*He spits.*) It's beyond me.

DOBELLE. I see.

POTTS. Pity about that gun.

DOBELLE (*returning to his train*). Well, there's nothing to be done, I suppose.

POTTS. Other lorry's still outside. They'll be in 'ere before they go, I guess.

(AUNT COLUMBA *appears once more, this time carrying her coat. She comes down.*)

AUNT. Oh well, if it wasn't touched this time that won't save it the next. I shall have to put a new lock on my door, I can see. All the keys in this house open all the doors. Oh, Captain Potts, please tell George I want to see him before I go. (POTTS *wanders off.*) What time is it? It must be very late. (*She goes and searches the drawers.*) Those are my roller skates, I do believe! How did . . . ? No they're not. I hope people will kindly remember that I have a championship to defend, and if anyone interferes with my skates I won't be answerable for the consequences. Some people don't seem to realize that skating may mean a lot to others.

(*She continues her search. The train runs round and stops in the station. She closes the hall door.*)

DOBELLE (*to the world in general.*) A most peculiar thing! I had quite forgotten the incident, it's so many years ago. I was driving with my uncle in one of those old-fashioned high dog-carts. We were coming back from duck-shooting and a rabbit ran across the road directly in front of us. I remember it distinctly now. My uncle rose from his seat, took a careful aim, and shot the horse through the head. It was a most surprising incident at the time.

(AUNT COLUMBA *stops her searching and presently she crosses quietly behind him.*)

AUNT. Roddy! (*She touches his arm.*)

DOBELLE. Eh – what?

AUNT. I am going away.

DOBELLE. Away. At this hour? Don't be ridiculous, Columba.

AUNT. I can't stay here any longer.

DOBELLE. Where will you go?

AUNT. That doesn't concern you. I shall catch the first train and put my bike in the van.

DOBELLE. Well, you know your own mind best.

AUNT. Roddy, I wish you'd try sometimes to understand my point of view.

DOBELLE. God forbid. I daresay if I understood it, you'd have ruined my life long ago as successfully as you ruined Captain Dopping's.

AUNT. I didn't ruin his life. His own dishonesty was quite sufficient to do that.

DOBELLE. Didn't you keep writing him offensive postcards to the mess until he was forced to resign from the regiment?

AUNT. I was only asking for what any gentleman would have returned without question – the mowing machine I gave him. When an engagement is broken off I say it's dishonest not to return the presents.

DOBELLE. I don't suppose the poor fellow had it to return. He had no accommodation for mowing machines. It was a damn silly present to give him anyway. But what's the use of arguing? I don't want to hurt your feelings, and, besides, I'm tired.

AUNT. Well, why don't you go to bed?

DOBELLE. I don't want to go to bed. I have been spending the night reading the *Inferno* and it has upset me.

AUNT (*goes upstairs*). Well, I think you ought to go to bed. (*She vanishes into her room and soon reappears with her bicycle.*)

DOBELLE. Columba, have you ever heard of Antenora?

AUNT. No. What's that?

DOBELLE. It's the Hell specially made for traitors to one's country. Have you any idea why Ruggieri, the Archbishop of Pisa, should be placed there, while Rahab, the harlot who betrayed Jericho, goes to Paradise?

AUNT. I'm sure there's a very good reason for it.

DOBELLE. It must have been a little difficult to know where one stood.

AUNT (*fixing her attaché case in her basket*). Well, talking of *Inferno,* there is one thing that really makes me uneasy about going away. That child, Roddy. Why don't you try and be nicer to her? Just for a little.

DOBELLE. Please, Columba!

AUNT. It's not much to ask of you. And you're not naturally a cruel person.

DOBELLE. I can't see how I'm being cruel to her.

AUNT. Of course you are. She sees nobody. She knows nothing. And she's just at the age when she needs companionship. She used to say her only friend was that Darrell Blake.

DOBELLE. God knows I don't want to make her life a misery. But I can't see what it has got to do with me. How can I do anything for her?

AUNT. You can send her to school.

DOBELLE. To school! To be taught lies and sophistries! To have illegal operations performed upon all her natural instincts. No, Columba! I'm not quite so cruel as that.

AUNT. But she must be educated somehow. I do my best, but you tie my hands so.

DOBELLE. Another convent, I suppose, is indicated. Perhaps even one on the Danube near Pressburg?

AUNT. There you go again. I know you're against religion, Roddy, but remember they only did what was right by Mary and the child according to their lights.

DOBELLE. I'm not against their religion. I am against their rightness. It is right that a woman should die so that a child's immortal soul should be saved from Limbo, therefore I say that I am against right. It is right that men should murder each other for the safety of progress. I admit it. That is why I am against right and believe in wrong. When I look back over my life, it's as plain as a pikestaff to me. It is always evil that seems to have made life worth while, and always righteousness that has blasted it. And now I solemnly say that I believe in wrong. I believe in evil and in pain and in decay and, above all, in the misery that makes man so much greater than the angels.

AUNT. Maybe you'll have ample experience of it before you're finished.

DOBELLE. Well, what do you offer me instead? A Paradise where I shall be expected to applaud the torment of my friends – who knows, perhaps even those of Mary. Keep it. I prefer to be damned.

AUNT. Mary was a good woman, Roddy. You've no right to talk like that.

DOBELLE. Who can tell? (*There is a knock at the door.*) But here we are arguing again. You'd better go. Come back when you feel better, and I'll do my best by the child in the meantime.

(*He starts the train and follows it out of sight. She stands in thought until the knock is repeated. She goes to the door and peers out.* GEORGE *and* POTTS *are there. They have lost much of their buoyancy.*)

AUNT (*letting them in*). Oh, it's you, is it? Been drowning your troubles in drink, I suppose, as usual.

GEORGE. No, but we've been giving them a damn good swimming lesson. Potts says you want to see me.

AUNT. Yes, come in. I have something to give you. Where are the others?

GEORGE. You mean Lanigan and the Bosch? Oh, down below. That German is off his rocker, you know. These foreigners! Anything knocks them over.

AUNT. Why, what's he doing?

GEORGE. Oh, going around. It's been a terrible night. And as if he hadn't done enough already, he's marching round objecting to everything. I declare to God I'd hate to be Lanigan out tonight with that fellow on the loose.

AUNT. Nonsense. They're hand in glove.

POTTS. Could I have . . . glass of water, please . . . voice gone.
    (*She indicates the carafe and he drinks.*)

GEORGE. First we carried poor Darry up to the isolation hospital. And then we came back and tried to reason with those fellows about the gun. It was no good, though. They took it off in one of the lorries. Poor Potts is terribly cut up. On such a day too.

AUNT. And Willie?

GEORGE. Oh, a very bad business. They took him off in the lorry as well. He was raving and swearing that he's going to get Lanigan. You wouldn't believe it was the same fellow. Seeing red.

AUNT. Well, what would you expect?

GEORGE. It's been a terrible night.

AUNT. Terrible. But not so terrible as it might have been. George, I've saved something for you.

GEORGE. Saved something for me?

AUNT. Yes. Trust a woman to be the only one to keep her head in a crisis. If it wasn't for me you'd have nothing left. Look.
    (*She proceeds to raise the tea-cosy. There is a knock at the door and she replaces it.*)

AUNT. What do you suppose that was?

GEORGE. Somebody wants to come in.

AUNT. Well, open it and see.

GEORGE. Me?

AUNT. Yes, go on.

GEORGE. Hadn't you better? It's your house.

AUNT. I will not. You're a man, or supposed to be one.

TAUSCH (*off*). Aal-lo!

GEORGE. It's the Bosch! Good God, what do you suppose he's up to now?

TAUSCH (*off*). Open, please.

(GEORGE *opens the door and* TAUSCH *and* LANIGAN *enter.*)

GEORGE. Both of them!

(*They all stand looking at one another for some seconds.*)

LANIGAN. Is Mr Dobelle about?

DOBELLE (*appearing*). You want me?

LANIGAN. I'm going now. I've told the men at the gate to let nobody through but the lighthousemen and anyone you give one of these passes to.

(*He sits at the table and commences to write.*)

DOBELLE. I see. How long must we have a guard?

LANIGAN. That depends upon headquarters.

TAUSCH. Commandant Lanigan, how often must I repeat that I do not wish to have either you or your men in my works. I do not require the type of protection you provide, and I will not have myself associated with you in the eyes of the public.

LANIGAN. I've told you we're here to stay whether you like it or not. These works are a national affair.

TAUSCH. And to the nation I will answer for them. They are in no danger now except from your presence.

LANIGAN (*to* DOBELLE). I'm leaving you half a dozen in blank. You must fill in the names of your tradesmen and visitors for yourself. I suppose six will be enough?

DOBELLE. I think so.

TAUSCH. Furthermore, I insist upon knowing whether you intend to surrender yourself to the law. It seems to me the most dignified course for you to take and it will save me the painful necessity of having you arrested. If you will not give me your honourable undertaking then I must assume the worst of your intentions.

LANIGAN. Ah, will you leave me alone. Haven't I had enough?

TAUSCH. Mr Dobelle, will you please oblige me with a piece of note-paper and an envelope.

DOBELLE. Try the drawer of the table.

TAUSCH. I thank you.

(*He sits and prepares to write.*)

AUNT. Well, goodbye, Roddy.

DOBELLE. Goodbye.

TAUSCH (*rising politely*). You are leaving, Miss Dobelle?

AUNT. I have nothing to say to you.

TAUSCH. To me?

AUNT. I hope for your own peace of mind you have as little conscience as you seem to have. We will not meet again. (*She pushes her bicycle off.*)

TAUSCH. Am I correct in thinking that the lady suggests there is something on *my* conscience?

GEORGE. Well, it was rather dirty work, you know, old man. Willie's right. You tricked those boys into this.

TAUSCH. That is monstrous, sir!

GEORGE. Mind you, I didn't see what happened. I'm no witness. I wasn't in the room at the time. But from what I've heard, it wasn't on the level.

TAUSCH. A crime has been committed. Are you accusing me, sir?

GEORGE. Ah, I don't accuse anyone. But it wasn't straight, you know. Leaves a bad taste in the mouth, old man. No! I'd have expected better. But then, of course – foreigners – you know. Not good sports. (*He shakes his head and, crossing to the table, he sits down silently beside* POTTS *and sinks into gloomy reflections.*)

TAUSCH. I never heard of such a thing. Even Commandant Lanigan appears to have some grievance against me!

LANIGAN (*rising and buttoning his coat*). I only said it was you wanted your works secure.

TAUSCH. I do. But did I ask you to commit a crime? You admit yourself that there is no excuse for what you have done. It is – I can use no other word – it is murder!

DOBELLE. Why not call it war? That's a well-known palliative.

TAUSCH. Pardon me, Mr Dobelle. In war there are certain rules that must be observed.

DOBELLE. I don't see that that's of much importance. From the point of view of the man who dies, it makes very little difference whether he is killed according to rules or not.

LANIGAN. Ah, what's the use of arguing! I was a rebel once. What I've done was war then. Now I'm on the other side and it's murder. I admit it.

DOBELLE. Don't try to explain, Lanigan. Your friends don't want it, and your enemies won't believe you anyhow.

LANIGAN. I'm not trying to explain.

TAUSCH. Well, I must say I admire your frankness, Commandant.

But I do not think that it will assist your position when I have made my report to the Attorney-General.

LANIGAN. When I took on this job I said to myself: 'Well, I'll last as long as God allows me.' So make your report and be done with it. If I don't get what's coming to me for this business, I suppose I'll be plugged sooner or later by somebody.

TAUSCH (*writing*). You need not be plugged, as you say, by anybody if you do not do these things.

LANIGAN. Somebody has got to do them . . . if the country's to go on.

TAUSCH. That is quite untrue. How can you say such a thing?

LANIGAN. Ah, never mind. I'm a physical-force man born and bred in the movement. I'm only doing my job – the job I'm able to do – the job that always seems to deliver the goods. There's no excuse for it, I daresay. I don't pretend to be clever like he was. He was the brains and inspiration of the movement in the old days against the British. But now we seem to have a damn sight too many brains, and inspiration always ends in trying to blow up something.

TAUSCH. And so you assassinate that inspiration!

LANIGAN. I suppose you think I enjoy that, when it means a bullet in my own back sooner or later. But enjoy it or not, I've always been taught that it's not words but deeds the country needs, so I'll go on doing what I can, no matter.

TAUSCH. A very fine attitude for young revolutionaries to adopt, maybe. But you are a man of responsibilities. The State cannot ignore the forms of justice.

LANIGAN. Forms! Do you think Blake wanted a lot of play-acting in court to find out what everybody knew already? And then they'd have tried to break his heart in jail in order to put a bit more venom into him for the next attempt.

TAUSCH. Ah! Quite a humanitarian, after all!

LANIGAN. I don't know about that. It was he that always had the wit to find the word for these things. Not me. But I only hope that when my time comes I'll be plugged fair and clean like he was, with none of the tomfoolery of law and justice and the torment they call 'Prepare to meet your God!'

TAUSCH. That is all you have to say before I send this letter to the Attorney-General?

LANIGAN. Ah, what more is there to be said? I'm a gunman. I

always was and I always will be. And if you ask me why, I declare to God I don't know. There's no glamour on my side, nowadays. But God help you all if I wasn't. It may be brains and inspiration that makes the country at the start, but it's my help you're always telephoning for before the end.

TAUSCH. Well, I am amazed!

LANIGAN. There are times when it's best to destroy the things that are nearest to us.

TAUSCH. I have heard that we are supposed to love our enemies in this life. But you would work upon the principle that we must kill our friends, eh?

LANIGAN. If there's any man could answer that, it's the man that has gone. And I believe that if ever I meet him again he'll bear me less ill-will for what's finished and done with, than those that are left behind. So, shot in an attack on the works, is my report. If you know better – well, I won't blame you for saying so. It'll be all the same, I suppose, for *they'll* get me in the end, if you don't. But, by God, they'll not touch this power house again! You'll see that I'm right there. Whatever happens now will be a personal matter between me and the likes of Willie Reilly. The works will be out of it. Good night, gentlemen. (*He goes. The lorry outside is heard to start.*)

DOBELLE. The Moor has done his work. The Moor may go.

TAUSCH. Mr Dobelle, that man is a scoundrel. But do you think that he is sincere in what he says?

DOBELLE. Maybe you are thinking that there are more ways than one in which a man may die for his country?

TAUSCH. Do you feel like that?

DOBELLE. No. I say, let my country die for me.

TAUSCH. Perhaps it would be best for you to make this report, Mr Dobelle. I would do it, but – I am a stranger. Perhaps . . .

DOBELLE. Denounce Lanigan, you mean?

TAUSCH. Some person will have to do so of course.

DOBELLE. There were only three of us there at the time. Willie was committing a felony and can say nothing of any weight. That leaves just you and I.

TAUSCH. I agree. Yes. Just you and me.

DOBELLE. Well, you can rule me out, I don't like the man, but hanging him won't bring back Darrell Blake.

TAUSCH. But murder. It is murder!

151

DOBELLE. Murder! Yes. The birth of a nation is no immaculate conception.

TAUSCH. But your feelings for your friend who is dead?

DOBELLE. He seems to have been Lanigan's friend too. There is no cure for death.

TAUSCH. Do you try to justify this man Lanigan?

DOBELLE. No. Yet when Lanigan dies he will leave behind him you and your works. When I die nothing will be left but the squabbling of female connections.

TAUSCH. *Das heisst* – you admire him, so?

DOBELLE. No, I hate him. Hate him like poison. But if I were to see him hanged, whenever I turned on your light I should feel more sorry for him than for my friend Darrell Blake. And I could not endure that. I prefer to continue hating him. Besides, would any jury accept the testimony of a man like me against Lanigan's? But they'll believe you, Herr Tausch. Oh yes, they'll believe you every time.

(TAUSCH *hesitates and then goes on with his letter.* GEORGE *gathers himself together and raises the tea-cosy.*)

GEORGE. Have some cold tea, Captain? We may as well. Oh!

POTTS. 'Ello! Where cher get that?

GEORGE. The last of the Mohicans. This must be what the old lady said she had saved for us.

POTTS. That was decent of her, George.

GEORGE. Not that it's much good, old man.

TAUSCH. A little give and take. A few words around the table. We were good enemies, Mr Blake and I, and we would have come to understand each other before long.

DOBELLE. You would never have understood Blake. He belonged to a different world that had no chance against yours – a world that must inevitably have been destroyed by you. You remember Li-Po? He was trying to embrace the Moon in the Yellow River.

TAUSCH. But I assure you, I would not think of destroying anything. We would have lived, side by side in harmony, respecting each other's point of view.

DOBELLE. Never with him. You'd always have been disturbing the waters with your machinery and drowning his moon in mud. No, in the end you would either have had to kill him or to give up your fight. You remember – he who establishes a despotism and slays not Brutus abideth but a little time.

TAUSCH. I wonder why the people whom we can like most easily are always on the wrong side? Why must Mr Blake be against me and Commandant Lanigan be my protector? Why must I have these monstrous doctrines foisted upon my shoulders?

DOBELLE. I told you, there are monsters in the mists that will glare back at you with your own face.

TAUSCH. Why always talk in parables, Mr Dobelle? You seem to wish to make everything appear unreal.

DOBELLE. If there was anything real in your sense of the word about tonight, was it not Lanigan's shot? That should satisfy even your thirst for reality.

TAUSCH. I see what you are at, Mr Dobelle. You wish me to believe that Lanigan's shot was part of my world – that he and I are truly on the same side.

DOBELLE. More than that. Lanigan is just yourself. He is your finger on the trigger. Denounce him by all means. The tribute to your works is not yet complete. For if he doesn't hang for Blake then Willie will hang for him, and I'm sure you'd like to save Willie. But before you denounce him, I say you must give me an answer to what he has said. And you won't do that. Because there is no answer, and you know it.

TAUSCH. Mr Dobelle, you drive me very far.

DOBELLE. Do you complain of this? What nonsense! Two more lives, Herr Tausch, but what of it! In this welter of blood one great factor will be borne in upon us. The works will remain. Man may perish, but they have been saved. Hallelujah!

TAUSCH. Enough of this.

DOBELLE. The inspiration that threatened them is no more. Nothing remains but the sordid squabble of Willie and Lanigan, in which the works will be forgotten and your programme will go through. I surrender, Herr Tausch. You are the victor after all.

TAUSCH. All guilt must be avenged on earth. I am going to send this letter, Mr Dobelle.

DOBELLE. Then why the delays of the post? The telephone is still at your disposal.

TAUSCH (*after a moment's consideration*). I do not know, sir, whether you regard me as a fool or a lunatic, but whatever may have been the effect of this evening's events upon other people, I, at least, have retained my common sense. I shall be glad to use your telephone.

DOBELLE. Do, sir. For the second time this evening.

(TAUSCH *glares at him for a moment and then crosses to the telephone, and takes up the directory.*)

GEORGE. I say, Potts, let's get rid of the damn thing. It makes me depressed.

POTTS. Same 'ere, George. I'm sick of the sight of it.

GEORGE. What do you say we chuck it away?

POTTS. Where?

GEORGE. Oh, anywhere. Into the sea. I don't want to see it again.

POTTS. What 'appens when the tide goes out?

GEORGE. Well, over the wall on to the old slag heap. Anywhere we'll be rid of it.

POTTS. Just as you say, George.

TAUSCH (*after some consideration, has thrown aside the directory and picked up the receiver*). Allo.

GEORGE (*rising*). Well, bring it along, Potts, old man. I'm bloody well fed up.

POTTS (*rising and taking the shell*). Only good for the slag 'eap, I'm afraid. Oh, we've been badly let down. Eight years' work gone up the spout.

(*They go off leaving the door open, through which the turbines hum merrily. It is a little lighter outside.*)

TAUSCH. Allo. Is that the exchange? Yes. I want Ballsbridge 586 please. Yes, that is right. No. Never mind. Ring till they answer, please.

DOBELLE. Until we had the telephone we were quite out of touch with civilization. (*Pause.*) Certainly if I were the Attorney-General I'd agree to prosecute anybody at this hour of the morning.

TAUSCH. Pardon. I speak with the German Legation. It is a matter for them what steps are taken.

DOBELLE. Oh, cowardly.

TAUSCH. Mr Dobelle, when I have telephoned I am going away and I do not think we will meet again – socially. I do not appreciate your satiric neurosis and I do not wish to lose my temper. But do not think, sir, that I have no answer to what you say. What I am doing here is greater than any of the considerations you fling at me – yes, greater even than the life of a man. I am not afraid to say it, even if that life must be my own. What is the life of a man beside the future of humanity? There is a purpose in this life, my dear sir, that transcends all personal feelings. Allo. My dear sir, you have only to go outside and look around you. Everything you see has its purpose in the scheme of things. You stand upon the sea wall and look down at the works below. What do you see? Allo. Yes. Yes, I wait still. The great river is there – the granite pier – the navigation lock – the turbine house beside the old slag heap. Everything with a purpose.

DOBELLE. Even the slag heap?

TAUSCH. Yes even – allo. Is that the Secretary? This is Tausch speaking, I have a report for the Minister. Yes, a serious report.

(*Outside there is a livid flash and a roar. In a moment it is followed by the sound of falling masonry. Then the lights go out. When silence comes again the sound of the turbines is no more and a red glow illuminates the sky behind the parapet.*)

GEORGE (*off*). Potts! Potts!

POTTS (*off*). Are you hurt, George?

TAUSCH (*dashing to the door*). The works!

GEORGE (*appearing outside*). It was a good one – a good one, Potts.

POTTS (*far away*). Bet-cher-life!

TAUSCH. What has happened to the works?

GEORGE. Blown to hell. Pure accident. Sorry, must be off.

(DOBELLE *begins to laugh as he lights a lamp.* TAUSCH *seizes* GEORGE *by the collar.*)

TAUSCH. Is anybody hurt? The night shift! Where are they?

GEORGE. Running like hell, old man. Can't be dead if they run like that.

(DOBELLE *picks up the dangling telephone receiver and speaks into it before replacing it.*)

DOBELLE. Did the Minister get that report?

(TAUSCH *releases* GEORGE *and dashes to the sea wall, over which he looks before returning. There is distant shouting from outside.* GEORGE *goes.*)

TAUSCH. *Du lieber Gott!*

DOBELLE. You were telling me – about a purpose – a purpose in this life – a purpose . . . (*He laughs quite hysterically.*) for the old slag heap!

TAUSCH. Please. Please.

DOBELLE (*lighting a lamp at the table*). You were explaining to me – your philosophy – excuse me – my satiric neurosis – it overcomes me . . . (*He laughs.*)

TAUSCH. My works! My works!

DOBELLE. Your works! Your memories! Brutus is avenged, O Octavius.

TAUSCH. Isn't it enough that a man has died and that my plant has been destroyed? Must we have laughter and jeers as well?

DOBELLE. It is not I – it is this land – this life. Take your works where they belong. Here is Hesperides – the garden where men may sleep.

TAUSCH. I think I go mad! . . . (*The shouting outside resumes.*) But I forget. Somebody may be injured. I must not give way. I will go down and search in the ruins. I must go at once.

(*He goes. The red glow in the court is streaked with the first sunlight.* DOBELLE *closes the door behind him as if to shut it all out.*)

DOBELLE. Yes, be off . . . search in the ruins. Search them well. Turn the scorched sod over. It will be all the same in the end. You'll never learn anything, and I'll never do anything. There's no end and there's no solution. (*He picks up the picture of his wife.*) Ah, Mary, have pity on me and on poor Tausch. No, not on Tausch. He's too great to need pity. But me . . . *Ah, Bice – la dolce guida* . . . take away this cursed gift of laughter and give us tears instead.

(*At the head of the stairs is a white figure in a long night-gown. He sees it with a gasp.*)

DOBELLE. Mary!

BLANAID. I'm frightened.

DOBELLE. Your voice! Why are you standing there looking at me, Mary?

BLANAID. Don't you know me, Father? (*She comes down.*)

DOBELLE. Know you! Why – what am I saying?

BLANAID. I saw a glare and then there was a terrible bang. Aren't you well?

DOBELLE. It's Blanaid! I didn't recognize you. You're so changed, child. You seem to have grown up suddenly.

BLANAID. I am not changed. Only you never look at me.

DOBELLE. I believe I don't. I wonder why. Stay with me for a little.

BLANAID. I was hoping you'd let me. In case there's another bang.

156

DOBELLE. There won't. It's all over now. (*Offering her a chair*.) Won't you sit down?

BLANAID. Thank you kindly.

DOBELLE (*sitting too*). I wonder what is the proper way to begin on meeting one's daughter for the first time?

BLANAID. I should say, 'Are you staying long in these parts?'

DOBELLE. I rather hope you are.

BLANAID (*kneeling beside him*.) Daddy, why do you never talk to me? Why do you hate me so?

DOBELLE. Because – because I'm an old fool. Because I thought that life had played its last trick on me. (*The lamp flickers*.) I'm afraid there's not much oil in that lamp.

BLANAID. Did I take her from you? (*He smiles*.) I'm sorry.

DOBELLE. I remember. That lock of hair used to do that.

BLANAID. When I grow up I'm going to try to be like her. I think I can. A Guide never gives up. Daddy.

DOBELLE. Yes, my dear.

BLANAID. Will you take my education in hand from now on?

DOBELLE. In what way?

BLANAID. I thought perhaps I might ask you questions from time to time.

DOBELLE. I'll do my best. If they're not too difficult.

BLANAID. May I ask one now?

DOBELLE. Well, only one. Then you must go to sleep and rest yourself. Well, what is it?

BLANAID. Do you know why people aren't happy?

(*There is a pause, during which she settles down and goes to sleep without really waiting for an answer. Through the cracks in the shutters the morning starts to shine*.)

DOBELLE. Well, I think that puts an end to my part in your education. I wonder, after all, do they want to be happy? The trees don't bother and they're not unhappy. And the flowers too. It's only men who are different, and it's only men who *can* be really unhappy. And yet isn't it unhappiness that makes men so much greater than the trees and the flowers and all the other things that can't feel as we do? I used to thank the Devil for that and call him my friend. But there's more to it than that. I suppose the Devil can do nothing for us until God gives him a chance. Or maybe it's because they're both the same person. Those glittering sorrows, eh? Asleep? Well, here endeth the first lesson. (*Pause, while the lamp sinks lower and his head nods.*) Darkness . . . death and darkness. Ah, can anything cure them? . . . I wonder.

(*He closes his eyes. Presently* AGNES *opens the hall door and comes in. It is morning outside and the sunlight floods into the room from behind her. She crosses to the window and opens the shutters with a sigh of intense satisfaction and smiles out at the flowers and the ivy that grow around the frame. Nodding her head, and with an approving click of her tongue, she softly hums a lullaby and surveys a new day. That is the end of this play.*)

CURTAIN

KITZBUHEL, 1930.

Fu - I loved the green hills

(ACT II)

EZRA POUND'S WORDS   WILLIAM ALWYN

Senza Ped. stacc.

Fu – I   loved the

green hills   and the white clouds   a-las he died   of

A FOURTH FOR BRIDGE

A War Play in One Act

ARMA VIRUMQUE

THERE is nothing like a war play to bring out the paradox of the conflict between the picture and the fact, especially if it is about a war in which the bulk of the audience is still committed to some partisan view of the issues.

Our conception of war as a subject for the theatre is usually melodramatic. Yet what we know of it from actual experience is, on the whole, quite the reverse. It is, of course, an abhorrent and loathsome thing, and entirely the fault of the enemy. At the same time it is difficult to close one's eyes to the fact that quite a number of people, whom we all know, had a much better time during the last war than they ever had before or since. That particular upheaval was a human disaster of the first magnitude, and the most widespread experiment in ruthlessness that the world has yet experienced. Yet on many occasions it evoked a most peculiar friendliness between the men who were engaged in killing each other, and a feeling of warmth – as between the more professional enemies at least – that was totally out of keeping with what was portentously called the 'War Effort'.

While a war is actually going on, few of us who are involved therein have any doubts as to how it started and what it is all about. It is brought about by Aggression, and Liberty is at stake. Sometimes our women and children are also concerned in the matter. This is perfectly clear to everybody. But after it has passed into history for a number of years a very odd change often takes place. We do not exactly come to the conclusion that it was about nothing at all. It would be fairer to say that we discover that it was actually about something else. This change of attitude is now legitimate in the case of the 1914-18 war – the 'Kaiser's War', as it was once called. The Kaiser is now generally recognized as rather a pathetic old gentleman who would probably have stopped it if he had not been cruising in the Baltic; while the real misdemeanants were a couple of parties called Schlieffen and Sasonov. On the other hand, 1939-45 is still widely regarded as having been a conflict between England and Germany, and little credence is as

165

yet given to the thesis that I heard expressed as early as 1940, that it would actually turn out to be a row between the United States and Russia, neither of which were combatants at that date. But there are signs that we will reach this point of view in due course.

Cynics and pacifists sometimes argue from these pecularities that wars never settle anything, but this is absurd. Of course they settle things. They settled American Independence, and they settled Slavery. They settled Tsarism, and they settled the Boers. That is to say, a hard-earned military defeat decided that the Boers should eventually have the whole of South Africa, instead of a couple of minor republics.

It is this aspect of war as a decider of problems that is becoming more and more evident as time goes on. What it usually settles today is the victor. A growing knowledge of this fact is the principal factor that makes war unpopular nowadays. Man has always known that war – in reasonable quantity – is good for his metabolism, and on the few occasions on which the Almighty has paid any attention to the second Collect, and given peace in our time for an unreasonably long period, we have had to invent a war – as in the Crimea – or promote private armies, as in the halcyon days of Carson and Home Rule, when everybody had a supremely good time. Peace is as undesirable a thing as Leisure, or Beethoven, or Money. In reasonable quantities it is all right, but too much is absolute hell.

The cheerfully realistic view of Man as an animal that shows considerably more dignity in hot conflict than in cold, is not only at variance with the views of the Sunday school. It also runs contrary to the conventions of the traditional war play – a fact that may partly account for the disturbing silence with which the following *morceau* was received when it was originally performed on British television. We had an uproarious time in the studio, where it was rehearsed in gales of uncontrollable laughter by a cast of ex-service men; but it was received by the public with a gloom that is normally reserved for public funerals.

Since then – to the best of my knowledge – it has only been performed by some company in Scotland which omitted to pay the usual royalties; so one can hardly decide as yet whether it is just a very bad play, or is another of those pieces that suffer from the fact of being a true story. But time, I hope, will repair this neglect, if not the missing royalties.

INTRODUCTION

This item – a squib about the War – is based on fact. I was shown the plane in Malta, where it actually landed after some arguments that now form part of the lore of the Royal Air Force. There have already been a number of plays that describe very accurately the physical circumstances of that extraordinary war, but none, that I can think of, that reflect its spiritual confusion, and the amusing chasm between theory and practice that confronted most of the fighting men.

Looking back on it now, from a reasonably safe distance, it appears to me to have been a superb example of the fact that War as a phenomenon can no longer be regarded, melodramatically, as a struggle between villains and heroes. It is a social disease, in which behaviour is much more important than the issues. All wars, at the time, seem highly important as a matter of right versus wrong. Yet how many of them manage to retain this aspect on the pages of our history books? The incidents, Yes: but the issues, No. We remember the Charge of the Light Brigade, but who knows or cares what the devil the Crimean War was all' about?

As for the late upheaval, we all said at the time that never had there been a struggle before, in which the issues had been clearer. But what, after all, were they? We fought the Germans on behalf of the Poles. And the Germans fought the Russians on our behalf. The Americans stayed out of it until they had cornered everybody else's external assets, and were finally forced by the Japanese to help us to beat Hitler. The Italians – with considerably greater cleverness than they were given credit for – fought on whichever side appeared to be winning. And the Jugo-Slavs fought most vigorously of all amongst themselves. It could probably never have been avoided, in view of the ponderous social tensions that were at work, without any machinery to control them. But it is time that we stopped talking about it as a Crusade, and looked at it from the clinical point of view of half a dozen friendly enemies trapped in an aeroplane. It will not be the official attitude, but it will certainly be a realistic one.

The play, so far, has only been professionally performed on television, but it is much better suited to the stage than to broadcasting. It should not be overplayed for farce, any more than *The Golden Cuckoo*. And, please Directors, forget all the Germans you have ever seen on the movies. There is only one thing more foreign to life than the Stage Whore, and that is the Stage German.

A Fourth for Bridge

CHARACTERS

THE GERMAN
THE HUSSAR
THE AIR FORCE TYPE
THE ITALIAN
THE YANK
THE PARTISAN
THE PILOT

SCENE

The interior of an Italian military transport aircraft,
in flight over the Mediterranean – 1942

THE PLAY

The interior of this aircraft is viewed as if sliced in half longitudinally, from the pilot's compartment to the door leading into the tail. At one end, facing offstage, the pilot is at the controls, with a co-pilot's seat empty beside him. He is a rascally-looking little man dressed in a variety of leather garments, and perpetually sucking at a cigarette. Affixed to the fuselage beside him is a large photograph of a girl in a bathing suit. A German officer, in the khaki shorts and tunic of the Afrika Korps, is standing beside him. He has a holster attached to his belt containing an automatic.

Behind him is the doorway, now open, which separates the nose from the main compartment of the plane. Along the major part of this area runs a metal seat with several small windows behind it. Overhead is a rack, from which a variety of equipment hangs down and swings rhythmically with the movement of the plane. Towards the tail end is a metal door, now closed, which opens outwards into space. Nearer to the tail, our view is blocked by a bulkhead in which is a small interior door marked 'UOMINI'. Another notice prominently displayed reads 'PERICOLOSO: FUMARE PROHIBITO'.

Towards the pilot's end of this central area, an American soldier is seated on some sacks, on the floor, and reads a fat volume. Lying against him is a sleeping figure of indeterminate size and sex, wrapped in a blanket. Towards the tail end an Italian officer yawns. He is neatly dressed, with shiny top boots and a blue-green uniform with rather elaborate shoulder cords, a tasselled forage cap, and a black belt holding an automatic pistol of formidable proportions. Beside him sit two British officers – one, a flight-lieutenant in khaki shorts and bush shirt, flying boots and a blue hat – the other a tank commander in corduroy trousers, a grey pullover, a gaily-coloured scarf, gym shoes, and a beret bearing a Hussar cap badge. The latter has a pack of cards which he idly shuffles as the flight-lieutenant glances through an Italian illustrated paper.

171

There is a continual hum of engines, which is louder whenever the door to the nose is open. At present this hum is augmented by some gay crooning that comes from a radio beside the pilot. The German peers ahead. Then he taps the pilot on the shoulder and indicates his cigarette with disapproval. The pilot pretends to put it away, but promptly produces it again, as the German goes through the door into the main compartment, and closes it behind him. The sound of the engines becomes fainter, and the music fades out altogether.

Passing along the compartment, the German first politely takes the American's book, looks at its title, registers interest, and returns it with a courteous salute. He then steps over the sleeper, moves to the rear end, and is about to enter the tail through the door, when he pauses near the Hussar, and looks at his costume with some surprise.

GERMAN. Excuse, please. What does this costume represent?

HUSSAR. Oh, just bits and pieces, old boy. 4th Hussars, actually.

GERMAN. *Ach* – the cavalry! It is the recognized costume of the English Hussars? Yes?

HUSSAR. Well, I wouldn't know, actually. We're not fussy.

GERMAN. I, too, am fond of horses. You ride much in times of peace, perhaps?

HUSSAR. Horses? Don't know one end of a horse from the other. Why do you ask.

GERMAN. Because I thought that you said – but never mind. I do not understand the system in your English army. What is your job?

HUSSAR. I've got a B echelon.

GERMAN. A B echelon? What is that?

AIR FORCE TYPE (*looking up from his magazine*). What's he talking about?

HUSSAR. Wants to know what a B echelon is.

AIR FORCE TYPE. He doesn't know?

HUSSAR. Apparently not.

AIR FORCE TYPE. Good lord!

HUSSAR. Hasn't got a clue.

GERMAN. Well, it does not matter. For you the war is over.

(*He turns to go through the rear door.*)

AIR FORCE TYPE. Whacko!

GERMAN (*turning back*). *Das heisst* . . . what is this word? Wacko?

AIR FORCE TYPE. Whacko! Why – er – (*To his friend*). How would you describe it, old boy?

HUSSAR. An expression of sympathy, old man. D'you know what I mean?

GERMAN. Sympathy? For whom?

HUSSAR. For you, old man. As you say, for us the war is over.

GERMAN. Please. I wish to understand. You are prisoners. I am not. Why then does your friend sympathize with me?

HUSSAR. Got a cigarette?

GERMAN. With pleasure. (*He offers him one before he remembers.*) But excuse. There is no smoking on this aeroplane. It is dangerous.

HUSSAR. It is an Italian aeroplane. There is always danger that it blow up.

    (*The* ITALIAN *indignantly lights a cigarette too.*)
    (*Shrugging his shoulders.*) *Macht nichts.* But I think we all wish to arrive safely in Sicily? Eh?

HUSSAR. Not particularly.

ITALIAN. What? You do not wish for Sicily? Then you have deceived me!

HUSSAR. Oh no, old man.

ITALIAN. You say to me, we must leave Pantelleria. Pantelleria is no good. So I arrange we go to Sicily. And now you say you do not wish for Sicily. So you have deceived me. Yes.

HUSSAR. I only said not particularly.

AIR FORCE TYPE. Don't be so touchy, old boy. Bad for the body.

ITALIAN. It is always so. I am Italian. The German he sneers. The English they lie, And all the time I do not feel very well.

    (*A spasm shakes him and he steadies himself.*)

HUSSAR. What's the matter?

ITALIAN. I feel terrible. It is the movement of the *macchina*.

AIR FORCE TYPE. Relax, old boy. You're exciting yourself.

HUSSAR. Just a touch of air-sickness.

ITALIAN. The movement is unpleasant.

AIR FORCE TYPE. I know. There was a time when I didn't like it much myself.

ITALIAN. I have not flown before.

HUSSAR. You'll get used to it.

GERMAN. You hear? He has not flown before! It is what I have learnt to expect. He is a parachutist, and he has not flown before.

173

HUSSAR. Well, he's got to learn, hasn't he? I expect it takes time to get round to the technical side.

AIR FORCE TYPE. Pasquale's a good type. A regular fire-eater . . . when he's on the ground, of course.

ITALIAN (*in trouble*). Oh!

HUSSAR. Very nice fellow. Maybe a short game would take his mind off it.

(*He holds out the pack of cards.*)

GERMAN. Excuse, please. I still do not understand. This man is your guardian?

AIR FORCE TYPE. Our guard, old boy. Guardians are only for minors.

HUSSAR. And loonies. We're taking him to Sicily.

GERMAN. You are . . .! But if he is your guard why are you taking him to Sicily?

HUSSAR. Quite simple, old man. We were in the bag on this Pantelleria.

AIR FORCE TYPE. Revolting little place.

GERMAN. So?

HUSSAR. So we didn't like it much. D'you know what I mean?

GERMAN. Yes. (*Pause.*) No, I do not know what you mean.

AIR FORCE TYPE. Terrible food.

HUSSAR. No accommodation to speak of.

AIR FORCE TYPE. Air raids galore.

HUSSAR. And not a fourth hand in the whole place.

GERMAN. A fourth hand? What is that?

HUSSAR. A fourth for bridge. We were teaching old Pasquale.

GERMAN. Bridge? Ah! That is a game of cards.

AIR FORCE TYPE. Bright fellow. Perhaps you play yourself?

HUSSAR. So we said to old Pasquale here, 'Pasquale, this Pantelleria seems a pretty dim place. What are we going to do about it?'

AIR FORCE TYPE. Can't sit quietly under those conditions.

HUSSAR. Self-help, old man, if you know what I mean.

AIR FORCE TYPE. If the unthinking lobster can grow a new claw in a crisis, surely we can manage to find a fourth for bridge?

GERMAN. The unthinking lobster?

HUSSAR. Rather a neat simile, old man. Congrats!

AIR FORCE TYPE. Glad you like it.

(*They shake hands.*)

HUSSAR. Anyhow, Pasquale saw our point. So we all packed up, and now we're going to try a prison camp he knows about somewhere in Sicily.

AIR FORCE TYPE. Good idea, don't you think?

GERMAN. Ah, I see. (*He turns to the door and then pauses.*) The hussar has never seen a horse. The parachutist does not fly. The prisoners of war require a fourth for bridge. And the explanation has something to do with a lobster. No, I do not see.

(*He shrugs his shoulders and goes into the Uomini.*)

AIR FORCE TYPE. Peculiar fellow.

HUSSAR. Afrika Korps type. Old Rommel makes them a bit pompous. Still, he seems to know something about the game. How about asking him to make up a rubber?

AIR FORCE TYPE. What do you say, Pasquale? Like to make up a rubber with the Jerry?

ITALIAN. Please, please, do not speak to me! I do not wish for conversation.

AIR FORCE TYPE. Poor fellow. He's looking terrible. Perhaps we'd better not press him.

HUSSAR. Nonsense. A nice brisk game is just what he needs. (*Confidentially.*) And it might be a good moment to try out that forcing spade convention. Maybe clean up a tidy bit of cash, too, if you know what I mean.

AIR FORCE TYPE. I get you. In that case what about the Yank over there? Then we could do without the Jerry, and maybe do better still.

HUSSAR. Hey, America! How would you like to join us in a short game of bridge?

(*The* YANK *makes frantic gestures towards the figure beside him.*)

What's the matter? Can't you leave your book and your boy friend?

(*More gestures.*)

AIR FORCE TYPE. Odd behaviour! What can he mean?

(*The sleeping figure stirs, sits up, turns over and sleeps again. It is a pretty girl in battle dress.*)

(*He whistles.*) Why it's a popsy.

YANK. Say, fella, don't do that.

HUSSAR. Trust the Yanks.

AIR FORCE TYPE. Fast worker, eh?

HUSSAR. Who's the cutie pie?

YANK. Don't talk like that. She don't like it.

HUSSAR. Why not?

(*The* YANK *disengages himself gingerly and comes down the plane.*)

YANK. Don't ask me. She's one of these Partisans. They don't like being called cute. Says she's a soldier.

AIR FORCE TYPE. A soldier?

YANK. Yeh! Been travelling with her for three days now, and, boy, am I a wreck?

AIR FORCE TYPE. You sly dog, I bet you are!

HUSSAR. Let's have her over.

YANK. Listen, pal. Take my tip and lay off that dame. Those girls are dynamite. Treat them like a woman and they go up in smoke.

AIR FORCE TYPE. Nonsense, old boy. The fair sex, you know. Always the same, underneath.

YANK. No sir, not those ones. They're tough babies. Like nothing I've ever come across, and I thought I knew a thing or two. This one talks psychology and says she's shot up a town in Poland, and brother I wouldn't doubt her.

AIR FORCE TYPE. Really? Who'd think it? Such a nice little piece.

YANK. Sure. That's the trouble. I'm not used to this. I can lay off dames if I have to. But to live with them night and day, and be expected to treat them like a man! That's not natural. Not when they look like that. Sam, I keep saying to myself, keep your mind on Tolstoy. But do I?

AIR FORCE TYPE. Well, do you?

YANK. Like hell I don't.

HUSSAR. Sorry to interrupt, old man, but just take a look at Pasquale.

ITALIAN (*holding his stomach*). Oh! Oh!

YANK. I guess that guy is just about passing out. What seems to be the trouble?

HUSSAR. Quite a simple complaint. The Folgore Division is sicking up.

AIR FORCE TYPE. Poor old Pasquale. I say, old boy. I've just thought of a little plan.

HUSSAR. What's that?

AIR FORCE TYPE. I have a feeling that old Pasquale is so disinterested in life at the moment, he mightn't mind giving up his gun if we put the proposition to him in the right way.

HUSSAR. I see what you mean.

176

AIR FORCE TYPE. Then we might clobber the old kite and go to Malta instead.

HUSSAR. To Malta?

YANK. Boy, that's a honey! Let's take over. I've never been to Malta. Who owns it?

HUSSAR (*gloomily*). The British Empire.

YANK. That's O.K. by me – so long as there's no Girl Scouts. But what about that Kraut?

HUSSAR. He's busy inside. Maybe we could lock him in.

AIR FORCE TYPE. No good. The fastening is on the inside. But I tell you what. I'll stand by and clip him one as he comes out. He'll never expect that. Meanwhile you chaps get the you-know-what and use it to popularize our point of view with the pilot.

(*He takes up a position behind the rear door.*)

YANK. Let's go. (*To the* ITALIAN) Say, bud, how are you feeling now?

ITALIAN. Please do not talk to me.

HUSSAR. Like us to hold your head, eh?

ITALIAN. *Basta! Basta!* You torture me. Leave me alone.

HUSSAR. We don't want to torture you, old man. Just want to make you comfortable.

ITALIAN. Basta, basta.

YANK. O.K. Take it easy. The belt's the trouble. Suppose we take it off and fix you up real comfortable?

HUSSAR. Much too tight round the stomach.

YANK. See. All we have to do is loosen it.

ITALIAN. Oh, leave me alone.

YANK. Take it easy. You'll feel a new man.

(*They take the belt and pistol and dash for the nose of the machine. Opening the door the engines grow louder and we hear the music as well.*)

(*Speaking above the noise.*) Howya, bud?

PILOT. 'Allo.

HUSSAR. Nice little place you've got here.

YANK. We kinda thought you'd like to know we're taking over.

PILOT. Ya ne ponimayu.

HUSSAR. By popular demand we have decided to go to Malta.

PILOT. What say?

HUSSAR. Mind if we turn off the wireless?

(*The* HUSSAR *turns off the radio. The music stops, leaving engines.*)

YANK. Malta!

PILOT. Malta? Oh no. Sicily!

YANK. That's where you're wrong, brother. All wrong. We're in charge now, and we say Malta.

PILOT. Sicily very nice. I have a nice girl there.
     (*He indicates the picture and clicks his lips.*)

HUSSAR. You'll find them attractive in Malta, too.

PILOT. Oh, no. See.

YANK (*showing the gun*). No, you see.

PILOT. This is a pistol?

HUSSAR. Exactly.

YANK. Rooty-toot-toot. That's what we're saying.
     (*Pregnant pause.*)

PILOT. What do I get if we go to Malta?

YANK. This is what you get if you don't.

PILOT. You mean you shoot me?

YANK. Sure. Right in the belly.

HUSSAR. Very painful.

PILOT. And who will pilot the arrow-plan if you shoot me?
     (*Awkward pause.*) Maybe one of you knows how to fly the arrow-plan, eh? Perhaps not.

YANK. See – that's not the point. We've got the gun. So what we say goes.

PILOT. But excuse. You have the gun, but I work the machine. I do not think you can shoot me until we are on the ground.

HUSSAR. Oh, so that's your line, is it? A hold-up?

PILOT. Si, signore.

YANK. You don't say! Well would you like to know what my answer is to that?

PILOT (*nodding his head*). Ya?

YANK (*after a pause*). So would I.
     (*The PILOT clicks the wireless switch, and soft music resumes.*)

HUSSAR. Better come behind and talk this over, old man.

YANK. What will you take to go to Malta?

PILOT. What have you got?

HUSSAR. You're a bit of a twerp, aren't you? We'll speak to you later.
     (*They go back to the main cabin of the plane. The music stops, leaving engines fainter, as they close the door.*)

YANK. Say, what do we do now? Take up a collection?

HUSSAR. We could do that. And then, of course, we could take it back off him as soon as we've landed. D'you know what I mean?

YANK. Boy, that would be a super double cross.

HUSSAR. On the other hand, he's probably thought of that himself. So probably he doesn't want money.

YANK. Well, it's going to be tough if he takes us to Sicily now we've stuck him up.

HUSSAR. True enough. We've got to tempt him somehow. I wonder if . . . Women! Let's try him with a woman.

YANK. You mean. . . ?

HUSSAR. Certainly I do. Wake up your friend and get her to persuade him.

YANK. Wake her yourself, brother. I wouldn't trust myself near her.

HUSSAR. Oh, very well, if you're as soft as all that. (*He shakes the sleeping girl by the shoulder.*) Excuse me, miss. Would you mind doing something for us?

PARTISAN. Why do you disturb me?

HUSSAR. Would you mind using your charms on the pilot. We're trying to persuade him to change his course to Malta.

PARTISAN. I am so cold. Where is the American? He will lend me his coat, I think.

HUSSAR. Sure he will. Give the girl your coat, chum. She's cold.

YANK (*taking it off*). Why mine? What's she got against me?

HUSSAR. It's your fatal charm, and good-quality wool. Now listen, my dear, we've got everything under control, all but one thing. So if you can use a few feminine wiles on the pilot, Bob's-your-uncle.

PARTISAN. Bob is not my uncle. You are mistaken.

HUSSAR. Well, never mind who your uncle is. Go and vamp the pilot and make him take us to Malta.

PARTISAN. What is vamp? I think it is to play the piano.

HUSSAR. Totally wrong, my dear. It means to drop a glance or two – to hint at certain matters – to make unmaidenly advances. Oh, you know.

PARTISAN. Oh? You wish me to ruin him?

HUSSAR. Well, I wouldn't put it quite that way. Just the odd feminine wile, You know what I mean?

PARTISAN (*after a little consideration*). But no. I am a soldier. In our army it is not allowed.

(*She sits.*)

YANK. There she goes. I told you.

AIR FORCE TYPE (*coming down the compartment*). I say, what's going on?

HUSSAR. Damn birdman won't change his course without a bribe. Says he's the only one who can fly the plane.

YANK. Say, bud, you can fly the kite!

AIR FORCE TYPE (*horrified*). Me?

YANK. You're in the Air Force, aren't you?

AIR FORCE TYPE. Don't be silly. I'm an administrative type.

HUSSAR. You might have known with those handlebars.

AIR FORCE TYPE. No need to get personal.

YANK. Aw, who cares whether you can fly it or not? We'll pull a bluff on this guy.

> (*They go back to the* PILOT'S *compartment. Engines and music once more. The* YANK *indicates the co-pilot's seat to the* AIR FORCE TYPE.)

You sit over there. Now look here, wop. You think you're pretty smart.

PILOT. I try to do my best.

YANK. I'll say you do. Well, believe me, brother, you're out of luck. Because this happens to be a distinguished ace of the Royal Air Force. How many missions did you say you've flown, Major?

AIR FORCE TYPE (*gingerly fiddling with the controls*). Major? Group-Captain! Let me see . . . about forty-five, I would say . . . not counting Berlin, of course.

YANK. Forty-five. (*He whispers.*) Draw it mild. Now listen to me, Nauseating. The Group-Captain is going to take over, and you're going to get a slug where you least want it. So get set.

> (*The* PILOT *switches off the dance music, leaving engines.*)

PILOT (*crossly*). I will take you to Malta.

YANK. Just as you like. It's all the same to us who takes us. Well, let's see her go around.

> (*The* PILOT *moves the controls. Those who are standing up stagger.*)

Well, that's fixed anyhow, You stop here, Group-Captain, and keep an eye on Son of Frankenstein.

AIR FORCE TYPE. Glad to, old boy. (*He tries some of the controls.*) Extraordinarily interesting, all these things.

YANK (*sotto voce*). Well, leave them alone and don't overact. Can I trust you?

AIR FORCE TYPE. Absolutely.

YANK (*going*). I hope so. (*Turning.*) Hey, what about that Kraut? Who's supposed to be taking care of him?

AIR FORCE TYPE. Good lord! He's still in the loo. Forget all about him.

YANK. We'll get back there at once.

(*The* AMERICAN *and the* HUSSAR *return to the main compartment closing the door behind them. As they enter, so does the* GERMAN *from the opposite end.*)

HUSSAR. Look! He's coming out.

YANK (*holding the gun*). Stick them up, Hynie. I've got you covered.

GERMAN (*raising them*). *Ach,* so!

YANK. Just in time! Now turn round and don't move while my pal takes that gun off you.

(*The* GERMAN *turns his back, holding his hands above his head. The* HUSSAR *moves towards him but stops by the* ITALIAN.)

HUSSAR. Look, Pasquale's sitting up.

ITALIAN. I am better now. The trouble has passed.

YANK. You reach for it, too, wop. This is a stick up.

ITALIAN (*rising*). I am much better. I feel good. Now I shall take back my pistol and my belt.

YANK. Oh no you won't.

ITALIAN (*advancing*). Yes please. It is not allowed in the Folgore Division to give away the pistol and the belt.

YANK. Stop there, fella, or I'll shoot.

ITALIAN (*advancing*). It is forbidden in the Folgore Division.

HUSSAR. Gosh, Pasquale's got some guts!

(*He and the* PARTISAN *cover their ears.*)

YANK. Get back. O.K. Don't say I didn't warn you.

(*He pulls the trigger several times. The gun clicks.*)

HUSSAR (*his eyes closed*). Is he dead?

ITALIAN. I will take it now, please.

YANK. Say, is this thing empty?

ITALIAN. *Certamento.* Otherwise it is dangerous to carry. Oh, do not throw it on the ground. That is not polite.

(*He picks up the gun from where the* AMERICAN *has thrown it, and puts it on, together with his belt. The* GERMAN *has turned.*)

YANK. I give up, And just when we'd fixed that pilot to go to Malta.

GERMAN (*his gun levelled*). Now will you all please to raise your hands?

HUSSAR (*as he does so*). There you are. This is what comes of being careless with firearms.

ITALIAN (*still blandly fixing his belt*). I am not careless. If I had been more careless this man would have shot me.

YANK. Best thing for you, you big phoney.

ITALIAN. If you insult me you insult the Folgore Division.

YANK. O.K., Gorgeous. Consider yourself insulted.

ITALIAN. Presently I shall spit in your face.

GERMAN. Silence, please. I am in command here. (*He frisks the Englishmen.*) You will all remain quietly here while I go to speak with the pilot. We will not go to Malta or to Sicily. We will go to the Côte d'Azur where my own division is resting.

> (*He goes into the forward compartment where music is heard again. He taps the* AIR FORCE TYPE *on the shoulder with the gun, and orders him aft. The latter raises his hands reluctantly and goes. Then the* GERMAN *takes his place in the co-pilot's seat and signals to the* PILOT *to swing around. Disgust of the* PILOT *as he does so. As everybody staggers, the lights fade out. For a while there is only music and the hum of engines. Then these fade and the lights come up again. In the main compartment, the* HUSSAR *and the* ITALIAN *sit at one end, while the* AIR FORCE TYPE *and the* PARTISAN *sit at the other.*)

AIR FORCE TYPE (*to the* PARTISAN). Has nobody ever told you that you're cute?

PARTISAN. Yes. My lover. He has told me.

AIR FORCE TYPE. Oh, so you've got a lover? Well, I'm not surprised, really.

PARTISAN. I have no lover. He is dead.

AIR FORCE TYPE. Dead? That's too bad. (*He coughs.*) Sorry.

PARTISAN. I shot him.

AIR FORCE TYPE. You?

PARTISAN. In Zoppot.

AIR FORCE TYPE In the . . . that must have been very painful.

PARTISAN. I said, in Zoppot.

AIR FORCE TYPE. I know. I heard you.

PARTISAN. Zoppot is a town in Poland, my country.

AIR FORCE TYPE. Oh, I see. Well, that clears that up. Not that it makes much difference to the poor fellow where you shot him if he's dead.

PARTISAN. He was no good.

AIR FORCE TYPE. I . . . er . . . think I know what you mean. Still, to shoot him. . . .

PARTISAN. No good for Poland, my country. That is why he has told me to shoot him. He is in remorse for Poland.

AIR FORCE TYPE. Remorse. By jove, that's a pretty human story. I mean to say . . . it's . . . pretty human, isn't it? No good for Poland. I bet if you were to write your reminiscences it would be a best seller. Eh?

PARTISAN. I write a book now. You would like to read it maybe?

AIR FORCE TYPE. Well, actually, I'm not much of a reading man, but if you insist . . . ah. . . .

PARTISAN. It is about the Death Wish.

AIR FORCE TYPE. What's that?

PARTISAN. It proves that death is the objective of the human race. In the subconscious mind we all wish to die . . . to creep back into the womb. That is why we act as we do. You agree?

AIR FORCE TYPE. Back into the . . . Oh yes, definitely.

(*He laughs mirthlessly.*)

PARTISAN. I do not like the way you laugh. I think you are not intellectual.

AIR FORCE TYPE. Oh, I don't know. Anyhow, I know a pretty girl when I see one. Come now, haven't you ever been in love, or something?

PARTISAN. Oh yes. But now there is no time. You would like to make love to me now, but what about the baby?

AIR FORCE TYPE (*startled*). What baby?

PARTISAN. The baby is a useless mouth. The mother is no longer able to be a soldier. So they both must die.

AIR FORCE TYPE. Hey, hold your horses. First there's a baby, and now everybody's got to die. I don't get this.

PARTISAN. It is the way of life. We must face the facts before we think of love. Perhaps I will read you part of my book now.

(*She commences to search in some sacks.*)

AIR FORCE TYPE. I shouldn't worry if it's too much trouble.

PARTISAN. It is somewhere in these things. I have written it in the internment camp.

AIR FORCE TYPE. You wouldn't rather have a nice game of bridge, by any chance?

(*She turns with a grenade in her hand.*)

PARTISAN. Oh, see what I have found.

AIR FORCE TYPE. Good Lord – a Mills bomb. Where did that come from?

PARTISAN. It is in the sack. You know how it works?

AIR FORCE TYPE. I should say I do! Look here, don't fiddle with it, please.

(*He hurries off.*)

I say, chaps. Something's got to be done.

HUSSAR. What's up, old man?

AIR FORCE TYPE. That's a terrible woman. You've no idea.

YANK. You're telling me.

AIR FORCE TYPE. Have you heard about the Death Wish?

YANK. Brother, I've taken a seminar in that.

AIR FORCE TYPE. Well, that's nothing. Now she's found a hand grenade.

(*General sensation. They all return to the* PARTISAN.)

YANK. We've got to do something right away.

HUSSAR. I don't like women with hand grenades.

ITALIAN. It is the end. We are faced with the final dilemma. Now if you had not interfered with me. . . .

YANK. Take it easy, bud. (*He approaches her.*) Good work, sister. Pretty smart to get that thing. Better let me have it, and I'll fix it so we go to Malta after all.

PARTISAN. I do not wish to go to Malta.

YANK. Well, I guess we can talk about that later. That's a good girl, let me have it.

PARTISAN. I do not think I will give it to you.

YANK. Look . . . we don't want to have to get tough.

PARTISAN. I do not think you will get tough. You see, I have taken out the pin.

(*Another general outburst.*)

YANK. Taken out the pin!

PARTISAN. Yes. If I let it go it will go off. See?

HUSSAR. No, no. Don't wave it about like that.

ITALIAN. Where is this pin? It must be put back at once. She does not understand the danger.

AIR FORCE TYPE. I'm afraid she does, old boy. That's the trouble.

PARTISAN. I have dropped the pin by mistake.

YANK. Look, fellas. Some of you see if you can find it on the floor.

(*The others start to search.*)

Now look, sister, it's all very well, but you don't want to fool around with that thing and blow yourself up with the rest of us. Now do you?

PARTISAN. It does not matter. I am tired of life. My country is betrayed by everybody.

YANK. Listen, honey, I don't know nothing about politics, but whatever you want we are all for it. Only give me that bomb and quit fooling.

PARTISAN. I am not a fooler and I will keep the bomb.

YANK. Give it to me, or I'll . . .

PARTISAN. If you touch me I will open my hand.

AIR FORCE TYPE. No, no.Don't do that, old girl.

YANK. I guess she would, too.

HUSSAR. Let her keep it if she wants it.

ITALIAN (*on the floor*). If we could find the pin. Let us keep looking for the pin.

HUSSAR. See here, my dear, we're all friends here. We're on your side.

AIR FORCE TYPE. That's right.

PARTISAN. Then let us all go to Poland.

(*General dissent.*)

ITALIAN. Poland!

HUSSAR. You're not serious?

YANK. I guess she is. I ain't seen her any other way.

AIR FORCE TYPE. Well, for one thing, we can't have enough petrol for Poland.

HUSSAR. You understand, my dear? Not enough petrol . . . gas . . . fuel. . . .

PARTISAN. Then let us go as far as possible. To Jugoslavia.

AIR FORCE TYPE. Tito! Not to Tito!

ITALIAN. Tito! This is the end. *Kaput!*

YANK. Look here, we've got to talk this over.

HUSSAR. Well, while you're talking it over, I'll just step up forward and tell them that flight to the Riviera is off. Don't want to land there, you know, before we've worked this out.

(*He goes through the door. Sound of engine and music. The others sit down gloomily.*)

GERMAN. I have told you to go away.

HUSSAR. Can't you turn off that damn thing?

(*The* PILOT *turns off the music.*)

Thanks. You may be in charge out here, old man, but there's

a girl inside with a Mills bomb in her hand, and she's talking about going to Poland. Thought you might like to know.

GERMAN. *Ach!* I will come and deal with her. A shot in the arm and she will put it down.

HUSSAR. And incidentally put us all up. She's taken out the pin, old man, so don't be rash.

GERMAN. *Davor behute!* I must come and see to this.

(*He rises.*)

HUSSAR. Thought you'd be interested.

PILOT. So what do you want now? For the third time you change your minds, eh?

HUSSAR. Well, Jugoslavia will probably do for the present.

PILOT. Jugoslavia. May the good Lord give me patience.

(*He pushes over the controls. Everybody staggers, as the lights fade out. Music.*)

(*When the lights rise, the music fades out and the* PILOT'S *compartment is in complete darkness. The others are sitting in a gloomy line in the main section.*)

PARTISAN. My hand is so tired. I cannot hold this thing much longer.

HUSSAR. Not as far as Tito anyhow.

YANK. Then why not hand it over?

PARTISAN. No, I cannot do that until we are agreed.

AIR FORCE TYPE. Agreed on what?

ITALIAN. Please will you throw it out of the window. We cannot find the pin.

PARTISAN. First I must have the gun of the fascist beast.

GERMAN. My gun? Never!

PARTISAN. Then I will have to take it from you.

GERMAN. Take it from me! A woman.

PARTISAN (*advancing*). If you shoot me I will drop this bomb when I fall.

AIR FORCE TYPE. No, no. Don't do that, dear.

ITALIAN. Please give her what she asks.

YANK. Yeh, don't argue. She's crazy.

GERMAN. Give her my gun? I . . . a member of the Afrika Korps. Never! Never till my dying breath.

HUSSAR. That means she's going to get it. (*She takes it.*) There, I told you so. That dying breath stuff always means a climb down.

(*She throws it out of a window.*)

186

PARTISAN. There.

ITALIAN. *Deo gratias.* And now the other after it.

GERMAN. She has taken my gun. I am disgraced.

AIR FORCE TYPE. Come now, my dear. You promised.

PARTISAN. I did not promise, but I am tired. How shall I throw it?
  (*She puts her hand out of the window.*)

GERMAN. Throw it backwards. Into the slipstream.

HUSSAR. No, throw it sideways – as far away as possible.

YANK. No – you're all crazy. Throw it downwards. That way it
  goes fastest before it bursts.

PARTISAN. I am sorry. You give me so much advice all at once
  that I have dropped it by mistake.

HUSSAR. Dropped it. Duck everybody.
  (*They all duck. Pause.*)

AIR FORCE TYPE. Are we still here?

YANK. Guess so.

HUSSAR. Did nobody hear it go off?

AIR FORCE TYPE. Probably just a dud.
  (*A distant bang and they all duck again.*)

YANK. Well, that's fixed that, thank God.

AIR FORCE TYPE. Now we can all get matey, eh?

ITALIAN. What do we do now?

GERMAN. I am disgraced. I have been disarmed by a woman and
  a Pole. I am disgraced.

HUSSAR. Absolutely, old man. Isn't it nice?

GERMAN (*after a moment's thought*). Yes. It is a relief. I find I am
  relaxed.

HUSSAR. D'you see what I mean? Now let's all get together and
  decide what we really want to do.

PARTISAN (*indicating the* GERMAN). You see he is pleased to be
  defeated in his plans. That is the Death Wish. We are all
  pleased to be defeated.

YANK. All except you, honey, eh?

PARTISAN. No, I also am like you. That is why I have thrown away
  the bomb. In my soul I do not wish for more. Listen, I will tell
  you something that is a secret. I am bored with Poland.

YANK. Put it there, sister. Now we're really getting somewhere.

ITALIAN (*suddenly*). And Mussolini makes me sick.

HUSSAR. Good for you, old man. And you can throw in our far-
  flung Empire.

ITALIAN (*delighted*). You mean it?

HUSSAR. Definitely. The farther it's flung the better.

AIR FORCE TYPE. Bloody nuisance, if you ask me.

HUSSAR. Glad you agree. Of course, I'm a conservative myself, so don't quote me.

AIR FORCE TYPE. Of course not. You can speak freely. (*To the* GERMAN.) How about Hitler, old boy? What's the form there?

GERMAN. I will tell you what I think. I think Hitler is a crazy lunatic. That is what I think.

(*Outbreak of pleased and surprised agreement.*)

ITALIAN. But not so crazy as Mussolini.

(*They argue together, giving exaggerated parodies of the Fascist salute.*)

HUSSAR. Oh, I don't know. You should see our House of Lords. That would open your eyes.

AIR FORCE TYPE (*roaring with laughter*). V for Victory! Go to it! Come off it!

YANK (*nervously*). Look fellas. . . .

HUSSAR. Anybody got a cigarette?

(*Cigarettes are produced, and mutually lit. After a moment's hesitation, even the* GERMAN *lights one, with a daredevil shrug of his shoulders.*)

YANK (*nervously*). Look, fellas, I don't think we ought to be talking like this.

HUSSAR. Why not, old man?

YANK. It don't seem right, somehow.

PARTISAN. You tell us now, please, what you think of the Stars and Stripes?

YANK. Not on your life! Not in this party.

ITALIAN (*beaming*). Oh, come. Just one little razzberry.

AIR FORCE TYPE. Don't let down the party.

YANK. Do you want me to lose my pants?

HUSSAR. Now don't rag him, people. Probably tougher for him than for the rest of us. Very particular about the old flag – out in the States.

YANK. Thanks, pal. I appreciate that. And I will say this about America . . .

HUSSAR. No, no. Not another word. Let's keep some illusions. The real question that we ought to be discussing is where we want to land.

AIR FORCE TYPE. That's right. What about that?

ITALIAN. Malta. We have agreed on Malta, so for the good of all, let it be Malta.

HUSSAR (*suspiciously*). Wait a minute. I don't much like that 'for the good of all' stuff. I know what you want. A nice quiet time in a P.o.W. Camp for the rest of the war, while we get sent back to the blood and sweat. Smart fellow!

YANK. Wait a minute. Are you hinting we don't all want to get back to the fighting as quick as we can?

HUSSAR. Yes, old man. That's right.

GERMAN. Natürlich.

YANK. You mean to say . . .?

ITALIAN. We will all be traitors to our cause. It will be very enjoyable.

(*A pregnant pause . . . while all look at each other.*)

YANK. Say, that's a pretty serious thing to say. In words, I mean.

AIR FORCE TYPE. Well, after all, what's the harm so long as we all sort of cancel each other out?

HUSSAR. That's one way of looking at it.

ITALIAN. On second thoughts, what we must do is to land in territory of the side that is going to win the war. If we don't do that, there will be a lot more trouble afterwards.

HUSSAR. I see what you mean.

GERMAN (*sadly*). Then we should go to the Côte d'Azur. The Fuehrer is bound to win. I am sorry to have to say it, but your people will not take the trouble to do anything right. I myself have observed this.

AIR FORCE TYPE. I know, old boy, but that's the very thing that makes me doubtful. In spite of all our activities in wrong directions, you still don't manage to lick us. Some gross incompetence somewhere.

HUSSAR. What I would suggest is some nice neutral country, like Franco-Spain where we can all get interned together. Then there'll be no favouritism.

PARTISAN. It does not matter where we go. It will soon be dark, and wherever we try to land now, we will be shot down.

HUSSAR (*rising*). Crikey, we never thought of the ack-ack, did we? And I bet that ass in front doesn't know any recognition signals.

AIR FORCE TYPE. That fixes it. We'd better go somewhere where they're damn bad shots.

YANK. That's the brightest notion yet.

PILOT (*appearing amongst them*). The worst shooting I know is over Gibraltar.

YANK. O.K. Then let's make for Gibraltar.

HUSSAR. Here! Who's shooting are you running down?

AIR FORCE TYPE. Taking a crack at our British gunners, eh?

PILOT. I only said what is my experience.

HUSSAR. Now if you'd said Tripoli –

AIR FORCE TYPE. That's right. It's notorious they can't hit a sausage over Tripoli.

ITALIAN. I deny it! I myself have seen the deadliness of our Italian flak at Tripoli.

AIR FORCE TYPE. Italian flak, pooh! If we're going to land anywhere I say let's have Italian flak.

ITALIAN. It is an insult!

HUSSAR. Suppose we try the French at Oran during the dinner hour?

PILOT. I still maintain that Gibraltar is laughable.

(*He laughs.*)

AIR FORCE TYPE. I'd like to know how any wop pilot is qualified to criticize Gibraltar.

PILOT. Excuse, I am not what you say. I am Russian.

PARTISAN. Ah, the Russian beast! The persecutors of my country! If I had known you were Russian I would not have thrown away my bomb.

YANK. Take it easy, kiddo. That's no way to speak of our Allies.

PARTISAN. He is no ally of Poland.

HUSSAR. Look here, chaps, let's not get confused about who exactly is on which side.

AIR FORCE TYPE. What's a Russian doing here anyhow – piloting Allied prisoners in an Italian aircraft? You've no *locus standi,* old boy.

PILOT. I will not be spoken to in this way. First I am conscript in Ruthenia and made to fight the Poles. Then I am taken prisoner by my own people and sent to invade the Finns. Then I am lost in Norway, and taken by the French to fight the Germans. Next, the French are the friends of the Germans, and I am told I must help the Ustachi against the King of Jugoslavia. Now I am told by Tito I am a traitor to Russia. So I fly the arrow-plan for Mussolini, and all I ask of you is to make up your minds . . . please . . . please . . . where you want to go to, and do not ask me what side I am on! That is all I ask.

HUSSAR. And very reasonable too.

YANK. Now, that's a mighty profound speech, fellas. That just goes to show, doesn't it?

AIR FORCE TYPE. Goes to show what?

YANK (*irritated*). How should I know what it shows? I guess it sort of puts the whole thing in a nutshell. Yeh, that's it. It puts it in a nutshell.

AIR FORCE TYPE. Makes you think.

YANK. Sure.

AIR FORCE TYPE. Definitely makes you think.

PARTISAN. In my book I have pointed out. . . .

HUSSAR. Never mind that, my dear. There's something else that has just occurred to me. Who's piloting this aircraft at the moment?

AIR FORCE TYPE (*indicating the* PILOT). He is.

YANK. Yeh! How about it, Revolting? What the hell are you doing in here when you're supposed to be in charge?

PILOT. Oh that is all right. She's flying on the stabilizer. Anyhow, I don't know where I am.

HUSSAR. Crikey!

PILOT. And I came here to tell you that there is no need to discuss where we go, because we have no more petrol and there is land ahead. So that is where we land. (*Pause.*) I think.

HUSSAR. Where is it?

PILOT. How should I know! You have pushed me around so much I have lost all my bearings two hours ago. But wherever it is, this is where we land. And now I think I go back to the controls.

AIR FORCE TYPE (*to the* ITALIAN). Well, if there's going to be any flak, let's hope it's yours, old man.

(*Violent arguments follow. The* PILOT *goes forward. Fade out lights into agitated music followed by many faint explosions and finally a crash. When the lights come on again everybody is on the floor and there is no more engine hum.*)

HUSSAR. Don't tell me we've landed?

AIR FORCE TYPE. Feels like it.

ITALIAN. Eureka! We are safe. We have come through all the troubles!

HUSSAR. And a lot of damn bad shooting, thank goodness.

AIR FORCE TYPE. Wonder whose it was.

ITALIAN. It cannot be Italy. Not Italy!

YANK. Look here, fellas. Pull yourselves together. God knows who's outside.

ITALIAN. That is true. I must put on my belt. But the pistol? Do I wear it or do I not?

HUSSAR. All depends on which of us are the prisoners.

AIR FORCE TYPE. Rather a problem, what?

PARTISAN. We will soon know. It is fate . . . one way or the other. It is fate.

GERMAN. My friends, this is very serious. For a time I think we have forgotten ourselves. Now we are back to the war, and to sanity.

HUSSAR. Back to sanity. Certainly a nice way of putting it.

GERMAN. You understand what I mean. In our quarrelling we have all forgotten for a time that we are enemies. But that is all over now. We must cease from quarrelling and be at war once more.

ITALIAN (*peering out the window*). It would be better if we knew where we are.

PARTISAN. It makes no matter. Prisoners or captors . . . we have all betrayed our flags in thought and deed. We will all be shot!
   (*General commotion.*)

AIR FORCE TYPE. See here, that's no way to talk, even in fun. Even if a few things have been said that shouldn't. . . .

GERMAN. It has all been most irregular.

YANK. Forget it. We're all in the same boat, so we'd better keep our mouths shut. Is that agreed? Whoever is outside, is it agreed we've none of us been talking to each other all the way across?
   (*General agreement.*)

ITALIAN. We are all enemies, I will swear it.

AIR FORCE TYPE. Whacko! Let's shake on that.

HUSSAR. Don't be silly, old man. We can't shake hands on the fact that none of us are speaking to each other. Don't make things more difficult than they are.

PARTISAN. It would have been better for us to have blown ourselves up as I suggested.

HUSSAR. Don't worry, my dear. We're bound to get round to that in time.
   (*The* PILOT *comes from the nose, where he has been disentangling himself.*)

PILOT. And now I think. . . .

HUSSAR. Ah, so there you are! That was a damn bad landing.

PILOT. . . . now I think I will open the door. Yes.

(*He opens the door to the outside world and peers out.*)

HUSSAR. Well? Where is it?

PILOT (*grimly*). I think. . . .

AIR FORCE TYPE. Doesn't matter where it is. Let's get out quick. And remember, chaps, not a word.

GERMAN. Heil Hitler!

(*He jumps out.*)

YANK. My country 'tis of thee.

(*He jumps.*)

PARTISAN. Zdravo.

(*She jumps.*)

ITALIAN. Avanti. Vincere. Duce!

HUSSAR (*stopping him*). That's enough.

(*The* ITALIAN *jumps.*)

(*To the* AIR FORCE TYPE.) Say something for England.

AIR FORCE TYPE. Taxi!

(*He jumps.*)

HUSSAR. Where did you say it was, old man?

PILOT (*stuttering furiously*). It's P-p-p-p-p

HUSSAR. Don't tell me. I can guess.

(*He shoves the* PILOT *out, and turns and sits down with a burst of maniacal laughter. That is the end of this play.*)

CURTAIN

THE GOLDEN CUCKOO

*An irrational comedy
in five scenes*

INTRODUCTION

The Golden Cuckoo is based upon the exploit of an old man called Francis Walter Doheny, who – oppressed as we all sometimes are by a sense of the injustice of life – went out one evening in 1926, and broke the windows of a Post Office in Kilkenny, calling this gesture the Saint-Edward's-Crown-Barker-Parsival-Ironore-Inoco-One-Man-Rebellion. There was a symbolic significance behind each word of this resounding title, and he also made it clear that his action was not inspired by any personal animus towards the Postmistress. Indeed, if he had heard that she had recently suffered the loss of her brother-in-law, he would have postponed his Rebellion to a later date, even at some inconvenience to himself. He then surrendered to a solitary policeman, and was conducted to the local lockup, singing his 'Rational Anthem'.

From confinement, he issued a statement to the Governor-General, the Provost of Trinity College, the Bishop, and the Bar (which is how I came by it) in which he explained the impelling reasons for his surprising gesture. Expecting to go to jail, as other rebels had done before him, he was utterly confounded when a humane and liberal-minded Judge insisted on turning the issue, not upon the injustice of life, but on the matter of Mr Doheny's sanity – an aspect of the case that had never occurred to him.

Now, it seems to me that this whole incident raises problems of some social importance, and all the more so if it raises a laugh. Rebellion against the tyranny of Monarchs and Invaders has long been recognized as a respectable thing. But what about the tyranny of Democracy, which in some of its facets can be even more sinister? At a pinch, Monarchs can be assassinated, but who can assassinate – much less identify – the Common Man? Rebellion is of little avail against the Herd. Yet it can hardly be denied that we live, today, in a community that is fundamentally dishonest, and is getting more so – a society that is subverting the Common Law for the convenience of the Policeman, and that maintains itself by a mass of regulations that have no basis in social morality at all, but are merely there to enable bad laws to operate – the currency and customs regulations, for example.

It is agreed, of course, that laws must be made by somebody, if we are to live in peace at all. It is, however, not so certain that any greater divine right attaches to them if passed by fifty-one per cent of a debating society, rather than by a King in Council. Nor does it necessarily follow that Democracy in office is any less dishonest than the Despot. Indeed, the reintroduction of mass murder as an accepted instrument of international argument, of the torture of prisoners, and of inquisition under penalty, lends colour to the view that the problem of the individual against the State, if it has altered at all, is rather more acute than ever.

In the circumstances, the thesis advanced by Mr Doheny – of the moral duty of the put-upon to break the law from time to time – assumes a significance which grows with the tendency of the State to become, itself, the biggest lawbreaker within sight. Maybe we have not all got the aplomb to select the Post Office windows as the best law to break, but we must admit that his selection was a gallant one, and did nobody any harm except himself.

Whether his personal grievance was legitimate or not is a question that does not really arise. He did what thousands have done before him – thousands who have had statues erected to their memories, without much enquiry into the rights and wrongs of their cause, and many of whose dependants are still collecting profitable pensions. His Independent Republic is a respectable and recognized answer. The only trouble is that Mr Doheny's was a One-Man-Republic, and here the herd instinct in all of us immediately takes offence.

What may be praiseworthy for a thousand men to do in armed conflict – probably slaughtering several harmless bystanders in the process – becomes absurd when it is done by one old man with a flagpole. What would happen – we hasten to ask – if everybody did that sort of thing? But this question is just an alibi. Everybody has not done it, and we need not pose that query until they do. At present, only Mr Doheny has done it. And is the measure of the rightness of his action, the number of people who have backed him up? Is it all a question of mathematics? Yes, says the Functionalist, because Mr Doheny, alone, is bound to fail. And since he fails, he must be wrong. In fact, goes on the Functionalist, I don't think that I like this play at all, because it seems to me to be on the side of failure, which is obviously immoral. The Author has obviously got no moral positiveness. So Mr Doheny suffered the most terrible and subtle of all punishments. He did not go to jail. He went to a lunatic asylum.

This is a subject that we may not wish to have discussed at the present stage of the world's history, but it can hardly be described as puerile. And one of the things that makes me glad that I ever tried to commemorate this heart-breaking old man is the fact that his memorial, in its last act, suddenly proclaimed its independence, too, and refused to accept the so-called happy ending that I originally attempted to impose upon it. I had set out to inveigh against the injustice of Society, and against the fact that its considerable rewards and punishments are largely allotted on a basis of chance. But if the only remedy of the unlucky Man of Resolution is that of a lunatic, this is far from being a happy ending, however one may treat it.

What the play itself proved was that I was wrong in being angry, and that my central character knew better. To a free spirit – he taught me – Justice is really quite a minor matter – a virtue only in the eyes of stock-jobbers and tradesmen, and not something for President Doheny to worry about in the proud security of his One-Man-Republic. It is impossible to punish, or even to be sorry, for one who does not deign to consider himself punished. His victory and his independence are matters of belief, and since he believes in them himself, there is no answer but respectful recognition.

Directors will see that this is actually a very serious play, that will probably go off the rails if allowed to betray the fact that it considers itself to be the slightest farcical. Let the audience laugh, by all means. But it should also be remembered that the highest art of comedy is sometimes to leave people wondering why they ever laughed at all.

The Golden Cuckoo

CAST OF CHARACTERS:

A BOY
MRS GOLIGHTLY, THE ACTRESS (LETTY)
MR CHAPLAIN, THE NEWSCASTER
MRS VANDERBILT, THE DAILY
MR PENNIWISE, THE LAWYER
MR HOOLEY, THE CABMAN
MR DOTHERIGHT, THE OBITUARIST
MR LOWD, THE EDITOR
MR GOLIGHTLY, THE REPORTER (PADDY)
MRS DE WATT TYLER, THE PHILANTHROPIST
MISS PEERING, THE POSTMISTRESS
A POLICEMAN
A PHOTOGRAPHER
A DETECTIVE
A HOSPITAL ATTENDANT

This play was first produced at the Dublin Gate Theatre by Longford Productions on Tuesday, 25 April, 1939, with the following cast: —

Mrs Vanderbilt, the help	NORA O'MAHONY
Mr Green, the Corporation official	HAMLYN BENSON
Mrs Golightly, the business woman	VIVIEN DILLON
Mr Pennywise, the lawyer	MICHAEL RIPPER
Mr Dotheright, B.A., the author	NOEL ILIFF
Mr Haybottle, the cabman	RONALD IBBS
Mr Lowd, the editor	ROBERT HENNESSY
Mr Golightly, the reporter	PETER COPLEY
Guard Bullock, the policeman	J. WINTER
Miss Peering, the postmistress	NANCY BECKH
Mme Subito, the foreign visitor	JEAN ANDERSON

Directed by the Author

Its revised version was first produced in the Gaiety Theatre, Dublin, on Monday, 25 June, 1956, with the following cast:—

Mrs Golightly, the Actress	MAUREEN CUSACK
Mr Chaplain, the Newscaster	NORMAN RODWAY
Mrs Vanderbilt, the Daily	MAUREEN POTTER
Mr Penniwise, the Lawyer	JOSEPH TOMELTY
Mr Hooley, the Cabman	SEAMUS KAVANAGH
Mr Dotheright, the Obituarist	CYRIL CUSACK
Mr Lowd, the Editor	NIALL MACGINNIS
Mr Golightly, the Reporter	MICHAEL MURRAY
Mrs De Watt Tyler, the Philanthropist	
	SINNETTE WADDELL
Miss Peering, the Postmistress	ANN CLERY
A Policeman	TRAOLACH O H-AONGHUSA
A Photographer	DONAL DONNELLY
A Detective	P. G. STEPHENS
An Attendant	DEREK HYDER

The production was directed by the Author
with settings by MICHAEL O'HERLIHY

The version printed here has not yet been produced.

205

SCENE ONE

MR DOTHERIGHT'S *residence is a partially-converted stable, containing an odd mixture of books and harness, crockery and sacks, furniture and garden tools. A horse box has been fixed up as a small study, and above this is a straw-filled platform from which comes an occasional cluck. An outer door leads to a yard, and an inner opening to the kitchen. Efforts have been made to make it homely, and it is not by any means uncomfortable. The curtain rises disclosing a small boy who appears to be supervising its ascent. He is as young an age as can be legally procured subject to local regulations and stage experience. He takes a look at the Audience to see that they are all seated and he is at liberty to make some helpful remarks if they are not. A cuckoo clock on the wall utters a single cluck. When all are comfortably seated the boy begins.*

BOY. Good evening. I'm glad you were able to come in time. In case you have not been able to study your programme, this is Act One – an old Coach House partly converted, as you can see, into a not very good residence for Mr Er – Whatshisname. That was one o'clock you heard and in a few minutes the action will begin with a knock at the door. (*Then louder*) A knock at the door. (*The knock comes*). Yes, that's right. And I shall go and let in the (*A goat whinnies off*) Leading Lady, Letty Golightly who has just come to live in the big house across the Yard. Don't mind that goat by the way. And a Mr Chaplain who has something to do with broad –
   (*He has gone to the door and opened it.* LETTY *steps in. She is young, attractive and fashionably dressed with an air of careless nonchalance.*)
LETTY. Mind your head.
BOY. – broadcasting.
   (*Chaplain follows her in, bumping his head. He is about thirty and wears a business suit.*)

207

LETTY. Oh, I did warn you.

BOY. She did you know.

CHAPLAIN. (*in pain*) It's quite all right. I enjoy it, really.

LETTY. You don't look as if you do. Shall I hold it or something?

CHAPLAIN. No thanks. I'll just sit down for a minute. (*He sits*). I say, is this somebody's bed?

BOY. Yes. It's Mr Duthery's bed. He's the Star. Well now that you've started so well, I'll leave you to go on with the Scene.

LETTY. Thank you so much for everything.

BOY. But I'll be back. I have to see about that goat.

(*He goes off with a friendly salute at the Audience.*)

CHAPLAIN. Who could that be? I mean – this Mr Duthery.

LETTY. Must be the old man the Agent mentioned. (*Looking at some papers*) Name looks like 'Do-the-right'. I understand he goes with the place. How's the poor head now?

CHAPLAIN. Oh never mind that. I'm sure it's good for the moral character.

LETTY. I don't see why . . . (*A cock crows from the loft*) Oh God! (*Pause*) What's good for the moral character?

CHAPLAIN. You'll have to get rid of him of course.

LETTY. I don't see why. Get rid of whom?

CHAPLAIN. The old man you say lives here. You'll probably want it for the car.

LETTY. That's just what I've been wondering. How did you know?

CHAPLAIN. Didn't you say you didn't see why you should get rid of him?

LETTY. No I said that about bumping your head being good for the – Oh do let's stop this conversation, Wystan.

CHAPLAIN. Suits me.

LETTY. You know why I've bought this place, don't you?

CHAPLAIN. (*nodding*) And I'm glad. I don't want to say a word against Paddy. I like him, Letty. Really I do. He's a very brilliant fellow.

LETTY. (*bored*) Yes. (*Pause*) You're always very fair to Paddy, aren't you, Sometimes too bloody fair.

CHAPLAIN. (*with a handsome smile*). Well. One can hardly be too fair to the husband of a woman one adores. Now, can one?

LETTY. (*reluctantly smiling back*) Maybe not. I like the way you have of keeping it from seeming sordid and mean. Thank you for that, Wystan. (*She moves around the room*). Anyhow, it's all over now. I've bought a place of my own at last. It's got to be a clean break. I'm bloody well fed up with Paddy. (*Her face lights up*). It's like opening a door and letting in – Oh, God, what's that?

(*The door crashes open and* MRS VANDERBILT *comes in. She hastily conceals a portable radio which she is carrying. She is a rascally old scrub woman in the sixties, wearing an apron under her overcoat.*)

CHAPLAIN. – a breath of cool, fresh air. Eh?

LETTY. Something like that.

MRS VANDERBILT. (*bustling across the room*) Pay no attention to me. I've been out at Confession.

LETTY. We just dropped in to – ah –

MRS VANDERBILT. To pay a call. I know. Suppose I get ya a nice cuppa tea?

LETTY. Oh please don't bother. We were just looking over the place.

MRS VANDERBILT. No bother at all. It'll be wet in a jiffy.

CHAPLAIN. Perhaps we'd better explain what we're doing here. This is the lady who has bought the house across the yard. And I am –

MRS VANDERBILT. Ah sure, amn't I in and out of the place an odd time myself, and heard all about her. I'm Mrs Vanderbilt, and she's the old man's new landlady. Gimme a hand now till I'm free of this Prayer Book.

(*She places the radio on a side table covered by a newspaper and presses* LETTY'S *hand affectionately.*)

Ah isn't she a gorgeous Mott! Me late husband – God rest his soul – would have had her stripped with a glance!

CHAPLAIN. (*attempting to come to Letty's assistance*) We must get better acquainted, Mrs Vanderbilt. I wish I had connections like you must have.

MRS VANDERBILT. (*looking at him with grave distaste*) Why?

CHAPLAIN. Oh never mind, Ma'am. Just one of my little jests. Er – what exactly was your husband?

MRS VANDERBILT. (*earnestly*) He was a dirty bum. Wait now – the kettle's on the boil. (*She goes into the kitchen*).

CHAPLAIN. What an enchanting inruption! Who do you suppose she is?

LETTY. I can't imagine. But I have rather a fellow feeling for her.

CHAPLAIN. Because her late husband was a bum? (*She smiles mirthlessly*).

209

LETTY. I always like your Gewohnlicherkeit, Wystan.

CHAPLAIN. You're a damn good actress. And I like your German too.

LETTY. (*emotionally*) Oh am I? Paddy says I'm a terrible actress.

CHAPLAIN. Paddy is a dirty bum – to borrow a phrase I've heard.

> (*He begins to embrace her, but half laughing, she breaks away as* MRS VANDERBILT *enters and starts to set cups.*)

MRS VANDERBILT. Pay no attention to me. You don't mind your tea as it comes? I've nothing to go in it at all.

LETTY. I prefer it any way, thanks. (*They both sit down as she pours out*). Are you a relation of Mr Do – the – the gentlemen who lives here?

MRS VANDERBILT. Duthery, Ma'am. Duthery is how he pronounces it.

CHAPLAIN. Duthery. I don't think I've heard that name. Is it Scandinavian?

MRS VANDERBILT. (*after a scornful look at Chaplain*) I'm no relation, Ma'am. Just a friend. I do for him, you understand. Just to oblige. And to please Father Feeley, of course.

LETTY. This is Mr Wystan Chaplain. You've probably heard him on the radio.

MRS VANDERBILT. I never listen to that thing.

CHAPLAIN. Come now, Mrs Vanderbilt. Don't tell me you're not one of my public? What's this you've got hidden under the newspaper?

MRS VANDERBILT. Father Feeley was just saying to me – (*He takes the paper off the radio*).

CHAPLAIN. Just as I thought. A radio! A good model too.

MRS VANDERBILT. (*louder*) Father Feeley was –

LETTY. Yes, a very good model. I've got one very like it over at the house.

> (MRS VANDERBILT *forcibly puts the paper back.*)

CHAPLAIN. Oh, excuse me. Letty, I believe we've discovered Mrs Vanderbilt's vice. She's a secret listener.

MRS VANDERBILT. (*with sudden venom*) You harness your clapper, you big gowger, or you'll find yourself with an ache where you least expect it.

CHAPLAIN. Who? Me?

MRS VANDERBILT. (*sweet again*) No, you'd hardly know Father Feeley, ma'am, and you a playactress. But he's a very broadminded man. He wouldn't hold it against you at all.

LETTY. (*taken aback*) Hold it against me!
    (*Another knock on the Door.*)

MRS VANDERBILT. Being on the stage – you know. For all, you're
a Protestant and respectably married. And your father has
money too. Though why wouldn't he, and he a Mason.

LETTY. Really!

CHAPLAIN. Mrs Vanderbilt seems to be well-informed on everybody's background.

MRS VANDERBILT. Just idle gossip, ma'am. Idle gossip. I pay no
heed to it at all.

LETTY. Isn't there somebody at the door?

MRS VANDERBILT. Ah, let them . . . (*Then changing her mind*)
That's right, ma'am. I'd better see who it is, hadn't I?
    (*She opens the door a few inches and somebody sticks a
foot in.*)
There's no one at home. The place is empty.

PENNIWISE. (*outside*) Is this where a man called Dotheright lives?

MRS VANDERBILT. No. There's no one of that . . . (*She glances at
Letty and then opens the door*). Why, yes, sir. That's right.
Mr Dotheright's residence.

PENNIWISE. I thought so.

MRS VANDERBILT. But he's not in. You'd better call another time.
    (*She tries to close the door, but he pushes in, and she
abandons the struggle.*)

PENNIWISE. Then I'm going to wait here till he appears. Come on
in, cabman, come in and sit down.
    (PENNIWISE *and* HOOLEY *enter. The former is a seedy little
Attorney's clerk in a black suit, and aged about fifty. The
latter is an elderly cabman in a variety of coats and mufflers,
with black crepe on his top hat.*)

HOOLEY. Don't mind if I do.

MRS VANDERBILT. You never know what sorts will turn up these
days.

PENNIWISE. (*to Letty*) Name of Penniwise. Do I know you? Your
face seems familiar.

CHAPLAIN. (*amused*) It probably is. This lady –

MRS VANDERBILT. She's just a woman that's dropped in.

PENNIWISE. Indeed. Well, I've dropped in too. And here I stay
till I get what I came for.

MRS VANDERBILT. Listen to that now. He'll be telling us next what
it is.

HOOLEY. He means we've lost the rest of the funeral.

PENNIWISE. That's not what I mean. If you hadn't stopped it would never have happened.

HOOLEY. The old man told me to stop. So I stopped. (*To Chaplain*) Anything wrong with that?

CHAPLAIN. No – so far as we have all the facts before us. It seems quite reasonable.

HOOLEY. (*to Penniwise*) There you are. You heard what the man said.

PENNIWISE. He doesn't know anything about it.

LETTY. Wystan, don't you think we really ought to be going?

CHAPLAIN. My dear, I'm getting more and more interested. What do you suppose will be the next to arrive?

MRS VANDERBILT. Ah, let them be. They stopped for a wet at some pub, and when they came out the hearse was gone.

PENNIWISE. It was not at some pub. It was at a newspaper office.

HOOLEY. The Comet Newspaper.

LETTY. The Comet? That's where my – Oh yes? So you stopped there.

CHAPLAIN. What a small world. We ought to hear some more of this.

PENNIWISE. There's nothing more to hear. Except that this man Dotheright who I'd never seen in my life before, but was sharing the cab with me – this man Dotheright insisted on going inside.

MRS VANDERBILT. I know. They still owe him something.

PENNIWISE. But to stop in the middle of a funeral!

HOOLEY. Well, he'd got to pay for his share of the cab, hadn't he?

PENNIWISE. He had no business to share a cab with me, if he had no money when we started out. And he needn't think he's going to dodge me now. The vehicle is still outside with the fare mounting up. But not at my expense! Here we stop until he produces his legal dues.

MRS VANDERBILT. Tell me, love, what's the time on your gold watch and chain?

PENNIWISE. (*looking at it*) Half-past two. Ttt – ttt!

MRS VANDERBILT. Well, since half the town seems to be dropping anchor here, maybe I'd better put on some sausages. Introduce yourselves.

> (*She goes out muttering*) I don't know who the hell they are at all. (*Shouting*) Take the beast out of my kitchen!

CHAPLAIN. Maybe we had all better introduce ourselves. This is Mrs Golightly – probably better known to you under her professional name.

PENNIWISE. (*suspiciously*) Professional?

CHAPLAIN. Letty Lowe.

(*Puzzled Pause as the* BOY *enters pulling a reluctant goat which he attempts to lead to the Horse Box.*)

HOOLEY. Oh, I know. She's on the movies.

CHAPLAIN. Of course! How smart you both are. (*To Hooley, archly*) You should get a prize. (*Then with some irritation*) Do we have to have that in here?

BOY. I'm sorry but it's not supposed to be in this Act at all.

CHAPLAIN. Then kindly take it away.

(*Now follows some extemporary business and ad-libbing while the animal is pushed and prodded into the horse box where, blocked in, it does whatever it likes for the remainder of the scene.* LETTY *is highly amused at all of this. When all is quiet, the scene continues.*)

BOY. I'm so sorry about this. Please go on.

PENNIWISE. Well – hm. Perhaps we'd better. (*To Chaplain*) May I ask what you're doing here?

BOY. He's a Mr Chaplain.

HOOLEY. That's right. Used to see him on the movies too.

CHAPLAIN. (*Irritated, as Letty laughs*) No, no. Not that Chaplin. Chap-lain. Wystan Chaplain.

HOOLEY. Ah. You're not a bit like the one I remember.

CHAPLAIN. Thank you so much.

BOY. Mr Chaplain is supposed to be a well known News Commentator.

CHAPLAIN. (*with a pained shrug*) "Supposed to be"!

HOOLEY. (*pointing at Penniwise*) He's a Solicitor.

PENNIWISE. Not a Solicitor. An Assistant.

BOY. He means a Clerk. The other one's a Cabman.

(*They shake hands all round with some disdain.*)

HOOLEY. I may only be a cabman, but if I had my rights I'd be living on the fat of the land. Solicitors is no good.

PENNIWISE. We've no time to go into your grievances now. (*To the Boy*) As for you. Maybe you'd be good enough to stop interrupting us with your remarks. Nobody wants you here.

BOY. Oh very well if you want me to go I'll go. But nobody out there will understand a word if I do.

213

PENNIWISE. (*Looking out where he is pointing*) Out where?

BOY. Oh never mind. Mr Dotheright will be on shortly, and he's the only character that matters. However, call me if there's any more trouble.

(*He goes off, as* MRS VANDERBILT *shouts from the kitchen.*)

MRS VANDERBILT. (*off*) Lay the table, ma'am. And you boys come in here and give me a hand.

LETTY. (*rising*) Really, Wystan, don't you think we'd better be . . . ?

CHAPLAIN. (*to Letty*) My dear, if these are the guests, what the hell will the host be like? I wouldn't dream of going yet.

PENNIWISE. (*calling out*) I don't want anything cooked for me. All I've come for is my . . .

MRS VANDERBILT. (*appearing*) I told you to come in here and lend a hand. D'you want me to raise my voice at you? You parchy old scrivener?

(*She goes again.*)

CHAPLAIN. Come along, Mr Penniwise. We'd better do as we're told.

HOOLEY. May as well have a bite while we're waiting.

PENNIWISE. I suppose you think that's all we'll get. But I've told you – not a foot will I stir out of this house until I've seen that man.

(*The men all go off muttering.* LETTY *lays the table, stopping for a few seconds to look in some puzzlement at the radio. Presently an eccentric-looking little old gentleman enters from the street, and locks the door behind him. He has a hunted look, but shows no particular surprise at the sight of* LETTY.)

LETTY. Oh! (*She pulls herself together*). How-do-you-do?

DOTHERIGHT. Would you kindly shut the window. (*She does so.*) Now put the catch on.

LETTY. (*after doing so*) Are you being pursued by anybody?

DOTHERIGHT. (*taking off his coat and hat*) It keeps out the flies.

LETTY. The flies? I don't quite follow.

DOTHERIGHT. They carry germs, and spread loathsome diseases.

LETTY. So you want the catch on. I see.

DOTHERIGHT. Why are you laying my table?

LETTY. So you're Mr Dotheright. I really ought to explain why I've called.

DOTHERIGHT. Is that your cab outside?

LETTY. (*shaking her head*) No.

214

DOTHERIGHT. (*disappointed*) Oh. (*Pause*) Then whose is it?

LETTY. I'm afraid it's your cab, Mr Dotheright. Indeed, I ought to warn you – there's going to be a little trouble.

DOTHERIGHT. Oh dear me. Sometimes it's difficult to avoid having a cab.

LETTY. There's Mr Penniwise inside, helping with some sausages, and he says . . . in fact, here he is now.

(PENNIWISE *and* HOOLEY *enter with some steaming dishes.*)

PENNIWISE. Ah, here he is at last. Have you any idea how much the fare is by now?

DOTHERIGHT. We will go into that presently. (*He looks in a dish.*) Sausages.

PENNIWISE. Over two pounds. And you needn't think I'm going to pay it. Here's Hooley the cabman – waiting.

DOTHERIGHT. He will be paid. Suppose we all sit down.

PENNIWISE. Paid, aye, but when?

DOTHERIGHT. Presently. When stockjobbers, shoulder-clappers, horse-copers and writers of scandal sheets begin to use a little honesty in their calling. For the present, we had better all – keep very, very calm.

PENNIWISE. Are you hinting that you have no money?

DOTHERIGHT. I have no money.

PENNIWISE. He has no money!

CHAPLAIN. (*entering*) Who has no money?

HOOLEY. *He* has no money.

LETTY. (*intoning*) Mr Dotheright has no money.

CHAPLAIN. (*putting down the plates*) So this is Mr Dotheright. We've all been getting quite worked up about you, Mr Dotheright, wondering what you were going to be like and – everything. Well, I must say you're all that I personally had hoped for.

DOTHERIGHT. (*To Letty*) Who is this person?

LETTY. Better ask somebody else.

HOOLEY. Why, you know *him*. He used to be . . .

CHAPLAIN. I know what's coming as if you'd said it already. So to avoid any further confusion, you, Mr Dotheright, may call me Wystan.

DOTHERIGHT. Wystan.

CHAPLAIN. Wystan, as a special favour. What is more, if these gentlemen are pursuing you for any money, don't let that bother you. I have some money.

PENNIWISE. (*brightening up*) Well! That makes things look a lot better.

DOTHERIGHT. (*puzzled*) You have some money? What is this money that you have? Mine?

CHAPLAIN. Oh no. It's my own money.

DOTHERIGHT. How did this gentleman's financial position get into the conversation?

PENNIWISE. Mr Chaplain can pay the cabman.

HOOLEY. That's right.

DOTHERIGHT. There, I knew there was some mistake. This gentleman – Wystan – (*he bows*) does not owe the cabman anything. It is I who owe the cabman something.

PENNIWISE. We know. But you can't pay him. He could. He's got money. Lots of it.

DOTHERIGHT. Then of course he could pay him if he has got lots of it. So could the other Mr Churchill. So could anybody for the matter of that.

PENNIWISE. But he will. Then you can pay him.

DOTHERIGHT. Oh. (*Pause*). But surely that shows some confused thinking. If I could pay him for paying the cabman, I would pay the cabman myself.

CHAPLAIN. I say, do let's stop this. The point is, Mr Dotheright, that I can probably spare the cash for a cab more readily than you can. However, I have no wish to force anything on you.

DOTHERIGHT. It had never occurred to me that you intended to use force, sir. May I ask how you come into this matter at all?

CHAPLAIN. Forget it, Mr Dotheright.

DOTHERIGHT. (*graciously*) Not at all. I am always delighted to discuss people's personal affairs if they wish it. Perhaps you would like to tell us what it is that you *do*, in return for all this money?

CHAPLAIN. (*stiffly*) Oh nothing very much. I interpret the news five nights a week, on the radio. That's all.

DOTHERIGHT. What for?

CHAPLAIN. For about a million people.

HOOLEY. That's right. I've heard him. I remember him now.

CHAPLAIN. (*with mock gallantry*) Thank you, Mr Hooley, I knew you were a man of affairs.

DOTHERIGHT. You mean, you tell them what is going on?

CHAPLAIN. More correctly, I help them understand it – to, er, think about it.

216

DOTHERIGHT. You must be a very remarkable man. So you help people to think. (*Pause*). And do they think?

CHAPLAIN. I would like to believe that I contribute to that end. But if you want the truth, Mr Dotheright, I sometimes wonder.

DOTHERIGHT. If there is any doubt on such a point, I am surprised that they continue to pay you. Unless of course, the fact that you are employed to guide their thoughts is actually to stop them having any thoughts at all.

CHAPLAIN. (*nettled by Letty's smile*) Really, I can't imagine why they employ me at all, Mr Dotheright. I must ask my superiors about it some day. Well, I think we must be going now. It was very interesting to have met you.

LETTY. No, no! I'm interested now. I want to hear some more.

DOTHERIGHT. And who are you, young lady?

CHAPLAIN. She happens to be your landlady.

DOTHERIGHT. Indeed.

PENNIWISE. I'll undertake she doesn't make a fortune out of that.

LETTY. I'm also an actress. A movie actress. Don't ask me what parts I've played, because you wouldn't have heard of any of them. Don't even ask me whether I'm any good or not, because I've never found out so far. And yet, they pay me a great deal. Don't you think that's very peculiar?

DOTHERIGHT. No more peculiar than other matters that have recently come to my attention. Did you by any chance call about the rent?

LETTY. Oh, no. I was only taking a look around.

HOOLEY. You should try one of them Shakespeare plays. They're good.

LETTY. (*to Hooley*) Of course, I'd love to. I've always wanted to play in Shakespeare. But what chance does one ever get? (MRS VANDERBILT *is serving.*)

HOOLEY. There's Ophelia, now. That's a nice part – if you don't mind them songs. They're a bit raw, if you ask me.

LETTY. (*dreamily*) Ophelia. I don't suppose I'll ever get the chance. (*She hums – with a smile at Wystan.*) "How shall I my true love know?"

HOOLEY. No, on second thoughts, not Ophelia. She's crazy.

MRS VANDERBILT. You mop up your slobber, you pauper-house cheat. Never mention the halter when you're supping with the hangman.

(*She goes into the kitchen. There is a brief silence.*)

DOTHERIGHT. Mrs Vanderbilt is given to these cryptic remarks. Pay no attention. It is best not to follow them up.

PENNIWISE. Look here – to get back to this loan you were offered –

CHAPLAIN. Oh please don't bring that up again. I'm sorry now that I ever suggested it. And really, Letty, I must be going, I have a commentary tonight, and I haven't prepared a line.

LETTY. What's the hurry? Haven't you said it all before?

CHAPLAIN. Maybe I have. But not in a towering rage. That requires a special technique. Well, I see you intend to stay, so maybe I'll see you later. Goodbye, all.

(*He goes.*)

LETTY. Goodbye, Wystan. And *do* cheer up.

PENNIWISE. (*to Dotheright*) Now you see what you've done. You've upset the man and lost your chance. Is that fair to me – I mean, is it fair to the cabman here?

DOTHERIGHT. The world we live in is unfair. I am, myself, the victim of a grave injustice. Only this afternoon.

LETTY. Is it something connected with that newspaper office?

DOTHERIGHT. Yes, madam.

LETTY. Would you like to tell me about it? Not that I want to seem inquisitive.

DOTHERIGHT. It is a painful story. And we really ought to have something besides these sausages. Ah eggs. I wonder are there any eggs yet. Excuse me. (*He rises and climbs a ladder.*) I have a hen somewhere up here. She hasn't laid as yet, but one of these days – Here, chook chook chook chook.

(*An indignant crowing is heard.*)

PENNIWISE If it's what I hear, you'll never get an egg out of that.

DOTHERIGHT. (*sternly*) Why not, pray?

PENNIWISE. Because it's a cock.

DOTHERIGHT. That is an allegation that always annoys me very much. I must ask you not to make it again. Where is the bird, and I shall demonstrate. I bought it in the spring from our local postmistress.

PENNIWISE. What as?

DOTHERIGHT. She assured me at the time that it was a fine young pullet. Here – chook chook chook.

PENNIWISE. Maybe she can tell a stamp from a money-order. But she certainly can't tell a cock from a hen. Or else she cheated you.

DOTHERIGHT. Sir I believe you are deliberately trying to upset me. I will not permit it.

LETTY. Oh please don't annoy Mr Dotheright. I'm sure it's a hen.

PENNIWISE. Bosh.

HOOLEY. (*to Penniwise*) What do you know about it, anyhow?

PENNIWISE. I have ears.

DOTHERIGHT. (*who has come down*) You seem to be an unusually intelligent young woman. Why are you so interested in my misfortunes?

LETTY. Because I have connections in that newspaper office.

DOTHERIGHT. Personal connections?

LETTY. Yes. Actually – well – yes.

DOTHERIGHT. An arid inhabitant of the outer office? – a young man in cycling knickerbockers with a quarrelsome face?

LETTY. That description would probably fit my husband.

DOTHERIGHT. (*embarrassed*) Ah. (*Pause*) It seems that I have committeed a faux pas.

LETTY. Not at all. I don't like him very much myself. What did he do?

DOTHERIGHT. (*settling down*) I shall tell you, madam. By profession I am a free-lance obituarist.

HOOLEY. A what?

PENNIWISE. He means that he writes death notices for the newspapers.

HOOLEY. Can he make a living out of that?

PENNIWISE. Obviously not.

LETTY. Never mind. What happened?

DOTHERIGHT. Only the night before last I was going the rounds of the local shrines of Mercury to find out – in the parlance of the day – whether there was "anything doing", when this young man handed me the report of the death of a certain prominent citizen, by name Boddy.

LETTY. Oh, I know him. At least my father does. He makes fertiliser.

HOOLEY. Fertiliser! Ah. I've got a horse outside. Called Mac after a fellow called Macintosh who . . .

PENNIWISE. We are not interested in your horse.

LETTY. Fertiliser and old Bibles.

HOOLEY. (*taken aback*) Horses are the friends of man.

219

DOTHERIGHT. You seem to be addicted to these truisms. Old Bibles and Almanacks?

LETTY. I didn't realize that Boddy was dead. My father knows him.

DOTHERIGHT. Such was my information at the time. And it was on that basis that I accepted the commission to pay a newspaper tribute to him to the extent of half a column. But on submitting my work to the person concerned, the article was rejected. On the ridiculous ground that the man Boddy was *not* dead, after all.

LETTY. I'm sure he's not. But I thought you said . . .

DOTHERIGHT. I said this to them. I am not concerned, I said, with the question as to whether or not this Boddy is alive. I have been commissioned to execute some literary work, and here it is. I shall expect to see it in print tomorrow morning.

HOOLEY. Fair enough.

PENNIWISE. Hey, wait a minute!

LETTY. And what did they do then?

DOTHERIGHT. They threw me out.

LETTY. Threw you out?

DOTHERIGHT. (*bowing to Hooley*) Both neck and crop. If I may be allowed the use of a cliché myself.

LETTY. You mean to say, they didn't pay you?

DOTHERIGHT. They wouldn't even discuss the matter.

LETTY. I understand the trouble now. You take that very much to heart.

DOTHERIGHT. I regard it as a matter of principle. I do not like being treated in a cavalier manner when I am prepared to adopt a reasonable attitude myself.

LETTY. (*rising*) I think it's a shame, Mr Dotheright. And I'm going to see what I can do about it.

PENNIWISE. What can you do about it?

LETTY. I'm going to talk to the Editor.

PENNIWISE. What good will that do?

LETTY. Probably not much. He's my father. Excuse me if I run along.

(*On her way out she bumps against the radio, and then pauses to examine it. With a dirty look at* MRS VANDERBILT, *who has just entered, she picks it up and carries it out.*)

LETTY. This happens to be my radio.

(*Exit.*)

DOTHERIGHT. What a curious young woman. Did I understand her to say that her father was the Editor of the *Comet* newspaper.

PENNIWISE. Delusions of grandeur. More to the point, whose is that radio she's just snitched?

DOTHERIGHT. Do you know anything about it, Mrs Vanderbilt?

MRS VANDERBILT. Divil a one of me knows. She brought it here herself.

(*She goes out.*)

DOTHERIGHT. Personally I never thought she was quite balanced. She would keep calling me Dotheright.

PENNIWISE. But you are Dotheright.

(*Pause.*)

DOTHERIGHT. Who is?

PENNIWISE. You are.

DOTHERIGHT. (*irritably after a few seconds' consideration*) Of course I'm Dotheright. Then she had no business to be so confusing. Especially when I'm upset over other things.

PENNIWISE. You obviously brought it on yourself – the way you talked to them. You should have kept a civil tongue in your head.

DOTHERIGHT. All my life I have found it difficult to meet with dishonesty and injustice and keep a civil tongue in my head. Whenever I meet with a snake, I know that I must put my foot on it.

PENNIWISE. Aye, and get yourself bitten on the leg.

DOTHERIGHT. Reason often tells us that it is more profitable to suffer wrong in silence. But then a strange childish voice speaks insistently in my ear and says, "Dotheright, you are a coward. You must speak out." And so I speak out.

PENNIWISE. And probably lose your job.

DOTHERIGHT. Invariably.

PENNIWISE. There you are.

HOOLEY. (*to Penniwise*) If everybody agreed with you, would we have done what we did in 1916?

PENNIWISE. I have no knowledge of what you did in 1916.

HOOLEY. (*sententiously*) We marched out into the streets of Dublin and hoisted the flag of liberty over the Post Office. That's what we did.

PENNIWISE. And what did you get for it?

HOOLEY. I got – Well – I got a medal.

PENNIWISE. Hah! Is that all? A medal.

221

HOOLEY. (*producing it from his pocket after some fumbling*) There it is. (*His voice changes.*) But if I had my rights I'd have a pension like all the others. Maybe a good job in the Sweepstakes – for services rendered to the rights of Man.

(*There is an uncomfy pause until the* BOY'S *voice is heard through the window.*)

BOY. Wear it, Hooley. You're supposed to be wearing it.

HOOLEY. (*suddenly enlightened*) So I am! By Jiminy, why shouldn't I be wearing it?

PENNIWISE. Who is this intolerable interrupter? Take his name, somebody!

BOY. My name is Alexander. (*His voice dies away.*)

HOOLEY. Alexander! That's a name to stir the troops! Look! I'm wearing it!

(*He pins his medal on to his outer coat. There is another pause while he stands up proudly.* DOTHERIGHT *rises.*)

DOTHERIGHT. This is a very solemn moment, Mr. Hooley – if that is the correct name. May I ask why you did not get your just deserts?

HOOLEY. Because of crookedness and rascality in them at the top. Because of dirty politics – that's for why. And nobody willing to take up my cause with them that matter. Ah, but what's the use?

(*He sits dejectedly.*)

DOTHERIGHT. Mr Hooley, you must speak out. What position did you hold in this Uprising?

HOOLEY. I was a Lieutenant in the Hibernian Rifles.

DOTHERIGHT. A lieutenant. Then Lieutenant Hooley, I drink a toast to you. (*Raising his cup.*) It is you who shall advise me what a resolute man should do in my position.

HOOLEY. You should go back to that office and kick up hell. That's what you should do.

DOTHERIGHT. Kick up hell. You think that is the proper procedure?

PENNIWISE. Don't be saying such things to the man.

HOOLEY. Well – it'll let off a bit of steam anyway.

PENNIWISE. You'll never get anywhere by causing trouble. If you want to, you can go back and discuss it with them reasonably.

DOTHERIGHT. But suppose they won't listen to reason?

PENNIWISE. There are other remedies – if you have any case at all.

DOTHERIGHT. What other remedies?

PENNIWISE. Well – I suppose you could go and see our Mr Phibbs about it.

DOTHERIGHT. A lawyer.

HOOLEY. Pah! Lawyers is no good.

DOTHERIGHT. You see, gentlemen, we have here two conflicting points of view – the constitutional and revolutionary. Which of them is right? Shall we all go back and find out?

PENNIWISE. What? Now? At this hour?

(*He feels for his watch.*)

DOTHERIGHT. (*crossing to get his coat*) Why not?

HOOLEY. (*rising and buttoning his coat*) That's right! Strike while the iron's hot.

PENNIWISE. (*suspiciously*) What exactly are you proposing? That's funny. I would have sworn I had my watch and chain when I came out.

DOTHERIGHT. Never fear, Mr Penniwise. We will begin with the constitutional. If that fails we will think again.

(MRS VANDERBILT *enters.*)

MRS VANDERBILT. (*briskly*) Well, boys, going out for a nice drink?

DOTHERIGHT. (*as they get into their coats*) No, Mrs Vanderbilt. We are going out to kick up hell – er, if reason fails.

MRS VANDERBILT. Maybe I'd better come too?

DOTHERIGHT. No. I don't think your presence would be any help at all.

PENNIWISE. I would have sworn . . . Um. Oh well, maybe I left it at home.

(*He gets into his coat.*)

MRS VANDERBILT. Whatever you say yourself.

DOTHERIGHT. (*pausing in the doorway*) And Mrs Vanderbilt, we all trust that Mr Penniwise in due course will find his watch again.

(*He waves his umbrella like a sword, and leads the other men off.* MRS VANDERBILT, *smiling blandly, continues to clear the table, humming to herself. The cuckoo emerges from the clock and continues to shout 'Cuckoo' until the Curtain is down.*)

SCENE TWO

Lowd's *room in the offices of the* 'Comet'.
Lowd *is talking to* Letty. *He is an expansive person with a firm belief in his own ability to manage other people and get his own way. A smiling wheedler or alternatively a roaring bully whenever it suits him, and yet not devoid of generosity. A bit of a rascal, yet not entirely without a sense of humour. In short, though he might prefer the world to be a better place, he is fully conscious of the fact that it is not, and he knows how to make the best of that state of affairs. He is, in fact, a crook with a conscience that is just sufficiently vocal to force him to justify everything he does in terms of a code of realistic common-sense.* Letty's *radio is standing on the floor.*

LOWD. Now, I'm a sane man – a normal, reasonable man-in-the-street. You know that my dear.

LETTY. Yes, father.

LOWD. A bit of an idealist in my own way. But at the same time I pride myself on having both feet planted firmly on the ground, and on being perfectly consistent.

LETTY. I know, father. But this old man says that he was given . . .

LOWD. Never mind him. It's Paddy I'm talking to you about. Are you really determined to leave him, and take this ridiculous place of your own?

LETTY. Daddy, I wish you'd try to understand. It's not just fancy that's making me get out. Marriage is far too important a thing to put up with second best.

LOWD. Of course it's important. That's just what I'm saying.

LETTY. So important that, if it's not right, it's liable to poison your whole life.

LOWD. It never poisoned mine. And, believe me, if Paddy's a crackpot, he's nothing to what your dear mother was.

LETTY. Father, it doesn't make things any better to hear you talking like that about mother.

224

LOWD. O.K. Let's talk about Paddy instead. I admit that he's got the social charm of an orang outang. And his ideas on most subjects seem to be those of an anarchist's apprentice. But you picked him, and you must have liked him once.

LETTY. Paddy's changed.

LOWD. I wish I could believe it.

LETTY. He used to be so sincere. But now life seems to have turned sour on him. He sees a dirty motive behind everything that happens. He says that every decent thing you try to do only turns round and kicks you in the pants.

LOWD. (*reflectively*) I'm sincere too. I think everybody agrees that about me.

LETTY. It's like as if he'd sold his soul to the devil.

LOWD. My dear girl, you must have a poor view of the devil as a business man. He'd never fall for that deal. Do you know something? I think you both ought to go and be psycho-analysed. I can give you an address . . .

LETTY. I don't need to be psychoanalysed. At least not yet, please God.

LOWD. It was only a suggestion.

LETTY. Father, I didn't come here to talk about me. I came to talk about an old man you're cheating. Now don't contradict me. That's the only word for it.

LOWD. Well it's not a nice word to use to your father – particularly after all the words I've avoided applying to your affairs. Now be fair. Is it?

LETTY. It's only a small sum, and he needs it. I'd pay him myself, only he wouldn't take it from me. It's a matter of *amour propre*. He wants to be paid for what he's done.

LOWD. French.

(PADDY *enters with a pile of proofsheets in his hand. He is a furious-looking young man in the middle twenties, wearing cycling breeches.*)

PADDY. Well –! What's going on here?

LOWD. Come in. Come in. We only need you, Paddy. Your wife's been telling me how to run my business in French.

PADDY. You should never have paid for those extras at St. Chad's. (*He looks at the radio.*) I see you've been having some music too.

LETTY. No. It's like you. Brr-oken down.

225

PADDY. No doubt that's why you carry it round. Quite a typical state of affairs.

LETTY. Paddy, I'm in no mood for you.

LOWD. Listen – will you please go away – both of you. I've still got work to do.

LETTY. I'll go, father. I see it's no good talking to you any more now.

LOWD. At the moment it would be a great kindness.

LETTY. Goodbye, Paddy.

PADDY. Goodbye, Letty. You're looking tired.

LETTY. I *am* tired.

PADDY. (*handing her a hip flask*) How about a little alimony?

LETTY. (*taking it*) Thanks, Paddy. Maybe I shall.

(*She goes out, forgetting the radio.*)

PADDY. (*surprised at her acceptance of the flask*) Well! Letty's coming on.

LOWD. She's going to leave you. You know that, I suppose?

PADDY. She *has* left me. (*Pause*) Is this where I'm expected to resign?

LOWD. Because you don't get on with my daughter?

PADDY. I suppose I should resign. Or would you rather give me the sack?

LOWD. Listen, Paddy, when I sack you it'll be for reasons connected with the paper. And God knows, there are plenty of them.

PADDY. (*grinning*) Yes, boss.

LOWD. For instance, how did this damn nuisance start about some unused hack work?

PADDY. Oh, that. I found a report of Boddy's death on your desk. I assumed it called for an obituary, so I handed it out to the first hack who happened to drop in.

LOWD. Damned efficient, aren't you, when nobody asks you.

PADDY. God dammit, you're always bawling people out for waiting to be told. How was I to know it wasn't on the level? It was in your own handwriting.

LOWD. O.K. O.K. Let's forget about it. The rules are the rules. (*The telephone rings.* LOWD *picks it up and listens absentmindedly.*)

PADDY. What did you write it for anyhow? The man's as much alive as we are.

(LOWD *puts back the receiver.*)

LOWD. Never mind. It should have been left on my desk.

PADDY. You might have warned me. Then it wouldn't have happened. Who was that on the phone just now?

LOWD. Nobody. They didn't answer.

PADDY. Maybe that's because you didn't say hello to them.

LOWD. I didn't want to speak to anyone. Oh, didn't I say hello? Well, maybe it wasn't important.

PADDY. So the old fellow's not been paid?

LOWD. Look, I've had all this out with Letty, and I don't want to hear anything more about it. There are a hundred and thirty-two hacks writing crap for this newspaper, and if any of them don't like to take the rough with the smooth, they know what they can do. Now for God's sake . . .

(The telephone rings. He lifts the receiver.)

PADDY. Hello.

LOWD. Oh – Hello . . . Yes . . . Oh, Mrs Tyler. *(He makes a face.)* . . . Delighted you've rung me up . . . Yes, Everything's set for this evening's ceremony. Both press and radio are covering it . . . Very well, just as you like. Tell me all about it . . .

(The telephone quacks in his hand as he holds it away from his ear, with a look of resignation.)

LOWD. I know now why the British left America. It was because they were tired of Mrs Tyler.

(Presently another phone rings, and he lays down the first on his desk, where it continues to quack. He shakes his head and picks up the other phone.)

LOWD. Yes, Miss Flintwhistle? . . . No, I don't think I can – WHAT? . . . Three gentlemen to see me? Have they an appointment? . . . *(He thumbs rapidly through an engagement diary.)* . . . Professor Somebody. And a Lieutenant? Never heard of them . . . Oh, wait a moment, though. This may be the Rotary Club Party . . . Yes, better send them up. *(He hangs up the second telephone.)* Don't go, Paddy. You may have to look after this bunch. It's about time you learnt how to handle the public.

PADDY. I'll take a few notes on your technique. Got a pencil?

LOWD. On the . . . Funny, aren't you? You'll never make a newspaperman, Paddy. I always said so. You've got the wrong attitude, and, I might add, the wrong trousers.

PADDY. My hands and my brain are the *Comet's*. My legs are my own concern.

LOWD. Shaw used to wear things like that. But you're not Shaw. Why can't you go out and turn in a good story once in a while? Just once in a while. Try it tonight. It's not much to ask. But I suppose a real newshawk has to be born.

PADDY. Like you?

LOWD. Yes. Like me. Why should I act coy about it? You've either got it or you haven't. I tell you, Paddy, there's a sort of extra sense that a good newspaperman has. I don't know what it is. But he can smell news before it happens. You've either got it or . . .

(PADDY *is gesturing towards the telephone, which has now stopped quacking.* LOWD *picks it up.*)

LOWD. Ah, yes. Mrs Tyler. Yes. That required a little thought. But I see your point, and I'm sure I agree . . .

(*Dotheright, Penniwise and Hooley file in, and he gestures to them to be seated. They are followed at some distance by the Boy who is carrying a large notebook.*)

LOWD. Yes . . . Yes . . . That's all been seen to. The whole party will be down there tonight. Reporters, photographer and a front-rank commentator It's all been laid on ⅄ . . Goodbye, Mrs Tyler . . . Goodbye . . . Goodbye . . .

(*He hangs up, turns to his new visitors with a genial smile.* PADDY *recognizes* DOTHERIGHT, *and is about to speak.*)

Now, gentlemen.

PADDY. Look here. This is . . .

LOWD. That's all right, Mr Golightly. These gentlemen want to see *me.*

PADDY. (*sitting down, with a sardonic grin.*) O.K. They're all yours.

LOWD. (*to the others*) That was Mrs Tyler on the phone – the wife of the American Senator. She's dedicating a memorial to some President this evening and wants us to cover the ceremony too. You made a note of what she said, Mr Golightly?

PADDY. (*arranging chairs*) In duplicate, Mr Lowd. (*He puts on a coat.*)

LOWD. I'll want you to go down and turn in a full report. Now gentlemen, I'm at your disposal. I – er – don't think I caught the names?

DOTHERIGHT. Alphonsus Maria Liguori Dotheright.

LOWD. (*uncomprehending*) Ah, yes, of course. I remember now.

DOTHERIGHT. B.A.

LOWD. And which of you is which?

DOTHERIGHT. That is my name.

LOWD. All of it – just you? Oh I see. I imagined it was everybody. Ha, ha.

DOTHERIGHT. (*grimly*) Am I right in thinking that you are the person in charge here? We want no underlings this time.

LOWD. I'm the Editor if that's what you mean. I presume you gentlemen want to see over the plant? Or – er – perhaps I'm wrong?

(*He starts at the sight of* HOOLEY.)

HOOLEY. (*suddenly*) Why don't you pay him what you owe him?

LOWD. What's that?

DOTHERIGHT. Three pounds and fifty pee.

HOOLEY. Plus tax.

LOWD. I don't follow.

DOTHERIGHT. Pardon my friend's abruptness. The matter arises in connection with some literary work I have been commissioned to execute for your paper.

LOWD. (*stiffening rapidly*) Oh! Is that what you've called about?

DOTHERIGHT. A certain obituary notice.

LOWD. You're not . . .

DOTHERIGHT. Concerning a certain Mr Boddy.

LOWD. Then you're not the Rotary Club! (*Turning on Paddy*) Did you know who these people are?

PADDY. Yes, Mr Lowd. But you said you would attend to them yourself.

(*He sits down and listens with exaggerated politeness, having taken off his coat.*)

LOWD. Take that grin off your face! (*Picking up his papers.*) I'm sorry, gentlemen, but I'm afraid I haven't time to go into that just now. Very busy.

HOOLEY. We won't keep you long.

DOTHERIGHT. I am a man of letters. And at the request of your periodical I have devoted a considerable amount of time to an intensive study of chemical manure – a subject that interests me not the slightest. But I am no longer insisting upon its publication. I am adopting a very reasonable attitude, as everybody agrees.

LOWD. You're not insisting on . . . Listen, I don't know what

you're talking about and I'm a busy man. So hurry on. I'll
remember you another time.

DOTHERIGHT. That is not what I'm asking for.

LOWD. O.K. It's a free country. Nobody's forced to work for the
Comet if he doesn't feel inclined.

DOTHERIGHT. My dear sir, you are persistently avoiding the issue,
which is the matter of payment for work already done.

HOOLEY. Aye – keep him to it.

LOWD. Are you seriously expecting to be paid for an obituary
on a man who isn't dead?

PADDY. We've got dozens of them on the shelves.

LOWD. (*shouting*) Shut up!

DOTHERIGHT. Whether Mr Boddy is or is not dead is a matter
quite outside my personal knowledge. Somebody may have
made an error of judgement, but –

HOOLEY. To err is human.

PADDY. (*to Hooley*) How do you think of these things?

DOTHERIGHT. But that does not affect the primary question of
contract.

LOWD. Listen, Mister, I keep books here. Books. Have you ever
heard of them? Places where I write down particulars of the
Company's money that I spend. Now, what do you suppose
will happen to me if I write down in my books: Paid to
Alaphonsius Flinkingirons the sum of three pounds –

DOTHERIGHT. – and fifty pee –

LOWD. – and fifty pence whatever it is –

HOOLEY – plus tax.

LOWD. Damn the tax.

HOOLEY. Oh you can't do that. That's compulsory.

LOWD. Will you kindly let me finish? I'm talking to this gentleman here, about a personal friend of mine who I happen to
know is at present enjoying a quiet holiday in Connemara
and IS NOT DEAD.

(*To Dotheright*) Do you follow me, my dear sir? Mr Boddy,
the well-known Manufacturer of –

DOTHERIGHT. (*nodding*) – of Chemical Manure –

LOWD. Ex-actly. This Boddy is in no need of an Obituary. Nor
is the *Comet* Newspaper. We're very much alive, Hah-hah!

DOTHERIGHT. So what?

LOWD. So what! You're not expecting me to pay you out of my
own pocket?

DOTHERIGHT. Well, will you?

LOWD. No!

PENNIWISE. There you are. You'd better come and see our Mr Phibbs.

LOWD. (*suddenly suspicious*) Wait a minute. What Mr Phibbs is this? How does he come into it?

PENNIWISE. I represent his firm – Messrs. Phibbs and Rooke, Solicitors.

PADDY. The majesty of the Law.

LOWD. (*Stiffening*) I told you to keep out of this. May I ask whether this gentleman is here professionally?

PENNIWISE (*after a cautious pause*) We all came here together.

HOOLEY. In my cab. I'm here professionally.

LOWD. (*after looking around*) That boy over there. The boy with the open notebook. What's he doing here?

PENNIWISE. Oh, he's nobody in particular. Nothing to do with us.

LOWD. What's your name, young man?

BOY. Peter.

LOWD. Peter. (*Pause*) Peter what?

(*Silence for a moment.*)

HOOLEY. That's not what he told us before.

LOWD. Before what?

DOTHERIGHT. Actually, that answer is not quite accurate. I seem to remember him telling us that his name is Alexander.

PENNIWISE. That's right. It struck me as unusual at the time. Alexander.

BOY. (*quietly*) That was two other fellows.

LOWD. *Two* other fellows? What the hell –?

DOTHERIGHT. There was only one as I remember. And I found him quite inspiring in some ways. Alexander.

HOOLEY. So now he's Peter. Well, all I can say is that somebody's a liar.

BOY. I'm not a liar. In fact I'm the only person in this mess who means exactly what he says.

LOWD. (*heavily*) Par-don me. *I* mean what *I* say. Invariably.

PENNIWISE. Schizophrenia! And at that age too.

LOWD. What are you doing with that notebook?

BOY. Just making some notes.

LOWD. Oh you are, are you. On whose behalf?

BOY. All these other people.

LOWD. What other people?

BOY. (*indicating the Audience.*) Out there. (*Pause while they all stare out and see nothing.*) Why don't you go on with the Play?

DOTHERIGHT. (*quietly*) A bookful of Notes. Peter. That's interesting.

LOWD. (*pulling himself together*) Ah, we've got something more to do than gossip with juveniles. I still want an answer from this gentleman as to whether or not he's here professionally?

DOTHERIGHT. Does it make any difference?

PADDY. Yes, Mr Dotheright, quite a big difference. You see, the *Comet* newspaper, in return for its kindness in allowing people to work for it, considers that it is entitled to steamroll its less-important contributors in small ways from time to time.

LOWD. That's not a bright way of putting it.

PADDY. Only in small ways of course. Let's be frank about this in fairness to Mr Dotheright. If these contributors choose to be nasty and bring solicitors along with them, they're liable to find themselves with no more work after the matter has been adjusted. You understand?

DOTHERIGHT. (*grimly*) Less-important contributors.

LOWD. I never put it that way.

PADDY. No, but we may as well face it. (*To Dotheright*) It's something I'm sure you ought to understand before your friend decides whether he is here professionally or not.

DOTHERIGHT. I don't like being spoken to in this manner.

LOWD. (*suspiciously*) Look here, I don't know what all this is getting at, but I tell you what I'll do. You go away quietly now and I'll find you another one to write.

DOTHERIGHT. May I ask what you mean by "another one"?

LOWD. (*searching on his desk*) In fact, maybe I can give you something right away. (*Pause.*) Yes, here we are. How's that? (*He hands* DOTHERIGHT *some papers.*) See?

PENNIWISE. Ah, that's more like it.

LOWD. Everybody happy now?

DOTHERIGHT. I am always ready and willing to work for a just wage –

LOWD. (*returning to his work*) Good. All the poop's there. Goodbye.

DOTHERIGHT. Nevertheless, the offer of this employment seems to

232

be quite irrelevant to the matter at issue, which, as I said, is payment for work already done.

LOWD. (*irritably*) Look, I'll give you a fiver for the lot, and we'll call it quits. Now be off.

PENNIWISE. Five pounds! Ah-ha! That seems very reasonable.

(*He and* HOOLEY *rise, but* DOTHERIGHT *stops them.*)

LOWD. And you'd better be going too, Paddy.

(PADDY *gets his coat again.*)

DOTHERIGHT. One moment, please. You mean that in consideration of your paper refusing to pay me what it owes me already, I am to continue to work for it at less than half the usual rate.

PENNIWISE. Och, have some sense, man! He's trying to do you a kindness.

DOTHERIGHT. I don't want his kindness. I don't even care very much about his money. All that I demand from him and his paper is a little honesty in their public dealings. Is that too much to ask?

PENNIWISE. Are you mad, Dotheright?

LOWD. Well, I'll be –! Give me back those papers and get out of here, the lot of you.

PADDY. You see! Now you've hurt his feelings. (*Indicating Lowd*).

DOTHERIGHT. I hope so sincerely, although I doubt it very much. But he has hurt my feelings, if that is of any consequence.

(LETTY *enters. She has assumed a new air of defiance. Maybe after a sip of her alimony.*)

LETTY. I've forgotten my – Oh, hello. Quite a crowd here.

LOWD. That's right. Come in, everybody. It's only my private office.

DOTHERIGHT. This room is full of germs. The windows must have been left open.

LETTY. Well I declare it's my old friend and tenant, Mr Dithery.

DOTHERIGHT. Duthery is the correct pronunciation.

LETTY. You've met my father, then? And my husband too. That's my husband over there. The one with the trousers.

LOWD. God give me patience. Paddy, haven't you gone yet?

PADDY. (*Putting his coat on.*) Yes, boss. I'm on my way.

LETTY. I came back for my radio, although why I can't imagine. It isn't working any more. (*She picks it up and puts it on the table where it bursts into crooning.*) Oh, I beg your pardon.

LOWD. Stop that thing!

DOTHERIGHT. We came here to give this gentlemen a chance to explain himself.

LETTY. That was a great kindness on your part.

PADDY. You can see how delighted he is.

LOWD. (*calling*) Flintwhistle! Where's Miss Flintwhistle?

HOOLEY. Pure waste of time. The man seems to be illegible.

DOTHERIGHT. You don't mean illegible, Lieutenant. You mean something else.

(*They cluster around the desk.* LOWD *rises on a chair, appearing above their heads.*)

LOWD. (*shouting*) Golightly! Get this clutch of twirps out of here. And turn that bloody thing off!

PADDY. Pull yourself together, boss. Is that the way to handle the public?

(PADDY *bangs the radio and it relapses into silence.*)

DOTHERIGHT. This paper spends roughly fifty thousand a year on something called Public Relations, and yet it won't pay three pounds fifty that it owes me. It's worse than dishonest, it's inconsistent.

LOWD. (*furious*) I resent that.

PADDY. Now you've done it!

DOTHERIGHT. Completely inconsistent. Not to mention the tax.

LOWD. Listen. I've put up with a hell of a lot but I won't be called inconsistent.

HOOLEY. Then tell us how you're not.

LOWD. I'm damned if I see why I should, but I will. Sit down! And don't you whisper in my office, Letty, it's rude.

LETTY. It would be ruder to say it out loud.

(*They all sit down in a row.* PADDY *takes off his coat as he does so.*)

LOWD. If Mr – Thing – here was a person of importance there's a great deal that I'd do for him. Certainly I would. And why?

DOTHERIGHT. You tell us.

LOWD. Not because I'm inconsistent but because you might be able to do one or two things for me in return. But you're all just like everybody else. You all want something for nothing. So listen here. If you want to be treated as an important contributor go ahead and be one. I'm not stopping you. In fact, I'll be delighted. I'll take you out to lunch at the Company's expense any time you call. But in the meantime

don't blame me if you're treated any other way. Blame yourself for not being important. There now – is that inconsistent?
(LETTY *is about to speak.*)

DOTHERIGHT. No. Let him finish.

LOWD. People are paid what they're worth in this world and it's
a damn good thing they are. I might have given you a few
bob out of kindness. What's-your-name, if you'd gone about it
the right way. But you've called me inconsistent and I'm
damned if I'll stand for that. So now I'm going to be consistent and pay you exactly what you *are* worth. And that's
sweet damn all. So get out of here, the lot of you, and don't
come back till you can make it worth my while to waste my
time. Go on, I mean it.

(*The telephone rings.* LOWD *lifts it. The* BOY *is pulling
agitatedly at* DOTHERIGHT'S *sleeve.*)

PADDY. (*sharply*) Hello.

LOWD. (*shouting into the receiver*) Hello! Oh? I beg your pardon.
Yes?

DOTHERIGHT. We will go, sir.

LOWD. Oh, Chaplain! (*He makes signs at Letty.*) Yes, we're going
to cover your tribute to those superannuated felons. Golightly
is on his way down. He left some time ago.

(*He gestures violently at* PADDY, *who is putting his coat on
again.*)

DOTHERIGHT. Yes, yes! But before taking any further action, may
I inform you, in the vulgar vernacular of the day what I
consider you to be?

LOWD. (*into the phone*) Yes. Yes.

DOTHERIGHT. Thank you, sir. You are a twister.

LOWD. I wasn't talking to . . . (*He lays down the phone.*)
What was that? Did you call me a twister?

DOTHERIGHT. Yes, sir.

HOOLEY. And put that in your . . .

LOWD. . . . pipe and smoke it. I know. I've heard that one too.

DOTHERIGHT. Come along, gentlemen. We will now follow in the
footsteps of our young – what did you say your name was?

PENNIWISE. We'll regret this, I'm telling you. Mr Phibbs will say
we should have taken his offer.

BOY. Actually I'm George! (*He leads them off.*)

PADDY. Where are you going, Letty?

LETTY. Out with my gentlemen friends. I don't know where, but I'm going along.

(*She picks up her radio and turns it on.*)

PADDY. Can you give me a lift?

LETTY. It will be a bore, but I will.

(*As they all file out, once again the martial music of the radio.*)

(LOWD *returns to the receiver.*)

LOWD. Flintwhistle, get me Hynie Phibbs at once. God dammit, Chaplain, are you still on the line? Get off! I know how to fix that bastard, Phibbs.

CURTAIN

SCENE THREE

*It is Evening and we find ourselves outside a small SUBURBAN
SHOP-CUM POST OFFICE next door to the entrance to a Pub.
In the window is displayed a mixture of periodicals, trinkets,
toys and cheap ornaments amongst which are a pair of unattrac-
tive china dogs. On the front of the building is affixed a small
plaque, at present covered by a piece of sacking, while over the
shop is the window of the bedroom of MISS PEERING, the
Postmistress, at present in darkness. WYSTAN CHAPLAIN is
engaged in arranging some boxes into a low platform below the
plaque together with a microphone on a stand and a cuelight
from which cables lead off into the door of the Pub, on the step
of which a cynical-looking Photographer with the fish-eyes of a
permanent hangover is sitting, smoking a cigar. To the side,
PADDY is reclining on a street seat, somewhat the worse for drink
and doodling in a notebook, while elsewhere a ponderous POLICE-
MAN hovers under a lamp-post, observing MRS VANDERBILT who is
seated on the kerb with a metal Supermarket trolley by her side.
Various passers-by pass by, without showing much interest in
these activities, while the Postmistress herself stands outside the
glass door of her shop observing the preparations with sour and
hostile eyes.*

CHAPLAIN. (*tapping the microphone and then speaking*) Hello
Control Room. Wystan Chaplain testing from the O.B. Point.
Are you getting me? A – B – C – D – E. Chaplain testing.
(*A light flashes.*) O.K. We'll give you a voice-test before we
go ahead.

MISS PEERING. Nobody gets into my Post Office after six o'clock.
I don't care whose Plaque it is. That's when I close.

CHAPLAIN. Quiet please. We need a couple more boxes . . . And
that Mrs Tyler ought to be here by now.

MISS PEERING. Nice kind of hour to pick for this sort of thing.
(*She slams the door behind her.*)

237

PHOTOGRAPHER. Keep an eye on that camera. (*He goes into the Pub.*)

CHAPLAIN. Where's Letty?

PADDY. How should I know? Running around somewhere in a cab with a bunch of creeps.

CHAPLAIN. Oh, not still with that lot!

PADDY. Last I saw of them they were all going into some Solicitor's office. I hadn't time to wait to see them thrown out.

CHAPLAIN. You ought never to have left her with that crowd. (*He goes into the Pub for more Boxes.*)

PADDY. They're just her style.

POLICEMAN. I'm keeping my eye on you.

MRS VANDERBILT. No more than mine's on you, Inspector.

POLICEMAN. I'm not an Inspector and well you know it.

MRS VANDERBILT. You will be soon, my lovely man. I can sniff quick promotion. Oh, there's muscle! That one's a buck of the best. (*She lifts the leg of his trousers. The* POLICEMAN, *in some embarrassment, replaces the trouser leg and grabs her trolley into which he peers.*)

POLICEMAN. Leave my leg alone! What's in this machine?

MRS VANDERBILT. Is them Parkgate manners? If you want me name and address, I'll leave you one of my scrivened visiting cards.

POLICEMAN. Be off in five minutes or I'll call the van. (*The* POLICEMAN *moves off nervously.*)

MRS VANDERBILT. (*Calling after him*) Don't be long, General. You'll be gorgeous in crepe.

(MRS TYLER *appears carrying a portmanteau.* PADDY *rises and approaches her.*)

MRS TYLER. Are all the arrangements complete? (*to Paddy.*) Will you take my portmanteau please? (*Paddy takes it reluctantly, half sobered by the majesty of her manner.*)

PADDY. Mrs Tyler, I represent the *Comet* newspaper. How about giving me an outline of what you're going to say on the air?

MRS TYLER. So that you can go away without waiting to hear me say it – eh?

PADDY. (*nonplussed.*) Well as a matter of fact it might catch an earlier edition.

MRS TYLER. I know. You wish to retire to some Public House, and avoid attending the ceremony which you are being paid to report.

PADDY. Well, they're all the same, aren't they?

MRS TYLER. You are a rather impertinent young man, and if you wish to hear what I have to say you must wait and listen. Now be careful with that receptacle. It contains a lot of literature.

(*She moves off to inspect the platform and peep at the Plaque.* PADDY *stares after her indignantly.*)

PADDY. Of all the old –

(*A horse's hooves and the clatter of a cab is heard approaching.*)

HOOLEY. (*off.*) There they are! Whoa up, Macintosh. Steady boy.

(*Presently* DOTHERIGHT *appears and approaches the door where* PADDY *still stands with the portmanteau in his hands.*)

DOTHERIGHT. Ah! A Post Office?

PADDY. Well met Dotheright! Hynie Phibbs showed you the door, I suppose. He wouldn't touch your case, eh?

DOTHERIGHT. (*turning*) He laughed at my case.

PADDY. He was kinder to you than you deserve.

(LETTY *enters.*)

PADDY. (*to Letty*) Hello, Lady Macbeth. Would you mind taking this?

(*He holds out the portmanteau.*)

LETTY. Yes, I would.

PADDY. That's not very wifely. Somebody's got to take it. I can't make any notes with this on my hands.

LETTY. Pooh! (*Letty moves to one side followed by Paddy who abandons the portmanteau, as they converse in undertones.*)

CHAPLAIN. (*entering*) Ah, Mrs Tyler at last! Good evening ma'am. Now look here everyone, I don't mind you looking on if you'll only keep quiet. We'll be on the air from here in a few minutes, and we've just got time to run through Mrs Tyler's routine.

MRS TYLER. Yes, where are my papers? We'll have them here, please.

DOTHERIGHT. Running through Mrs Tyler's what?

CHAPLAIN. (*shouting*) Her routine. Please don't interrupt.

POLICEMAN. (*approaching Mrs Vanderbilt*) Are you still here! Now you take heed, or I'll have to move you on.

MRS VANDERBILT. Quiet, as a mouse.

CHAPLAIN. Now on the cue, which I shall get in my headphones, I shall read the introductory material that will take the programme over from the Studio, and leave it with Mrs Tyler. Then when I say . . . let me see now. What is Mrs Tyler's cue?

(*Enter* PENNIWISE. *He is met by* DOTHERIGHT.)

PENNIWISE. What's going on here?

DOTHERIGHT. I don't understand it at all. He says he is running through this woman's routine.

PENNIWISE. I know this place. A Miss Peering is the Postmistress.

POLICEMAN. Ssssh!

(MRS VANDERBILT *slips past carrying the camera. The* POLICEMAN *grabs it and* MRS VANDERBILT *vanishes.*)

DOTHERIGHT. Whatever it is, it requires absolute silence. Was that Mrs Vanderbilt I saw just now?

CHAPLAIN. Ah, here we are. When I hear the cue "In the words of Jefferson: A Rising now and then is a good thing and as necessary in the political world as storms are in the physical" – I shall give you the signal, and you go ahead.

MRS TYLER. (*reading from a script*) "Where would we be today without our Rebels? Would we be living in a free land where the rule of law guarantees the rights and liberties of even the humblest?"

DOTHERIGHT. (*interested*) Would you repeat that, please?

MRS TYLER. Where the rule of law guarantees the rights and liberties of even the humblest?

DOTHERIGHT. Ah. That is what I thought you said.

CHAPLAIN. Pay no attention to this gentleman, Mrs Tyler. I know him.

MRS TYLER. No, no. I'm interested in his reactions. (*To Dotheright*) You are probably one of those conventional people who don't like to admit that our rights and liberties have been won for us by Rebels?

DOTHERIGHT. No, madam. I took exception to the ridiculous proposition that the rule of law guarantees us anything.

PHOTOGRAPHER. (*entering*) Where the hell is my camera?

POLICEMAN. Would this be it?

(*They go off, ad libbing.*)

CHAPLAIN. What are you laughing at? I can't hear a word of the programme above all this chatter and noise. (*To Dotheright*) And you're the worst.

PADDY. The old boy made a perfectly reasonable remark – the first we've had this evening. And I propose to report it in full.

LETTY. Shut up, Paddy.

PADDY. Shut up yourself.

CHAPLAIN. I shall just have to go and listen for the cue in the car. (*He hurries off.*)

LETTY. You're drunk.

PADDY. Not on clichés anyway.

DOTHERIGHT. Is that corner-boy presuming to compliment me? Because, if so, I do not require it.

MRS TYLER. What is the matter with this person?

PADDY. He's just been done out of a small sum of money by my newspaper. Just a small sum.

DOTHERIGHT. A very small sum – a very small breach of one of the smallest of the Ten Commandments. "Thou shalt not kill" is the only one that is slightly smaller.

MRS TYLER. Well he can sue, can't he?

PADDY. Some solicitor has turned him down.

DOTHERIGHT. These vendors of justice with their writs and their flim-flams, are only valuable because of their hard names, I tell you people, the talons of jailors and attornies are too sharp not to scratch the skin of those who shake hands with them.

PENNIWISE. What do you mean – Vendors of Justice? You don't buy justice. It's free for all.

DOTHERIGHT. That's not what Mr Hynie Phibbs says.

PENNIWISE. Ah, just a small advance for costs, of course. That's reasonable enough when you have no visible assets.

DOTHERIGHT. Just a small advance, and then a long retreat.

PADDY. De minimum non curat lex.

DOTHERIGHT. Latin. (*To the Public at large.*) That means "The law does not bother much about unimportant people".

PENNIWISE. That's not the correct translation.

DOTHERIGHT. May I ask you a question, madam?

MRS TYLER. I suppose we have time. But –

DOTHERIGHT. We live, we are told, in a society where man is rewarded according to his deserts – where wealth is the crown of ability, industry and thrift, and where poverty is the proper penalty of ignorance and improvidence. (*She nods.*) I have got no money, and that is because I have been careless and indifferent, and have not troubled to learn this thing that is called What's What. But what about my friend, Mr Penniwise, who has always played the game, and ought to be better off for it? Are Lieutenant Hooley's services to Society any less

241

valuable than those of my landlady, Mrs Golightly? Yet she, I understand, is in receipt of a salary from the motion picture industry that proves her to be equivalent of two Bishops and three Rural Deans. I have been working this out from Whitaker's Almanack. Or was it Poor Robin? Yes – Poor Robin I think it was that.

LETTY. (*laughing helplessly*) How right he is. And I still don't play Ophelia!

CHAPLAIN. (*hurrying back*) Mrs Tyler, Mrs Tyler, would you please get ready before we hear the cue.

MRS TYLER. Ah yes. We mustn't forget that we have work to do, must we. Would somebody please bring that portmanteau over here.

(*Nobody does, so* CHAPLAIN *grabs it while at the same time trying to adjust his headphones. Various passers-by stop to look on.* MRS TYLER *opens the suitcase and gets out some pamphlets.*)

PENNIWISE. You know, Dotheright, there's something in what you say. It doesn't seem fair, does it?

DOTHERIGHT. It is not fair, my friend. It is a lie that is told to us poor fools who, like the bath-keeper's ass, are content to bring home the fuel that keeps our master's fires alight, and live ourselves on the smell of the smoke.

PENNIWISE. I'm sure the times are hard for everybody.

DOTHERIGHT. Whether the times be hard or good, I have noticed that pimps and jobbers dine better than honest craftsmen should, and that the same cold wind blows through an empty purse.

PENNIWISE. (*thoughtfully*) Maybe I shouldn't have given up my writing?

LETTY. What writing? Is this the secret in your past, Penny?

PENNIWISE. (*stiffening*) Och, a lot of soft nonsense. I've forgotten it now. I was thinking of getting married at the time. She was a bonnie lass – so gay and bright.

(*He looks up at the upper window which lights up.*)

PADDY. (*nauseated*) Lord! Reminiscences!

LETTY. Shut up, Paddy. Why didn't you get married, Mr Penny?

PENNIWISE. Because there was the future to think of. I was going into the professions and had a career to consider. How could I get married?

DOTHERIGHT. And so you took the wiser course.

PENNIWISE. I suppose so.

DOTHERIGHT. And here you are now.

(*Meanwhile* CHAPLAIN *has been getting* MRS TYLER *into position, as she adjusts her glasses.*)

MRS TYLER. Let me see, now.

PENNIWISE. Aye. Here I am now.

CHAPLAIN. Sssh! Quiet please.

MRS TYLER. (*reading*) It is a great pleasure and privilege to be here on behalf of my husband, the Senator, to unveil this Memorial on the wall of the humble birthplace of his distinguished ancestor – the great English Rebel and Reformer of the 14th century, Watt Tyler.

CHAPLAIN. Yes Mrs Tyler, but it should be the 15th century. And that's not the proper opening is it?

MRS TYLER. Oh, are you sure? 15th century?

CHAPLAIN. Definitely but I'll go and check. And I repeat, Mrs Tyler, you mustn't begin until you get the cue from me.

(*He dashes back into the Pub. Some more onlookers gather round.* MRS TYLER *continues, unheeding.*)

MRS TYLER. Our American Revolution which we celebrate once a year on the Fourth of July – don't interrupt – is an expression of protest against tyranny and injustice – where's he gone, that man?

(*As some of her listeners indicate to her what has happened she gets into an inaudible discussion with some of them, and distributes some pamphlets from her portmanteau.*)

MRS TYLER. As our late President Tyler said in – er –

(*She starts to look through the script and makes some marks with a pencil.*)

DOTHERIGHT. You have squandered your days in rummaging the earth for small and unimportant things. And what has it profited you more than any of us?

PENNIWISE. (*in reminiscent mood*)

Lift up your eyes and see the budding hedgerows.

Ours are the meadows and the rowan trees.

This is our Earth. We can rebuild the Heavens,

And in a greener land, reset the seas.

(*Pause, while his Companions look at each other.*)

HOOLEY. (*entering*) I like that bit. "The blooming hedges".

PENNIWISE. (*crossly*) Budding hedgerows.

LETTY. Who's was that, Penny?

PENNIWISE. (*with a touch of apology*) Nobody's ma'am. It's just my own. She was nicer when I wrote it for her than she is today.

(*He gazes up at the window.*)

LETTY. Not Miss Peering? (*They all look up.*)

PENNIWISE. Yes, Ma'am. (*He sniffs.*)

PADDY. (*after another pause*) Well; I bet there's not a dry seat in the house.

LETTY. Stop it, Paddy. Stop it!

PADDY. Cheer up, Penniwise. I got married, and you can have my future.

(*He draws a hip flask from his pocket.*)

LETTY. Oh, I can't bear it. I can't. I can't.

(*She bites back her tears, and runs off, after grabbing the flask. PADDY stares after LETTY.*)

HOOLEY. Is there something the matter with her?

PADDY. Yes. Me. It's nice to be a bit of a shit. Helps you to feel sort of at home in this world of ours.

PENNIWISE. I think there's virtue in all of us.

HOOLEY. There's only one virtue that matters, and it's Courage. We learnt that when we occupied the Post Office.

DOTHERIGHT. Yes, Lieutenant, and let us add that there is only one Evil that matters – Injustice. Injustice is the supreme sin – not in those who commit it, but in those who submit to it. For to do so is to ignore the eternal verities and to admit that Life itself is evil. That is the Sin against the Holy Ghost.

(*The BOY is crossing the forestage leading the Goat on a tether.*)

BOY. (*with a bland smile*) He's right, you know. You have to occupy the Post Office. (*He goes off on the other side.*) Pause.

PENNIWISE. Was that Alexander?

PADDY. No. It was George – Saint George Washington with his Dragon.

CHAPLAIN. (*rushing to the Platform*) You're on the air, Mrs Tyler! Go ahead.

MRS TYLER. (*now completely confused*). When in the course of human events, no that's not the place, where is it? As our great President Tyler remarked just a moment please . . . Alas for the days of heroism. Where are the young men now who would do as those men did . . .

(DOTHERIGHT *has pushed his way up beside her as she struggles with* CHAPLAIN *over the script.*)

DOTHERIGHT. Excuse me, madam. I have a short announcement to make. I myself propose to hold a Rebellion.

MRS TYLER. I beg your pardon?

CHAPLAIN. Go away! Don't you know we're on the air!

DOTHERIGHT. A Rebellion. The days of heroism have not gone. Would any of you people care to join me?

(*The Onlookers hastily withdraw to a distance.*)

MRS TYLER. Will somebody please do something about this man?

(HOOLEY *and* PENNIWISE *get up beside them.*)

HOOLEY. See here you . . .

PENNIWISE. Dotheright, you'd better come away.

DOTHERIGHT. I will not come away. I agree with everything that has been said. We have been invoking St Peter when what we ought to invoke is Saltpetre. Like the philosopher, Diogenes, we must publicly deface a spurious coinage.

CHAPLAIN. Will you stop interrupting Mrs Tyler?

VOICES. That's right. Ah, get down.

(CHAPLAIN *takes hold of* DOTHERIGHT, *who clings on to something.*)

DOTHERIGHT. I am not interrupting. I tell you, I agree with her. Madam, I appeal to you.

VOICES. Ah, throw him out.

(*Angry Voices rise.*)

(MISS PEERING *looks out of her window and blows a whistle.*)

MISS PEERING. This noise is disgraceful.

(MISS PEERING *goes in again.*)

PADDY. (*excited*) Wait a minute. Wait a minute. Give us a chance of a headline! Any statement, Mrs Tyler, before you throw this rebel out of your revolutionary gathering?

CHAPLAIN. You keep out of this!

PADDY. Be careful now. I'm the Press. Will you not let the man have his say, Mrs Tyler? How many times have you demanded as much for yourself?

MRS TYLER. If the gentleman has a grievance I'm sure he is entitled to ventilate it. But please remember we are on the air.

PADDY. Come on, Dotheright, what do you propose?

DOTHERIGHT. (*with quiet reason*) I propose a Democracy dedicated to the triple slogan, "One Truth, One Law, One Justice" – a

Commonwealth where men shall be given to dignity, and not Dignities to men, and where Liberty and Equity shall be as free as the winds of Heaven.

HOOLEY. (*enthusiastically*) Triple Crown Dotheright; That's him!

PADDY. (*writing madly*) A Bellows full of Angry Wind! How's that for a Headline?

DOTHERIGHT. In furtherance of which I propose to occupy the Post Office.

PADDY. (*after a surprised silence*) Well folks, here's your chance.

CHAPLAIN. What right have you got to occupy a Post Office?

DOTHERIGHT. Precisely the same right as many others before me.

MRS TYLER. This is most extraordinary behaviour.

CHAPLAIN. (*grabbing the microphone*) Cut the whole thing! Do you hear me, Control Room? Cut – Cut – Cut!

VOICES FROM SOME OF THE ONLOOKERS. Let's get out of here. I'm off. So am I. Going to be trouble.

DOTHERIGHT. Don't go, ladies and gentlemen. As participants in this large event, you shall all be given jobs – maybe even in my Cabinet. Mr Hooley here – he has military experience. He shall be Minister for War.

(*As the strains of "Parsifal" are heard approaching from a Radio, he pulls down the awning, half of which remains attached to its rod, which he waves in the air.*)

CHAPLAIN. We'll have to start all over again. Control Room, have you cut?

(*Pause.*) My God! Then do!

DOTHERIGHT. Let us unfurl a new flag, dedicated to Sir Herbert Barker, who in the cause of Science was able and willing to put his own neck out of joint. (*He waves the flag.*)

(LETTY *enters, carrying the Radio and wearing the Horse's hat. Putting the Radio down she distributes straws from the nosebag to the departing Public in a fantastic parody of the mad Ophelia. The* PHOTOGRAPHER *appears from the Pub and hastily starts fiddling with his lens.*)

LETTY. Up the Rebels! That's Rosemary. That's for remembrance.

CHAPLAIN. Oh God! Stop this infernal row. We're still on the air.

LETTY. There's Fennel for you. And Columbine. And there's a Pansy.

PHOTOGRAPHER. (*receiving his*) Are you referring to ME?

MRS TYLER. (*at the mike*) Where would we be without our Rebels? Would we be living today in a land where . . . ?

(DOTHERIGHT *has got up beside her and is attempting to take the microphone. The* PHOTOGRAPHER *tries to fix his camera in position.*

MRS TYLER. Let it go. Let it go. Would we be living today . . .

DOTHERIGHT. (*into the microphone*) We must be angry men, unshamed of our anger. We must be mountains who will not be molehills.

(*Continuing to background*) What are our only weapons? They are words – big-bellied words, billowing like galleons out of Espanola – words that strike fire from flint. We shall speak to the great unknowing world how these things came about. (*Meanwhile.*)

CHAPLAIN. Stop behaving like a fool Letty. This is all your fault.

(HOOLEY *makes off with the nosebag and the Hat.*)

HOOLEY. No violence, please. That's Mac's supper. And his Hat!

LETTY. I would give you violence, but it withered all –

CHAPLAIN. Shut up!

LETTY. – when my poor old Father died!

CHAPLAIN. I told you to shut up!

PADDY. (*interfering*) Are you criticising my wife's performance?

CHAPLAIN. Yes!

PADDY. Well, I think it's very good.

CHAPLAIN. Deplorable!

(PADDY *strikes* CHAPLAIN *who goes down like a stone, knocking over the Radio which is suddenly silent, as the voices of the departing public die away.*)

LETTY. (*affectionately*) Did you really like me, Paddy? (*She indicates Chaplain on the ground.*) That much?

PADDY. Absolutely star quality.

MRS TYLER. (*Exhausted*) – when – in the course of human – events –

PENNIWISE. Look out!

MISS PEERING. (*appearing again in the window with some domestic receptacle in her hand.*)

There now! Maybe that will cool your chatter.

(*She empties it over* DOTHERIGHT'S *head, and blows her whistle again.*)

DOTHERIGHT. That, gentlemen, is our baptism by Grace. Here now is our baptism by Fire!

(*He raises the rod and smashes the glass in the doorway.* MISS PEERING *screams and slams her window shut as all the others are galvanised into activity except* CHAPLAIN *who*

247

remains prostrate. Police whistles are heard, off, as PADDY
picks LETTY *up and carries her off as she shouts*:)

Up with the Barricades. Revolution! Revolution!

PADDY. Out of my way, you nitwits. (*They go off in the opposite
direction to the sound of the whistles.*)

PENNIWISE. To the cab, everyone. Quick!

(*He leads the others off – including* MRS TYLER – *towards
the Cab.*)

MRS TYLER. Taxi! Taxi!

DOTHERIGHT. I hereby proclaim my Triple Crown Four Man
Republic, and occupy the Post Office.

(MRS VANDERBILT *pulls open the door from inside and he
enters.* MISS PEERING *reappears at her window. The* PHOTO-
GRAPHER *runs madly about trying to find his flashing
apparatus, and finally disappears into the Pub.*)

PHOTOGRAPHER. My flash! My flash!

DOTHERIGHT. Mrs Vanderbilt! How did you get in here?

POLICEMAN. (*appearing at last*) What's going on?

(DOTHERIGHT *hastily closes the door and leans against it.*)

MISS PEERING. He's inside! He's the one that did it!

POLICEMAN. (*shaking the door*) Come out of that! Come on. I've
got your name!

DOTHERIGHT. (*trying to hold the door against him*) Go away,
fellow. We do not recognise you any more.

POLICEMAN. (*pushing*) Well, I recognise you.

DOTHERIGHT. Oh dear me, dear me. To arms! To arms!

(*The* POLICEMAN *slowly pushes the door in and pulls him
out by the collar.*)

POLICEMAN. Come on, now. No more trouble out of you!

DOTHERIGHT. (*as he is dragged out*) What? Am I alone? Is it only
a One-Man Rebellion?

(*He ceases to resist.*)

POLICEMAN. Are you coming quietly, or shall I call the van?

DOTHERIGHT. No, sir. It is unnecessary to call the van. I surrender.
But only to superior force, you understand. (*He hands over
his flag.*) You will note, my dear sir, that there are no signs
of alcohol upon our person. Report us and our cause aright to
the unsatisfied. Now, officer, you may conduct the Republic
to the Bridewell.

(*He breathes on the* POLICEMAN *as the* PHOTOGRAPHER, *at last
ready, dashes forward to get the final shot, tripping over*

248

CHAPLAIN *and the Radio on the way. As he falls flat on his face the flash bulb goes off, and the overturned Radio breaks forth again into the brassy strains of "Parsifal".* DOTHERIGHT *stalks off with the* POLICEMAN.*)*

CURTAIN

SCENE FOUR

ANTEROOM OF CENTRAL CRIMINAL COURT

There is a Telephone Box in which PADDY *stands. Beyond this is a bench on which sit* PENNIWISE, MRS TYLER, HOOLEY *and* MRS VANDERBILT – *in that order.*

PADDY. (*looking out of the booth*) When do they reach this damn case?

PENNIWISE. The man said, any time now.

MRS TYLER. Is there still no word that I can go?

PENNIWISE. Mr Phibbs is doing the best he can.

PADDY. (*into the phone*) Any time now. (*He comes out.*) Oh cheer up, Mrs Tyler. You're not being charged with anything – so far.

MRS TYLER. Then why did he take my name?

PADDY. Just as a witness. An important one.

MRS TYLER. I was asked to take part in a broadcast. That was all. Is that an offence in this country? If so my husband, the Senator will have something to say about it.

PENNIWISE. They just want to find out what happened and why.

HOOLEY. We all know what happened but nobody knows why.

(*Pause.*)

HOOLEY. We shouldn't have been caught running away. That's the trouble.

PADDY. Certainly not in that cab. They wouldn't catch *me* doing that.

PENNIWISE. (*irritated*) Look – we've been over all of this already. Let's wait and see what we're asked, and answer as truthfully as possible. The only question that matters will be one of damages. Who broke the glass in that door?

HOOLEY. We all know who did that.

MRS TYLER. Well it wasn't me. And if I'm expected to pay I don't mind saying that there will be questions asked in the American Senate.

PADDY. There'll be questions asked there any way. Who was preaching Rebellion – eh?

(*An uncomfortable pause.*)

HOOLEY. "Mr Dotheright has no money". I seem to have heard that somewhere.

PADDY. In fact, the whole thing was just a dreary little brawl that none of us knows anything about. (*He sighs.*) Oh dear! And I quite enjoyed it at the time.

PENNIWISE. Then you must be as daft as that lunatic.

(MISS PEERING *is shown in by the* POLICEMAN.)

POLICEMAN. Wait in here, please.

(*He goes. There is an uncomfortable silence as they move politely along to make room for her. But she sits down at the end of the line. Realising that she is next to* MRS VANDERBILT, *she then rises and moves along to the other end beside* PENNIWISE.)

HOOLEY. (*after a cough*) We're all sorry, Mum, for what happened last night.

PADDY. Everybody was acting from the highest possible motives.

MISS PEERING. Indeed! I suppose that's why five pounds worth of tenpenny stamps are missing from my till.

MRS TYLER. We never heard about that!

MISS PEERING. (*with added indignation*) Not to speak of two antique china dogs that I can't find anywhere.

PENNIWISE. Believe me, Isa, none of us here knows anything at all about that. We can vouch for everybody, that is . . .

(*He coughs.*)

(*All eyes turn slowly on* MRS VANDERBILT, *who remains blandly composed.*)

MISS PEERING. Is that so?

PENNIWISE. Isa – we're sorry. We had no idea there was going to be anything in the way of – um – larceny.

MISS PEERING. (*a little coyly*) It's a long time since I've seen you, Angus.

PENNIWISE. Yes, Isa. A long time.

MRS TYLER. If there's anything that Mr Penniwise can do, Miss Peering, he'll only be too anxious. Won't you, Mr Penniwise?

HOOLEY. For the sake of ole lang sang.

PENNIWISE. Well – er – of course – mm!

(LETTY *enters briskly with* CHAPLAIN. *He has a black eye.*)

LETTY. Well, thank goodness we've been able to fix that.

251

PENNIWISE. What have you been able to fix?

MRS TYLER. Are they letting us all go now?

LETTY. Not just yet. But the case is going to be taken by Judge Bland instead of that awful old sour-puss who usually sits in the Police Court.

HOOLEY. Judge Bland. Who's he?

CHAPLAIN. Oh, a very reasonable man. We're lucky to have him. If anybody understands the situation Bland will.

LETTY. Yes, that's what everybody says. If we can arrange amongst ourselves that the damage will be paid for, Judge Bland isn't the kind of person to be hard on the – er, Professor.

PENNIWISE. Hard on him! *We're* the ones to be worried about. Not him.

CHAPLAIN. The Judge is going to see us all in a few minutes. So be ready to come along when I call.

LOWD. (*Entering*) So here you all are – my friends, family and helpmeets! I've been wanting to meet you all ever since I heard that broadcast. One of the most remarkable I've ever listened to. Congratulations, Wystan. Best thing since, "The Fleet's Lit Up".

CHAPLAIN. There are times when I distinctly dislike you. (*He hurries off.*)

MRS TYLER. Mr Lowd, this is no time for flippancy.

LOWD. Don't worry, Mrs Tyler. I'm arranging to do a little personal hunger-strike outside whatever jail they lock you up in. Special comfort facilities have already been laid on. As for you, my friend – (*To Paddy.*)

PADDY. You needn't look at me like that. I'm not being charged. I'm the Press.

LOWD. Not for long, the way you're going.

PADDY. Furthermore, it was I who got your daughter away. Only the people in the cab had their names taken.

LOWD. It was quicker to run, I suppose?

PADDY. Much quicker. But don't bother about them either. Everything is being fixed. Everything except old Dotheright. You'd better see about him yourself; otherwise there's no knowing what he may say about you.

LOWD. You don't have to tell me my business. I know what has to be done. Excuse me.

(*He goes, followed by* MRS VANDERBILT.)

LETTY. What do you mean – fix Dotheright?

PADDY. He'll have to be paid what he's owed. And quickly too. Then he can't bring the *Comet* into this mess.

LETTY. But then the whole thing becomes meaningless and absurd.

PADDY. Exactly. As if it wasn't that already.

LETTY. He won't be able to fix Dotheright.

PADDY. Oh yes he will. Maybe it'll cost a little more than the original amount, but he'll be fixed. The *Comet* won't be mentioned.

LETTY. It's not true. The Professor wasn't after money. He was after something far more important.

PADDY. He'll take money just the same.

LETTY. What will you bet?

PADDY. Anything you like, my dear. Against – against a bottle of Irish.

LETTY. It's a bet. Ssssh.

(DOTHERIGHT *enters with the* POLICEMAN.)

POLICEMAN. Wait here. You'll be wanted presently.

LETTY. Good morning, Mr Dotheright.

DOTHERIGHT. (*coldly*) Mr Dotheright regrets that he is not at home.

LETTY. You're not going to give up your Republic, Professor, are you? You still have friends, you know.

DOTHERIGHT. Yes, madam, we still have friends, although I don't see many of them around. I have, for instance, a gallant fighting cock to join my Cabinet. And you have a horse – a horse, if we are not mistaken, called Waterproof.

HOOLEY. Mac.

DOTHERIGHT. An animal of great accomplishments. In the space of a few hours he can effect what it has taken the late Mr Boddy a lifetime of experiment to manufacture. We will appoint him Minister for Transport. The Right Honourable Waterproof.

(PADDY *laughs.*)

PENNIWISE. It's a disgrace for you to be encouraging him.

DOTHERIGHT. Ah, good evening, Miss Peering. Do you know anything about the price of plate glass? I hope that I broke enough to secure a Jury trial.

MISS PEERING. Don't you speak to me, you thief.

DOTHERIGHT. Madam, perjury has not been entirely absent from your own affairs. Neither larceny nor drunkenness had any share in mine.

PENNIWISE. Now, now! You mustn't offend Miss Peering!

DOTHERIGHT. We have noticed that it is usually those who give most offence to others who are the first to be offended themselves. And those whom the world can most easily spare are always the most solicitous about saving their own lives.

MISS PEERING. Angus, I won't stay here and listen to this.

PENNIWISE. Don't pay any attention, Isa. You mustn't take him seriously. Why, he doesn't even understand the laws of economics!

DOTHERIGHT. They say that when Hannibal besieged Casilium, one mouse was sold for two hundred pence, and he that drove the bargain got his price and then died of hunger. He understood the laws of economics, no doubt.

PENNIWISE. Oh, a very high and mighty line. You don't care about money – don't even know what it is, I suppose?

DOTHERIGHT. Yes, sir, I do. It is what we gain on the devil's back and spend under his belly. There are sixty-three ways in which to get it, and a hundred and forty-five ways in which to lose it. If we are covetous we never seem to have it. If we are prodigal we cannot keep it. For it we live in hope of dead men's shoes, damning ourselves to leave our thankless children rich in that which will be worth nothing when to-morrow comes. For it we study to die wealthy rather than to ripen honourably, while all the time honesty is so scarce a commodity that we lay it up carefully to be used only on special occasions.

(LETTY *gives him a round of hand-clapping to which he bows politely.*)

PENNIWISE. Maybe so, but where have your fine ideas led you? What are you now, I'd like to know? An old . . .

LETTY. Oh stop! Please!

DOTHERIGHT. And what are you, who for the sake of this thing, have forgotten how to write your poetry? You are a sorry little lawyer, dancing on a tightrope with a bag of silver in each hand to keep you even for fear of breaking your neck. And under you are lawyers upon lawyers like yourself in their gowns whipped with silk, all staring upwards to see which way the money will fall.

(LETTY *nods approvingly.*)

254

MISS PEERING. What does he mean, Angus?

PENNIWISE. Och, just a lot of highbrow talk.

DOTHERIGHT. (*reflectively*) What mighty brows we would possess if all men's faults were written on their foreheads.

(*Pause.*)

LETTY. (*quietly*) Now are you answered?

(DOTHERIGHT *crosses and sits down to make a few notes, meanwhile* CHAPLAIN *enters.*)

CHAPLAIN. We've got to go in and see the Judge now, in his Chamber. Not Dotheright – but anybody else who has been called.

MRS TYLER. Now a united front, please everybody. And remember, I have some very important friends elsewhere who had better be kept in mind.

MISS PEERING. Doesn't he want to see me too?

PENNIWISE. Better leave it to me, Isa. You come along and wait outside.

MISS PEERING. I suppose it's the last I'll see of you, Angus?

PENNIWISE. No, no. We've got to have a long talk afterwards.

MISS PEERING. Very well. So long as you remember.

(*As the others go,* LOWD *enters, looking very pleased with himself.*)

LETTY. Don't worry, Professor. It'll be all right.

PADDY. Wait a minute, Letty.

LETTY. What is it?

PADDY. Maybe there'll be some news about our bet. (*To Lowd.*) How about it? Did the old man take his cash?

LOWD. Of course he did.

PADDY. Letty, you've lost. (*To Lowd.*) How much?

LETTY. Oh no!

LOWD. Just a matter of five pounds. No trouble at all.

LETTY. I can't believe it.

PADDY. Make it Bushmills, my dear. And don't worry. You can have a good stiff one out of it, yourself.

LETTY. I don't believe it. I can't believe it!

LOWD. (*crossing to Dotheright with a smile*) Well, my old friend. You're becoming quite an important figure. You'll be having lunch with me, one of these days.

LETTY. If this is true, Paddy, I'll never believe in anything again.

PADDY. Then what a pair we'll be. Oh, cheer up, Letty. I won't be able to enjoy that drink if you don't cheer up.

LOWD. We're certainly indebted to you for an exclusive front page story.

DOTHERIGHT. That isn't the only debt you owe me.

LOWD. What's this? Haven't you got it yet?

DOTHERIGHT. Got what?

LOWD. Why, the money of course. I gave it to your wife not five minutes ago!

DOTHERIGHT. You are under some delusion, sir. I have no wife.

LETTY. Oh!

LOWD. No wife – But that queer old lady who goes around with you. I met her in the corridor, and she said she was your wife.

DOTHERIGHT. I have no wife.

LETTY. Paddy, he never took it!

LOWD. But she promised me she'd fix everything with you – said I could leave the cash with her.

DOTHERIGHT. (*after shaking his head*) We have nothing to do with any such transaction.

PADDY. Better try him again – quick.

LOWD. The Confidence Trick! And pulled on me! (*Pulling money from his pocket*) Here, my dear fellow, you must take it now.

LETTY. Careful, Professor.

PADDY. Shut up, Letty. You're trying to foul up our bet.

(DOTHERIGHT *takes the proffered notes, glances at them and hands them back.*)

LOWD. What's this?

DOTHERIGHT. Pieces of paper.

LOWD. (*hardening*) Ah! Not enough, eh? Going to get tough with me. Well, I suppose you're entitled to . . . this once. Well, would an even tenner square us up and leave us friends?

DOTHERIGHT. It would not, sir.

PADDY. Try more.

LETTY. Ssssh!

LOWD. Well, how about fifteen pounds? Not a penny more!

DOTHERIGHT. The correct amount was three pounds and fifty pence plus tax. But I am not interested in that any longer.

LOWD. Look here. Suppose we put it this way. Here I'm giving you three pounds and fifty pee. And I'm also giving you fourteen pounds and whatever-it-is just for yourself.

LETTY. Twelve pounds and fifty pee.

LOWD. O.K. Whatever you say. I'm giving you all that along with it. Understand it now?

DOTHERIGHT. Why?

LOWD. Why what?

DOTHERIGHT. Why are you giving us all this along with it?

LOWD. Why because I like you, Alaphonsius. Because I want to make sure you get a good solicitor.

DOTHERIGHT. Mr Hy –?

LOWD. No, not Hynie Phibbs if you don't want him. You can spend it on Portland Cement for all I care.

DOTHERIGHT. (*thinks for a moment*) Portland Cement. I still see no reason why you should give thirteen pounds and whatever it is for nothing.

LETTY. Twelve pounds and fifty pee.

LOWD. (*shouting*) Never mind the exact amount! I'm getting sick of offering you jobs and money, and having them thrown back in my face. What's the game?

PADDY. Quite simple, boss. He's a sorehead and he wants to have a grievance. If you pay him off he won't have it any longer.

LOWD. Ah!

DOTHERIGHT. That is quite untrue. In proof of which, I shall accept what I am legitimately owed. My One-Man Rebellion does not require a personal grievance to justify it.

LOWD. Here, let's stop this gab. I've got twenty pounds here. But that's the outside limit. Will you take that and shut up about the *Comet* owing you money?

DOTHERIGHT. I will not take twenty pounds or a hundred or a thousand pounds. I will take three pounds and fifty pence and not a penny more or less. – Plus tax.

LETTY. Good for you, Prof.!

DOTHERIGHT. Do not think, sir, because the world is full of money-grubbers who will take anything they can lay their hands on that you can stifle my protest by a larger sum any more readily than by a lesser.

LOWD. (*fumbling in his pockets*) Suffering cheese, what is this? Three pounds, and twenty – thirty – forty – four pounds. Here!

DOTHERIGHT. (*looking at it*) I will not take four pounds.

LOWD. Well, give me change.

DOTHERIGHT. I have no change.

LOWD. Holy smoke, has anybody got change of a pound?

DOTHERIGHT. Why cannot people understand that what I have done is not for purely personal reasons. It is for humanity – and in obedience to my voices.

257

LOWD. Your what?

DOTHERIGHT. It would be quite impossible to explain such a matter to you without losing my temper. So if you will excuse me I will go and sit down quietly in the next room.

LOWD. Hey, you can't go now. I want to get this fixed up. Wait till I get some change.

DOTHERIGHT. Excuse me please. I have much of real importance to keep in mind. I have shortly to plead my defence at the bar of Society, and then go to jail to prove my point. However, I shall no doubt see you in jail sooner or later. Come and talk to me there, if talking is permitted. Good afternoon. (*He goes off.*)

LOWD. What are you sniggering at?

LETTY. Excuse me, father. I think I'll have to go and sit down quietly, too.

(*She goes out swiftly after* DOTHERIGHT, *as a quiet, soft-spoken man with a thin moustache and an unruffled but sceptical manner approaches* LOWD. *He is a plain-clothes man, but not one of the old stage type, in a bowler hat. He is one of the smoother products, and all the more sinister on that account.*)

LOWD. I've made him the offer before witnesses. That puts me in the clear.

(*The telephone rings.*)

PADDY. That'll be the news room again.

LOWD. Keep them posted.

(PADDY *goes into the telephone box and closes the door as he talks into the phone. But soon he is watching* LOWD.)

MAN. Excuse me, sir. Are you Mr Lowd?

LOWD. Yes, my man.

MAN. Might I have a word with you? (*He produces an identity card.*)

LOWD. You may have several, if you're not too long about it. (*looks at card.*) Oh! The C.I.D. I didn't know they bothered themselves with Police Court cases.

MAN. Not as a rule, sir. But there's something that puzzles us a little.

LOWD. (*laughing*) I'm not surprised. Mr Dotheright is a tangle of puzzles. Maybe an Alienist would be of more help to you than me.

MAN. Oh, we're not interested in him, sir. But somebody's been looking through his papers and found this.

(*He hands a document to* LOWD.)

Is that your handwriting, sir?

LOWD. Why, yes. (*Pause.*) Yes. It is. (*He hands it back.*)

MAN. This is a draft newspaper report of the death of a Mr Boddy.

LOWD. Ah, yes. I know he was upset over that. It was a silly mistake on the part of somebody in our office. We offered to pay him in full for his work, but he simply wouldn't take the money. Seems to prefer to have a grievance. (*He gives a mirthless laugh.*)

MAN. This report isn't a mistake, sir. Mr Boddy passed away in the West yesterday afternoon.

LOWD. What?

MAN. He's dead.

LOWD. Good Lord. How extraordinary. Poor Boddy. What did he die of?

MAN. We don't know, sir. But it's something we'd like to ask you about.

(PADDY *opens the door slightly and watches through the glass as he telephones.*)

LOWD. Me? Why me?

MAN. This Mr Boddy died yesterday afternoon. But this report of his death appears to have been written by you several days ago. May I ask how you knew he was going to die before it happened?

LOWD. Heavens! You're surely not suggesting that I could have anything to do with his death?

MAN. I'm not suggesting anything, sir. Merely checking up.

LOWD. Well I don't remember anything about it.

MAN. A pity, sir. It's rather important that you should be able to trace the source. Otherwise, I'm afraid . . .

LOWD. Otherwise what?

MAN. Otherwise I'm afraid I shall have to ask you to come along with me to our office, sir.

LOWD. (*getting desperate*) Inspector, I can't possibly come along to your office at the moment. In fact, you've no right to ask me. I've told you all I know about it and you have no right whatever –

MAN. (*interrupting him*) I only asked for your help, sir. Of course you're perfectly within your rights to refuse to give it. Nobody can force you to come to Headquarters without a warrant.

Good morning, sir.

(*He turns to go, but* LOWD *stops him.*)

LOWD. Good God, man, don't take me up like that. You don't have to go and get a warrant.

MAN. I didn't say I was going to do that, sir.

LOWD. No, but I know what you mean. Look, Inspector . . . it's all a little embarrassing, but I see I'd better tell you the truth.

MAN. Yes, sir. Perhaps you had.

LOWD. It really *is* a coincidence, Inspector. I know nothing whatever about Boddy's movements except that he was away on a holiday. It was this that gave me the silly idea of starting a rumour that he was dead. That's literally what happened.

MAN. Indeed!

LOWD. I had no intention of publishing it, of course. But you know, Boddy and I both have – er – had – extensive interests in – er – one or two businesses.

MAN. Chemical manure for instance?

LOWD. Exactly. I'm in that too – although it's not generally known. In fact, I've been recently buying up all the stock I can get. So I thought – you know – er – Boddy being away – er –

MAN. You thought that if a rumour got around the stock exchange that he was dead, you might be able to snatch a block at a bargain price?

LOWD. Well – er – I don't deny that the Market might have been a bit easier. Maybe it wasn't very – er – ethical.

MAN. Maybe not.

LOWD. (*beginning to gabble*) I'm sure you know the Market as well as I do. And after all I did nothing about it and even if I had, that's a very different matter from having him die.

MAN. Of course, sir. In quite a different category.

LOWD. Look here, you do believe me, don't you? You don't suppose I'd invent such a story against myself if it wasn't true?

MAN. I'm sure the Authorities will take that fact into consideration, sir. You'll make a statement of course?

LOWD. Good Heavens, do I have to?

MAN. Yes, sir. There'll have to be a statement. There's rather more in this than Chemical Manure you know.

LOWD. What do you mean? What more is there?

MAN. Well, sir, the Government is very sensitive about anything

260

connected with Nitrates. They make explosives too, you know.

LOWD. Explosives!

MAN. Didn't you know Mr Boddy was in Explosives? I'm afraid a lot of people will want to know what exactly was behind his death.

LOWD. God! Take me to the Station at once. I've got to make a statement about this right away. This can't go any further.

MAN. Very good, sir. I have a car outside.

LOWD. (*halting*) Not a Black Maria?

MAN. Oh no, sir. Just a taxi. No cause for alarm.

PADDY. (*coming out*) Boss –

LOWD. You go to the devil.

    (*As* LOWD *and the* DETECTIVE *leave,* CHAPLAIN, HOOLEY *and* PENNIWISE *come in from the other direction.*)

CHAPLAIN. Well, thank God that's over.

PADDY. What is?

PENNNIWISE. We're all well out of it.

HOOLEY. A bit of all right, if you ask me.

    (LETTY *follows.*)

LETTY. What's happened?

PENNIWISE. The Judge has had a private talk with us all.

HOOLEY. Very fair.

PENNIWISE. He understood the situation at once when it was explained to him.

CHAPLAIN. We're all going into Court and he's going to dismiss the case . . .

PENNIWISE. And any other possible cases.

HOOLEY. And say no more about it.

CHAPLAIN. On terms that the damage is paid for.

LETTY. Oh, thank goodness. They never could have put him in jail, poor man, could they? That would have been scandalous.

CHAPLAIN. Exactly what the Judge thinks. He seems to be a most sensible fellow.

PENNIWISE. Mrs Tyler is on her way to the Cunard Line already.

LETTY. Oh, what a relief to know that he won't be locked up.

PENNIWISE. Not in jail, anyhow.

LETTY. What do you mean?

CHAPLAIN. Well, you can scarcely expect them to let him loose, can you?

HOOLEY. After what he's done?

CHAPLAIN. (*defensively*) Now listen, my dear, he was really a very reasonable Judge. He doesn't want to punish the old fool if he's not responsible for his actions. And you know quite well that he's not.

LETTY. He is! He is! You've no right to tell the Judge that he's not.

PENNIWISE. What else could we tell him? Do you want to get us all into trouble?

CHAPLAIN. It's awkward enough as it is. And if there's no explanation for what occurred . . .

LETTY. You mean you told the Judge that he was crazy – just to get everybody out of a jam. Is that what you did?

CHAPLAIN. We're trying to do the best for everyone.

PENNIWISE. And he *is* crazy. That's the literal truth.

HOOLEY. As mad as a hatter if you ask me.

LETTY. "Quite a reasonable Judge". And it was I who got the case before him! Oh, what have I done?

CHAPLAIN. There's no other solution. He'll have to go to the . . .
     (DOTHERIGHT enters.)

LETTY. Hush – keep quiet. You mustn't even think of such a thing.

PENNIWISE. Well, somebody's got to tell him.
     (*Pause. The* POLICEMAN *enters.*)

POLICEMAN. Come on, now. The Court is sitting.

CHAPLAIN. Just a moment while we explain the situation to Mr Dotheright. Listen, old man. There's not going to be any question of your going to jail.

HOOLEY. You don't have to do a thing like that you know. Not even for us.

DOTHERIGHT. I am not doing it for anybody else. I have a higher command. I am doing it for Heaven – for my voices.

PENNIWISE. Now don't talk rubbish, Dotheright. Really.

CHAPLAIN. We've managed to explain things to the Judge. He's being very sensible.

PENNIWISE. We've got him to agree that you weren't responsible for your actions.

DOTHERIGHT. Not responsible! But surely the question of drink –

PENNIWISE. Oh no. Not drink.

CHAPLAIN. Even if you do have to go to another place, it won't be for long, I'm sure.

DOTHERIGHT. "Other place" – "not responsible". Why, you talk almost as though I was supposed to be ins – (*He bites back the words.*)

(*Pause.*)

PENNIWISE. Yes, that's right. So you see there's no question of your going to jail. Isn't that good news?

DOTHERIGHT. Ins-pired? No? Ins-urgent? Eh? Insolent? Insignificant- Insincere? Then – what?

CHAPLAIN. Dotheright. Let's not mince words. You're insane.

DOTHERIGHT. INSANE!

LETTY. Oh, no!

PENNIWISE. It's the only possible defence.

DOTHERIGHT. Insane! You have been talking to him about me? He spoke of insanity and you did not deny it?

CHAPLAIN. Now look here, we're only doing the best we can for you. You ought to be thankful at getting off so lightly.

DOTHERIGHT. You did not deny it!

PENNIWISE. You won't be long in the asylum.

DOTHERIGHT. Asylum!

LETTY. (*in tears*) Oh, Prof! It's all my fault.

DOTHERIGHT. Asylum! My curse upon you all for pleading so well! You called me mad! You cats-pew on the carpet, you itch in the groin! May the wind make bagpipes of your bones.

POLICEMAN. Come on, you can't shout here.

DOTHERIGHT. I am betrayed. Oh Heaven – betrayed!

CHAPLAIN. Now, listen to me, please. Surely you realise that –

LETTY. Yes, yes – we've betrayed you. All of us. We did it, Professor.

DOTHERIGHT. But my voices – my voices? Do they not want my – my services?

(*He grows very calm as he gazes upwards.*) Is there nobody up there?

LETTY. Oh, be angry, Professor. Please be angry. Roar out and curse us all. I tried to interfere, but Paddy's right. Every decent thing you ever do only turns round and kicks you in the pants.

DOTHERIGHT. (*turning to her grimly.*) No, it is not you that has betrayed me, child. Better for Heaven if it were. It is something far more terrible than that. For men and women can forgive each other. But when the Lord himself chooses to mock His servants, who is there to forgive Him?

(*He lowers his eyes and holds out his wrists to the* POLICE-MAN.)

263

Come, my good fellow. Do your duty. Take me to the mad-house.

(*He moves off with the* POLICEMAN.)

CURTAIN

SCENE FIVE

A few weeks later, MR DOTHERIGHT'S *residence again, but now the place has an air of not having been lived in for some time. Amongst the cups and saucers on the dresser two china dogs are unobtrusively standing.* PENNIWISE *and* MISS PEERING *are sitting in silence when* WYSTAN CHAPLAIN *arrives from the street.* PENNIWISE *is dressed informally.*

CHAPLAIN. Anybody in?

PENNIWISE. Only us.

CHAPLAIN. Oh, Mr Penniwise.

PENNIWISE. You know my fiancée, Miss Peering?

CHAPLAIN. Your fiancée?

MISS PEERING. (*rather archly*) Yes, Angus has persuaded me to marry him. Aren't we a pair of silly old things?

CHAPLAIN. Well, I can't say I'm surprised. My congratulations, both of you. Where's Mrs Golightly? Did she ask you to come here this afternoon?

PENNIWISE. Yes. We both got postcards.

MISS PEERING. Some sort of a party, we imagined.

CHAPLAIN. I wonder where she can be. Well, never mind. We can wait, I suppose. What are you both doing with yourselves these days?

PENNIWISE. Oh just enjoying my retirement. I've left Mr Phibbs, you know, and after we're married I'm going to settle down in the Post Office.

MISS PEERING. And write poetry.

PENNIWISE. (*modestly*) Well, maybe so. Maybe not.

MISS PEERING. I hope you've managed to come through your little bit of trouble, Mr Chaplain?

CHAPLAIN. Kindly don't mention that deplorable affair ever again.

PENNIWISE. Anyhow, you don't seem to have got the push.

CHAPLAIN. Of course I got the push – as you call it. But only for a week or two. It's beyond me!

265

PENNIWISE. You mean they liked it?

CHAPLAIN. They detested it. They were raging about it. But it seems to have had the best rating for months. There's even been a demand for a Repeat. So now it seems they're having to have me back. I never heard such nonsense!

MISS PEERING. Oh, you must go back, Mr Chaplain. It wasn't your fault, you know.

PENNIWISE. Of course not. You did your best to stop it. All the same I've heard it said that my fiancée was the hit of the evening. And it was her first appearance too – on the Wireless.

CHAPLAIN. And might well have been my last. However – we'll see. Maybe I shall go back if they give me a rise.

MISS PEERING. It's wonderful how nice everybody has been. Quite restores one's faith in human nature, doesn't it.

CHAPLAIN. Not mine, I'm afraid. And here's the cabman. We only needed him.

(HOOLEY *enters, dressed in a magnificent new coat with brass buttons and braid. Also his medal.*)

ALL. Oooh!

HOOLEY. Well? Whatcher think?

CHAPLAIN. Hooley, you look magnificent. Where does it come from?

HOOLEY. Had it specially made. My own design, too.

CHAPLAIN. I'd know that. You must be doing very well.

HOOLEY. As a matter of fact, I am. I've got my pension now.

CHAPLAIN. A good one, I've no doubt?

HOOLEY. Best that's going. And about thirty years of arrears along with it. Don't know how she managed it.

CHAPLAIN. Who?

HOOLEY. That Mrs Tyler and the Old Comrades Association.

CHAPLAIN. Ah, I see. I see. Santa Claus has been at work. Or is it Aunt Sally?

HOOLEY. I haven't got an Aunt Sally.

CHAPLAIN. Oh yes you have, with a finger that's longer than Coincidence.

(*There is a knock at the door.*)

(*He opens the door and* LOWD *enters. He is dressed in golfing clothes.*)

CHAPLAIN. Ah Hello, Lowd.

LOWD. Is something going on over here? I was at the house looking for my daughter, and I noticed you coming in.

266

CHAPLAIN. Some sort of a reunion, it seems. Letty asked us over.

LOWD. I wonder what she's up to now.

PENNIWISE. Got quite a holiday look, you have.

LOWD. Why wouldn't I? I've got a holiday – a long one.

MISS PEERING. Well, that's nice, isn't it.

LOWD. I'm glad you think so.

CHAPLAIN. Does this mean you've got the sack too?

LOWD. I prefer to say that I've resigned. Matters became a little complicated over at the *Comet*.

MISS PEERING. You mean, because of this scandal over some swindle on The Stock Exchange?

LOWD. We don't have to go into that again. I'm rather tired of the subject. As a matter of fact, a little rest is doing me no harm at all. Getting some golf at last.

CHAPLAIN. Anyhow, you satisfied the Police. That's something to be thankful for.

LOWD. Of course I satisfied the Police. The man died of a chill on the chest. My contribution was just an unfortunate coincidence.

MISS PEERING. (*Intensely*) How do you know it was that, Mr Lowd?

LOWD. What do you mean?

MISS PEERING. How do you know that when you were thinking out that wicked trick, Providence didn't give you foreknowledge of what was going to happen?

PENNIWISE. That's right. People do sometimes have visions, you know.

LOWD. Visions! Do I look like the sort that has visions? (*Pause.*) Yet, you know, it's a funny thing. I used to say that the sign of a good newspaperman is that he can smell news before it happens. Funny if it turned out that I was right.

HOOLEY. Um. There's many a true word spoken by mistake.
    (LETTY *enters.*)

LOWD. My God! An original remark from you!

LETTY. Oh hello everybody. I'm so glad you were able to come. And father too! That's nice.

PENNIWISE. Good afternoon, Mrs Golightly.

LOWD. (*grimly*) What's going on?

LETTY. My, but you're looking fine, Lieutenant.

HOOLEY. Glad you like it.

LETTY. I asked you all over to hear the good news. We're getting the Professor out of the looney bin.

(*General sensation.*)

PENNIWISE. What? He's coming out?

HOOLEY. Well, I'll be . . .

LETTY. Yes, isn't it wonderful? Paddy and Mrs Vanderbilt have got him outside in a car. I've been to see the Judge, and he says that if he's got enough to support him, and if two or three respectable people will join in a bond for his good behaviour, he'll allow him to come home.

PENNIWISE. A bond for his good behaviour? And may I ask who's going to give that?

LETTY. I thought we might all like to join in.

HOOLEY. Us?

LOWD. I expected something like this.

LETTY. For the sake of old times. After all, we're his friends, aren't we?

(*Pause.*) Aren't we?

(*There is a pregnant silence.*)

PENNIWISE. Out of the question as far as I'm concerned. I'm getting married to Miss Peering, and that's enough responsibility of my own, without taking on that sort of thing.

MISS PEERING. Yes indeed. I don't see how Mr Dotheright's future behaviour has got anything to do with us.

LETTY. I see. Well – I'm not really surprised. Congratulations anyhow.

PENNIWISE. Thank you.

LETTY. What about you, Wystan?

CHAPLAIN. (*upset*) Me? Look, I've only just got back my job, and I've got my public to think of.

(*Pause.*) Really, Letty, I don't want to seem narrow-minded, but damn it all . . .

LETTY. That's all right, Wystan. You don't have to explain. If you don't want to, you needn't.

HOOLEY. Now there's no use asking me. I'll tell you that straight before you start.

LETTY. Why not?

HOOLEY. Because it's unnatural – see. I risked all for others once, see. And I've had little enough luck ever since. Now you want me to risk it all again. Maybe you'll think I'm mean, and maybe I am. But it's natural to be mean, see and I'm natural.

LETTY. Well that's a better answer. Thank you, Hooley.

PENNIWISE. What right have you to talk to us in that superior way, as if we hadn't got a right to say no. You're the member of the party with no responsibilities. Why don't you give the bond yourself?

LETTY. Of course I shall, if you all feel this way. And so will Paddy. We can't allow him to go on being locked up.

HOOLEY. That would be too bad.

LOWD. (*approaching*) Excuse me, but why can't we allow him to go on being locked up?

LETTY. Oh, father. I was almost forgetting you.

LOWD. You didn't answer Penniwise's question. What right have you got to make everybody feel mean by putting on that tone of voice to three decent, honest men? Why can't we leave him locked up?

LETTY. You'd like to help him, father, wouldn't you?

LOWD. Me? Help that four-footed friend?

LETTY. After all he's done.

LOWD. "Done" is right! He nearly gets us all into jail, loses me my job, plays hell with Chaplain's career, and now you've got the neck to suggest that I go bond for his good behaviour! What do you take me for?

LETTY. Rather a rascal, father. But a nice one.

LOWD. (*not really annoyed*) Rascal! Well I resent that.

LETTY. Haven't you been saying so to the police at the top of your voice for the past month?

LOWD. That was for a very special reason.

LETTY. Of course – to prove that you were just a nice old crook, and not a murderer. And everyone's loved you for it, daddy. We don't care if it gets you the sack. We love you, daddy, far more than we ever did before.

LOWD. (*backing away*) Well, I care about getting the sack. And you needn't think that you're going to kiss me, and then pick my pocket.

LETTY. Oh, come on. You wouldn't miss twenty pounds or so. Just to keep the old man in comfort.

LOWD. I don't give a damn about the old cod's comfort.

MISS PEERING. Really, Mr Lowd!

LOWD. I've got my own comfort to worry about.

LETTY. (*following him*) Now, daddy . . .

LOWD. Besides, I'm a crook. You said so yourself, and that lets me out. You don't go round asking crooks for charitable donations.

LETTY. Of course we do. You used to say that they're the ones who like to have their names at the head of the list. Say forty pounds.

LOWD. No, No! I won't! It's absurd – and completely inconsistent.

LETTY. Of course it's inconsistent – just like all that money you spent on bringing up a thankless child. Wasn't that inconsistent? But you did it, daddy, and I don't believe you're even decently ashamed of it.

LOWD. In your case it appealed to my sense of humour.

LETTY. Well, my goodness, what would be funnier than this? Why, it'll tickle you to death afterwards, every time you think of how you've paid him out for his treatment of you. Come on, where's your cheque book?

LOWD. Look here, if I give you forty pounds . . .

LETTY. Make it fifty.

LOWD. (*struggling with his pocket book*) O.K. O.K. But understand this – I will not go bond for his good behaviour. That's flat and final. Will you take it or leave it?

LETTY. I'll take it.

LOWD. (*flinging the money at her*) Then take it, and let me out of this bughouse before I start acting Napoleon.

LETTY. (*taking it*) But you've ben doing that for years, daddy. Still, thanks a lot for the money. You're a better man than . . .

LOWD. Than Gunga Din – don't say it! I know that's the next to come.

LETTY. Now, daddy, don't shout. You'll make him nervous.

(MRS VANDERBILT *and* PADDY *come in, helping* DOTHERIGHT. *An attendant follows.*)

LETTY. Well, Prof. darling, how are you feeling? Put him down in that big chair.

(*They do so.*)

DOTHERIGHT. (*weakly*) I am Mr Dotheright, and I propose to go home.

MRS VANDERBILT. Of course you're going home, love. Who's got the better right?

DOTHERIGHT. You wouldn't say that if you knew who I was.

MRS VANDERBILT. Why, who are you, love?

DOTHERIGHT. (*mysteriously*) Mr Dotheright.

PADDY. And don't you forget it!

DOTHERIGHT. (*to Letty*) Why do your eyes glisten so? Am I to give you sixpence for that tear? Well, I shall see what I can do. Bread also is reserved for those who can pay.

MRS VANDERBILT. Lay out on yer wad, and I'll finger a prayer for you in Saint Adam and Eve's.

PADDY. (*as Dotheright shakes his head*) No penny, no Paternoster.

MRS VANDERBILT. Cheer up, my old fireflint. Next week you'll be skipping round like a gamecock without the loss of a feather. (*To Miss Peering.*) I hear tell you're getting married, ma'am. Well, I've got a nice wedding present for you.

MISS PEERING. A wedding present! That's kind of her, Angus.

(*She is presented with the two china dogs.*)

MRS VANDERBILT. In place of the ones you lost.

MISS PEERING. Angus! Look!

(MRS VANDERBILT *trots out as* PENNIWISE *pacifies his indignant fiancée.*)

PENNIWISE. That's all right, my dear. Thank you, Mrs Vanderbilt.

MISS PEERING. But, Angus, they *are* the ones I lost!

PENNIWISE. Now, now, my dear! Let's not have any more scenes. I lost a watch once; but I say nothing.

DOTHERIGHT. Who is that person who breathes so heavily in the corner?

LETTY. That's my father, Mr Lowd.

DOTHERIGHT. Mr Lowd of the *Comet* newspaper?

LOWD. Mr Lowd, late of the *Comet* newspaper.

DOTHERIGHT. Late?

PADDY. He's lost his job, Prof.

DOTHERIGHT. Tt-tt-tt. I am not surprised. I feared he would come to this. But what is he doing here? Does he wish us to believe that he has mended his ways?

LETTY. Yes, Prof. darling. He's turning out to be quite a reformed character.

DOTHERIGHT. Nonsense! Only the pox converts the whoremaster, and then only when it kills him. But ah, poor fellow, I suppose it is the fault of his environment. Let me see now. (*He feels in his pocket.*) Only fifty pee, I fear. Still, it may assist. Here you are, my poor fellow. You have it. Try not to spend it on drink.

(LOWD *stares at him speechlessly while* LETTY *carries the money over.*)

LETTY. There you are, daddy dear.

PADDY. Aren't you going to thank the President?

LOWD. (*after swallowing several times*) Thank you, Mr Dotheright, for all you've done for me.

DOTHERIGHT. You're welcome. And you had better be off. Respectable employment is often hard to find.

(*He closes his eyes.*)

LOWD. (*slowly*) Perhaps I had.

LETTY. Au revoir, daddy. You're very sweet – really.

(*She kisses him swiftly.*)

LOWD. (*after a pause.*) All merciful suffering Providence! Where's the way out? Where's the bloody –

(*He goes, slamming the door.*)

DOTHERIGHT. (*shaking his head*) Tt-tt-tt. Poor fellow. Poor fellow.

LETTY. And now – what about the rest of you? You'd all better go too. He ought to have rest and quiet.

CHAPLAIN. I'm sorry you seem disappointed in us, Letty. But in the circumstances I really can't see . . . (*He dries up.*)

LETTY. Of course, Wystan. You're much too good a man to see anything as difficult as this. Goodbye.

CHAPLAIN. You mean it? Goodbye?

LETTY. Yes, Wystan.

HOOLEY. Come on. The cab's waiting.

(CHAPLAIN, PENNIWISE *and* MISS PEERING *go out.* HOOLEY *pauses in the doorway and comes back.*)

HOOLEY. Maybe there is something I can give the Professor. Here, you can have it.

(*He removes his medal and gives it to* DOTHERIGHT.)

LETTY. Your medal! Not that, Hooley?

HOOLEY. It's better for him to have it. I'll tell you no lie, ma'am. I never occupied any Post Office.

DOTHERIGHT. What's this?

HOOLEY. Mind you, it's not that I didn't want to strike a blow for freedom. I was always one for doing the kind of thing he did. In theory, at least. But – well, you know how it is, when it comes to the point.

LETTY. Oh, Hooley, I know indeed.

HOOLEY. Maybe I will some day yet. And if I ever do he can give it back to me, Eh?

272

DOTHERIGHT. Well, do not geld yourself when the sun is in Scorpio, or your stones may not grow again by the spring – if at all.

LETTY. Thank you for that, Hooley.

HOOLEY. (*suspiciously*) I wonder what he meant by that? Oh well – the old nag's getting restless. Ta-ta so. (*He goes.*)

LETTY. Well, Prof. darling, it seems that all you're left with are the Publicans and Sinners. The happier people seem to have other things to do.

MRS VANDERBILT. (*re-appearing with cups*) Dirty chancers – that's all they are. Now let's have a nice bite of supper.

PADDY. Still no eggs I suppose from that fraudulent bird up there. (*She proceeds to load the table with many delicacies from her shopping-bag.*)

PADDY. Mrs Vanderbilt, I've always admired your work, but this time you seem to have excelled yourself.

MRS VANDERBILT. Ah, times is good for them that knows where to look for it. I have a job now charring for the Parish Priest. Rest easy there while I go and wet the tea. (*She goes off again to the side.*)

ATTENDANT. Now what about this bond, ma'am? We're supposed to be on our way to the Judge, you know.

LETTY. Yes, I know. We'll come along in a minute.

DOTHERIGHT. (*struggling up*) I must go home now.

LETTY. But you are at home, Professor. Don't you recognise it?

DOTHERIGHT. No, I am not at home. That place where they put me is my home. It is time for me to go back.

LETTY. No, no, it's all right – truly. You don't have to go back there any more.

DOTHERIGHT. My child, nobody wants your bond, I am going back where I belong. I prefer the company there, if you will forgive my saying so.

LETTY. Please don't talk like that, Professor.

DOTHERIGHT. (*sitting again*) Yes, my dear – very good company. And I may add, they all fully recognize my official position. Indeed, you will be interested to hear that one of my closest friends is the Archbishop of Canterbury.

PADDY. You don't say?

DOTHERIGHT. A most intelligent man, although sometimes a little peculiar in his behaviour.

LETTY. Prof. – I don't know how to explain, but –

273

DOTHERIGHT. (*kindly*) You don't have to explain. You don't believe that he really *is* the Archbishop. You think that he is an impostor.

LETTY. (*confused*) Well perhaps – in a way –

DOTHERIGHT. Like the rest of your world, you believe that you can distinguish the real Archbishop from the false one. But it is harder than you think.

PADDY. By God, he's right! We're all impostors. Every one of us.

DOTHERIGHT. Excuse me, my friend is not an impostor, whatever the other gentleman in Canterbury may be. I know this from certain matters he has let slip in the course of our talks. That is why I propose to go back to him. Goodbye.

(*He rises.*)

LETTY. But you mustn't go back – you mustn't! There's no justice in life if you go back there and get locked up for what you've done.

DOTHERIGHT. Justice? Do you suppose that I care about Justice? Am I a Stockjobber or a Bank Official that I should bother my head over the balancing of payments and accounts? I have left all these things behind.

LETTY. You can't leave them behind. Aren't they what you fought for?

DOTHERIGHT. If so, I have learnt better from my new friends. Justice is of little importance when you know that you have been right.

LETTY. But Heavens above –

DOTHERIGHT. (*sharply*) And please do not mention Heaven to me. That is a somewhat delicate subject. I have offered my services to Heaven, and had my proposal ignored. Very well, If Heaven does not choose to pay its debts any more than the *Comet* newspaper, I have nothing more to say. I shall remain where I have been sent.

LETTY. Oh, Paddy!

PADDY. (*after a pause*) Rather a difficult case, eh?

DOTHERIGHT. As for you young people, let me give you a word of advice before I go. You have not been very happy with each other in the past, and that is because you, also, have been concerning yourselves with justice. You want to love each other in return for your virtues – not a very difficult feat, if I may say so. But you should leave that to your Employers, and love each other for your faults. It may be the advice of a lunatic, but you will find it most rewarding.

LETTY. You're not a lunatic, Professor. You're a Saint.

DOTHERIGHT. I have sometimes wondered about that. Indeed, once or twice I have tried to put it to the test by attempting some simple miracle. But never with any success. As a Saint, I am a failure. But as a Madman – ah, there at least, I am in the forefront of the field. So let us all be happy in the facts, whatever, they may be. For to be otherwise is to die twice. Now, fellow, I am ready.

(*He moves towards the door following the Attendant.* PADDY *follows him.*)

PADDY. (*passionately*) Damn you, Dotheright! How can we be happy in the facts if we have pity? Either the facts or pity, I say – but not both.

LETTY. (*surprised*) Paddy, I never heard you use that word before.

DOTHERIGHT. Why not, my friend? Call Heaven's bluff as I do, and give up neither. That's the only way we have to answer back. Try it and see.

PADDY. (*shouting*) O.K. Don Quixote. I'll try it, if you'll go on trying for your miracle. The one's just about as simple as the other.

DOTHERIGHT. Indeed, you quite inspire me.

(*He pauses in the doorway.*)

LETTY. (*to Paddy*) If he ever succeeds, will you pay me that bet you owe me? I think I've decided what I'll have.

(*She approaches* PADDY *in a menacing manner, and he backs his way into the Horse Box. There is a rustle of straw overhead as the* BOY *sticks his head up and looks down.*)

PADDY. Whatever it is, remember there's got to be a miracle first.

(DOTHERIGHT *solemnly makes a sign of benediction from the doorway, at which an indignant clucking arises from the loft, as the* BOY *drops an egg on* PADDY'S *head below, where it gently breaks.*)

PADDY. God dammit! What the hell . . . ?

LETTY. (*overcome with laughter*) Good old Nick, the King of the Goats has turned up trumps!

DOTHERIGHT. A very remarkable bird!

(*He looks at his hands in some surprise, bows politely and follows the Attendant out as* PADDY *wipes his head, and the clock starts to strike.*)

BOY. (*with a wave of his hand to the audience*).
     That is the end of this play.
                              Curtain.

1 August, 1978

NINE RIVERS
FROM JORDAN

*The Operatic Libretto
based upon some sections of
NINE RIVERS FROM JORDAN
by the same author*

CAST OF CHARACTERS

Lieutenant Jean L'Aiglon, of the Free French Army *Lyric Tenor*
Captain Father Angelino, an Italian Priest *Baritone*
Major Mark Lyon, United States Army Medical Corps
Lyric Tenor
Captain the Reverend Lucius Bull, an English Padre *Bass*
Members of an Inter-Allied Graves Identification Mission

Sergeant Abe Goldberg, U.S. Army, their driver *Bass-Baritone*
Private Don Hanwell, of the Royal West Kents,
   Dispatch Rider *Baritone*

The Righteous Twelve

Andy, the Highlander (British Army) *Tenor*
Copperhead Kelly, the Irishman (British Army) *Tenor*
Tom Tosser, the tea maker (British Army) *Tenor*
Phil, the Signalman (British Army) *Tenor*
Little Jim Clap, the Medical Orderly (British Army) *Baritone*
Simple Simon, the sock washer (British Army) *Baritone*
Peeper Johnny, 1st Artilleryman (British Army) *Bass*
Jim Gunn, 2nd Artilleryman (British Army) *Bass*
Sergeant Pete Fisher (British Army) *Bass*
Bartolomeo, an Italian Prisoner of War *Tenor*
Matte, an Italian Prisoner of War *Tenor*
Taddeo, an Italian Prisoner of War *Bass*

Otto Suder, a German Prisoner of War *Tenor*
The Dead Man *Tenor*
A Muezzin *Tenor*
Leader of the Bedouins *High Baritone*
An Italian Woman *Soprano*
An Italian Woman *Mezzo-Soprano*

279

The Salt Woman		*Dramatic*
The Pieta	Sung by the same person	*Soprano*
The Third Eve		

Recorded Woman's Voice	*Pop Singer*
Recorded Radio Announcer	

Chorus of Displaced Persons	*SATB*
Chorus of Jewish Chalutzim	*SATB*
Chorus of Bedouins	*TB*
Chorus of Mourning Women	*SSAA*

This opera musically, dramatically and symbolically, attempts to deal with the unprecedented moral problems caused by the circumstances of the Second World War. The use of many different languages in the libretto, the rapid changes of scene and the geographical extent of the action, mirror the universal involvement and confusion of those years. In the opera, actual happenings and imaginary events are juxtaposed.

SYNOPSIS

Don Hanwell, a British soldier stationed in the desert by the Dead Sea, is warned by a mysterious woman not to carry a weapon, as it is ordained that man will meet his death according to the arms he bears. Don heeds her warning and goes weaponless for the rest of the war, but this fact, coupled with Don's general indifference to questions of right or wrong, causes him to allow a German prisoner, Otto Suder, to escape. Subsequently, Suder becomes a guard at Todenwald, a German concentration camp.

In a scene on the Brocken, legendary site of the Walpurgisnacht, an allegorical trial takes place to fix the guilt for the atrocities committed at Todenwald. Don himself feels guilty for his part in Suder's escape years before. Though the verdict of the court is that all mankind is guilty, it pronounces that if Suder dies God will forgive everyone else. Don, feeling it is his duty to kill Suder, takes a Mill's bomb and sets out to find him.

In the last days of the war Don and a companion, Copperhead Kelly, find Suder, disguised as an English soldier, trying to escape into Italy. When Don announces he has come to kill him, Suder tricks him into taking his identification papers and convinces a mob of D.P.'s that Don is a Nazi and he, Suder, is a British soldier. Copperhead Kelly makes no attempt to come to Don's defence and Don feels betrayed. A woman in the mob takes the bomb from Don and gives it to Suder, who then throws it in an attempt to kill them all but succeeds only in killing himself. Don calls upon Heaven for an explanation of his betrayal and, in a dialogue with God, who speaks with the voice of Copperhead Kelly, is finally made to realize that, though we must accept all of life, both good and bad, we ourselves have the personal responsibility for making the choice between right and wrong and, though we are all 'dirty', we are not all damned.

'But in the last days it shall come to pass,
'That the mountain of the house of the Lord
'Shall be established in the top of the mountains.'

Micah, Ch. IV, v.1.

PROLOGUE

(The curtain rises, disclosing a snow-filled valley. Pine trees mount the slopes to the rear toward the summit of a giant massif shaped like the head of a man. A broken road-sign hanging at an angle from a tilted pole reads – ENNERO. To one side, at the higher level, can be seen a bombed-out cemetery, its broken vaults and gravestones lying in grotesque attitudes amongst the tumbled earth and snow. On one of these vaults a mass of debris overhangs an alcove, masking the interior. To the other side, the ground appears to fall away toward the bottom of the valley, along which runs a road which crosses the stage. On one of the upturned tombstones, a hatless man in a British battledress is seated with his back to us. A broken stake bearing a British-type steel helmet and a scrap of torn paper is stuck in the ground close beside him, while on a wall above the road there is fixed some sort of memorial plaque with an inscription in Italian. Along the road a column of filthy and emaciated D.P.'s, of both sexes, is slowly plodding its way through the slush. Some are pushing small handcarts displaying Italian flags. Others stagger under sacks of loot. Some wear the striped uniforms of the concentration camps.)

THE D.P.'S   Lang ist der weg und veery
Zur Heimat da prigione.
Gebrochen zu der Brenner ziehn –
Gefangen, perduti – nichts persone.
Dort Sammelt sich der grosse Hauf
Mit passi sanguinosi
Sporchi und spaccati we trudge
La via dolorosa.

(As the D.P.'s thin out and disappear down the road they disclose an American truck halted on the road with a steaming radiator. At the wheel is a stout, good-humoured American sergeant, Abe Goldberg, wearing a very long woollen scarf and a woollen cap

*with the brim turned up at the front. Four allied officers –
members of an Inter-allied Graves Identification Mission – are
in the vehicle. The leader is* MAJOR MARK LYON *of the U.S. Army
Medical Corps. The others consist of* CAPTAIN THE REVEREND
LUCIUS BULL, *an English Padre,* CAPTAIN FATHER MATTEO
ANGELINO, *an Italian Priest and* LIEUTENANT JEAN L'AIGLON *of the
Free French Army.*)

L'AIGLON.   Pourquoi l'arrêt?

ANGELINO.   Perché questa fermata?

GOLDBERG *(gruff).*
             Can't you see the kettle's boiling?

LYON.   But the view's O.K.
             We must be in the saddle of the Pass.

BULL.   A saddle fit for centaurs.
             And a graveyard, too.

L'AIGLON *(pointing).*
             Les tombeaux! Voici la dessus.

LYON.   Let us get down and stretch our legs.
             Maybe there are soldiers buried here.
(He and Angelino dismount.)

BULL.   What is that writing on the wall?

LYON.   Some sort of a plaque.

ANGELINO.   Iscritto — Italiano.

LYON.   Can you read it, Father Angelino?
             An inscription – to an Unknown War, I think.

BULL.   La via dove.
             What kind of bird is that?

ANGELINO.   No, no, no.
             It is not pronounced that way.
(Reading.)

             SIA SACRA,
             AGLI ITALIANI
             LA VIA DOVE PASSARONO
             I FANTI

L'AIGLON.   Translate, if you please.

ANGELINO.   It means, my dear L'Aiglon,
That we have crossed the Brenner
And are now in Sunny Italy.

(*The others dismount with the exception of* ABE GOLDBERG, *who lights a cigar.*)

BULL (*dismounting*).
I should have brought a thicker overcoat.
For May in Sunny Italy.

QUARTET.   A May day. A May day.
Chill as the Pleiades
High in the Brenner
Chatters a noontide
Under its shroud.
Falcon and vulture
Lazily circling
Far in the panoply
Over this couch
Of the dark and the dead.
M'aidez! M'aidez!
Silent the snow
On the steps of the altar.
Deep in the pinewoods
Poltergeist – partisan
Whisper a question
That hangs in the air.

LYON.   It might be West Cummington and the road to the
Berkshires.
Lord! I wish I were home.

L'AIGLON (*to the seated figure*).
Tell me, my man,
Who bombed God's acre here,
And why?

DON (*the Man*).
(*without turning around*)
How are the dead raised up?
And with what body are they come?

L'AIGLON. An enigmatic answer.
(*To* BULL) Your man, I think, cher Bull.

BULL (*to* DON).
An Englishman.
Don't you know, fellow,
How to address an officer?

LYON. What does it matter, Lucius?
The war is over,
Or will be in a day or two.

BULL. Is this then the final victory,
When tombs must open
And the dead shall rise again?

L'AIGLON. A resurrection manque!
Poor bodies. They must have dreamt they heard the
trumpet.

ANGELINO. A premature salute on Gabriel's bugle!

L'AIGLON. Ah, zut alors! Why should they sleep till Doomsday.

BULL (*laughing*).
Sewn in corruption, and raised in glory.
Here are the first fruits of them that sleep.

(*All three join in the laughter.*)

LYON (*somewhat upset by this irreverence*).
Gentlemen, gentlemen!
We are here to find and catalogue our valiant dead,
Not to make sport of Holy Scripture.

BULL (*embarrassed*).
Yes, yes. You are perfectly right.

ANGELINO. It needed a layman to remind us!

L'AIGLON. Suppose we get on with the job.
There is a soldier's grave.

(*He approaches the stake beside the seated figure.*)

BULL. A recent burial, I think.

LYON (*taking out his notebook*).
Can you make out the name?

286

L'AIGLON. It's British.
A vous, mon Capitaine Taurus.

BULL. Hanwell, D.R.
Lance Corporal in the Buffs.

LYON (*writing*).
The Buffs?

BULL. The Royal West Kents.
A famous regiment.

(GOLDBERG *looks up from his own thoughts and presently starts to get out of the truck.*)

LYON. And the religion, please?

BULL. It says here – Rationalist.

L'AIGLON (*laughing*).
An honest Englishman, at last!

ANGELINO. Basta, basta, signori!

Do not waste time,
I see a soldiers' cemetery in the hollow over there.
Let us go down and do our work
While the machine recovers from the boil.

LYON. Yes, gentlemen. This way, please.

(*To* GOLDBERG, *as he passes.*)

We'll be back in five minutes.

(*The four officers go off down the hill as* GOLDBERG *approaches the seated figure beside the grave.*)

THE D.P.'S (*in the distance*).
Lang ist der weg und veery
Zur Heimat da prigione.

GOLDBERG. Don Hanwell – of the Buffs.
That is a guy I knew once in the desert.
How come he's here?

DON (*turning*).
A small world.
It's a small world.

287

GOLDBERG. He was a nice guy when sober.
Fond of a jag, and sometimes free with other
    people's dough;
An easy-coming, easy-going, goddamn son-of-a-bitch
Playing a game of crooked crap,
With eyes that smiled away
The taste of angostura on his lips.
A book-toting, pixilated Limey
That couldn't pass a cathouse if he had the cash.
But all the same, I liked him.
He was a thin, blond character –
Like you.
I liked the crazy bastard.

DON. Hello, Abe.

GOLDBERG. Yeah, he sure was like you.
He looked like you,
And by Christ, he sounded like you.
I guess too he WAS you.

DON. How are you doing, Abe?

GOLDBERG. He knows my name.
Abe Goldberg – PFC
When first we was together in the Middle East.
Now Master Sergeant, with a Purple Heart.

DON. Where do you hang it?

GOLDBERG. On my arse, bud.
What d'ya expect?

(offering his hand)

You goddamn son-of-a-bitch,
I'm glad to see you.

DON *(taking his hand)*.
Still carting gypsum for the birdmen?

GOLDBERG. Nix on that.
Now I'm a master cabby for a bunch
Of International Morticians
Riding around looking for graves.
As for you, old pal,
What's this about being dead?

DON (*indicating the grave*).
>> Read what it says.

GOLDBERG (*reading the paper on the stake*).
>> Hanwell, D. R. – Rationalist.
>> Yeah, that's you all right.
>> Gee, it must be tough being dead.

DON.
>> Here at the top of the Pass
>> To have been canonized by death,
>> Dead in my prime
>> At the summit of the Brenner!

GOLDBERG (*sceptically*).
>> No kidding.
>> How does it feel?

DON.
>> Here beyond the grasp of those two dismal sirens
>> Excuse and Explanation,
>> Safe in a womb that will not drive me forth in
>>> nine months time,
>> I am a spirit,
>> Infinite, eternal and unchangeable,
>> And this the New Testament in my blood.

>> I shall not live to be a burden unto all my dear ones,
>> Nor disappoint my children with the no's of
>>> parenthood.
>> I shall not live to be a bore in all the clubs,
>> Nor the worst of these – the fellow
>> With something on his mind.

>> Not for me the queues, the questionnaires,
>> The threats of lawyers and inspectors.
>> Not for me the potbelly and the gobs,
>> That creep on others in the evening of their days
>> And stay to mock them in the looking glass.

>> Maybe for you, but not for me
>> The contribution to the spring sowing
>> Of the next field of dragon's teeth.
>> High in the noontide of my days
>> Far from the interchange of tide and planets,
>> I have put on eternity.
>> So do not presume to grieve for me.

GOLDBERG.   Sure Don, sure.
You're as dead as mutton and live as lamb.
But kidding aside,
What's it in aid of?
This resurrection racket has been worked before.

DON.   High in the hills I died.
And yet, I did not die.
Yet there was one who fell and lies below.
No contradiction here, only a miracle.
Don't you understand, Abe?

GOLDBERG.   I liked you better back in Palestine –
Those days we trucked the gypsum from the
    Dead Sea
Back to the base at Lydda.

DON.   In that vulva of the Earth,
There was a voice that set us on our way.
Didn't you hear it, too?

GOLDBERG.   Boy, there was nothing to hear down there
Except the sound of silence.
Not a bird in the air, not a breaker on the beach,
Not a bleat from a Beddo's goat.
Nothing but salt – salt and gypsum.
Great pillars of it, standing there like Lot's wife
Looking back at the Cities of the Plain.

(The scene slowly changes to the headwaters of the Dead Sea. The truck remains where it was, with the two men seated in it, but the white snow-clad mountains change into cliffs of salt, with the barren shore of a dull grey lake in the background. To one side, what had previously been the buttress of the vault now assumes the appearance of the ghostly statue of a giant woman, gazing out across the waters. For a moment there is silence.)

SCENE 1 – THE JORDAN

GOLDBERG.   Wogs! Wogs! Where the hell are them
friggin' wogs?

(From one side comes a train of eight Bedouins carrying sacks of gypsum. They are singing a popular song, and all seem supremely amused. They are ragged and dirty, but have an air of child-like levity that seems oddly at variance with their condition of obvious poverty. They are scrofulous but basically a happy bunch, swinging readily from smiles and laughter at one moment into extremes of passionate emotion at the next.

The light has that yellow quality of early morning in the desert and comes from a low angle at the start of the scene, casting long shadows that shorten as the sun rises.)

DON.   Have you got the cash?

GOLDBERG.   Yeah. But you'd better do the talking.

DON *(to the leader)*.
Hi, George. That for us?

LEADER.   Gypsum. One pound and half each sack.

DON *(climbing out of the truck)*.
Let me take a shuftie.
One pound on each is all you'll get.

LEADER.   One pound and half. Very good.
Very cheap. Quais ketir.

DON.   Maalish. One pound is what it costs
And what you'll get.

LEADER.   One pound and quarter.

DON.   One pound. Take it, or push off.
Yella!

A MUEZZIN *(chanting in the distance)*.
ALLAHU AKBARU. ALLAHU AKBARU.

291

LEADER.   Aw ri. One pound.

(GOLDBERG *climbs out of the truck, pulling out a roll of paper money which he hands to Don.*)

GOLDBERG.   Tell them to throw it in the truck.

DON.   Into the lorry, George.

LEADER.   No load lorry. That cost more.

DON (*waving the money in his face*).
              Filoos. Filoos.

LEADER.   Baksheesh.

THE ARABS (*excitedly*).
              Baksheesh. Baksheesh.

DON (*acting tough*).
              Mafeesh baksheesh.

THE LEADER.   No baksheesh, no load lorry.

(*Shouts of agreement.*)

DON.   Ah stanna shwaya.
              Take it easy.

GOLDBERG.   Then dump it there, you sons-of-bitches,
              And we'll load it ourselves.
              But look in each sack before you pay him.

(*As each sack is brought forward and dumped, DON looks inside and pays a simple bill on each to the leaders, singing sardonically as he does so.*)

DON.   Oh we're just black bastards
              But we do love our King,
(*sack*)
              Every night at the flicks
              You can hear the buggers sing;
(*sack*)
              From Sollum to Tobruk
              Quais ketir, Bab-el-Louk,
(*sack*)
              Oh you can't fuck Farida
              If you don't pay Farouk.
(*sack*)

GOLDBERG.   Boy, but that sure is a song
                    To end the British Empire.

DON.   It's wasted on them.
                    They think it's the Wog National Anthem
                    Sung in English.

                    Oh this is the song
                    That you've heard the Gyppos sing,

(sack)

                    And we'd sing just the same
                    If we'd Rommel for a king.

(sack)

                    You may have a tarboosh,
                    A gamel a gamoos,

(sack)

                    But you can't fuck Farida
                    If you've got no filoos.

(sack)

(Chattering and laughing the Beddoes move off quickly, grabbing the money from their leader. ABE *throws them a couple of packs of cigarettes, which they seize upon with many ingratiating nods as they go.)*

DON.   Let's get this stuff loaded before the sun gets high.

GOLDBERG *(as they start to load the sacks into the truck).*
                    Gee, but I like it here this hour of day.
                    Look at the light catching that tower
                    Up on the skyline.
                    Do you know what that is, Don?
                    Jerusalem.

DON.   Jerusalem!
                    It's a Yank Y.M.C.A.?
                    Is that what you mean by Jerusalem?

GOLDBERG.   I guess you don't appreciate this country, Don.
                    Your taste's peculiar.

DON.   Here is a graveyard, Yank –
            A rubbish heap of tombs and cemeteries
            Of phony promises and empty skies –
            The greatest fraud the world has ever known.
            There's nothing here –
            Nothing – nothing – nothing

GOLDBERG.   Little you know what's here –
            Up in the caves above the Lake –
            Under the waters of that Asphalt Sea.

DON.   The Garden of Eden, I suppose?
            Don't kid yourself.
            If anything is there
            It's only Sodom or Gomorrah.
            Take your choice.

GOLDBERG.   Would you like to bet on that?

DON.   What are we doing here – fighting for a boneyard,
            A strip of sand and seaweed?
            Let Rommel have it.
            Who else wants it?

GOLDBERG (*thoughtfully*).
            I guess we want it.
            This is my country,
            My promised land.

DON.   You can have it.

GOLDBERG.   Maybe we will have it – some of these days.
            Down there, on the beach,
            There are Jews – like me.
            See over there – those boys and girls
            Working the potash.
            Some day there'll be more.

DON.   Sticking up factories and restaurants.
            Now I know what the Sphinx is smiling at . . .
            My pal – the new Crusader.

GOLDBERG.   I'm no crusader.
            But I guess I know why I'm in this war.

294

DON. You're in it like me –
Because you were pushed into it.
My God, why can't you fellows act your age?
Don't talk to me of Right and Wrong.
We're all right and we're all wrong.
I'll tell you my war aims, buddy –
To sit out the rest of it
In a comfortable prison camp.
That's for me.
I took the Blitz and I can take that, too.

GOLDBERG. Brother, you're as loaded as that truck.
Come on, let's take a look at the Jordan before
we go.

DON. I've seen the Jordan – what there is of it,
besides the mud.
Once is enough.
It's over there. Those potash kids will show
you where.

GOLDBERG. I guess I'll take a look.

DON. Careful you don't get baptised.
I'm for a simple can of beer . . .

(GOLDBERG *laughs and goes off.* DON *pries open a beer can.*)

DON (*calling after him*).
. . . and watch the skies for doves descending.
You know what birds can do.

(*Presently the Pillar of Salt comes to life.*)

THE SALT WOMAN.
This is my beloved son . . .

DON (*looking up*).
Christ! Was that a dove?

SALT WOMAN. . . . beloved son.

DON. A bird over the Dead Sea.
No! No!
No feathers in this Earth's arsehole.

SALT WOMAN. This is my beloved son . . .

DON.   . . . in whom you are not at all well pleased.
That's what my mother used to say.
Where are you, lady?

(he notices the pillar)

Blimey, it's you!
A fine figure of a woman.

SALT WOMAN. Vox clamantis in deserto
Parate via domini rectas.

DON.   Can't you speak English, ma'am?
I never learnt that Double Dutch.
I'm a secular type.

SALT WOMAN. Whom shall I send?
And who will go for me?
Who will go down into Egypt,
And fetch the pearl
That we have lost in Eden?

DON.   That's better, ma'am.
I'm just a Veteran of Foreign Bars,
Whole overseas and half seas over,
Cheek by the Arab and jowl by the Jew,
Under the harrow and over the worm.
Suppose we introduce ourselves?
I am the grin on the face of the Sphinx.

SALT WOMAN. I am a prayer in the mouth of Eurydice.

DON.   I am a dog in the blessed manger.

SALT WOMAN. I am a ballad of good counsel.

DON.   I am the waste places of Jerusalem.

SALT WOMAN. I am the shadow of a staff in a weary land.

DON.   I am a traveller on the road to the hills.

SALT WOMAN. I am a salt tear in the eye of the sun.

DON.   I am the lost son of my mother.

SALT WOMAN. I am the lost rib of my husbandman.

DON.   I am the hungry generations.

SALT WOMAN. I am the seed for the sower.

DON. I am the fast riding dead.

SALT WOMAN. I am the voice of one crying in the wilderness.

DON. I am data.

SALT WOMAN. I am errata.

DON. I know you, Mrs Lot.
They left you here when you were naughty.
Like all the girls,
You had to take a peek in the wrong direction.
What were you looking for? – I've often wondered.

SALT WOMAN. Only a pearl.
Will you find it for me?

DON. Why pick on me?

SALT WOMAN. The pearl of innocence.

DON. Innocence?

SALT WOMAN. When you were a little child
And dwelling in the pleasures of your father's
house,
From the West your parents sent you forth
Bearing your load unaided.
And they girded you with adamant
That is not crushed by iron
And wrote their promise on your heart,
That it should not be forgotten.
'If you will go out into the Wilderness
And find the pearl your parents threw away,
Then you may put on your bright robe
And, with your brother who has gone before,
Be heir in our kingdom.'

DON. If that's an offer, it's a fair one, ma'am.
What do I get for wearing out my feet of clay?

SALT WOMAN. An answer.

DON. Death's the only answer in the end.

297

SALT WOMAN. No, my son.
                    Death is not the answer
                    Unless you carry a weapon.
                    That is all that is forbidden.

DON.   A weapon? Who needs a gun?
                    They only get a soldier into trouble.

SALT WOMAN (*emotionally*).
                    O my son! Remember that!
                    By the weapon that you carry you will
                        meet your end.

DON.   Don't worry, ma'am. I've got no gun.
                    So tell me, gypsy lady,
                    What's in my hand?
                    You read them?

SALT WOMAN (*reading his hand*).
                    Over earth. Over fire.
                    Over air. Over water.
                    To a summit – from a depth
                    Where all is white
                    To where it shall be white again.

DON.   And how will I know when I'm there?

SALT WOMAN. By the dove, my son. By the dove.
                    At the end of your journey you will find a dove.

DON (*disgusted*).
                    I'll get the bird!
                    I know what that involves.
                    Still, maybe we'd better get started.
                    Can't frig around here all the day.

(*He goes to the truck and blows the horn.*)

SALT WOMAN. Facite in solitudine semitam domini nostri.

(*From the direction of the Dead Sea,* ABE *approaches, leading a train of young Jewish workers of both sexes. They are dressed in denims; some carry picks and shovels, singing as they slowly advance.*)

GOLDBERG.   Shir hamaalot;
               B'shuv adonay et shivat tziyon
               Hayinu k'cholmin.
               Oz yimoe s'chok pinu
               Ul'shonenu rino.

CHORUS.   Oz yomru vagoyim
               Higdil adonay la'asot im ele,
               Higdil adonay la'asot immonu
               Hayinu s'mechim.

DON (*turning from trying to crank the engine*).
               Aw, put a sock in it, you Yids!
               Am I supposed to have the gift of tongues?

(*The* SALT WOMAN *makes a gesture before stiffening into rigidity,
and the chorus immediately becomes intelligible.*)

CHORUS.   Turn, O God our exile,
               As waters in the dry land,
               And they that sow in tears
               In joy shall reap.

A MUEZZIN (*in the distance*).
               Rise up to prayer. God is most great.
               There is no God but God,
               And Mohammed is his messenger.

DON.   Thanks, lady, thanks for the translation.

(*He starts the engine with a roar, and climbs to his seat with*
GOLDBERG. *When the initial sound dies down we hear the*
BEDOUINS *and the* JEWS *in the distance.*)

CHORUS.   Though on his way weeping he goes,
               He shall come home with ringing cry,
               Bearing his sheaves with sounds of joy.

BEDOUINS (*in the distance*).
               In the name of the merciful, the compassionate
               Lord of three worlds and of the Day of Fate
               For all our sins we ask remission,
               And for our service,
               Your commission.

299

CHORUS. Bearing his sheaves with ringing cry!

(The scene fades as the truck starts to move with a wave of the hands from the occupants.)

SALT WOMAN *(joyfully)*.
Now the springing plough is upon the hill,
And youth on the slopes receives the Sacrament
That sears the furrow on the brows of men.

SCENE 2 – THE NILE

(The scene changes to the Libyan desert. A hot, brown expanse at the end of a hot, brown Christmas Day. Centre is a war-scarred triumphal arch defaced by inscriptions in smeary white paint — DUCE! AVANTI!! VINCERE!!! W IL 1924. To one side a stunted tree is hung with old cans and rags. To the other side appears the nose of a Sherman tank. Twelve soldiers are engaged in various chores. They include three Italian prisoners who are cooking on a stove made from a large can. A British sergeant, in command, is pulling up old German traffic signs – ARMEE NACHRICHTEN LAGER — HY — BAD UNTER-SUCH STELLE — and hammering in new ones in English — TAC 35 — MINES. KEEP OUT. WHO'S YOUR HITCH HIKER? Two artillerymen are sponging the muzzle of the tank's gun. A medical orderly is going through a pile of German haver-sacks and pocketing a selection of the contents. A sapper is brewing tea. A signalman fiddles with a wireless receiver. Another is washing his socks in a basin, and hanging them to dry like decorations on the tree. A red-headed Irishman of ingratiating but insincere affability is writing a letter on a sheet of V Mail. A Highlander in battle dress is playing the pipes. It is evening, and the scene changes to moonlight as it proceeds.)

ANDY *(the Highlander)*.
The Caesars were a randy crew
Ye ken the story o'm.
They tauld this tale tae Goy and Jew
That a' roads lead tae Rome.

300

But for a' the havering o' the runts
An' the bletherin' blarney o'm
We hear the same frae a' oor fronts
There's nae road leads tae Rome.

COPPERHEAD KELLY (*the Irishman*).

(*petulantly*)

Ah, will ye dry up!

LITTLE JIM CLAP (*Medical Orderly*).
Put a sock it it, Andy.
Give us a bit o' quiet for Christmas.

PEEPER JOHNNY (*First Artilleryman*).
A hot, brown No-el. Coo!

TOM TOSSER (*the tea-maker*).

(*indicating the sock-washer*)

While shepherds wash their socks by night.
Hey, Simple Simon,
Whatcher want with them?
Are you expecting Santa Claus?

SIMPLE SIMON.
My feet are giving me hell.

SERGEANT PETE.
Rommel is what your crimps will get –
Not Santa Claus.
Been 'ere before, at Marble Arch,
And got a bloody nose from Rommel,
That old fox.

LITTLE JIM.
Pete was a copper back in Civvy Street.
A blue look-out, 'e was.

(*Laughter*).

PHIL (*the Signalman*).
This time we've won a victory,
So Monty says.

JIM GUNNER (*Second Artilleryman*).
To 'ell wiv 'im.

301

SIMPLE SIMON.
I've 'ad this fuckin' war.

TOM TOSSER. A nice P.W. job –
I'd buy it like a shot.
Look at them bleedin' Eyties, cookin' chow.
For them the war is over;
For us, nothing but blood and shit.

BARTOLOMEO, GUIDO, TADDEO *(Italian prisoners).*
Grazie, grazie.
Mussolini kaput.
Long way to Tipp-ar-rrarie, eh?

TOM TOSSER. A 'ell of a long way, Bart-ollow-meo
I've arf a mind to clip you one.

ITALIANS *(not understanding).*
Molto grazie.
Sigaretto
Amico

(Each shakes his own hands over his head and smiles.)

SERGEANT PETE.
Leave 'em be, Tosser.
They'll be Our Gallant Allies in a month or two.
Just wait an' see.

PEEPER JOHNNY.
Where's our B Echelon?
We're out of ammo, an' we want some fags.

TOM TOSSER *(throwing him a packet).*
'Ere, Gunner. 'Ave a V for Victory.

PEEPER JOHNNY.
'Oo smokes this camel dung?

LITTLE JIM. 'Ow's the war doin', Phil. Any news in the paper?

PHIL. Another SNAFU in Algeria
But here it says 'The Spirit of the Eighth
Is simply fine.'

LITTLE JIM. Aw, shit. I meant the Russians.

JIM GUNNER. That's right. 'Ow's Uncle Joe?

PHIL (*turning over the page*).
　　　　　The P.M.'s made another speech.

TOM TOSSER. Winnie's a wet.

JIM GUNNER. An' so is Monty if yer asking me.

ANDY. Oh, we've had two Heiland laddies.
　　　Now we've got two Irish paddies.

ALL (*in unison, except* COPPERHEAD).
　　　An' they aint no effin' good
　　　For the Eighth Arm-ee.

COPPERHEAD KELLY.
　　　Ah, divil take your blather!
　　　You've made me spoil me letter.

TOM TOSSER. Keep it down, boys.
　　　Copperhead Kelly's writin' 'ome.

PHIL. Read it to us, Copperhead.
　　　Your picture of the Desert Rats.

COPPERHEAD KELLY.
　　　Dear Mother, dear Mother
　　　I'm writing to say . . .

ALL. Down along, down along,
　　　Derry down day.

COPPERHEAD KELLY.
　　　The Hun's on the run
　　　And I'm now on my way . . .

ALL. With Jim Gunner, Peeper Johnny,
　　　Old Andy the Arse'ole . . .
　　　Simple Simon, Tom Tosser . . .
　　　Jim Clap, Phil the Po . . .
　　　Three Roman sopranos . . .
　　　A morte fascisti . . .
　　　An' Peter, the pride of them all . . .
　　　An' Sergeant Pete Fisher an' all.

(*Laughter and applause.*)

303

COPPERHEAD. Do youse want to hear it, or do youse not?

(DON HANWELL *appears, escorting* OTTO SUDER, *a soldier in the uniform of the Afrika Korps.*)

JIM GUNNER. Well if it aint 'Anwell, the Don R.

SERGEANT PETE.
　　　　　Where you been, Despatch Rider?

PEEPER JOHNNY.
　　　　　Seen our lorry anywhere?

DON.　　　Sorry, fellows. No fags, no coffee.
　　　　　Your truck has had it.

PEEPER JOHNNY.
　　　　　The 'ell it 'as.

SERGEANT PETE.
　　　　　Wot 'appened?

TOM TOSSER. 'Oo's yer Narzie friend?

DON.　　　Here was this fellow in a rozzer's cap,
　　　　　Cool as bedamned, standing on a crossroad
　　　　　Like it was Oxford Circus,
　　　　　Directing all our traffic up a detour
　　　　　On to a minefield.

(*Laughter.*)

LITTLE JIM.　Well, aint 'e a caution!

DON.　　　Blew the tracks off seven Shermans
　　　　　Before we got him.
　　　　　Clobbered a squad of Free French.

TOM TOSSER. Bet that scared the Froggies.
　　　　　Good for 'im, I say.

(*Sounds of agreement.*)

SERGEANT PETE.
　　　　　What 'appened then?

DON.　　　They sent me back on the motorbike to look for
　　　　　　　tires,
　　　　　And dump him in a cage.

SIMPLE SIMON.
    Should 'av plugged the blighter full of 'oles.
    Let's do it now.

SERGEANT PETE.
    Ah stanna schwire.
    'E's only doin' 'is job.

PEEPER JOHNNY.
    Dontcher know there's a war on?

SERGEANT PETE.
    Hey, wop. Spaghetti for the 'Un.

ITALIANS.   No food for 'im.
    Tedeschi, 'ee no good.

SERGEANT PETE.
    Give the man chow, Toddy.
    That's an order.

(*Grumbling, the three Italians hand over a plate of food.* SUDER *takes it in some surprise, and starts to eat.*)

SUDER.   Danke sehr.

DON.   What's to be done with him?
    It's not my job – escorting prisoners.

SERGEANT PETE.
    That's your 'eadache, not ours, thank Gawd.

PEEPER JOHNNY.
    Well, if the truck 'as bought it
    We may as well doss down.

LITTLE JIM.   'Ow about it, Phil?
    Our good-night song.

(PHIL *fiddles with his receiver, which presently lights up.*)

RADIO.   ... wishing you all a brisk good morning from
    the Pacific Service ...

PEEPER JOHNNY.
    Ah, cut it out.

TOSSER.   'Oo wants the B.B.C.?

LITTLE JIM.   Get us Marlene.

(As the radio breaks in on the Belgrade transmission, the men proceed to settle down for the night.)

RADIO *(a woman's voice).*
>   . . . ein Leid geschehn,
>   Wer wird bei der Laterne stehn?
>   Mit dir Lili Marlene,
>   Mit dir Lili Marlene.

TOM TOSSER. 'Ow's that for a nice bedroom voice?

(As the music of the song concludes, all curl up in the moonlight except DON *and* SUDER.*)*

SUDER.   One woman singing three nations to their sleep.
            It is a strange world we live in.

DON.   And a crazier war.

SUDER.   But do not fear the New Order, my friend.
            The Führer knows how much we owe to you
            And what we still must learn.

DON.   You learn from us?

SUDER.   You heard that silly song.
            It is ours, not yours.
            We Germans sing of lonely soldiers
            And dream of home.
            Your poets sing of Empire
            And of lesser breeds without the law.
            Those sentimental lullabies are ours, not yours.

DON.   'Wish me luck when you wave me goodbye.'
            That's what our doxies sing.
            A Land of Hope and Theory.

SUDER.   We Germans have no hatred for your country.
            We have so much in common.
            Why do you fight us?

DON.   Common!
            I'm glad you call it that. Fight!
            So far, we've hung no washing on your
                Siegfried Line.

306

SUDER (*rising*).
>We should not fight.
>And so, perhaps,
>I go.

DON.
>Go?
>Go where?

SUDER.
>Back into the desert.

DON.
>You can't do that.
>You're a prisoner.

SUDER.
>We're both prisoners of a stupid situation,
>Expected to kill each other for reasons most absurd.
>But you and I know better.
>And so I think you will not stop me
>If I go.

DON.
>Don't be too sure.

SUDER.
>With what will you stop me?
>I do not think you have a gun.

DON.
>No. I have no gun.
>She said I mustn't carry one.

SUDER.
>Who said this?

DON.
>A salt lady by a sea that cannot drown.
>So now I'm a soldier that cannot shoot.
>It makes a sort of sense to me.
>A man dies, she said, by what he carries.

SUDER.
>So if I go, you cannot shoot.

DON.
>I might shout
>And wake one of those twelve Apostles over there.
>Some of them shoot all right.

SUDER.
>I think not.
>They are your friends and you are an Englishman.
>And I have noticed that the English
>Are much more interested in their enemies
>Than in their friends.
>It is something that I like about your country

But do not understand.
And so good bye, my enemy.
We will meet, I hope, in the New Order.

(*He stands hesitantly, looking back at* DON. *In the distance the sound of men's voices is heard.*)

CHORUS.   In der lybischen Wüste die Fünfte einst stand
Die Fahrzeug' begraben die Schnauze im Sand.

SUDER (*softly*).
The song of the Afrika Korps.

CHORUS.   Sie sprachen von Deutschland, von Bier und von
Wein
In der lybischen Wüste da gibt es kein.

(DON *turns to the radio and switches it on. A woman's voice breaks in.*)

THE ANNOUNCER.
. . . wishing you all in the Forces wherever you may be a pleasant good morning from the Overseas Service. Our first recording is from Mrs Gladys Crumb for her son, Sapper Crumb, in the Far East.

DON (*turning off the radio*).
Aw, to hell with that crap!

(SUDER *turns and walks away.* DON *stares after him for a moment, and then lies down to sleep.*)

DON.   You can go.

CHORUS (*continuing*).
Fahr mich nach Neapel, nach Rom und nach Hause
Da gibt es Bier, auch Wein und auch Brause.
Der Sandsturm ist trocken, die Sonne brennt heiss,
Und das Mädel in der Heimat von allem nichts
weiss.

(*The curtain falls.*)

SCENE 3 – The Sangro

(To begin with, the stage is dark.)

ANDY.　　　　　But noo ye'll hear the pipers play
　　　　　　　　Afore St Peter's dome,
　　　　　　　　While Scotland tells the world today
　　　　　　　　That 'Ooer road led tae Rome.

(The effect of a moving panorama. DON is on the forestage, covered with dust and oil. His uniform has degenerated since desert days and but for his British helmet it would be difficult to identify the force to which he belongs.)

DON.　　　　　The wind has blown us onwards from the
　　　　　　　　　sands of Alamein –
　　　　　　　　On from the sunbaked Shermans, leaguered
　　　　　　　　　when daylight fades –
　　　　　　　　From runners and wrecks, sunk to their bellies
　　　　　　　　　in the shale,
　　　　　　　　And rusty Dannaert wire along the Barrel Track.

TOM TOSSER.　Hit 'em for six!
　　　　　　　　Good hunting to you all.

DON.　　　　　Out of Bizerta through the wine-dark sea,
　　　　　　　　We sent them reeling.

CHORUS.　　　Colpite duro.

THE TWELVE.

　　　　　　　　Garibaldi's friends.

DON.　　　　　From Syracuse and Gela –

CHORUS.　　　Kilo five fifty-five –

DON.　　　　　Through olive orchards on the heights of Etna
　　　　　　　　To where the grass grows green
　　　　　　　　Under Apulian pines

CHORUS.   Kilo three hundred

THE TWELVE.   Dichiarate tutti

CHORUS.   Zivilbevölkerung ist verboten!

DON.   Across the bloody Sangro
                        Over Cassino and into Anzio

CHORUS.   Labore! Duce! Vincere!
                        Kilo fifteen – kilo eleven – kilo five
                        La Porta Maggiore! !
                        Roma! Roma! Roma!

SCENE 4 – THE TIBER

(Flashing lights and the sound of motor horns and traffic. The arch reappears, in the guise of the Porta Maggiore. Beneath the outline of the dome of St. Peter's, a statue is dimly illuminated. Presently we see that it is Michelangelo's PIETA. *People pass and repass, amongst them the three ex-prisoners of the previous scene, together with the rest of the Twelve, under the leadership of* PETE.)

VARIOUS VOICES.
                        You wanta nice girl, Tommee?
                        I got plenty here.
                        Sigaretto please. Biscotti.
                        Tedeschi kaput.

PIETA.   E tu mammina cara
                        Pensi sempre al tuo Figliol.

(DON *meets* COPPERHEAD KELLY, *who greets him warmly.*)

COPPERHEAD KELLY.
                        Caed mile failte, Donnach!

VARIOUS VOICES.
                        I take you catacombs – Arco Triompho –
                        Il Papa – Red 'ot Mama – Santa Pieta.
                        Postcards – Holy medals.

COPPERHEAD KELLY.

> I never thought the day would come
> We'd meet in Rome.

DON. Hello, Copperhead

COPPERHEAD KELLY (*taking his arm*).

> My old segotioner – I know ye well.
> You let that fella go at Marble Arch.
> I saw you – but I never breathed a word,
> now did I?

DON (*disengaging himself*).

> I wouldn't have him mix with runts like you.

COPPERHEAD. Oh, there's a thing to say about your friends.

VARIOUS VOICES.

> Clean whoreshops thisa way
> Americano prophylactic very handy.
> You coma to this address and see
> A spectacle you never saw before.

DON.

> This is a happy day for everyone.
> Bring on my friends and let us drink to victory –
> The thief, the pederast, the exhibitionist,
> The public nuisance and the crooked cop,
> The voyeur and the postcard king,
> The worshipper of underclothes,
> Three pimps,
> And you – Copperhead Kelly, who never would
> betray a pal without a kiss –
> Together we have taken Rome.

COPPERHEAD. Ain't you the one for blarney!

> We have our little faults – I'll not deny.
> Who hasn't?
> But after all, we're on the right side, Don.
> Now aren't we?

DON. I don't know what that means.

COPPERHEAD (*seemingly angry*).

> The only thing that matters.
> But that's a queer soldier, now,
> Who doesn't know his enemies
> And never totes a gun.

GOLDBERG *(appearing).*
>Maybe you'll need one
>In the place we're heading for.

DON *(as* COPPERHEAD *disappears).*
>Why, Abe, you old bastard.
>It's good to see you.
>What are you doing here?

GOLDBERG.   Just looking round, I guess.

DON.   You'll never get a better chance at half the money.
>Come on in, Abe, and let me show you St. Peter's.

(Together they approach the PIETA, *who is now fully visible.)*

GOLDBERG.   I guess I won't.
>That lady at the door –

DON.   She's from your country, Abe.
>A fellow citizen.

GOLDBERG.   It's you she wants to talk to.

DON.   She doesn't talk.
>They only say she does.

GOLDBERG.   Oh, yeah?
>The strangest women seem to want to talk to you.

SCENE 5 – THE MEUSE

(As women's voices are heard in the background the lights change upon the statue, who now appears as a ragged D.P. clasping in her arms the emaciated body of a man in the striped uniform of the camps. He is dead. Other women D.P.'s surround her.)

WOMEN'S CHORUS.
> Rachel m'vaka al banecha
> Ki enenu

PIETA.
> Not seven sorrows is my load,
> But seven and seventy.
> Where is the grief to equal mine?

ABE.
> Speak to her, Don.

DON.
> Tell her to stop this whining.
> Others have died.
> We all must die –
> If not this way, then in another.
> Dry your eyes, woman.

PIETA.
> He thinks my tears are for the dead.

ABE.
> Tell him. Tell him.

PIETA.
> My tears are not for this, but for myself.
> I mourn the killing, and I mourn the damned.
> I mourn my people, and I mourn for you.
> This lament is for the living –
> Not for the dead.
> Who grieves for dust?
> This clay is not the thing I loved,
> Yet it is dearer far,
> Than what they made of him before he died.
> O desolation!
> What wretchedness can equal this –
> That he is better dead.

(*She has laid the body on the ground, and now approaches* DON.)

DON.
> War is war, dear lady. I'm sorry.

PIETA (*taking him by the hand*).
> Three things there are that must be opened –
> Two eyes that will not see,
> And a gate that will not yield.
> Come with me, my son.

SCENE 6 – THE RHINE

(The lights change again and we are in a forest, in the midst of which still stands the arch. But now it is surmounted by a black flag, and bears the inscription RECHTS ODER UNRECHTS – MEIN VATERLAND. It is closed by a grim, studded gateway on which a smaller notice reads JEDEM DAS SEINE.)

DON.
The mountains are struck with magic.
Where are we now?

PIETA.
Another milestone on your way.

DON.
Where's Rome?

ABE.
Brother, it's far behind.
We've passed the Côte d'Azur
And through Lorraine,
We're camping now amongst the Boche.

PIETA.
There is a gateway.
Open it.

ABE.
The name is Todenwald.

DON *(impatiently)*.
I've heard of Todenwald.
I've heard of Holloway,
And Alcatraz.

ABE.
I've been to Alcatraz,
And boy, this ain't it.

PIETA.
Open and see.

DON.
A concentration camp.
I know all about these places.
What's more, I know the boys who write them up.

PIETA.
Open the gate.

ABE.
He's not the curious type.
He doesn't want to take a look.

314

DON.　　　　　You think not?

(As he approaches the gate there is a shriek of terror, and a chorus of ragged women rushes on, and crouches to one side. They are followed by OTTO SUDER, *who stops before the gate.)*

SUDER *(politely).*
　　　　　Excuse please. You cannot pass this way.

DON.　　　　　Well, well! Otto Suder!
　　　　　My old pal – the enemy.
　　　　　Forgive me, Otto, if we don't fraternize today.
　　　　　I mustn't talk to you.
　　　　　Non-combatants at home don't like it.
　　　　　So YOU oblige my friends.
　　　　　And show them what's inside.

SUDER.　　　　I do not know what is inside
　　　　　Nor do I care to know.

DON.　　　　　Then let me open up.

SUDER.　　　　I'm sorry.
　　　　　My orders are to guard the gate.

DON *(with a laugh).*
　　　　　It MUST be grim.
　　　　　What does that welcome sign suggest?
　　　　　'Jedem das Seine.'

ABE.　　　　　'To each what is coming to him.'

PIETA.　　　　Open it. Open!

THE WOMEN.　Broken in pieces are the gates of malachite,
　　　　　And cut in sunder are the bars of steel.
　　　　　And the blind shall come forth from the Sepulchre
　　　　　And the dead from the house of tears.

*(*SUDER *draws a gun as* DON *makes another movement toward the gate.)*

DON.　　　　　Now, none of that.
　　　　　Listen, Suder, if there's nothing there . . .

315

SUDER (*shouting*)
> What's there is none of my business – nor of yours.
> My orders are to guard the gate.
> My duty must be done.

(*From the rear, he is hit smartly over the head, and falls in a daze. PETE appears.*)

SERGEANT PETE.
> England expects each man to do 'is dooty.

(*The remaining eleven of his companions emerge, fully armed.*)

JIM GUNNER. Wot's this?

TOM TOSSER. Another bloody clink.

LITTLE JIM (*opening up his haversack*).
> Let's liberate. I need a bit o' liberation.

ANDY.
> Nae one can pick a lock like Little Jim.

PEEPER JOHNNY.
> Don't wait to pick the lock.
> Blow the friggin' thing off.

(PETE *levels his rifle and fires at the gate. It creaks open ponderously, disclosing the end of a building. No one appears and for a moment there is silence, until from somewhere inside a thin wavering wailing starts, at first unintelligible, but gradually growing louder.*)

CHORUS. Heil! Heil! Viva! Viva!

PETE (*calling*).
> 'Oo's there?

TOM TOSSER. Coo! What a stink.

LITTLE JIM. There's someone there. I 'ear crying.

PHIL. Who's there?

TOM TOSSER. Sounds like a child. Come out, chum. Yer free.

CHORUS (*growing louder*).
> Heil! Heil!
> Viva! Viva!

PHIL. That's not crying. They're cheering something.

316

SIMPLE SIMON.
> Yer crazy. That's not cheering.

BARTOLOMEO.
> Viva-viva!
> You hear?

SERGEANT PETE.
> Come out, 'ooever you are.

LITTLE JIM.   Maybe they can't walk.

PHIL.   Then let's go in and carry them.

SERGEANT PETE.
> Come on.

(The wall of the house becomes transparent, disclosing row upon row of what appear to be shelves. From each of these, packed tightly together, thin twigs of arms wave feebly in the air. Here and there a skull-like face looks down with pits for eyes. The twelve soldiers disappear inside.)

CHORUS.   Heil! Heil!
> Viva! Viva!

DON.   Like twigs in a breeze.
> It IS cheering.
> What's it for?

ABE.   For us, I guess.
> Why don't you cheer them back?

(He moves to the gate, and as each soldier emerges carrying a limp bundle of dirty rags and bones, the scene assumes the semblance of some grotesque reception.)

ABE *(announcing).*
> His Honour, the Mayor of Prague.
> His Grace, the Lord Archbishop of Gran.
> Professor Ludvig Marwitz, faculty of Humane
> Letters, University of Heidelberg.
> And wife.
> Alois Mayer, Clockmaker of Mainz.
> Chaim Berkowitz, partisan of the
> Warsaw Ghetto.

317

DON (*stepping forward*).
>   Make them stop that dreadful cheering.

ABE.
>   Charles Ernest Joseph Leopold,
>   Grand Duke of Schwartzburg-Sonnderhausen-
>   Saxe-Altenburg.

DON.
>   Stop them cheering.

JIM GUNNER (*moving off with his load*).
>   Out of my way, soldier.
>   We're busy.

ABE.
>   Colonel Heinrich von der Hausen,
>   Suspect of Rastenburg.

CHORUS.
>   Viva! Viva! Viva!

ABE.
>   Rabbi Aaron Meshullam, Chacham of the late
>   community of Salonika.
>   His Excellency, Doctor Hermann Schindler,
>   Vice-Chancellor of the Austrian Republic.
>   Rachel Kaplan, a child.

(*The last of the Companions,* COPPERHEAD KELLY *brings up the rear with a piled wheelbarrow.*)

ABE.   What's this?

COPPERHEAD KELLY.
>   The heavy luggage.

(*He tips the wheelbarrow, and a flood of old boots and shoes comes tumbling down.*)

DON (*passionately*).
>   Where's Suder? I must find Suder.

COPPERHEAD KELLY (*abandoning the wheelbarrow and running to* DON *eagerly*).

>   He's on the Brocken.

DON.   What's that?

318

COPPERHEAD KELLY.

> A summit where the witches dance.
> Let's go.
> You'll find him there.

(The chorus of women, now in flying cloaks and witches hats, flourishing broom sticks, breaks into a wild dance around DON.)

ABE *(shouting).*

> Hey, give us a ride, someone.

THE WITCHES.

> The way is wide, the way is long.
> A crazy ride with a crazy throng.
> The pinchers pinch and the broomsticks tear.
> The children choke and the mothers swear.

COPPERHEAD KELLY.

> On we go, over stick and straw.
> As belch the witches, so farts the law.

(Screaming and dancing, they bear DON *along with them.)*

DON.   Where are you taking me?

COPPERHEAD KELLY.

> To the Last Assize.
> To Justice . . . a dream of a Midsummer Night.

CHORUS.   Peace with Honour.
> Smrt Fascismu.
> Sieg oder Siberien.
> Up the Rebels.
> Lend to defend the Right to be Free.
> With-Liberty-and-Justice-for-all.

COPPERHEAD KELLY.

> Make way for a witness –
> A gold-star witness –
> The witness for the Prosecution.

CHORUS.   Viva! Viva!

PIETA.   Testimony! Testimony!

CHORUS.   Viva! Viva!

SCENE 7 – THE WESER

(The lights change, disclosing the summit of the Brocken. The gate has become a prehistoric cromlech, on the top of which dangles a long white beard. The tree that was in the desert is now a twisted bush on which hang pistols, bayonets and a Mills bomb. The D.P.'s are sitting in rows applauding the dance of the Witches and Devils. In a stone dock we can see SUDER'S empty tunic, stuffed to represent a man, together with the SS helmet. COPPERHEAD, donning white gloves and a white MP helmet, takes his place behind the prisoner. On an outcrop of rock ABE takes his seat, where he is joined by the PIETA's DEAD MAN, who carries a sackfull of papers. The four officers of the first scene occupy the Press Box, where they record the proceedings in enormous notebooks.)

COPPERHEAD KELLY.
        Silence in the Court!
        The Court sits for the Last Assize.

(The dance concludes, and the Witches and Devils take their seats around the Jury Box. THE DEAD MAN rises.)

THE DEAD.   Your Honour, I am the Prosecution.
        And this, the Testimony.

(He empties piles of paper of all colours and sizes from the sack, mixed with old boots and shoes.)

CHORUS OF JURY AND M.P.'S (The Twelve).
        Sentence first and trial afterwards.

COPPERHEAD KELLY.
        Silence!

ABE *(rising).*
        Your Honour, I object.

CHORUS.   Objection overruled.

ABE *(rising).*
        Your Honour, for the record, may the Press
           hear the objection?

CHORUS.   No! Sentence first and trial afterwards.

ABE.   What kind of Court is this?
               Where's the Geneva Convention?

THE DEAD (*opening a book*).
               I quote Geneva, Mr Goldberg.
               The People versus Paul.
               What is man's first birthday gift under
                   the law?
               A sentence.
               The rest is trial.

(*Wild cheering*).

ABE.   Then the trial is a fraud.

THE DEAD.   Contempt of Court!

JURY.   Contempt. Contempt.
               Throw him in the dock.
               Sentence first and trial afterwards.

DON (*to* COPPERHEAD).
               Who's the Judge?
               Where is he?
               I see nobody.

COPPERHEAD KELLY (*indicating the cromlech*).
               Yes. That's him. Judge Nobadaddy.

ABE.   Contempt or not, this trial must be on
                   the level,
               Or who can take the rap for Todenwald?

THE DEAD.   Who allowed it?
               Ladies of the Jury,
               We stand appalled before the presence of
                   the Absolute.
               That Absolute is Todenwald.
               A crime against the Human Race.
               Not only those who made it,
               But those who have allowed it to be made,
               Must be condemned.

FULL CHORUS. Guilty. Guilty.
               Throw them in the dock.

L'AIGLON *(rising)*.
> Please, Your Honour, for the record may the
> > Press be told
> Who the Defendant is?

CHORUS.   Otto Suder.

BULL.   Is that the party in the dock?

(COPPERHEAD leans forward and peers under the empty helmet.)

COPPERHEAD KELLY.
> The face appears familiar.
> If it's not him, it's good enough.

(Applause. BULL *shrugs his shoulders and sits down.)*

ABE *(persisting)*.
> My client's case is not that he allowed
> > this crime,
> But that he did not know.
> My client says he did his duty.
> If, for not knowing, he gets it in the neck,
> Then all who did not know are guilty too.

JURY & M.P.'S.
> Guilty! Guilty!
> Sentence first and trial afterwards.

THE DEAD.   The argument is sound.
> And all these other parties to the charge.
> Amend the Affidavits,
> And let us start again.

(Amid applause, he tears up the Charge Sheet, and is presented with a great roll of paper, a copy of which he flings at ABE. *Amidst shouting and confusion, most of the onlookers are shepherded toward the dock.)*

VARIOUS VOICES.
> I object.
> I wasn't there at all.
> I'm not well.
> My brother is the Senator.
> This congestion is disgraceful.
> I was a Boy Scout.
> Save us, lady – save us.

COPPERHEAD KELLY (*struggling with the crowd*).
Silence! Silence!

THE DEAD.   Present or absent, all must be condemned.

ABE (*thumbing his way wildly through the papers*).
But this is crazy.
Half the human race!

THE DEAD.   Why not?
It's damned already.

PIETA (*intervening*).
No, no.
This is too much.
Not all the human race –
But as it was before.
One only.
One can stand here for all.

CHORUS.   Yes. One for all.
Otto Suder – Suder alone.

(*The crowd sweeps backwards from around the dock, exposing* DON, *who is behind it, alone.*)

DON.   This is a nightmare.
There's no one on the Bench,
And no one in the Dock.

(*He knocks over the empty tunic, and holds aloft the helmet. There is a long silence.*)

LYON.   He's right.
There's absolutely no one there.

ANGELINO.   Nessuno.

BULL.   The man's escaped again.

(*The wailing of the D.P.'s breaks out once more.*)

323

SCENE 8 – THE DANUBE

CHORUS.   Hoch! Hoch!
             Viva! Viva!

DON.   Stop! Stop that wailing!

CHORUS.   Who let him go?
             Who let him go?

COPPERHEAD KELLY.
             He let him go,
             He there.

(*All fingers point at* DON, *who stands alone.*)

DON (*distressed*).
                 Twigs in a breeze. Twigs in a breeze.
                 Why must I have this wailing in my ears?

COPPERHEAD KELLY (*insidiously*).
                 Is it because you are the guilty one?

ABE. (*indignantly*).
                 What's the man guilty of?
                 Didn't he set them free?

DON.   I set nothing free
             But corpses.

ABE.   Your righteous twelve broke down the gates.

DON.   That's true enough.
             Those thieves – those pimps – those queers
             On the side that happens to be right –
             They broke them down – not I.
             They did it well – not I.
             I deserve nothing.

CHORUS.   Guilty! Guilty!

COPPERHEAD KELLY (*smoothly*).
             No! Not yet,
             Since only he can find the one we want.

DON.   Find Suder?
        Why?

COPPERHEAD KELLY.
        You must kill him.

WHISPERS.   Kill. Kill. Kill.

DON.   What good will that do?

COPPERHEAD KELLY.
        For Todenwald there must be payment.

DON.   To whom?

COPPERHEAD KELLY (*pointing at the Prosecutor*).
        To him – the Dead.
        And . . .

(*He looks upwards, and then points again.*)

DON.   So I must do what Suder did?

COPPERHEAD KELLY.
        If you don't,
        It will all happen again.
        You must kill the killer.

DON (*passionately*).
        And who will kill the hangman?
        And tell me, where does guilt end?

PIETA.   Nowhere, my son – for all are guilty.
        But if Suder dies, God will forgive the others.
        That is the promise that I bring.
        That is the promise of forgiveness.

DON.   I'd like to sleep at night again.

THE DEAD.   Bring Suder back.
        And I will let you sleep.

(*He sinks to the ground.*)

DON.   Not only Todenwald is open now.
        So are my eyes.
        Give me a knife – a gun,
        And I shall do what must be done.

325

COPPERHEAD KELLY *(with a smile of triumph).*
> He needs a weapon.

(The PIETA *crosses to the tree and takes the Mills Bomb from its branches, which she gives to* DON.)

PIETA.   Go. Go, my husband! Go!

CHORUS.   Go. Go.

(He takes the bomb and stuffs it in his haversack. Sinking on the ground behind the prostrate Prosecutor, the PIETA *takes him in her arms, answering once again the posture of Michelangelo's Pieta.)*

SCENE 9 – THE INN

(The curtain rises once again on the Brenner Pass as in the Prologue, except that as yet there has been no appreciable bomb damage. The tombs stand intact, and as the dawn comes up we can see on the other side of the stage a truck with COPPERHEAD *at the wheel, and* DON *by his side. In the distance the singing of the D.P.'s is heard as they approach.*
To the side of the road a woman D.P. is brooding over the body of a dead man, who lies before her – almost naked. Her attitude is that of the Pieta, although her clothes are rags.)

D.P.'S.   A morte, a morte i traditori
                 Che hanno venduto il nostro onor'.

DON.   Whose singing is that?

COPPERHEAD KELLY.
> Only the D.P.'s.

*(*DON *has dismounted from the truck and is staring at the road sign.)*

DON.   Nothing but Italy ahead.
              The sun will soon be up.

COPPERHEAD KELLY.
> We're the first to top the pass.

326

D.P.'S.   E tu mammina cara,
           Pensi sempre al tuo Figliol.
           Sorridi e prega il Signor
           Che il tuo figliolo vive ancor!

DON.   Down the white road from Innsbruck I can
           see lights.

COPPERHEAD KELLY.
           That means the war is over.
           Sieg heil!

DON.   No! No! Not till we find a man.
           No peace with Suder in the hills.
           You said he would be here.

COPPERHEAD KELLY.
           He must be somewhere near.
           He can't go any further.

THE WOMAN. Se la miseria è il sale della vita
           Io sonno la moglie di Loth.

DON.   So you sing too, my lady,
           Like the others.
           But what's the song about?

COPPERHEAD KELLY.
           About Lot's wife –
           A lady that you met before,
           Beside the Salt Sea.

(He gets out of the truck and wanders away out of sight.)

DON.   Another Eve. A third, perhaps.
           I've come a long way from that Pillar of Salt
           Who was the first.
           I have crossed my rivers, lady,
           To end my business here.
           Is this your man?

THE WOMAN. Once I had a man.
           They took him from me into the mists of nowhere

327

	And gave me back – gave me back This thing.
DON.	Weep, woman, weep.
THE WOMAN.	I do weep. But not for him. But for what they made of him.
DON.	You shall not weep alone. I have an apple here. It's one your namesake gave me on the Brocken The night the witches danced.
THE WOMAN (in distress).	That's no apple. That is an evil thing. Spit it out. Throw it away.
DON.	Throw it away? Throw away my knowledge of Good and Ill? This thing is hard to come by, And harder still to throw away.
THE WOMAN.	Man dies by what he carries.
DON.	Is this how Adam sinned in Paradise? Was that apple forced into his mouth As this was forced on me? Is this the sin for which I must be threatened – That I exact a price for Todenwald? Is this my end – because I carry it? Answer me! What fraud on man is this – That he should die for fighting such a thing? If I permitted Todenwald – did He?

(He points to Heaven.)

Answer!
Where's your thunder?

(The sound of something falling is heard from somewhere amongst the tombs. He turns and listens.)

THE WOMAN.	Fight evil, but know it not. For knowledge is the poison in the seed of Adam.
DON.	Who's there?

Whoever you are – come out.

(Raising the bomb.)

Come out before I blow you out!

THE WOMAN. You have won the war
But your enemies were right.
Your path, too, leads to Hell.

(SUDER appears from amongst the tombs. He is wearing British battle dress.)

DON. Who are you?

SUDER. A Partisan.

DON. You're no Partisan.
You're Otto Suder – the man I'm looking for.

SUDER *(smiling).*
We met before in happier days.

DON. Happier for whom?

SUDER. For the world, I think.
But you have had your way.
My country is destroyed.

DON. "My country – right or wrong."
I saw those words not long ago above a gate.
Well – your country's wrong,
So now regrets are out of date.
"To each what's coming to him."
But this time there is death in my hands.

SUDER. I regret nothing.

DON. And learnt nothing.

SUDER. Just that we were right.
The Führer's words,
Only the strong can live.
The man with the gun
Is always God.

DON. I'm not God,
But the sooner it's over the better.

329

SUDER.   Of course, Sir.

(SUDER *approaches* DON, *and holds out his papers and his dog tags.*)

> Well, here are my papers and my dog tags.
> Take them, and send them to my home.

DON (*taking them*).
> I'll see they get them.
> Now move over there.

(*He pulls the pin out of the grenade and throws it away.*)

D.P.'S.   A morte, a morte, i traditori
> Che hanno venduto il nostro onor'.

THE WOMAN (*running to* DON).
> No, no, no. Throw it away.
> It is poison.
> You have eaten the fruit of the Forbidden Tree.
> Spit it out.
> Throw it away,
> While there still is time.

D.P.'S.   A morte, a morte i traditori.

DON (*holding the grenade above his head*).
> It was a woman gave me this, and told me what
>   to do.
> So you don't try to put me off.
> Out of my way!

(*The* D.P.'s *have appeared, trudging up the road, carrying bundles and pushing carts. When they see* SUDER *and* DON *they set up a shout of joy and rush forward, surrounding* SUDER.)

D.P.'S.   Ecco! Ecco Inglesi!
> Viva! Viva!
> Wir sennen frei.

DON.   Stand back, you fools!
> That man's a Nazi.

SUDER.   I am Handwell, of the Royal West Kents.
> Disarm that collaborator.

330

DON.   Tell them, Copperhead,
            Tell them who I am.

SUDER.   Careful! He has a bomb.

(*A swarm of men advance upon* DON.)

D.P.'S.   Smrt Fascismu! Stravo! Stravo!

DON.   Copperhead, you bastard,
            Can't you lend a hand?
            Where are you, Copperhead?

(*The* D.P.'s *seize* DON *from the rear and try to grasp his arms.*)

D.P.'S.   Smrt Fascismu! Stravo!

SUDER.   Look at his dog tags and his papers.

(*As the* D.P.'s *drag these from his pockets and examine them,* COPPERHEAD *appears on the mountain. The Woman approaches* DON *and snatches the grenade from his outstretched hand.*)

D.P.'S.   A morte! A morte!

THE WOMAN. Not this man . . .

(*She crosses to* SUDER *with the grenade.*)

            . . . but Barabbas.
            Man dies by what he carries.

(*She gives the grenade to* SUDER, *whose eyes glare with excitement.*)

DON.   Copperhead – you up there –
            Tell them who I am.

COPPERHEAD. They say we are all members of one another.

DON.   Judas! Judas!

THE WOMAN. But not with a kiss.
            Not with a kiss this time.

(COPPERHEAD *disappears. As* SUDER *raises the grenade to throw it, there is a gasp of horror from the* D.P.'s, *who abandon* DON *and*

331

run for cover. The women advance upon SUDER. DON *takes shelter behind a grave stone.)*

DON.   Watch that bomb!

SUDER.   You have had your wish.
            The New Order has gone and there is nothing
                left to live for.
            So let us all go out together.

(With a shriek, the women fling themselves upon him in fear and supplication, embracing his legs and smothering him frantically. Suddenly the grenade, which SUDER *has clasped to his bosom, goes off, and the stage is plunged in darkness. After some more shrieks and the sound of falling masonry, there is silence.)*

DON.   Whitebeard! Whitebeard!
            Where the hell is Whitebeard?
            Is there nobody up there?

COPPERHEAD KELLY'S VOICE *(in the darkness).*
            Who is this that flings blasphemies upon the air
                of the morning?
            Whose feet blacken the carpet of my sanctuary?

CHORUS.   Mea culpa.
            Mea culpa.
            Mea maxima culpa.

THE WOMAN. Tribuat nobis omnipotentes et misericors Dominus.

COPPERHEAD KELLY.
            What is this spate of unintelligible words –
            This spectacle of bended backsides –
            To whom are these oblations offered?

DON.   God forgive me, but it sounds like Copperhead.

(The rays of the rising sun strike upon the mountain, showing COPPERHEAD *somewhere on the heights.* SUDER *lies dead, and on all sides the* D.P.'s *are crouched in prayer.)*

COPPERHEAD KELLY.
            I am the Lord, and there is none else.

DON.   It's not the Lord. It's Judas.

332

COPPERHEAD KELLY.

> The Lord made Judas, and the Lord made you.
> I form the light, and create darkness.
> I make peace, and create evil.
> I, the Lord, do all these things.

DON.

> And more – whoever you may be –
> You have created Man, and set him in the way
>   of temptation.
>
> You have sent him out from Eden to do your work,
> And damned his soul for being there.
> You have (*staring down at* SUDER) . . . bidden
>   him to fight for life
> And plagued him with a Pity for the things he kills.
> Is that enough?

THE WOMAN (*in distress*).

> You ask forgiveness in your prayers
> But cannot give it to your lonely Lord.

DON.

> I do not ask or grant forgiveness
> So if you are going to strike me down,
> Do it now, or let me be at peace.

COPPERHEAD KELLY.

> Suder has peace, if that is what you want.

(Don is silent.)

> Well, hang your helmet over the clay
> And we will say that Don is dead.
> Will that conclude the reckoning?

(The sun has risen and it is now high morning.)

DON.   If Don is dead, then who am I?

COPPERHEAD KELLY.

> My rider,
> Who neither forgives nor is forgiven.
> Go now,
> Forgetting good and evil, which is MY concern,
> And knowing only night and day.
> Let the damned rest, and fling your accusations

At the Lord instead.
He will survive.

(DON *covers his face in momentary terror. Then he looks up.*)

DON.   There was to be a dove . . .

COPPERHEAD KELLY.
          Bury the bones
          And be off about MY business.

(DON *suddenly smiles, as* COPPERHEAD *fades out into a passing cloud.* THE WOMAN *approaches with a piece of broken timber, which she places in the torn earth above the grave.*)

THE WOMAN. Here is an unknown warrior.
          Baptise him in your name,
          And in His name
          And in honour of a dove that never comes.

(DON *suddenly comes to life, drags* SUDER *to the grave, and after throwing some earth upon him, places his steel helmet on the timber.* THE WOMAN *writes a name upon a piece of paper, which she places on the marker.*)

DON.   This is crazy.
          But he's dead and I'm alive,
          Whoever I may be.

THE WOMAN *(as they work).*
          Cheer up.
          He killed himself.
          You are not him.

DON.   I'll do as I'm told.
          But if he's me, by God, I'll pay him my respects.
          If he's the devil himself
          I shall salute my enemy, dead.

(DON *stands back and salutes the grave.*)

THE WOMAN *(bringing flowers).*
          See.
          You have cast forth the fruit of the Forbidden Tree.
          Oh, thank God!

DON. (*turning to the* D.P.'s *who have by now stood up and have resumed their line.*)

> Be off.
> The men of law will soon be here
> To ventilate the cesspools.

(*The* D.P.'s *move off, unmasking* ABE GOLDBERG *as they go. He is sitting in his truck, as in the Prologue.*)

D.P.'S.
> Lang ist der weg und veery
> Zur Heimat da prigione.
> Gebrochen zu der Brenner ziehn –
> Gefangen, perduti – nichts persone.

GOLDBERG.
> Boy, you've sure got dirt on your face.

DON. (*wiping it and making it worse*).
> I'm told we all are dirty,
> But it seems we're not all damned.

(*The four Officers are seen returning.* THE WOMAN *returns to the body which she covers with her shawl, and picking some wild flowers, begins to spread them on the heap.* DON *sits down on the grave where he was in the Prologue.*)

GOLDBERG.
> Aw, nuts to all that.
> There ain't no Santa Claus.
> And here's the brass coming back.

L'AIGLON.
> Tout prêt.

LYON.
> All aboard.

ANGELINO.
> Avanti!

BULL.
> Let's go.

GOLDBERG.
> Say folks – before we leave,
> What have you got down for that one over there?

BULL (*consulting his notebook*).
> Hanwell, D. R., Rationalist.

GOLDBERG.
> Hanwell's not dead.
> That's him – sitting on the rock.

L'AIGLON. *(laughing).*
> Clearly a resurrection!
> That will require a special form.

LYON *(annoyed).*
> Lieutenant, if you please!
> Let us be serious.
> The entry stands.
> Drive on.

(ABE shrugs his shoulders and starts the engine. THE WOMAN rises from beside the body and points to the inscription as the truck moves off.)

GOLDBERG. It's in the Book –
And so it must be so.

D.P.'S. Sorridi e prega il Signor.

ANGELINO. SIA SACRA AGLI ITALIANI
LA VIA DOVE

D.P.'S. DOVE.

DON. *(rising and starting to laugh).*
> What's that about a do-ve?
> DOVE, DOVE.
> By God, I never noticed it.
> You are there, my dove!

(He points to the inscription.)

(Shouldering his haversack and preparing to follow.)

> I bind unto myself this day
> This undiminished legacy –
> The lips of song, the feet of clay,
> The frosts of autumn and the flowers of May,
> The darkness of the night, the sins of noon,
> The promise of an ending not too soon.

(He sets off down the road, as THE WOMAN comes forward and begins again to spread her flowers.)

THE WOMAN. The flowers of spring are growing on the graves.
Within the birch trees magic stirs.

336

Blest be this signpost to the heavenly ladder –
This shepherd of the sheep – and of the adder.

DON AND THE WOMAN.

The miseries that match content,
The blessings and the chastisement.
These things unto myself I bind,
Leaving both good and ill behind.

(DON *leaves.*)

(THE WOMAN *looks after* DON *and waves her hand.*)

COPPERHEAD KELLY.

I have harnessed the unicorn to the plough.
And now he shall bend his back to the furrow.
In famine he shall save you from starvation
And in war from the power of the sword.
But keep him hungry till his work is done,
Will the wild ox bray, while he has grass?

(*The curtain falls as* THE WOMAN *continues to wave.*)

TAIN BO CUAILGNE

*A Pageant
of the great
Cattle Raid of Cooley
and of the high deeds
of
CUCHULAINN
Champion of Ulster*

―――――

THE SETTING

This Pageant was written for production on a full-sized football arena with appropriate seating accommodation on both sides, and entrances and exits at each corner.

It is intended to open in daylight, with darkness falling in the course of the action until the conclusion, which should be played entirely in artificial light.

The only structural scenery required (apart from decoration and masking for electrical equipment) is an erection near the southern end (which must not form a visual obstruction) representing the Palace of Rathcroghan. To the south of the centre of the field is a non-inflammable Rostrum upon which is a primitive Rock Altar. The grass around this area must be protected from burning. In the centre a section of the field is coloured or decorated to indicate the River Dee. The ford of Ardee is represented on a raised structure, dead centre. Further to the north stands the Pillar Stone of Ard Cullin, a rough megalithic pillar so constructed that inside there may be concealed a life-sized figure or dummy, dressed as a replica of Cuchulainn, invisible until required. On a slope, to the far north stands a column representing Emain Macha.

CAST

STAR PART:
    CUCHULAINN

LEADING PARTS:
SHANAHAN TOPPERT	— The Speaker or Narrator. The clerical Historian who writes the Tain in Clonmacnois.
MAEV	— Queen of Connacht.
FERDIA	— Champion of Connacht.
BRICRIU	— The antagonist or Counter-Commentator.
THE MORRIGAN	— A bird-witch. She must also be an accomplished dancer as well as an actress.
LAEG	— Cuchulainn's Charioteer. Must be able to manage horses.
FINNAVAUR	— 'Of the fair Eyebrows'. Daughter of Queen Maev.

MAJOR SMALL PARTS:
FERGUS MAC ROY	— Herald of Ireland.
AILEEL	— Consort of Queen Maev.
EEVER	— Wife to Cuchulainn.
FEDELMA	— Prophetess of Connacht.
MAC ROTH	— Connacht Herald.
SUALTAM	— Ulster Herald, and supposed mortal father of Cuchulainn.
DARA MAC FACHTNA	— The owner of the Brown Bull. (Ulster accent).
LOCKA	— Handmaid to Queen Maev.

342

MACHA	— A Goddess.
LU	— A God. Representing the Sun.
CUROI	— King of Munster.
LEWY	— Son of Curoi, King of Munster.
ERC	— King of Leinster.
CONOR MAC NESSA	— King of Ulster.
NACHRANTAL	— Champion of Connacht.
LECH	— Champion of Leinster.
CALATIN	— A Wizard of Connacht.
BEVE	— Calatin's daughter (handsome).
THREE CRONES	— Calatin's misshapen daughters.
FIACHA	— Champion of Ulster. Must be an accomplished (or better still, trick) horseman, and able to gallop without stirrups.

MINOR SPEAKING PARTS:

FERCARTNA	— Munster Herald,
ANNI	— Wife to Calatin.
RORY	— Ferdia's Charioteer. Able to manage horses.

NON-SPEAKING (*but Acting*) PARTS:

DECLAN	— Leinster Herald.
CALATIN'S 21 WARRIOR SONS	— Able to mime.
CALATIN'S 3 MISSHAPEN SONS	— Able to dance.

DANCERS, MIMERS *and* OTHER SPECIALISTS:

DANCERS AT RATHCROGHAN	— About 12.
BEASTS AT RATHCROGHAN	— About 12.
THE RED BULL	— A male dancer.

343

THISTLES, PUFFBALLS,
and miscellaneous
WRAITHS — About 40. All dancers.
CROWS — About 20. All dancers.
FOUR TRUMPETERS
CROWD PARTS:
COURTIERS *and*
SERVANTS AT
RATHCROGHAN — About a dozen.
ULSTER CHAMPIONS — About half a dozen.
THE HOST OF LEINSTER ⎱ Indefinite.
THE HOST OF MUNSTER ⎰
CHARIOTEERS
THE GREY OF MACHA ⎱ Cuchulainn's Horses.
THE BLACK SAINGLEND ⎰
HORSES FOR THE
OTHER CHARIOTS — As required.

Note: The various animals paraded before Maev and Aileel are
mimed or danced by Players. They include the Red Bull.
The BROWN BULL OF COOLEY is an enormous
garlanded, brazen property, drawn on a truck. It is constructed so that at the required moment its great mouth
opens and it belches smoke, and its eyes light up.

RECORDED EFFECTS
(Apart from speech and music)

THE ROARING OF THE BULL OF COOLEY
THUNDER
THE HOOF BEATS OF A GALLOPING HORSE.

SOME NOTES ON COSTUMES AND SPECIAL PROPERTIES

Cuchulainn must be a dark man, wearing a crimson cloak with a brooch of gold. He slings on his back a crimson shield with a silver rim, wrought with the figure of a great Dog. He has a long sword belt, looped several times around his body, sufficient to encircle the Pillar Stone.

Ferdia is a fair man. He wears a tunic of striped silk, braided with gold spangles, and an apron of brown leather. He has a crested helmet studded with carbuncles and carries a shield with bosses of bronze.

None of the above insignia should appear to be heraldic in the modern sense. The shields are round.

All fight with sword and spear, but Cuchulainn also possesses the GAE BOLG, a terrible weapon that is thrown in some way by the foot.

The spear of the God Lu is a celebrated mythological weapon signifying the light of the Sun.

Shanahan Toppert reads from a book, bound in skin — THE BOOK OF THE DUN COW.

The banners of the four provinces raised at the end are as follows:

ULSTER: A red right hand on a yellow or golden field.

CONNACHT: A black bird with wings outstretched on a white or silver field.

LEINSTER: A deer on a green field.

MUNSTER: A boar on a blue field.

(*These should not be standards attached to the pole at one end, like a modern flag, but hung from a short cross bar more in the Roman manner.*)

BREAKDOWN

The Pageant is in four parts, separated by music.

There are seven sections in each part. The entire running time should be a little under two hours.

A section described as ACTION is one in which the players have spoken lines, but which depends principally upon the visual performance of a relatively few characters, rather than on dialogue.

A section described as DIALOGUE depends principally upon the spoken word, and care must be taken to have no more action than can be synchronised with the recorded speech.

A section described as DANCE, depends mainly upon specially rehearsed dances, rather than upon dramatic production. MIME, on the other hand, refers to stylised movements in the nature of dance, but intended to convey a story, in lieu or in support of dialogue.

A section described as PRODUCTION is a self-contained number, combining dialogue and mass movement, and usually requiring special treatment as a production item in its own right, together with its own music.

A section described as BATTLE is also mainly a mass item, but owing to the numbers involved and the nature of the action, it had probably better be handled fairly realistically, accepting a certain amount of confusion and *ad-libbing* as inevitable.

On the above basis, the sequence of scenes is as follows: —

PART ONE: Scene 1 — Musical.
                       Scene 2 — Formal Introit.
                       Scene 3 — Production.
                       Scene 4 — Narrative.
                       Scene 5 — Dialogue.
                       Scene 6 — Dance, followed by dialogue
                                        and mime.
                       Scene 7 — Action.
                       Musical Interlude — Sunset.

PART ONE

THE PILLOW TALK

1.

*A Military Band plays a martial introduction.
It is not in view.*

2.
(FORMAL INTROIT)

As the band concludes, FIACHA *the Champion, enters on horseback from the North West and gallops at full speed down the field to the Rock which he mounts, horse and all. From the summit he blows a blast upon a trumpet.*

Meanwhile, FERGUS MAC ROY, *Herald of Ireland, drives in with his* CHARIOTEER *by the South East and comes to the Rock. Here, the* CHARIOTEER *leaps out and holds the horses' heads while* FERGUS *mounts the Rock.* FIACHA *rides down, and gallops off by the South East.*

A TRUMPETER *on foot enters by the S.W. Entrance and runs to the centre of the southern end of the field.*

A TRUMPETER *enters by the E. Entrance and another by the W. Entrance and they stand to east and west of the field respectively.*

Another TRUMPETER *appears on the top of the slope to the far North.*

FERGUS (*in the direction of the Presidential Box*).
        In ainm Dé agus in ainm marbh –
(*The* TRUMPETER *answers from the East.*)

FERGUS (*in the opposite direction*).
        In the name of God and of the Dead Generations. . . .
(*The* TRUMPETER *answers from the West.*)

349

FERGUS (*to the South*).
> Eachtra Tána Bo Cuailgne.

(*The* TRUMPETER *answers from the South.*)

FERGUS (*to the North*).
> The tale of the Cattle Raid of Cooley.

(*The* TRUMPETER *answers from the North. The last note is held until a Band has begun the National Anthem. At its conclusion all four* TRUMPETERS *play a fanfare together.*)

3.

The drone of War pipes is heard through the last notes of the fanfare and then the Pipe Band leads the head of the Procession through the South East Entrance.

> *First comes Munster, led by* CUROI *in his chariot, followed by the host of the South.*)

FERGUS. I, Fergus Mac Roy, Herald of Ireland, call
> the men of Desmond, of Thomond,
> of the Decies and of all fair Munster. I call
> Curoi the King, Lewy his son, Fercartna his
> Herald, and all the hosting of the South.

(*Connacht follows, led by* MAEV *and* AILEEL, *in their chariot.* FERDIA *does not carry any weapons at this stage.*)

FERGUS. I call the Rosses, Croahan, Breffni, the bloody
> plain of Moytura and all of wide and windy
> Connacht. I summon Maev the Queen, Aileel her
> consort, their daughter Finnavaur of the Fair
> Eyebrows and their seven exiled sons, the Manes.
> I call Mac Roth the Messenger, the black Morrigan,
> Ferdia and Nachrantal, Fedelma the Prophetess,
> Locka the maid, the Clan Calatin and all the hosting
> of the West.

(*Ulster follows, led by* CONOR MAC NESSA *in his chariot.*)

FERGUS. I call Dalriada and Oriel, Iveagh, Muirhevna,
> and the black hills of Ulster. I call their
> king, Conor Mac Nessa, Sualtam his Herald,
> Bricriu of the Poisoned Tongue, Fiacha the warrior,

the Charioteer Laeg, Dara Mac Fachtna, owner of the
Bull, the Red Branch Knights and all the hosting of the
north.

(*Leinster follows, led by* ERC *in his chariot. Amongst them is*
SHANAHAN *carrying the Book of the Dun Cow.*)

FERGUS.   I call Offaly, Fingal and Bregia, Moy Mel, the
Happy Plain, Royal Tara, Meath and all of gracious
Leinster. I summon Erc the King, Declan his Herald,
the Champion Lach, Eever, the Maid of Lusk, Shanahan
Toppert chronicler of Clonmacnois and all the hosting
of the East.

(LU *and* MACHA *in the last chariot end the procession.*)

FERGUS.   I salute Lu of the Long Arm, the heavenly one,
Slaughterer of Balor, wielder of the spear of light,
And with him, the daughter of Red Hugh, Macha swifter
than the horses of Ulla whose curse begins the Tain.

(*The Procession moves around the field, and the pipers finally
march off by the South West Entrance. Munster ends up at the
South end of the field where they camp and squat on the ground.
Similarly, Connacht halts on the West side, while* MAEV, AILEEL
*and their Court move on to the Palace of Rathcroghan. The
Ulstermen camp on the north end, where they are joined by their*
TRUMPETER, *Leinster gathers similarly on the east side –* EEVER *a
little apart from the others – while* SHANAHAN *brings his book to
the Rock where he opens it and prepares to read.*

LU *and* MACHA *drive to the Rock where* MACHA *mounts the
rostrum and faces north.*)

4.

SHANAHAN.   I, Shanahan Toppert, Clerk in holy orders
Of the flock of the blessed Ciaran,
Cloistered in this sanctuary of Clonmacnois,
Have written the story of the Cattle Raid of Cooley
In the Book of the Dun Cow.
In those days, many years ago,
The men of Ulster lay under a curse

Laid upon their shoulders by the Goddess Macha.
Whom they had offended by the cruelty of their King.
(*He seats himself while* MACHA *mounts the Rock and faces north.*)

MACHA.   For the shame that you have put upon me
In the bearing of my brood
Ulster is cursed.
In the hour of her necessity
May her warriors be helpless as a woman in childbirth
And as weak as I was when they tormented me.
Four nights and five days
May this debility corrode them in their need,
And their children after them
To the ninth generation.

(*There is thunder. The Ulstermen throw up their arms and scatter in terror, some up a slope to the north, some to the sides, where they lie down and cover their heads, except* FIACHA, *who has been coming south across the field to meet* FERGUS *who is on his way north, at the completion of his Introduction. The Ulster chariots are driven off by the North West Entrance, followed by* DARA *and* LEAG.

    MACHA *descends and remounts the chariot with* LU.)

FIACHA.   Fly, royal Fergus;
Fly with me to Connacht.
Our King has brought this thunder on the North
And Connacher is for the dark.
We must seek service in another Rath.

FERGUS.   What will become of Ulster now, Fiacha?
Scattered the Red Branch,
The Warriors of Emain ride no more
And fire is turned to water.

(LU *is driving his chariot on the way out with* MACHA, *but halts it while close to* FERGUS.)

LU.   Whither away, Fergus? Why run, Fiacha?
I will send you a Champion
Who rides by right over all maledictions,
Because his Father is a God.

FERGUS.   What son of Ulster has such a Father?
None that we know of.

LU.   My son – the son of Lu –
                The Hound of Cooley –
                The lad Cuchulainn.

(*He points to the South East Entrance. There is a trumpet call, and the boy* CUCHULAINN *enters – a small, solitary figure. There is laughter, and* LU *and* MACHA *drive off.*)

FERGUS.   That is no God's son.
                That is Setanta, son of Sualtam,
                A blower of trumpets,
                A common carrier of unimportant tidings,
                Whose lineage is mortal as my own,
                How can he defend Ulster?

(*From all sides of the field, wild laughter.*)

LU.   Only the Gods know who their children are.

(LU *and* MACHA *drive off by the South East.*

FERGUS *and* FIACHA *join the men of Connacht and there is a general exodus from the field of all except* SHANAHAN, FERDIA, *the Court of Rathcroghan including* BRICRIU, *and the* MORRIGAN. CONOR *and* SUALTAM *sleep beside the Pillar of Emain Macha. The Prophetess* FEDELMA *comes to the Rock from Rathcroghan. The chariot of* MAEV *remains beside Rathcroghan but those of* CUROI *and* ERC *are taken off by the South West and South East Entrances, respectively. The extras leave by the entrances nearest to their respective camps.*

CUCHULAINN *has come to where* EEVER *sits and he talks to her before moving on at her direction to the centre rostrum which she indicates.*)

5.

(CUCHULAINN *has come to the centre Rostrum where he meets* FERDIA, *who has also come there from his camp. Together they practice feats of arms with weapons which they find there. Meanwhile* BRICRIU *has come to the Rock, and stands behind* SHANAHAN – *a Mephistophelean figure with a sardonic leer.*)

SHANAHAN.   It was to school Cuchulainn went
                    To learn the art of weapons.

BRICRIU.	A pity. Fighting is an unprofitable employment. Sensible men employ others to do it for them.
SHANAHAN.	Who are you?
BRICRIU.	I am Bricriu.
SHANAHAN.	A soldier too?
BRICRIU.	The Gods forbid! – a realist.
SHANAHAN.	What is that?
BRICRIU.	A man of some perceptions. I can see the real intent behind all high professions, and the subtle shades of meanness in the things we do. I can analyse all effort in the most revealing way, and offer arguments against the vain display of talent or ability. I am a Thinker and carry my rapier in my mouth.
SHANAHAN.	The kennel of a poisoned tongue. Beware of Bricriu, People of Ireland For he is always with us.
BRICRIU.	And, like the poor, am blessed.
FERDIA (*to* CUCHULAINN).	I am Ferdia of Connacht. Who are you?
CUCHULAINN.	Cuchulainn of Muirhevna.
FERDIA.	Cuchulainn? That's a funny name. The Hound of Cullann. Are you a dog?
CUCHULAINN.	Once in the embered days of Bealtaine When in the train of Connacher, my King, As a young lad, I followed him to Cooley. There, coming late, to the house of Cullin, the Smith, I slew the Hound that sentried at his gate And bayed me from the feast. 'Boy, you have robbed me of my watchdog' cried the smith. 'What shall I do for such another beast?' 'Forgive your guest, Cullin' I said, 'For injuring my Master's host.

'I shall become your hound myself
'And prowl your threshold till another whelp
'Is grown to dogdom'
And so I got my name.

BRICRIU.   He claims to be a dog! I hate pretensions
         in the very young.

(BRICRIU *moves across to the centre Rostrum.*)

FERDIA.   What brought you here?

CUCHULAINN.   The same as you – to earn my right to arms.

BRICRIU.   Come, tell the truth, Tripehound.
         A woman sent you here.

CUCHULAINN.   Yes, it was a woman – a woman whom I met in
         Leinster,
     What shame is there in that? To win a woman,
         a boy must be a man.

BRICRIU.   And by what tests will you achieve this graduation?

CUCHULAINN.   When I can leap the salmon weir of Lusk and
     have slain three times nine men and with each
     blow sparing one of the nine –
     When I can work without sleep from Samhain
     to Candlemas and from Candlemas to Bealtaine
     and from Bealtaine round to Samhain once again –

BRICRIU.   — then you will be qualified for matrimony. I see.
     How odd these women of Ath Cliath are in their
     requirements.

CUCHULAINN.   She has the six gifts of womanhood –
     The gift of beauty, and the gift of voice,
     The gift of silver speech, the gift of needlework,
     The gift of wisdom, the gift of chastity,
     And her name is Eever.

(BRICRIU *returns to the Rock where* FEDELMA *is standing.*)

BRICRIU.   She needs to be a hero to marry with a fellow
     such as this.

FEDELMA.   There never is a fool like a clever one, and
     you are the cleverest fool of all, Bricriu.

This boy shall be a Champion. I hear his
praises on the winds of tomorrow. Great
warriors and their charioteers shall bell
his deeds from mouth to mouth, till poets
build his monument. He will give such
combat at the Ford that Centuries shall hear
it ringing down the years.

BRICRIU.   In Connacht, prophecies are three a penny,
               Fedelma.
               Here comes another. Do you not see the Morrigan
               skimming the boglands like an evil crow?
               She is a sorceress too.

(THE MORRIGAN *approaches the men at the centre rostrum fluttering like a bird.* FEDELMA *returns to Rathcroghan.*)

FERDIA.   Let us swear to be friends, Cuchulainn – now and
               forever.

CUCHULAINN. Friends we are. Let's pledge it to the Death.

THE MORRIGAN. Not to the death, my lovely lads. A little less
               than that – a little less.

FERDIA.   Why so Morrigan?

THE MORRIGAN. Death cannot be the end of Friendship, but
               the end of Friendship may perhaps be death.

CUCHULAINN. Stop speaking riddles.

THE MORRIGAN. Swear by the summer, lads, for friendship
               is as fleeting as the Sun and cannot bear
               the cold. Wait for the winter's winds
               before you promise more. The frost kills
               more than apple-blossoms.

FERDIA.   Away! Away!
(THE MORRIGAN *invests them each with a shield and a sword
which have been concealed behind the Rostrum.*)

THE MORRIGAN. Champions you wish to be. Champions you are.
               Champions must kill. What would you, Champions,
               slay?

CUCHULAINN. Not each other, anyway.

356

THE MORRIGAN (*laughing wildly*).
>A Gift and a Geas for all who graduate. What
>will you have, Ferdia, to take away?

FERDIA.   Give me the gifts of the body, that I
>be strong, and fleet of foot.

THE MORRIGAN. This I give you – that you will overtake all
>that you pursue.

FERDIA.   I thank you, Morrigan.

THE MORRIGAN (*her hand on his head*).
>And this, the Geas, I place upon your head –
>that you must never refuse to fight for a
>woman whom you love.

FERDIA.   An easy yoke, I take it gladly.

THE MORRIGAN. And you, Cuchulainn – what do you desire?

CUCHULAINN.   Grant me the gift of weapons.

THE MORRIGAN. This I shall do (*handing him the Gae Bolg*).
>Here is the last – the final weapon –
>the weapon that will end all battles –
>the Gae Bolg. Do not use it until you must
>for it is a terrible weapon.

CUCHULAINN.   I thank you, Morrigan – even if I never use it.

THE MORRIGAN (*her hand on his head*).
>And this, the Geas I give to you as well –
>that you must never refuse the offer of hospitality.

CUCHULAINN (*laughing*).
>Is that all? That is an easier load than Ferdia's.
>How can I be conquered now?

THE MORRIGAN. No man can be conquered, Cuchulainn, who
>does not eat his own strength.

CUCHULAINN.   I am content. No man will ever eat himself.
(*With another wild laugh,* THE MORRIGAN *goes dancing and
fluttering off. The two Champions shake hands.*)

FERDIA.   Farewell, Cuchulainn.

CUCHULAINN.   Farewell, Ferdia.

BOTH.   Blood brothers. For all time.

FERDIA.   Brothers.

CUCHULAINN.   Brothers.
(*They part,* FERDIA *going back to the camp of Connacht.*
CUCHULAINN *goes to* EEVER, *whom he picks up forcibly and carries
away with him to the Pillar Stone, where they lie down together
and go to sleep.*)

BRICRIU.   All time indeed!
Ha! Ha! Do they not know that Time is Sand
Running through the channel of an hour-glass?
They swear by Sand – these warriors.
They try to weave the waters of the Boyne,
And whistle jigs for all the milestones of
    Muirhevna.

SHANAHAN.   A gift for every hero.
A Geas for every brow.
And so they part.
And now the years flow by
And we must turn the page to Connacht
And to the Court of Maev.
(BRICRIU *has gone back to Rathcroghan.*)

6.

(*Music. Dancers have entered from the South West Entrance,
and now dance before* MAEV *and* AILEEL. *Their beds are prepared
by* LOCKA, *and as the Dance concludes, they retire to rest.*
BRICRIU *seats himself between the couches.*)

BRICRIU.   That will be all, Locka. Now you may leave
their Majesties.
(LOCKA *moves off and sits down upon the step of the Palace.*)

AILEEL (*wishing him to go, too*).
Good night, Bricriu.

BRICRIU.   How true. What a good evening it has been.
            You are so much to be envied here in Rathcroghan.
            I'm sure there is not a Court in Eire so fortunate
            as that of Maev and Aileel.

MAEV.   We will be more fortunate when we can get to
            sleep.

BRICRIU.   Yes indeed. And with nothing whatever to
            disturb your dreams. An ideal marriage, if
            I may so observe. I hope you realise how
            lucky you are.

AILEEL (*sitting up irritably*).
            At the moment, I am *not* in luck.
(*He lies down again.*)

BRICRIU.   Oh yes you are. An ideal wife –

MAEV (*sleepily*).
            Thank you, Bricriu.

BRICRIU.   – So much better fitted than you are to
            assume all the responsibilities of married life –

AILEEL (*sitting up*).
            What's that?

BRICRIU.   – leaving you with nothing whatever to do
            but to enjoy yourself.

AILEEL.   I don't like that way of putting it.

MAEV (*sleepily*).
            It's true enough.

BRICRIU.   A butterfly's existence. As for Maev –
            is she not happy with a husband who is so well
            connected. She need have no social
            fears whatever?

MAEV.   What's that?

AILEEL (*lying down*).
            It's true enough.

BRICRIU.   Both very lucky people.

MAEV.   Who says that Aileel is better connected than I am?

BRICRIU (*innocently*).
        Well – some people say so.

AILEEL (*sleepily*).
        Of course.

MAEV.   It is a lie! My father was High King of Ireland.
        What was *his* Father, I would like to know?

AILEEL (*sitting up*).
        Whatever your Father was, he was glad enough
        to get you married to me.

MAEV.   He had no fears whatever about getting me married.
        I was much the most marriageable of all his
            daughters.
        I had many offers all my girlhood and I turned
            them down, for I was the most choosy woman in
            Banba.
        A husband fit for me had to be brave and generous
        to match my valour and my open-handedness. Above
        all he must never be a jealous man, (*rather coyly*)
        for it was clear that I would have the men running
        after me all my life.

AILEEL (*smugly*).
        And so you found these qualities in me.

MAEV.   If I did choose you, it was I who made the decision
        and – I may add – gave all the presents.

AILEEN (*sitting up*).
        You can hardly have done that, my dear, seeing
        that I was the only one with any cash.

BRICRIU.   Ah yes. She is a fortunate woman indeed,
        who has a rich husband.

MAEV.   Rich! I had always twice the money that one had.

AILEEL.   If so, this is the first time I have heard of it.

MAEV.   Why one could hardly move in my Father's palace
            for serving men.

360

> And as for maids – he used to say they'd eat
> him out of house and home.
> So when I left for your small holding,
> He put a Province in my purse.

AILEEL. That's true. A strip of mountainy waste on
which the neighbours pastured goats. It took
a man to drive them off.

MAEV (*sarcastically*).
A man! Moryah.

AILEEL. I had the choice of at least two Kingdoms.
But I let them go to my unenterprising brothers
and took my Mother's place in Connacht so as
to look after you.

MAEV. Your Mother never owned a pigsty, let alone
Connacht.
And as for looking after me, I suppose that's what
you call living on your wife for the rest of your
life?

AILEEL (*furious*).
I live on you! Why should I do that, seeing that
there's nothing that you've got that I haven't
got – and better.

MAEV (*rising and ringing a bell*).
We'll see about this. Rouse up the house. Scullions
arise and fetch my pots and pans.

AILEEN (*doing likewise*).
Fetch mine as well.
(*From all parts of the house, servants come running, carrying the
things demanded. The Dancers form a jury and applaud each
exhibition.*)

MAEV. Bring out my jugs and plates and pitchers.

AILEEL. Bring mine as well.

MAEV. Display my rings and jewellery.

AILEEL. And mine too.

MAEV.   Show him my cloaks and hats.

AILEEL.   Empty my wardrobe.

MAEV.   I have horses.

AILEEL.   Mine are as good as yours.
(*The Animals dance on.*)

MAEV.   I have fine rams – fetching the price of
half a dozen bondsmen.

AILEEL.   And so have I.

MAEV.   As for noteworthy boars – what can equal these?

AILEEL.   None, except mine.

MAEV.   Then wait! Produce my cattle and let us end
this argument.

AILEEL.   Drive on my herds with them.
(*When the Red Bull, Finnbennach, appears in* AILEEL'S *herd
there is a sudden silence, followed by a triumphant outburst of
applause.* MAEV *raises her hands and there is silence again.*)

MAEV.   Stop! Stop! What is my Red Bull, Finnbennach,
doing over there with your herd?

AILEEL (*smugly*).
That is where he now belongs.

MAEV.   He is mine – not yours.

AILEEL (*patting him*).
Do you suppose that such a Bull as this
would condescend to remain in the herd of a
woman?
The White-horned One has chosen Aileel for
his master.
(*Loud applause.*)

MAEV (*aghast*).
He is yours?

AILEEL.   Yes, my love. And that, I think decides the matter.
(*Applause.*)
Thank you, my loyal jury, for your verdict.
You may retire now to your fast-cooling couches.

362

(The Animals dance off and the Court, including AILEEL *returns to rest with the exception of* MAEV, BRICRIU *and* MAC ROTH.)

MAEV.   Oh to be so defrauded – and by a Bullock.

BRICRIU.   To whom are you referring, Queen?

MAEV.   To whoever or whatever the cap fits.

BRICRIU.   You need a better bull.

MAEV.   Yes. But where shall I find one?

7.

MAC ROTH.   Royal Lady,
    Madam,
    I have heard of such an animal.

MAEV.   Mac Roth, my Herald, what is this you say?
(The Brown Bull commences to be drawn in on its truck by the north-west entrance. DARA *is in attendance with* LAEG *as his herdsman.)*

MAC ROTH.   In the far north, on the lush pasturage of Cooley
    They say there crops a great Brown Bull,
    The peer of which Erin has never seen.
    They say that fifty brats can play upon its back
    And when it rages it can stamp its herdsman
    Thirty feet into the ground.
    Madam, it is a very notable Bull.

MAEV.   Who owns this animal?

MAC ROTH.   A simple fellow, Madam. A farmer known as
    Dara son of Fachtna.

MAEV.   Then run to Dara now, and buy this bull for me.

MAC ROTH.   He may not sell it, Madam.

MAEV.   Then borrow it. And if he will not lend,
    Take it by force. If you lack the power

Then send for me and I will bring all Ireland
In my train. This bull I mean to have.
Hasten, at once.

MAC ROTH. Madam, I go.

MAEV.　　　Away.
(MAC ROTH *hurries off towards the north.* MAEV *returns to her
bed. There is music.*)

MAEV.　　　Draw down the curtains of the day
And let us sleep.
Lu in his chariot is harrowing the west
And now the gulls of micaed Deilginis
　　Are beating the Pleiades with painted wings.
The sun, that for a yellow day
Has warmed the fields of Scythia and Rome
Keeps his last blessing
For the island that he loves the best.
Good night.
Pack up another store of unremembered sins
And set your dreams to work
Until the gong sounds in the Orient.
(*She lies down to sleep. The music swells and concludes.*)

END OF PART ONE

PART TWO

THE HOSTING OF THE FOUR GREAT FIFTHS

8.

(SUALTAM *wakes in Emain Macha, and sets forth to call on* DARA. MAC ROTH *arrives in* COOLEY *and is greeted by* DARA.)

MAC ROTH. Son of Fachtna, I am Mac Roth.

DARA (*dryly*).
    A name I never heard tell of hereabouts.

MAC ROTH (*proudly*).
    I am the Chief Herald of Connacht. . . .

DARA. Think of that now.

MAC ROTH. . . . and I bring you good news.

DARA. Sowl, I'm the best judge o' that meself. Yer sellin' something, eh?

MAC ROTH. Dara, I do not sell. I have come to buy your Brown Bull.

DARA (*sceptically*).
    Is that a fact?

MAC ROTH. Seven cumals, I shall offer.

DARA. The baste is not for sale.

MAC ROTH. Ah! Then thrice times seven cumals and every one the value of a female slave.

DARA (*shocked*).
    A female slave in Cooley? Where's yer dacency, man?

MAC ROTH. Still not enough?

365

DARA. The baste is not for sale.

MAC ROTH. Then for the hire of your Bull you shall have fifty
heifers.

DARA. Fifty?

MAC ROTH. And of the smooth soil of Moy Ai as many acres as
you furrow here. And a chariot of bronze the worth
of one and twenty bondsmen.

DARA. Away home. Yer daft.

MAC ROTH. And best of all – the gratitude of my Mistress.

DARA (*suspiciously*).
Mistress?

MAC ROTH. Maev of Rathcroghan. That is the Queen who sent
me here.

DARA (*relaxing*).
Oh a Lady is it! In that case, you can borrow
the baste an' welcome.

MAC ROTH. And the fee. . . ?

DARA. Nathin at all, man. Nathin at all. I'm not the man
would disoblige a lady.

MAC ROTH. Nothing at all?

DARA. You should have spoke yer mind to start with, an' not
deeved me with yer crack. The Serving Man will
see ye down the lonie.

MAC ROTH (*taken aback*).
Well – thank you very much.

DARA. Be off with him, Laeg.
(DARA *returns to his business, and* LAEG *escorts* MAC ROTH *to the*
BULL *where, with the attendants, they start to make it ready for
removal.* SUALTAM *arrives.*)

SUALTAM. What is happening here?

MAC ROTH. We take this Bull to Connacht.

SUALTAM (*surprised*).
Indeed? A decent man, this fellow, to let you lead a
prize like this from Ulster.

MAC ROTH (*indifferently*).
A decent man, no doubt.

SUALTAM. Though tart of speech perhaps.
It is the Northern way.

MAC ROTH. The North!
In Dara it's the frosts of Thule.

SUALTAM. But still – a very decent man.

MAC ROTH. And sensible.

SUALTAM. What do you mean?

MAC ROTH. He knows, of course,
That what we cannot hire, we can take.
The mention of our Queen alarmed the man.

DARA (*stopping his work and coming back*).
What's that? Ye think I care about yer Queen,
When all I minded was til' oblige a lady?
Ye'd take it, so you would?
Then off, my boy!
You'll get no Bull from me.

MAC ROTH. No Bull?

DARA. No Bull.
(MAC ROTH *half draws his sword, but puts it back again when*
DARA *and* LAEG *seize their sticks.*)

MAC ROTH. (*drawing himself up*).
The Queen, my Mistress, will be told of this.
She'll come, no doubt, herself.
And in her train, a host of better arguments than
mine.
Slan lath. (*He goes*).

DARA (*calling after him*).
No Bull!

367

9.

(The Servants of the Bull run away in terror by the North-west entrance.)

DARA.　　Call out the North!
　　　　　Heads will be bloody here by dayligone.
　　　　　Go with him, Laeg! Fetch help.

(SUALTAM and LAEG hurry off.)

SUALTAM.　　To Ard Cullin!
(MAC ROTH is ringing the great bell of Rathcroghan.)

MAC ROTH.　　Connacht awake! Dara Mac Fachtna will not give
　　　　　　　up the Bull of Cooley.
(DARA is trying to pull the BULL away towards the north, by himself. He does not get it very far. SUALTAM is awakening CUCHULAINN at the Pillar Stone. LAEG is beating on a drum.)

SUALTAM.　　My son! My son! Ulster is in danger.
(MAEV is rising furiously from her couch. AILEEL sleeps on.)

MAEV.　　No Bull! This is not to be tolerated.
　　　　　Summon my people, while I clothe myself for war.

CUCHULAINN.　　Run to Emania, Father.
　　　　　　　Take my wife with you to a place of safety.
　　　　　　　And while you rouse up Connacher Mac Nessa,
　　　　　　　'Tis I will hold the bounds of Ulster.
(SUALTAM and EEVER leave for Emain Macha. LAEG stays with CUCHULAINN who proceeds to divest himself of shirt after shirt.)

MAEV.　　Call back my exiled children. Call the Manes.
　　　　　Call Leinster – Tara. Summon the fiery South.
　　　　　Fair words have failed, so lightning shall be loosed.
(The Connacht trumpeter blows a blast upon his horn, and as LOCKA robes MAEV in her battle array, the Seven Manes enter from the West, followed by FERGUS, FERDIA and FIACHA, and they come to Rathcroghan. Drums beat.)

10.

(The section opens with the War-Dance of Connacht by the Seven Manes. While it is going on the dialogue proceeds.)

BRICRIU *(indicating* AILEEL*).*
> Your husband, madam.

MAEV *(shaking* AILEEL *by the shoulder).*
> Wake, up, wake up. Is this a time for sleeping?

AILEEL *(taking one look).*
> Yes.

(He lies down again.)

MAEV.
> Get up, you soiler of the sunlight . . . you squalid cul-de-sac.

BRICRIU.
> He'll never forgive you, madam, if you allow him to miss this.

MAEV.
> Locka! Fetch me a bucket of water from the river. I'll soon arouse this languid dandylion.

(The Trumpet of Leinster is heard, as LOCKA *hurries off to the Ford with a bucket. The host of Leinster enters on foot from the east, led by* ERC, *and comes to Rothcroghan. Drums beat as they march. Meanwhile* SUALTAM *is trying to arouse Emain Macha, where* CONOR MAC NESSA *is sunk in a torpor.)*

SUALTAM.
> Rise and defend yourselves, Men of Ulster.
> Your frontiers are in peril, and your cattle will be gone.

EEVER.
> It is the curse of Macha that is on the north.
> The weakness is upon them.

CONOR *(sleepily).*
> Enough. Enough.

SUALTAM *(shaking* CONOR*).*
> Rise and defend yourselves, Men of Ulster.

*(CONOR *rises sleepily and draws his sword, with which he strikes down* SUALTAM. *Then, covering the body with a cloak he cuts off the head and places it upon the top of the Pillar of Emain.)*

CONOR.　　　Death to him who disturbs his King.

SUALTAM'S HEAD.
　　　　　　Rise and Defend yourselves, Men of Ulster.
(EEVER *sinks down in despair.* LAEG *has been helping* CUCHULAINN
to don his armour.)

CUCHULAINN.　Who are you? Are there none awake in Ulster save
　　　　　　ourselves?

LAEG.　　　　I am Laeg, a herdsman. Too humble to be noticed
　　　　　　by the curse. Let me stay, and be your Charioteer.

CUCHULAINN.　There still is time to fly.

LAEG.　　　　No. I will stay with you.

CUCHULAINN.　Brave lad! I'll take you in my service. Come arm
　　　　　　me. Arm!
(LAEG *helps* CUCHULAINN *to dress for battle.*)
(*At Rathcroghan* ERC *salutes* MAEV.)

ERC.　　　　Greetings Maev, from Erc, King of Tara. I bring
　　　　　　to your hosting the men of Leinster and of Meath.
(*War Dance of the Men of Leinster. As it concludes, the Trumpet
of Munster is heard and* CUROI *and* LEWY *lead on the warriors
of the South through the south-west entrance. Drums beat as
they march.*)

HEAD OF SUALTAM.
　　　　　　Rise and defend yourselves, Men of Ulster.

CUCHULAINN (*giving the Gae Bolg to* LAEG).
　　　　　　This is my final weapon, Laeg.
　　　　　　Keep it secure until I call for it.
　　　　　　But now, a chariot.
　　　　　　Go, fetch me a chariot.
(LAEG *hurries off by the North West entrance. At Rathcroghan*
CUROI *greets* MAEV.)

CUROI.　　　Greetings, Maev, from Curoi, King of Munster, and
　　　　　　from my son, Lewy. I bring to your hosting the
　　　　　　men of the South.
(*War Dance of the Men of Munster. At its conclusion,* MAEV

370

*enters her chariot and leads off the Host in procession. Drums
beat.* FERDIA *remains behind, talking to* FINNAVAUR.)

MAEV.   Forward, my friends and Allies.
           Forward on the Foe.

BRICRIU (*in the Palace*).
           The time's propitious.
           Nobody is there. Some disability is on them all.
           I almost am disposed to go myself.
(MAEV *halts her chariot beside* FEDELMA, *whom she meets on the
way.*)

MAEV.   Stop! Here is my Prophetess.
           What do you see, Fedelma?

FEDELMA.   I will look into the future, Queen.
(*She covers her face with her hands, and sways from side to side.*)

BRICRIU (*to* FERDIA *who remains in the Palace with* FINNAVAUR).
           Hello! ! Not gone, Ferdia?

FERDIA.   I do not fight with Ulstermen.

BRICRIU (*leering*).
           Who would blame you, with so much
                better to attend to!

FERDIA (*stiffly*).
           Their Champion is my friend. I will not fight with
                him.

BRICRIU.   What Champion?

FIDELMA.   I see your Host be-crimsoned.
           All is red.

MAEV.   How can this be? For Conacher is in his sickness
                in Emain, and the best of his warriors are here
                with me.

FEDELMA.   I see your Host be-crimsoned.
           I see a man with light upon his brow –
           A wolfhound on whose forehead victory sits –
           A dark man girded round with adamant –
           The Battle-fury boiling in his blood.

He will make slaughter at the Ford
And those that stay behind will curse you, Maev,
For summoning their playmates
To so notable a feast.

MAEV.   Slay that crone, and let her see what crimson is.
(FEDELMA *is struck down as the army moves off.*)

FEDELMA.   I see red. I see red.

11.

(*As the Host of* MAEV *begins its march,* CUCHULAINN *goes into his Battle-Fury.*)

CUCHULAINN'S BATTLE FURY.
            Masu e in riastarde,
            Betit colla dóene de,
            Betit eigme de im lissu,
            Betit buind ri harissu.
            Betit Corrthe do im lechta,
            Bud fórmach do rigmartra.
            Ni maith far-arlith in cath
            Ar leirg risin foendelach.
            Atchiu cruth inn foendela ich
            Nóe cind leis i foendelaib,
            Atchiu fadb leis na bretaig,
            Deich cind ina rosetaib.

(CUCHULAINN *in his fury descends upon the Ford, where he finds* LOCKA *filling her bucket.*)

CUCHULAINN.   Ah, contumelious Queen, so you would cross my
                    Ford
                And foul our meadowlands!
                Here is your welcome.
(*He kills her.*)

LOCKA.   O, my heart's blood!
                Why have you done this to me?

CUCHULAINN.   Are you not Maev?

LOCKA. My name is Locka.
Do not mistake my face the next time,
For you will see it again –
The day you die.

(*She dies, as* MAEV'S *Host arrives at the Ford and the drums
cease to beat.*)

MAEV. Who is this fellow who has killed my waiting
woman?

CUCHULAINN (*crestfallen*).
I am Cuchulainn. It was you I should have slain.

CUROI (*stepping forward*).
Stand aside, murderer of maidservants.

HEAD OF SUALTAM.
Rise and defend yourselves, Men of Ulster.

CUCHULAINN. I am at fault. But I will not stand aside.

CUROI (*advancing upon him*).
Dog you may be but I am a wild boar.

12.

(*The Drums beat.* CUROI *advances through the Ford and fights
with* CUCHULAINN. CUCHULAINN *slays him. The Drums stop.*)

LEWY (*astonished*).
This juvenile has killed my father!
(*He hurries to the body and picks it up in his arms.*)

MAEV. This is too much!
Forward my seven sons
And clear the Ford.

(*Drums beat. The Seven Manes advance upon* CUCHULAINN *and
are all slain in rapid succession.*)

BRICRIU. Is this according to the plan?
The Boar is dead, and all is not happy with the herd.
The situation calls for conversations on a
higher level.

13.

(The Army withdraws a little. As MAEV *comes to the Ford,* BRICRIU *follows.* MAEV *and* CUCHULAINN *greet each other.)*

MAEV. Boy, you have slain the King of Munster
And my seven sons.

CUCHULAINN. Send all your troops to cross this Ford
And I will add a column to your catalogue.

MAEV. Would you slay me too?

CUCHULAINN. You most readily of all.

BRICRIU *(amid general horror).*
This is a lamentable business
And must be faced with common sense.
This should be an affray of champions.
The Queen requires her faithful commoners.
But Champions can be spared.
(General agreement; except among the Champions.)

MAEV *(to* BRICRIU*).*
What is it you propose?
*(*BRICRIU *consults in whispers with* MAEV *for a moment and the latter archly agrees.)*

MAEV. Cuchulainn, will you fight my champions
single handed?

CUCHULAINN. I shall. With pleasure.

BRICRIU. But not to-night, to-morrow we begin.

CUCHULAINN. Agreed.

BRICRIU *(to* MAEV*).*
And while he fights, the army steals the Bull.
Better to lose a man or two a day.
Than half a regiment in one bloody brawl.

MAEV.   Agreed.
           To-morrow, we shall meet again, Cuchulainn.
(CUCHULAINN *retires to the Pillar Stone and flings himself upon the ground falling asleep at once.*)

14.
(ACTION)

BRICRIU.   This is really a sensible solution –
           More sensible the more I think of it.
           He sleeps. Now is the time to steal across
           And kill him.
(*After a moment's hesitation, the Army commences to creep forward. But then* LU *appears galloping down from the North West in his chariot. As he crosses between the Army and the Pillar Stone, the tribes fall back in dismay.* DARA *goes off by the North West leaving the bull in the field.*)

VOICES.   It is a God! See, it is Lu!

LU.   Yes, it is Lu
           And you shall keep your bargain with my son.
           Cuchulainn sleeps,
           But there is still a sentry at the Ford.
           Who dares to cross?
(*The Host of the Four Fifths falls back, carrying off its dead. Those still in the Palace slip away too. There is music in the air. As* LU *drives off by the North West* CUCHULAINN *still sleeps by the stone.*)
     Meanwhile SHANAHAN *sings, and during the second verse he closes the Book and leaves the field by the eastern entrance.*)

SHANAHAN (*singing or reciting to the music*).
           Anois is ea thógann an oíche a leinbh chun hucht;
           Cosúil le máthair is ea chosnann sí ar chontúirt
           lad bhíonn brónach tuirseach d'éis fad-shiúil –
           Míleadha tréana milse aoibhne na mór-Chúige.
           A oíche álainn, is tú a gcara lán de ghrá;
           Socraínn tu a gcroí led dhorchas fairsing mór;
           Tir'mionn tú a súile; glanann tu a n-anama de
               chrá;

375

Is iad i eim codhladh' gan fhios gan aithne,
gan mhothadh, gan anál.

(*As the music builds and concludes, there is nobody left upon the field, except* CUCHULAINN *unless it is dark enough for him to get away unseen and return after the Interval*).

END OF THE SECOND PART

INTERVAL

PART THREE

THE FORD OF ARDEE

(A Band has been playing during the interval. Before it has quite concluded, SHANAHAN *has returned to the Rock with his Book.* CUCHULAINN *still sleeps at the Pillar Stone or alternatively comes back there again in the darkness).*

SHANAHAN.   Day breaks on Cooley and the hills of Mourne.
        The testing time of Champions has begun.

*(*LAEG *drives in from the North-west in* CUCHULAINN'S *Chariot drawn by the Grey of Macha and the Black Sainglend. He comes to the Pillar Stone and dismounts. A Trumpet sounds in the South-East, and* NACHRANTAL *marches in, followed by* BRICRIU *and a group of skirmishers.* DARA *returns to his bull.)*

LAEG.   Wake up Master. It is morning and the first of
        the Four Fifths is on its way.

*(*CUCHULAINN *rises and buckles on his sword and takes his shield.)*

LAEG *(holding up the Gae Bolg).*
        Will you need this, Master?

CUCHULAINN.   Not the Gae Bolg. I can fight this fellow without
        that.
        Who are you?

NACHRANTAL.   I am Nachrantal, Champion of the Queen of
        Connacht.
        I claim the right to be the first.

CUCHULAINN.   The first to die?

NACHRANTAL.   The first to cross the Ford.

BRICRIU *(to the skirmishers).*
        Now, while they are engaged, you men will
        circumnavigate the storm and liberate the Bull.

This is the tactic of the indirect approach which
I myself shall supervise from a position of
security.

(*He retires to the Rock, where he prepares to comment.*)

NACHRANTAL (*advancing*).
Yield or die, Dog of Cullin.

CUCHULAINN. Neither shall I do, Nachrantal.

(MAEV *in her chariot has come to the Rock followed by* LECH,
ERC, FERGUS *and* FIACHA. FERDIA *and* FINNAVAUR *have returned
to Rathcroghan where they sit talking. Drums beat, and as the
Champions fight, the Skirmishers slowly advance around the side
upon* DARA *and the* BULL. CUCHULAINN *kills* NACHRANTAL *and the
Drums stop.* BRICRIU *whistles the Skirmishers back and they come
scampering home.*)

BRICRIU.   Back, skirmishers! Beware of that Dog.
(NACHRANTAL *is borne off by the West.* THE MORRIGAN *flutters in
from the South.*)

16.

BRICRIU.   That was too short a fight.

CUCHULAINN. (*calling out*).
Who's next? See, the crows are gathering.

THE MORRIGAN.
My lovely pupil! Did you take me for a bird?
I have come to help you.

CUCHULAINN. I don't need your help.

THE MORRIGAN (*fluttering around him*).
Say that you love me, lovely boy.

CUCHULAINN (*striking at her*).
Be off, crow, be off!

THE MORRIGAN (*screeching as she flies off*).
Aaaah! Gratitude. Gratitude. Gratitude.
Caw. Caw. Caw. Caw.

MAEV.   Fergus – advance.
(FERGUS *draws his sword but is restrained by*
FIACHA.)

FIACHA.   No, Fergus, Ulster cannot fight with Ulster.
(FERGUS *shrugs his shoulders and sheathes his sword.*)

MAEV.   Cowards! Where is my best of Champions Ferdia?

BRICRIU.   At home, talking with your daughter, Finnavaur.
But what about the Corcu Osraige –
The Folk of the Deer from Leinster?

ERC.   Yes, it is Leinster's turn.
I call for Lech of Ossory.

LECH.   For me?
Do you suppose that I, a man of fifty battles
Would condescend to fight a beardless boy?

BRICRIU (*calling out*).
Cuchulainn, assume a beard for Lech of Ossory.

CUCHULAINN (*calling back*).
Let him advance and I will fight him as I am.

LAEG (*laughing*).
Come Master. Let us oblige him with a beard.
I will give you one.
(*He smears some blue-black substance on* CUCHULAINN'S *chin.*)
(*The Morrigan flutters around* LECH.)

CUCHULAINN.   What is this upon my chin?

LAEG.   Raspberry juice. (*calling out*)
Now my Master has a beard.
The Gae Bolg? Cuchulainn.
(*He offers the Gae Bolg.*)

CUCHULAINN.   No. Not this time either.

THE MORRIGAN.
Courage, Lech.
I shall help you to destroy this thing
That spurns old friends.

LECH.   Very well. Have at him! (*Drums begin*)

379

NO! No drums please. (*The drums stop*)
We do not care for such vulgarities in Leinster.
(*They fight. This time* THE MORRIGAN *trips up* CUCHULAINN *and he is about to be slaughtered on the ground when by a superb gesture, he flings a javelin and kills* LECH *instead.* LAEG *drives away* THE MORRIGAN *clucking and cursing. The skirmishers, who have again advanced towards the Brown Bull, hastily retreat once more.* LECH *is borne off by the East Entrance.*)

BRICRIU.   Back again, skirmishers!
              The People of the Deer have done no better.

MAEV (*getting furious*).
              Where is Ferdia?

BRICRIU.   Still at the Palace.
              A public service is required of Finnavaur.

17.

(*In Rathcroghan* FINNAVAUR *is pouring out wine for* FERDIA.)

FINNAVAUR.   Why did you stay behind, Ferdia? Was it because
              of me?

FERDIA.   No, Finnavaur. I must admit that there were other
              reasons.

FINNAVAUR.   I'm glad. Women should be of little account with
              warriors.
              We are so small – so unimportant in our views –
              seeing everything in terms of personalities, when
              principles are so much more important.
              I admire a man who gives no thought to women's
              whims.
(*She fills his goblet.*)

FERDIA (*indulgently*).
              Oh, I don't know. Some of your sex are very
              sensible.

FINNAVAUR.   That is another thing that draws me to you. You
              know the way to speak to women, Ferdia – not

380

as a warrior's recreation, but as a human being,
like yourself. You understand women, Ferdia, in
a way no man that I have known has ever done.
It sometimes frightens me – you understand
women so well.

FERDIA.   Oh, I don't know. It's simply that I don't look down
on women – at least not on women of intelligence,
like you.

FINNAVAUR.   That is your great attraction. You are not a bore,
like other men.
You can have no idea what bores other men are –
and the greater the celebrity, the greater the
bore. Take Cuchulainn, for example – always
boasting of his prowess as a hero. Who cares if he
could conquer you?

FERDIA.   Is that what he says?

FINNAVAUR.   Continually. But what does that matter to a
woman?

FERDIA.   Cuchulainn is no greater a warrior than I am.
I could cross that Ford against him any time I
chose.

FINNAVAUR.   That is not what everybody says. But I don't mind.
I know that you have other reasons for not
fighting him, and that is enough for me.

FERDIA.   We are blood brothers, Finnavaur, plighted in
friendship.
In college we were boys together. As men we raced
with Death again and again – horses in double
harness.

FINNAVAUR.   I know. But that is what my silly woman's tongue
cannot explain to other people, Ferdia. Does this
pledge mean that he may seek the good of Ulster
by fighting at the Ford, while you may not
pursue the good of Connacht by taking arms
yourself? He may fight you and yours, but you
must not fight him. Is that the meaning of
your pledge?

381

FERDIA (*confused*).
Well, – it's quite a problem, Finnavaur.

FINNAVAUR. Then let us have some wine, while you explain the answer to me.

(*She pours out more wine.*)

18.

(*Meanwhile, at the Rock,* CALATIN *has entered, and is gathering together his twenty-one sons to fall upon* CUCHULAINN. ANNI, *his wife, follows in some distress, with* BEVE, *her daughter.*)

CALATIN. Draw your swords, my gallant sons. Let the Clan Calatin show its metal.

ANNI (*flinging her arms around his neck in terror*)
Don't go, my husband. Let the lads go if they must, but not you. I can have other children, but never such another husband.

CALATIN. What, shall I send my children into battle, and stop at home myself! Am I the greatest Wizard in all Connacht, whose spells have staggered thousands, or am I just a father for your brood?

BEVE (*answering him back angrily*)
Have you no sense, Father? – no responsibilities towards those that are coming?

CALATIN. I can never owe more to my children – living or coming – than they owe to me. Forward, my sons. And let us have drums again, in the grand old style.

(*With a dreadful shriek,* ANNI *releases him, and turning away she hides her eyes in* BEVE'S *arms. Drums beat. The Clan assails* CUCHULAINN *amidst the cheers of the Four Fifths.* CUCHULAINN *is hard pressed and suddenly from the southern ranks,* FIACHA *leaps forward.*)

CUCHULAINN. Help me, Fiacha, Help!

FIACHA.   I am of Ula too!
           My kinsman needs my help
           And I must give it.

CUCHULAINN.   Brave lad.
              Lay on!

(FIACHA *dashes through the Ford, and joins* CUCHULAINN *in the fray. Together they hew down every man of the Clan. With a despairing shriek* ANNI *is led back to the south-west entrance by* BEVE. *The drums stop, as* CUCHULAINN *and* FIACHA *embrace each other. Again, the skirmishers return without capturing the Bull, although this time they have almost reached it.)*

CUCHULAINN.   Thank you, my countryman.

FIACHA.   The time of the curse is almost gone.
           Hold the Ford, Cuchulainn,
           While I rouse the Red Branch
           From its sleep.

CUCHULAINN.   Go, and the Gods go with you.
              Rouse up the North, Fiacha,
              And tell my wife, Eever
              I shall be with her, soon.

(*The bodies of the Clan have been borne off by the South-West.* FIACHA *goes to Emain Macha and rouses* CONOR *who goes drowsily with him out of sight. But* EEVER *rises and comes down to the Pillar Stone, bearing a basket of food and wine.)*

19.

(*In Rathcroghan,* FERDIA *rises from* FINNAVAUR'S *kiss.*)

MAC ROTH.   The Clan Calatin is slain.
             No one could cross that Ford but Ferdia.

MAEV.   Where is Ferdia?
         Let him be brought.

(*All the host cries out for* FERDIA.)

FINNAVAUR.   Say that you love me, Ferdia?

FERDIA.   Yes, I love you. Why should I deny it?

FINNAVAUR.   Then go and fight for me.

FERDIA (*taken aback*).
          Fight for you?

FINNAVAUR.   You have said that you love me.
          If you will not fight for Connacht,
          Go then and cross the Ford for Finnavaur.

BRICRIU (*after a solemn pause*).
          There is a Geis upon you, Ferdia,
          Never to refuse to fight for one you love.
          You must go, Ferdia.
(FERDIA'S *Chariot has drawn up at Rathcroghan, driven by* RORY.)

FERDIA.   It is true. My Geis I must obey.
          I swear, Finnavaur, upon my honour as a Knight
          That I shall not return till I have crossed the ford.
(FERDIA *mounts his chariot and comes to the Ford. A hush falls
on the battlefield, as the Army sits down upon the ground in
silent groups.*)

FERDIA.   Greeting, Cuchulainn. You are welcome here.

CUCHULAINN.   Since this is my country and my Ford
          It were more fitting that I should welcome you.

FERDIA (*struggling with his feelings*).
          Cuchulainn, they have put a Geis upon me,
          And I must cross.
          Yet we are Brothers, and we must not fight.

CUCHULAINN.   No stranger to Ulster shall cross this Ford in arms
          Be he my brother or be he not.

FERDIA.   There was a time, Cuchulainn
          When you would not have spoken to me thus.

CUCHULAINN.   Time dies as readily as Man.

FERDIA (*turning in agony to those behind him*).
          Release me from my Geis.
(FINNAVAUR *is with her Mother, watching from the Rock.*)

FINNAVAUR *(prompted by her mother)*.
>I do not release you, Ferdia. You must fight.

HALF THE HOST *(calling out)*.
>You are not released.

THE OTHER HALF
>Fight, Ferdia.

FERDIA.
>Cuchulainn, I swear I have no wish to break our
>Bond.
>Why then, must you oppose me?

CUCHULAINN.
>Stay where you are, Ferdia, and my sword shall do
>the same.
>But cross the Ford, and you are challenging Ulster.
>And Ulster is Cuchulainn.

FERDIA *(turning in despair to the South)*.
>Finnavaur, I must obey my Geis.
>But for this springle you have placed me in
>I swear, when I have slain my friend
>I shall return to Connacht, and slay you.

(FINNAVAUR *cries out, and hides her face.*)

FERDIA.
>What weapons do you choose, Cuchulainn?

CUCHULAINN.
>Let the choice be yours, Ferdia.

FERDIA.
>Then let it be spears.

CUCHULAINN.
>So be it.

(CUCHULAINN *and* FERDIA *mount their chariots, and their fight with spears is mimed. There are no drums this time.* BRICRIU *orders off the skirmishers as before. After a time a trumpet sounds and the battle stops. The skirmishers lie down on their stomachs, taking cover.*)

FERDIA.
>A truce, Cuchulainn. See the sun is setting.

CUCHULAINN.
>A truce, Ferdia, till the morning.

RORY (FERDIA'S *Charioteer*).
>Food and drink for my master, Ferdia!

(*As the two Champions dismount and meet in mid-stream, servants run forward bearing food and wine, and* EEVER *comes to the Northern side with the same.*)

FERDIA.   Share my food, Cuchulainn.

CUCHULAINN. And you my flask.
(EEVER *brings him a flask, which he hands to* FERDIA. FERDIA *in his turn gives* CUCHULAINN *bread. Each Champion returns to his own side, where he then lies down upon the grass.* MAEV'S *skirmishers are now camped around the Bull.*)

BRICRIU.   How gallant these contenders sound today.
            But it will not continue.
            When next they fight
            Their manners will be rougher.
            That is the way of war.
(*A Trumpet sounds, and the Champions rise and again face each other.*)

FERDIA.   Cuchulainn, I have sworn to cross the Ford.
            You will not suffer me to pass?

CUCHULAINN. I am a man who has slain his son for Ulster.
            If you were Lu himself, I would not treat you
                otherwise.

FERDIA.   Then we must fight again.

CUCHULAINN. So be it.

FERDIA.   Hound of Cullin, man of Fate,
            Together we have learnt the craft of battle.
            So choose this time the order of our fighting.

CUCHULAINN. You came to the Ford.
            Let yours be the choice.

FERDIA.   Then swords this time I say. And on our feet.
(CUCHULAINN *bows, and they fight. This time the fight is grimmer.*)

FINNAVAUR. Who wins?
            Who wins?

MAEV.   Are you hoping it is not your lover?

LAEG.   A truce?
(*Trumpet call.*)

RORY.   The trumpet sounds.
(*Silently they turn and go each to his own bank, refusing the food*

386

that is brought. Meanwhile, during the conflict, the skirmishers of MAEV *have driven off* DARA, *and are gathered round the Bull.* DARA *leaves by the North-West.*)

BRICRIU.   As I opined, this time they have not parted friends.
            The earliest casualty in war
            Is always Brotherhood.
(*The trumpet sounds again, and both heroes rise and face each other for the last time.*)

CUCHULAINN *(grimly).*
            This time it is for me to choose the weapons.

FERDIA.   Then choose and let us get to work.

CUCHULAINN. Let it be as each man wills.

FERDIA *(after a terrible pause).*
            So be it.
            All is free.
(*For a time* CUCHULAINN *fights with a sword,* FERDIA *with a spear. Then* CUCHULAINN'S *helm is knocked off and blood runs from his forehead. A gasp of excitement runs through the onlookers.* CUCHULAINN *pauses in midstream.*)

CUCHULAINN. Laeg. Give me my weapon – the Gae Bolg.
(LAEG *takes it from the chariot.* FERDIA *passes his hand across his face.*)

FERDIA.   Rory – a stone. Something to place before my
                stomach.
(RORY *brings him a flat stone, and helps him to place it under his tunic.*)

CUCHULAINN. Are you ready?

FERDIA.   Ready indeed.
(*They fight for the last time,* CUCHULAINN, *as before with his sword, until* FERDIA *raises his shield above his face to ward off a blow from above. With that,* CUCHULAINN *drops the Gae Bolg and looses it upon* FERDIA *from below with his foot.* FERDIA *falls with a terrible cry.*)

FINNAVAUR *(in tears).*
            Oh, I am saved.

(CUCHULAINN, *after staring for a moment at the body, drops his sword and shield and picks up* FERDIA'S *remains, which he carries over to his own side of the Ford.*)

CUCHULAINN. Look, men of Erin, your Champion has discharged
          his oath.
        Ferdia has crossed the Ford.
        May this great soul rest in peace for evermore.
(*He sinks to the ground, holding* FERDIA *in his arms.*)

FINNAVAUR. And yet I loved him truly!

LAEG (*as the Host begins to advance*).
        Rise up, Master, or the Host of Erin will be on us.

CUCHULAINN. What is there to rise for now?
        Ferdia has fallen by these bloody hands.
(*But except for* FERGUS *and* RORY *who are at the Ford, the host of Erin is not advancing upon* CUCHULAINN. *It is moving to receive the Brown Bull, now being pulled triumphantly to the south by the skirmishers.*)

FINNAVAUR (*coming to the Ford*).
        Oh, my grief!
        Where is my man – my fair one – my golden
          brooch?
        The shield with the rim of gold?
        The ring of whitest silver on his arm?
        The soft-folded girdle round about his waist?
        Where is the kiss that once was on my lips?
        Let heaven burst, and the unbridled sun
        Sweep from its bed, and drown me in its tears.
        He is gone!
        And I prayed for his going.
        I loved him –
        Yet I praised the Gods when Ferdia fell!
(*There is outburst of dancing and cheering from the Host, as it seizes the Bull, and led by* MAEV, *they escort it back to Rathcroghan. The great bell is rung, and each Province disperses in its own direction by the usual entrance, leaving only the Court of* MAEV, *and the Red Bull, which has been brought on, garlanded from the south east.* AILEEL *is roused by* BRICRIU, *and preparations are on foot for an orgy, when silence falls again.*)

20.

(CUCHULAINN *rises and signals to* FERGUS *and* RORY *who bear*
FERDIA *to his chariot. A single piper is with them now.*

EEVER *crouches by the Pillar Stone, to which* LAEG *brings*
CUCHULAINN'S *chariot and the weapons from the Ford.* FINNAVAUR
still stands at the Ford, in tears.

DARA *comes creeping back from the north, with a group of the*
Brown Bull's Attendants.)

CUCHULAINN. Woman, if I could only grieve for Ferdia
　　　　　　　My grief would be a happy one indeed.
　　　　　　　But what are half a dozen years
　　　　　　　Stolen from the Death Sentence
　　　　　　　That hangs above the race of man –
　　　　　　　On you and me, as well as Ferdia?
　　　　　　　We should be happy he has won the race
　　　　　　　That once was promised him.
　　　　　　　We should crown his forehead with the colours he
　　　　　　　　　has earned.
　　　　　　　O Ferdia, you were fleet of foot indeed.
　　　　　　　For you have paced the bare-ribbed runner
　　　　　　　Whom we all pursue
　　　　　　　And caught him at the post.

(*The piper commences to play a dirge, and the Chariot moves off*
towards the south east, led by RORY, *and followed by* FERGUS *and*
FINNAVAUR.)

CUCHULAINN. But what of me?
　　　　　　　What I have murdered is not Ferdia
　　　　　　　But Friendship.
　　　　　　　I have slaughtered the warm clasp of hands –
　　　　　　　The pledge of brotherhood –
　　　　　　　And in the name of Duty.
　　　　　　　Cursed be Duty!
　　　　　　　What duty can be worth this paradox?
　　　　　　　Where are our promises now?
　　　　　　　The quips in College courtyards?

The pennies squandered in the Pumprooms?
The songs sung out of harmony?
The deadly quarrels that were worth
The sprees of reconciliation?
Gone, like the winds on Nephin
And as stable.
O Ferdia, we swore to put the Shannon in our
    pockets
And drink it after Samhain.
If such things as these are mortal
Let men die!

(With a crash, the victory dance breaks out at Rathcroghan, around the Brown Bull.

CUCHULAINN *returns wearily to the Pillar Stone, where he lies down with his head in* EEVER'S *lap.)*

21.

(At Rathcroghan the celebration reaches its climax by facing the Brown Bull with the Red. The latter professes great readiness to attack the Brown, dancing round it in an aggressive manner. Then DARA'S *voice is heard, calling the Bull, and for the first time its roar is heard. It opens its mouth, and smoke pours from its throat and nostrils. Its eyes blaze with light, and with a shriek of terror, everybody runs away by the South-West entrance and the lights go out – the Red Bull being the last in the rout.)*

In the gathering darkness DARA *and the attendants run the Brown Bull as rapidly as possible back to·the North and out by the North-West entrance.)*

INTERLUDE: DIRGE BY UNSEEN PIPERS

END OF PART THREE

PART FOUR

THE END OF CUCHULAINN

22.

(Before the lights rise on SHANAHAN, LOCKA *has come to the Ford and crouches there, with her head covered, looking like a heap of rags. The lights first rise on* SHANAHAN, *and the Rock. Rathcroghan is now empty. The warriors of Munster under* LEWY *are in a group to the South.)*

SHANAHAN. And so the Brown Bull of Cooley
     Was captured and was lost again.
     But this is not the end,
     For blood cries out for blood
     And cannot hold its tongue.
     Lewy of Munster murmurs for a Father,
     And from the West
     The mis-shapen brood of Calatin
     Hatched after their Father's death
     Follows their sister, Beve,
     To the making of mischief.

(The six mis-shapen ones – three males and three females – come from the South West entrance to dance and weave spells around a cauldron that they bring with them. One of the men carries a dead dog which he places in the cauldron. BEVE, *their only surviving normal sister, goes to the Pillar Stone where* CUCHULAINN *lies with his head in* EEVER'S *lap.* SHANAHAN *shakes his head sadly and leaves the field carrying the book.)*

BEVE.   Do you know who I am, Cuchulainn?

CUCHULAINN. Nor do I care.

BEVE.   I am Beve, daughter of Calatin
     Whom you slew with all my brothers at the Ford.

CUCHULAINN. Go away.

BEVE. There is still another battle to be fought,
Cuchulainn.
The Hosting of the South is on its way.

23.

(*Strange tremulous music. From both southern ends of the field
come Dancers dressed as Wraiths, Puffballs, Thistles and Leaves.
As they dance* CUCHULAINN *sits up and watches.*)

BEVE. Do you see, Cuchulainn?
The warriors of the Four Fifths are on the march.
You must go out and fight again.

EEVER. Do not listen to her, husband.
No one is there.
Nothing but leaves and puffballs,
Dancing in the air.

(*The roar of the Bull is heard in the distance.* CUCHULAINN *rises.*)

CUCHULAINN *(struggling up)*
No. I hear the roaring of the Bull.
My enemies are coming.
Fetch me my armour, Laeg.

BEVE. Yes, yes.
Go out and fight.

EEVER. Stay with me, husband.
There is no one there.

CUCHULAINN. My chariot, Laeg.
My chariot!

(*The Grey of Macha breaks loose from the chariot and trots off.
He must be subsequently recaptured on the field and taken out
by the North West Entrance.*)

LAEG. You are deceived, Cuchulainn.
Even your horse knows it.
The Grey has broken loose
And runs away.

CUCHULAINN. Must I be baffled by a mutinous horse?
My sword, you scullion!
Cuchulainn knows his enemies
And will fight.
(BEVE *hurries to the men of Munster.*)

EEVER *(trying to hold him back).*
Cuchulainn!

CUCHULAINN *(flinging her off)*
Blood and maledictions!
Unfruitful nag, be off
After your kind!
(*He tears himself away, sword in hand, and tries vainly to come
to grips with the dancing wraiths, who presently flutter off, as
LEWY and his men prapare to march north. EEVER, in despair,
retires to Emain Macha, where she waits and watches. The music
has ended.*)

24.

(*At the Ford* CUCHULAINN *finds a woman washing clothes in the
river. When she looks up she has the face of* LOCKA.)

CUCHULAINN. Where have they gone?
Woman, who are you?

LOCKA. Don't you remember my face?

CUCHULAINN. It is the face of one I slew, here by this water.
It is Locka the maid.

LOCKA. Yes, Cuchulainn.
Now you have seen my face again.

CUCHULAINN. What is this that you are washing?

LOCKA *(holding up a blood-stained tunic).*
A bloody tunic. Do you know it?

CUCHULAINN. It is mine.
(*He hurries away over the Ford, and comes to the cauldron of
the Mis-shapen ones. The three female crones sit around it. The*

393

males are sitting on the Altar step. LOCKA *gathers up her washing
and wanders off by the North.*)

1ST CRONE (*stirring the pot*).
> Share our poor food, stranger.

CUCHULAINN. That I will not.

2ND CRONE. If it was a great feast you would share it with us.
> But we are poor
> And the great always despise the poor.

CUCHULAINN. That is not my reason.

3RD CRONE. Then show us that you are not too proud,
> Cuchulainn.

CUCHULAINN. So you know my name?

1ST CRONE. Who does not know the Hound of Cullin?

2ND CRONE. And the Geis that is on him
> Never to refuse the offer of hospitality.

3RD CRONE. Come and join our humble table, Champion of
> Ulster.
> You have a long way to go.

CUCHULAINN. Never to refuse –
> Yes, I must remember my Geis.
> I must share your brew.

(*They deal out the concoction and* CUCHULAINN *and the* CRONES
taste it together. THE MORRIGAN *is fluttering around in a great
state of excitement.*)

CUCHULAINN (*in some disgust*).
> What is this that I have eaten?

1ST CRONE. Do you not recognise it, Hound of Cullin. It is
> Dog.

(*On the Rock the three males set up a howl of triumph, and
dance off after the crones, carrying the steaming pot.*)

THE MORRIGAN.
> Dog, Hound of Cullin, Dog!
> You have eaten yourself.
> Haha! Haha!
> Where are your sinews now?

25.

(*Drums beat, and the troops of* LEWY *advance upon* CUCHULAINN. LAEG *hastens after him in the Chariot, now drawn by the Black horse only.* CUCHULAINN *mounts the Chariot and his enemies form a square of shields,* LEWY *in the middle.*)
(*Around the square, the Chariot gallops. The drumming stops.*)

LEWY (*shouting*).
                Give me that spear, Cuchulainn.

CUCHULAINN.   My need of this spear is greater than yours, Lewy.

LEWY.   Give me that spear or I shall satirise you for
                meanness.

CUCHULAINN.   No man shall call me mean. So take it.
(*He flings the spear at the square of shields. One picks it up, and* LEWY *flings it back killing* LAEG.)

LEWY (*as he throws*).
                Do you take it back?

LAEG.   Oh Master, I am slain.
                Master – take care.
(LAEG *falls out of the Chariot.* CUCHULAINN *picks up the reins and gallops around the square again.*)

LEWY.   Give me your sword, Cuchulainn.

CUCHULAINN.   No Lewy. I am not bound to grant more than
                one request a day.

LEWY.   Give me your sword.
                Would you refuse a Bard his orison?

CUCHULAINN.   Take it.
(*He flings his sword at the square. One takes it and* LEWY *flings it back, loosing the Black horse and wounding* CUCHULAINN *in the stomach. The Black horse gallops away. And it does not matter where it goes.*)

LEWY *(as he throws).*
> Do you take it back?

CUCHULAINN. The Bolg, Laeg!
> My weapon – the Gae Bolg.

THE MORRIGAN *(cackling).*
> Your charioteer is dead.

CUCHULAINN. A drink, then. Fetch me a drink.
> My chitterlings are scattered by this novice.

THE MORRIGAN.
> To the river, Hound of Cullin –
> And further than the river.
> Ha! Ha! Caw. Caw. Caw!

26.

(Weird music. From nowhere THE MORRIGAN'S *Crows gather and dance in a wide circle around the Pillar Stone while* CUCHULAINN *struggles upwards and binds himself to it with his belt. The square breaks up and the warriors approach* CUCHULAINN, *led by* LEWY. *Others place the body of* LAEG *in the abandoned chariot and draw it off to the South.* FERCARTNA, *the Munster Herald goes reconnoitering towards the north.)*

CUCHULAINN. If I must die
> Let me die standing up.

(The hoofbeats of a horse are heard through the music.)

CUCHULAINN. Hoofbeats on the wind!
> Where is my Grey –
> The Grey of Macha that deserted me?
> Where are all the men of Ulster?

THE MORRIGAN *(approaching).*
> Nowhere Cuchulainn, You are alone.

CUCHULAINN. Still I will die fighting.

(He draws a dirk and strikes at a warrior who approaches. The Dance stops as do the hoofbeats. The warriors advance upon

CUCHULAINN, *crowding around him, with shouts of triumph.*
Behind their screen, the dummy figure concealed in the Pillar
Stone is substituted for the live player, who assumes the cloak and
headdress of one of the assailants for the purpose of getting
away unseen.)
(FERCARTNA *comes running from the north and approaches* LEWY.)

FERCARTNA. Peril in the North, Lewy!
I saw sparks of fire coming out of the mist
And then a great wind lifted the hair upon my head
And flung me on my back.
Yet the wind of the day was not great.

LEWY. Make haste to end Cuchulainn.
These are the Ulstermen – coming out of their
sickness.

(*He pushes his way into the throng around the stone. Then there*
is a loud cry from LEWY *and the assailants draw back to a*
distance, disclosing once again CUCHULAINN *apparently still lashed*
to the Pillar.)

LEWY (*shaking a stump in the air*).
Rogue, you have struck off my hand.

THE MORRIGAN.
Take his hand too!

(LEWY *strikes off* CUCHULAINN'S *right hand. From the north come*
thundering hoof beats.)

LEWY. Quickly! Quickly!

(THE MORRIGAN *dances forward and with a screech places a crow*
upon CUCHULAINN'S *shoulder.* LEWY *picks up his sword with the*
left hand. Then LEWY *advances, and with a blow of his sword,*
strikes off the figure's head.)

27.

(*A trumpet blares in the North, and* FIACHA, *entering from the*
North West, gallops wildly round the field on the Grey of Macha
like a circus rider shouting and waving his sword. LEWY *and his*

men with THE MORRIGAN *and her crows run frantically away to the south as* LU *in his Chariot approaches the Pillar Stone from the Southern Entrance.*)

(*Meanwhile the Red Branch Knights, following* CONOR MAC NESSA *in his chariot, enter from the North West Entrance.*)

THE HEAD OF SUALTAM.

         Forward, the Red Branch Knights of Ulster!

(*The Red Branch Knights line up to the north of the Stone as* CONOR *dismounts and bows to* LU *who has also dismounted with a golden casket in his hand.*)

(FIACHA, *having driven off the enemy, returns to the Stone and leaps from the Grey,* FERGUS *follows.*)

CONOR.   Conor Mac Nessa, King of Ulster,
            Greets the great God, Lu.

LU.   Pick up the head. Pick up the hand.
            I have come for the soul of my son,
            The Hound of Ulster.

(CONOR MAC NESSA *picks up the head.* FERGUS *picks up the hand.* LU *opens his casket and* CONOR *shakes the breath of the severed head into the open top.* LU *closes the top, raises the casket proudly above his head and returns to his Chariot. From all sides the people are now coming with faggots to the Rock Altar. They pile these around it.* FERGUS *and the three Provincial Heralds take up their places to north, south, east and west of the Rock holding furled banners.*)

LU.   Blazon the blood-red hand upon the oriflamme
              of Ulster, Fergus Mac Roy.
            Fly, bird of the Morrigan, over the silver fields of
              Connacht.
            Men of the Deer, unfurl the verdant fields of
              Ossory.
            And Munster raise the Boar of Kerry.

(*Funeral Music. The four standard-bearers now unfurl their banners in succession. The Red Branch Knights carry the body shoulder-high and place it on the summit of the pyre.* EEVER *follows with the head, which she puts, last, upon the top.*)

LU.   Ireland is one in honouring her warriors.
            From north and south and east and west
            Come, Gaels and gather at this pyre,

Where burns the meanest part of Lu's beloved.
Bring torches, Irishmen,
And carry to your homes
This flaming dust that never shall be quenched.
(*The flames of the pyre leap into the air as* Lu *drives off by the North West holding the casket aloft.*)

28.

(*The music changes to a march and from all quarters of the compass the warriors and people of Ireland come marching in with unlit torches and by fives and tens the torches are lit from the flames. The scene changes to a sea of burning torches marching and counter marching, singing as they go, until finally they march off leaving nothing to be seen except the flaming pyre.*)

THAT IS THE END OF THE PAGEANT.

Appendix

Introducing the enigmatic Dean Swift
in a play designed either for Stage
performance, public Reading or Broadcasting.

THE DREAMING DUST*

Some years ago, while engaged in writing a Radio Feature on the subject of the celebrated Jonathan Swift, I spent a great deal of time in reading through all of the major authorities. In the course of this work I discovered to my annoyance that the more I read, the more confusing and self-contradictory the whole subject became. A great many books have, and continue to be written about Swift, and what struck me most forcibly at an early stage of my enquiries was that however satisfactory most of the available commentaries may be to writers of academic Dissertations, to a man of the Theatre who had to make sense of the story, they were, on the whole a total loss.

In those days one of the most popular features of the Higher Criticism lay in the cult known as 'Semantics' – that is to say, a study of Literature that concerned itself primarily with the precise meaning of Words, rather than with anything about the Writer himself. His character, his personal experiences and his behaviour were considered to be irrelevant in relation to the merits of his work. In short, anything in the nature of a biographical approach was considered to be highly suspect, unprofessional, and inadmissable.

This was all very well from the angle of the English Departments, but for a Dramatist whose principal concern is usually the depiction of Character on the stage, this picayune pose of certain Professors of English was poisonous in the field of Drama for the simple reason that it tended to rule out one of the most important elements of good playwriting, namely: Motivation.

In the case of Dr Swift, I found myself confronted not only with one character whose reactions to most situations were not

*I have used parts of the Introduction to *The Golden Cuckoo and Other Plays* (1954) in this volume. I decided also to revise the section on *The Dreaming Dust*, and give it here.

merely unusual but positively inexplicable. All very well one says – he was a Genius, and that excuses everything! But before long it became evident that it was also going to be necessary to explain the behaviour of his Patron, his Uncle, his supposed secret Wife, her Duenna, his Mother, his Archbishop, and most of his best friends – an entire cast of uncontrollable eccentrics.

There could only be one explanation of this. It was more probable that there was something wrong or missing from the facts as reported in the books than that human nature had gone crazy in the gravitational field of the Dean of St. Patrick's. But how – one may ask – had not the same point occurred to the many eminent authorities who had had to cope with these problems during the past two hundred years? They include Forster, Scott, Churton Collins, Craik, Dr Johnson, Monck Mason, Leslie Stephens, Hone and Rossi, Hayward, Harold Williams, Davis, Edith Sitwell and Uncle Tom Cobley and all. Such an array of heavy names is impressive, to say the least of it. But how many do they actually amount to?

I set to work – and it soon became a fascinating pastime – analysing the source from which each Biographer in turn had drawn his information. And in the end, a startling fact emerged. There were not so many authorities as it first appeared. On the whole, each eminent writer was accepting, and sometimes elaborating, what had been written on the subject by his predecessors. And in the ultimate analysis, the only original authority on the Dean's early life and parentage was Dr Swift, himself. It was his word alone, as embodied in a very curious document now in the Library of Trinity College, Dublin, that was the basis for the mountain of literature that has since been written. And however excellent such an authority may be on any point where he wishes to be informative, nothing worse could be found, if he had anything to conceal.

Shaw used to object strenuously to any independent investigation of his youth. But as soon as he saw that the enquirer was going ahead with it anyhow, he would immediately bury the writer under a heap of voluntary information. Why this was so, I do not profess to know – unless it was the best way to make any further enquiries seem unnecessary. Swift had the same trick to a greater degree. In fact, he did his best to save all trouble to his future Biographers by writing the text for them himself – always in the third person, particularly in a document in which he made a number of lying claims about his ancestry, showed considerable doubt about giving the year of his birth (which he finally deleted) and told an absurd story about having been kidnapped and taken from Dublin to Whitehaven by a nurse, soon after he was born. Here his distracted Mother allowed him to remain for almost three years, because – forsooth – she did not want him to risk the return journey at so tender an age. And when, finally, he was brought back to his birthplace, she was no longer in Dublin herself. He also included a date for his Father's death, which is ascertainably untrue. His 'father', in fact, was dead well over nine months before the future Dean was born.

This is hardly the place to go into the matter in any greater detail, or to describe the manner in which a play about Swift steadily developed into a play about the search for Swift. It is sufficient to state that, while there is now no direct evidence to prove that my solution of the Swift tangle is the true one, it *could* be the true one, and is in line with the known facts. It is the only explanation that I can find which motivates the behaviour of all the characters. To that extent, I believe as a Dramatist that it must be true. But whether it is true or not, it is perfectly clear that the books are wrong.

When originally produced on the radio – that is to say by the most universal means known to science, and to the largest audience then possible – it produced no critical reactions whatsoever. Nobody takes seriously what they hear on the radio, apart from News and invasions from Mars. In stage form, it evoked very little more response. But then I read a short paper on the subject to the Old Dublin Society, which published it in its journal, at which point the reactions were catastrophic. I had invaded the realm of scholarship, and violent as the reactions of an audience may be to a Point, they are nothing to the reactions of the owners of any literary Tom Tiddler's Ground, towards inter-meddlers from other departments.

One would imagine that at this distance, it is not a matter of any very great importance to suggest that Swift was a bastard. But unfortunately it involves the statement that a great many books to which many years of study have been devoted, are at fault in their facts, and that more than one respectable tome has been written without a proper check of the original documents that it quotes. In the circumstances it is perhaps not surprising that I have got myself into a lot of hot water over Dr Swift, and have since made matters worse, by writing a tome of my own – a volume studded with footnotes and terminating with a Bibliography, which, God knows, has made heavy reading.

So much for the story itself. Since the play has turned out to be more interesting as a search for an answer than as a straight piece of biography, I have taken the opportunity of constructing it in an unusual way. The enormous success of dramatic Readings in the United States has opened up some entirely new avenues by which the cost of scenery and scene-changing can be largely eliminated. What there is room for today is a type of play with a small cast of star parts, that can be toured with ease, carrying only props, and maybe some additional lighting equipment, and that can be performed in places where there is not a regular theatre at all – a play that can be staged with an elaboration or a simplification that depends only on the taste and resources of the Manager – from a Cathedral interior with organ and choir, to a broadcast with no scenery at all.

This is an attempt to construct such a play. Furthermore, it is intended as an Actors' Play, in which the doubling up of parts is deliberate. The mechanics of performance are intended to be shown. And if this means that it requires a cast of Ruth Drapers, so much the better. Good Troupers are not given enough opportunities of showing their versatility these days. So here they can do so, several times over in the same play.

Being tragic in the extreme, it should be played for as many legitimate laughs as possible. And there are a good many to be had.

January 1979